Children, families, and government

Perspectives on American social policy

Children, families, and government

Perspectives on American social policy

Edited by

EDWARD F. ZIGLER, SHARON LYNN KAGAN,
and EDGAR KLUGMAN

CAMBRIDGE UNIVERSITY PRESS

Cambridge
London   New York   New Rochelle
Melbourne   Sydney

Published by the Press Syndicate of the University of Cambridge
The Pitt Building, Trumpington Street, Cambridge CB2 1RP
32 East 57th Street, New York, NY 10022, USA
10 Stamford Road, Oakleigh, Melbourne 3166, Australia

First published 1983
Reprinted 1985

Printed in the United States of America

Library of Congress Cataloging in Publication Data
Main entry under title:
Children, families, and government.
Includes index.
1. Children–Government policy–United States–
Addresses, essays, lectures.   2. Family policy–United
States–Addresses, essays, lectures.   3. United States–
Social policy–Addresses, essays, lectures.   I. Zigler,
Edward Frank, 1930– .   II. Kagan, Sharon Lynn.
III. Klugman, Edgar.
HQ792.U5C43   1983   362.8′2561′0973   82-23444
ISBN 0 521 24219 3

This book is dedicated to two courageous public servants,
Elliot Richardson and Patricia Harris,
who have demonstrated that concern for the quality of child and
family life transcends political party affiliation.

Contents

vii

Part VI. The future

Foreword

Margaret Mead said it so well when she testified during my U.S. Senate hearings on families in 1973: "As families go, so goes the nation."

She recognized that basic American truth – that strong families are a necessary foundation for the strength and stability of our country. If we look at almost every major social problem – whether crime or violence, or a young person who cannot study in school, or an adult who cannot hold a job, or a person involved with drugs – whatever the problem is, it will not be fully solved without strong families.

It is in the family that we begin to be good citizens, to love our country, to obey the law, to work hard, and to get along with our neighbors. It is the family that teaches these bedrock values.

When I chaired the Senate Committee on Children and Youth, and later when as Vice President I chaired the Task Force on Youth Employment, I came to believe that if we want our children to become good, productive citizens, contributing to society, the best thing we can do is ensure that we have strong and loving families.

As Michael Novak put it: "What strengthens the family strengthens society. One unforgettable law has been learned painfully through all the oppressions, disasters and injustices of the last thousand years: if things go well with the family, life is worth living. When the family falters, life falls apart."

Despite this, however, the sorry fact remains that the United States has a large, unfinished agenda when it comes to children and families. For that reason, I am delighted that Professors Zigler, Kagan, and Klugman have compiled this book. I hope it will serve to revive what I regard to be one of our most vital debates: How can we support and strengthen families?

Difficult challenges ahead

This question has never been more timely. American families are finding it increasingly difficult to cope with their problems. Recent research highlights just how severe this pressure has become:

> George Gallup found in 1980 that nearly half of all Americans believed family life had worsened during the preceding 15 years. Only 7% saw family life as better.
>
> A 1980 Louis Harris poll reported that 63% of working mothers felt they did not have enough time for themselves, and many worried that they had less time for their family and children.
>
> The divorce rate continues to climb: 4 in 10 marriages now end in divorce.

These pressures come from all sides. First, enormous economic, cultural, and social changes have altered the pattern of family life in most societies. Daniel Yankelovich, in *New Rules,* wrote about how the "giant plates" of American culture are shifting beneath us, creating tremendous dislocations in people's lives. He predicts that the process of reconciling our traditional value for family life with the new personal freedom Americans have come to expect will be "the preeminent question" our culture will confront.

Second, major changes in our communities are affecting families. Substantial economic and demographic shifts have created upheavals in many areas. Continued economic turmoil has forced many families to the edge of financial ruin. High rates of mobility have frustrated the development of stable neighborhoods.

Third, American families will be affected by the dramatic redefinition of government's role now under way in Washington. Cutbacks in federal funding for education, school lunches, day care, special programs for handicapped children, health care, job training and employment, and many other programs will deny families the help they need so badly.

Finally, new private sector issues will arise during the next decade that will create new problems. For example, the movement of industry from the frostbelt to the sunbelt threatens to disrupt and uproot many families. Questions of adequate child care and flexible working hours for the rapidly growing number of single-parent families and working parents will be crucial concerns for many families.

The role for public policy

As this book makes abundantly clear, public policy influences the way we respond to these challenges. That does not mean we should have a national family policy. It does mean that when government touches family life – as it does every day – we should make sure it supports and maintains rather than undermines and weakens American families. For example:

> The tax system should not penalize marriage.
> Welfare policies should not encourage fathers to abandon their families so that their wives and children can eat.
> Economic policies should not foster unemployment and thereby weaken the ability of families to support themselves as well as their self-esteem.
> Programs for the elderly and handicapped should help these people stay in their communities, cared for by families, not in institutions staffed by strangers.
> Housing policies should not be allowed to discriminate against families with young children.

The point is, before government acts, we should ask the simple question: How will this affect our families?

Yet there is also a more direct role for government to play than simply ensuring that policies do not negatively affect families. We have a special obligation to affirmatively invest in families and children. Nowhere is this principle better underscored than in the Head Start program. Head Start, by providing a comprehensive range of health, nutrition, education, and other services, enables children to get a fair chance in life who might otherwise not. And by directly involving parents in the direction and operation of local programs, Head Start makes certain that the services meet families' needs as well.

Other programs make a similar investment in our children – and thus in our future: The education programs for handicapped children; school breakfasts and lunches; the special food program for women, infants, and children; the Title I education program for disadvantaged children; Aid for Families with Dependent Children; day care; and adoption assistance all help strengthen children and families.

Today's children and America's future

As a nation, we can make no more important investment. The youngsters growing up today belong to the so-called baby bust generation, a far smaller group than their baby boom predecessors. By the time these children reach maturity, the United States will have to master some very serious challenges, and today's youngsters will have to carry a staggering burden.

Over the next two decades, the United States must modernize its industrial base, upgrade its military defenses, and cope with a steadily rising proportion of retired citizens. This will require the best-educated and best-trained workforce in American history as well as policies that give every child a full opportunity to develop skills and contribute to the community.

It will also require a stable and healthy society. And that means the United States must be just in providing education and opportunity for all. Yet today almost 30% of all American children are born into poverty. Millions lack regular health care, and a young person from a poor family is nearly twice as likely to be unemployed as other youth.

The tragic disparity between rich and poor is an affront to our conscience and a threat to the harmony of our society. A people cannot act together unless they are bound together. And the strongest bond is the chain of trust. As Lincoln once said, "With public trust, everything is possible. Without it, nothing is."

Americans today are counting on the next generation. Our economy, our retirement, our defense, even our stability as a society – everything that matters will face gigantic tests in the coming years. Our nation can only pass those vital tests if the American people are up to the job.

There can be no doubt about it: The generation that is young today may be the most hard-pressed and heavily burdened generation in our nation's history. It is not only a matter of justice and compassion to give these children a chance at the fullness of American life. It is also in our own self-interest. We should prepare them for the job they must do – by feeding, and healing, and educating, and training the young today.

As Alan Pifer, former head of the Carnegie Foundation, put it: "We should be concentrating our attention as a nation on the quality of our present children – those who bear the heavy burden later on."

Our future depends on their fitness – to be teachers, workers, artists, scientists, soldiers, wage earners, and productive citizens in every field – in the new world that awaits us.

We know that the best way to invest in children is to have strong families. The goal should not be to replace families with agencies, but to make public policies work for families. The task is not to choose between public and private means, but to form a partnership between government and the private sector in behalf of families. Most of all, families need the concern and help of their communities.

I believe this book can help inform scholars, practitioners, advocates, and policy makers about issues that confront children and their families. I am hopeful it will spur renewed debate and action. We in the United States have an unfinished agenda for children and families that demands such debate and action.

Walter F. Mondale
March 1983

Acknowledgments

We would like to acknowledge The Bush Foundation, whose financial support made this book possible. We express our gratitude to Gwen Mood, Elizabeth Schreiber, and Tamar Siff for their assistance in all phases of the preparation of this work. For their help in this effort, we would also like to thank Carol Buell, Brad Fuller, Theresa Glennon, Melissa Maier, Susan Muenchow, Wendell Piehler, Judith Prusski, and Jacqueline Wilcox. We also wish to acknowledge the assistance and support of our editor, Susan Milmoe.

Part I

Introduction

1   Creating social policies for children and families: an overview

Sharon L. Kagan, Edgar Klugman, and Edward F. Zigler

Concern about social policy as it affects children and families is currently being generated in many different arenas. Scholars, aware of the myriad of unmet needs of children and families, are working toward influencing policy through research and analysis. Practitioners, concerned about the welfare of individual children or families, are coming to realize that advocacy to alter legislation is an accepted, if not essential, component of their professional responsibility. Policy makers, themselves aware of the complexities of constructing and passing legislation, acknowledge the need for systematic investigation of the policy process. The press for a better understanding of the nuances of policy formation and implementation, predicated on accurate scientific knowledge, has been a major factor in precipitating this volume.

Another factor that led the editors to undertake their effort was the desire to facilitate the new relationship between social policy and research in child development. If an effective collaboration between the two disciplines is to develop, an exploration of the complexities of each and an understanding of the major obstacles to bridging the gap between them is necessary.

One key obstacle is that no single definition of social policy exists. This problem stems in part from the interdisciplinary nature of policy studies. Social policy researchers and analysts draw on work in political science, law, economics, sociology, history, psychology, and anthropology, and their work is both enriched and complicated by the different orientations of these disciplines. Dialog between members of various disciplines, separated into different departments at universities, is infrequent and often impeded by the differing vocabularies and assumptions of each.

A second obstacle to bridging the gap between social policy and child development research is divergent goals. Whereas social policy theorists and practitioners usually want their findings to be applied, child develop-

3

ment researchers have, in the past, worked toward the refinement of theory rather than its application. Clearly, differences in mission coupled with differences in methodology lead researchers to question their appropriate role in the political process.

Recognition of the growing interest in the relationship between child development research and social policy and of its inherent difficulties led the editors to bring together the work of individuals who have both reflected upon and acted in the two domains. This volume does not set forth a unified vision of the direction of social policy for children and families. It does not present a single definition of social policy, nor does it present grandiose plans for ending the schism between disciplines. There is no strategy for manipulating the political process and no unique formula for extracting social relevance from empirical research.

Rather, this collection of essays provides a view of the state of the art of constructing policies for children and families. Theorists and practitioners present major issues, alerting the reader to complexities and nuances of studying, analyzing, formulating, and evaluating social policy. Readers are left not with a completed portrait, but with a palette of different perspectives from which they may create their own vision of child and family policy.

Several assumptions guided the creation of this volume. The editors began with the premise that social science can, and in fact must, inform social policy. Social problems are endemic to a democratic society, and if they are to be ameliorated, the best knowledge available must be utilized in that effort.

Second, the editors acknowledge the existence of vast bodies of literature postulating systematic and rational approaches to the creation and analysis of social policy. That this literature exists reflects scholarly attempts to impose order on what the editors consider basically idiosyncratic processes. Because policies emerge often as a consequence of compromise, the editors do not advocate one system of policy study or subscribe to one mode of analysis. Rather, the editors elected to include a series of unique case studies that collectively explicate the malleability of the policy-making process.

The third assumption that guided the development of this work was that policies are very much a product of their time. Conceived during the late 1970s, this book was intended to provide an apolitical vision of the current state of child and family policy in the United States. The 1980 presidential election, and the subsequent economic reforms and devolution of power to the states, have reflected a changed zeitgeist. This volume will be born in a political climate committed to minimal government intervention rather than in an era characterized by a willingness and desire for government involvement in child and family policy for the needy. While the effect of various political and socioeconomic tides is crucial to the very nature and existence of child and family policy, the important point is that policy is not a free-standing entity, but rather a reflection of the values of the times. To be understandable, the study of policy cannot be removed from the study of political, social, and economic climates.

The fourth assumption, emanating from the preceding three, is that policy making should no longer be envisioned solely as the responsibility of those in national or state capitals or city halls. Rather, policy making is influenced by many individuals and groups: scholars, practitioners, lobbyists, interest groups, and seemingly apolitical organizations. Whereas federal and state policies are formalized by agents of governments, individuals in local programs interpret policy and in so doing recreate policy daily. Policy making, in the editors' opinion, is an ongoing, dynamic series of negotiations and bargains, affected by a myriad of players.

Although these assumptions are not necessarily held by all contributors to the volume, the editors, in conceiving the collection, tried to ensure that they would be addressed specifically and then more generally within the context of social policy development. Therefore, the volume includes chapters that explore (1) the nature of the policy-making process; (2) the effects of changes in the socioeconomic climate on child and family policy; (3) the influences on the policy process; and (4) the translation of social problems to social policies.

The nature of the policy-making process

The development of social policies for children and families is a long and arduous challenge even for seasoned policy makers. The process of policy construction has received considered attention by theoreticians and practitioners. Two parts of the volume address the development of policy, first from a conceptual perspective and then from a pragmatic one. In part II, Conceptualizing Policy Development, two approaches to policy analysis are discussed. Theodore Marmor, after presenting models of analysis, explicates contemporary approaches to political science. Garry Brewer reviews phases of the policy process, including initiation, estimation, selection, implementation, evaluation, and termination. Brewer reconsiders this framework in light of children's policy, with special emphasis on the problematic phases of initiation and estimation. This chapter highlights a recurrent theme in discussions of the policy process – that is, can a rational model of policy analysis take into account the nuances of a complicated and often unpredictable process?

Pragmatic aspects of policy construction at federal and state levels are treated in part III. Federal legislative processes, including recent modifications in the budget procedures, are presented by Pamela Ebert-Flattau. J. Lawrence Aber points out the crucial role of the state in developing policies for children and families. Using Massachusetts as a case study, Aber demonstrates the changes in the state's responsibility during the past decade. John Hansan provides an account of the relationship between the states and the federal government in the area of human services. Hansan suggests that our current system of intergovernmental relations was determined early in our country's history, and that whereas the relationship between states and the federal government has changed, it was and continues to be rooted in our collective value system.

Offering a slightly different perspective on the process of policy, Carol Mershon Connor discusses various conceptions of federalism from a historical – ideological perspective. She then demonstrates how fiscal reform in the past two decades has altered the balance of power between state and federal levels of government. The section concludes with a chapter by Stephen Heintz, who discusses Reagan's new federalism. Heintz, after reviewing the history of federalism, espouses dual and equal sovereignty between federal and state governments.

The effects of changes in the socioeconomic climate on child and family policy

That policy reflects changes in the zeitgeist is a recurrent theme in many of the chapters in this volume. Peggy Pizzo, in her review of American federal policy, discusses the content and rationale of federal policies as they have emerged since 1900. Pizzo documents the origins and dimensions of federal policies and the perspectives about the changing and appropriate role of the federal government. In the discussion of specific policies, Pizzo demonstrates how key policy issues are treated depending on the general climate of the decade.

Urie Bronfenbrenner and Heather Weiss demonstrate how radically attitudes toward services for children and families have changed over time. Their chapter presents the implications of "deficit model" policy formulation and postulates new policies that are more appropriate to changing family patterns. The concluding chapter, by the editors, explores the current status of American child and family policies. The chapter identifies criteria that may guide future policy development and suggests strategies that will foster their implementation given the current political–economic climate in the United States.

Influences on the policy process

That the policy process is not influenced only by politicians, elected representatives, or political scientists is evidenced throughout the volume and is specifically treated in part IV. Particular emphasis is given to the role of advocates and advocacy movements in two chapters. Catherine Ross chronicles two major approaches to advocacy: (1) the single-issue campaign and (2) broader, more general efforts to change public attitudes wherein children and children's issues become the "metaphor of human potential and social justice." As such, this chapter demonstrates just how the policy process may be influenced by broad-based constituencies. Ellen Hoffman provides a more recent picture of the advocacy process, detailing how it and the central players have changed since the mid-1960s. Hoffman's account vividly describes who are advocates, how they have functioned, and how they might function given current challenges.

Policy is not only influenced by advocates, but is shaped by current societal and demographic trends. In their chapter, Nicholas Zill II, Heidi Sigal, and Orville G. Brim, Jr. explain how social indicators can be an effective data base for influencing policy.

Susan Muenchow and Susan Shays Gilfillan present another perspective on policy influences. In their discussion of social policy and the media, they present the crucial role, often overlooked, that the media play in shaping public policy. The authors illuminate various examples of and issues related to the media's powerful contribution to policy making.

The translation of social problems to social policy

In order to more closely explore the subtleties of policy development, eight studies, each addressing a particular social problem, are presented in part V. The contributors, usually taking a historical perspective, document how policies have emerged as a consequence of the existence of social problems, how they were structured to ameliorate the problems from which they were generated, and how they accommodate the prevailing political–social context. The case studies presented do not address the myriad of child and family-related problems. Rather, they provide a sampling of issues and a sampling of policy strategies.

Gwen Morgan discusses the existing chaos in child day-care policy, highlighting the need for a family-oriented perspective to child-care policy. Throughout the discussion, Morgan identifies various influences of policy and chronicles how the dilemmas of child-care policy have been exacerbated over time. Jeanette Valentine and Edward Zigler present a review of the development and modification of the Head Start program. They demonstrate how Head Start is the best example of the utilization of child development knowledge in the framing of social policy. The chapter also points out the important role of advocates in influencing the policy process.

The next three chapters discuss educational policy from various perspectives. Edmund Gordon and Carol Yeakey discuss practices of educational equity in light of status and functional differences among youngsters. The chapter provides an in-depth analysis of the basis on which fundamental educational policies are formulated. It explores the relationship between knowledge about learning and children, on the one hand, and school practice, on the other, indicating that the schism between theory and practice still prevails. John Goodlad presents a discussion of factors that shape the school's curriculum. He demonstrates how shifts in curriculum, one key element of educational policy, reflect changes in the broader society. Seymour Sarason directly addresses the relationship between research and educational policy, using Public Law 94–142, the Education for All Handicapped Children Act, as an example. This essay explores the consequences of policy made in the absence of sound conceptualizations about schooling.

Edward Zigler in his chapter on child abuse provides an overview of the need for and problems associated with establishing federal policies. Zigler chronicles the relevant areas of research, demonstrating that, despite much attention, the child abuse problem continues to elude both researchers and policy makers. Juel Janis provides the reader with a detailed account of the emergence of children's health policy in America. The chapter demonstrates the policy process and points to the fact that, despite legislative efforts, the status of children's health in America continues to remain a great concern. David Musto provides a historical review of the evolution of American drug policy. The chapter clearly documents changes in public reaction to drugs over time as well as bureaucratic efforts to deal with the problem. The chapter concludes with a view toward the future.

The chapters of the volume may be read as individual analyses. Each is complete in itself and offers an account of the policy process. Taken together, the chapters provide a rounded view of child and family policies. It should be pointed out that no author has endorsed the creation of a comprehensive child and family policy. A single system is neither politically feasible at the present time nor reflective of the pluralism that characterizes family patterns in the United States.

Rather than advocating a single process, a single mode of analysis, or a single uniform set of policies, the editors through this compilation of chapters have sought to support a variety of approaches to child and family policy. We believe that an appropriate function of research is to define viable options on specific issues and that the policy-making process is a series of negotiations and bargains, struck by competing special interests and influenced by individuals and institutions. Finally, we acknowledge that policy making is an interactive process, shaped by and shaping the society.

2 Slouching toward Bethlehem: American federal policy perspectives on children and their families

Peggy Pizzo

Writing in *The Children's Cause,* Gilbert Steiner says, "A children's policy will be successful enough if it concentrates on ways to compensate demonstrably unlucky children whose bodies or minds are sick or whose families are unstable or in poverty" (1976, p. 255). Reasonable people disagree whether the population outlined by Steiner *should* be the only one of concern to federal policy. But in the 80-year history of federal policies benefiting children, "unlucky children" – whether their unluckiness originates in chance or in systematic exclusionary economic or political policies, such as racism – *have* been the primary focus of federal activity. In defining a manageable scope for the encyclopedic possibilities to which a discussion of federal policies for children and families lends itself, the author has chosen this population, and in particular the young "unlucky child," as the organizing focus for this chapter.

This chapter also discusses the contents and rationales of federal policies for children and families as they have emerged since 1912, when federal policies specifically shaped to benefit children were first enacted. It documents the origins and dimensions of federal policies and the perspectives about the appropriate role of the federal government that those policies reflect. Then it analyzes common elements of federal policy that seem to arouse consensus and support, as well as aspects that give rise to policy maker hesitation or hostility.

The concept of public policy seems at times distant, complex, and highly ambivalent. For purposes of this chapter, public policy is defined as a course of action consciously selected by publicly funded institutions (particularly government) from among several possible methods of approaching a concern brought to the attention of decision makers within those institutions. Policy – a definite, if general, course of action – is chosen to guide both present and future specific decisions and activities addressing this concern. Policy typically develops from discussion and debate about alternatives (hence, the "options paper," which is the nuts and bolts – or for those more inclined to culinary metaphors, the meat and potatoes – of federal policy making in the executive branch).

The policies most emphasized by this chapter are those that authorize, guide, and determine the amounts of fiscal resources distributed by the federal government to accomplish desired objectives for the "unlucky child" and his or her family. Other policies safeguarding the civil rights of both children and adults or setting standards for industry that protect children from injury caused by unsafe consumer products, or from mental or emotional harm caused by industry-sponsored television shows and commercials, provide important examples of the ways in which the federal government has acted or is considering action on behalf of children and their families.

Most federal activities conducted on behalf of children and their families achieve one or both of two basic objectives: (1) *knowledge* – investigation of the conditions under which children and families live, compilation of useful data, the delivery of that data back to the American public, the production of new knowledge, and, whenever possible, new breakthroughs that help us bring up children more safely and more effectively; and (2) *help* – the provision of financial assistance, services, or protective regulation to children and their families. Two corollaries are the subsequent evaluation of the performance of those programs in meeting the objectives mandated for them by the U.S. Congress and the continuing effort to improve and strengthen federal programs for children and their families.

Proposals for federal policy in this sensitive area often evolve with strongly held rationales both for and against federal activity. To the extent that proposals for activity become policies, it may be presumed that the rationales and the advocates arguing for action were more persuasive.[1] Why some proposals succeed in reaching policy status and others do not will be discussed in this chapter.

Finally, although those policies reaching the preschool child will be of primary concern, a range of programs from public assistance to health care, nutrition, child care, and protections against abuse or neglect of children will be discussed here. Education and youth unemployment will not.

Many of the public policies that touch the lives of young children are not federal in origin. States and local government by custom and law establish policies that influence the functions and operation of hospitals in which babies are born; the procedures followed in the adoption of children; the content and methods of public school instruction; the location and scope of services offered by publicly funded child health clinics; the type of traffic safety standards protective of children and penalties for nonobservance of these standards; the public response to child mistreatment; and processes for removal of children to safer havens when their own families inflict or appear likely to inflict violence upon them. The almost 62 million children in the United States in 1980 and the more than 30 million families (Children's Defense Fund, 1982) who cared for most of them conducted their affairs within a veritable ecology of public policies set up to give children a better start in life, to safeguard them from danger and illness, and to develop new knowledge and new awareness about childhood, its pitfalls, its promises, and its potentials. For the last 350 years American colonial and state legislatures, local schoolboards, county commissions, city halls, and town meetings have been the principal forums for American policy debates about children and their families.

In the last 80 years, however, for diverse reasons that shall be examined later, these debates have emerged in two other powerful and intermittently attentive forums – the executive and legislative branches of the federal government, to wit, the White House and its federal agency offshoots and the Congress of the United States. A central impetus for federal actions, decade after decade, has been the slowness of state governments to respond effectively to some acute childhood problem or need or the exclusionary policies of some states that denied some children – black and Hispanic children, for example – essential human services made available to other children. Considerable debate and struggle over the appropriate role of the federal government in situations like these resulted in federal policy – executive orders, statutes, regulations, services – intended to provide similar opportunities and human services for children in all 50 states. During the eight decades of focused activity for federal policies regarding children, there appears to have been three "peaks" – times when federal activity on behalf of children has been highest. The first peak occurred in the first third of this century, during the period 1910–1925, the next during the decade 1933–1942, and the third during the period from 1965 to 1980. For purpose of discussion, these periods of intense federal policy interest are examined within the context of the years 1900–1929, 1930–1959, and 1960–1980.

Federal policy, 1900 to 1929

In the first third of the century, certain events fused to produce a climate particularly responsive to federal policy making for children: (1) the election of a popular chief executive interested in children's issues; (2) the spread of grassroots movements among those persons living and working in hardship conditions; (3) a parallel movement among highly educated and concerned segments of the populace determined to improve social conditions; and (4) evidence both of authentic harm and of ways to correct or prevent that harm. A similar combination occurred later in the century – during the mid-1960s – and once again provoked intense federal activity.

In 1904, an energetic chief executive, Theodore Roosevelt, was elected president in his own right. While serving as police commissioner of New York City and the governor of New York State, Roosevelt, together with Jacob Riis, had crusaded against oppressive conditions harmful to children in New York (Morris, 1979). The domestic policy concerns of the new Progressive movement, whose formalization as a political party Roosevelt presided over less than a decade after this 1904 election, reflected social changes that presaged interest in "unlucky children," that is to say, white children from immigrant or rural American backgrounds. Among these changes were the increasing education of women and their entrance into "high-minded civic activities" on behalf of the poor; a mothers' movement composed of women concerned about maternal and child mortality and pure food and drug laws; the startling new phenomenon of urban settlement houses in slum neighborhoods organized and lived in by articulate, well-bred women who chose to dedicate their lives to the poor; the beginnings of successful unionization among the working classes; and the increasing awareness of the nation as a whole about the aftermath of the pioneer movement westward, which had peopled millions of acres beyond the Mississippi with families in crammed cabins, sod houses, and huts, isolated by seldom-traveled miles from physicians, nurses, schools, and other amenities. Finally, and importantly, breakthroughs were occurring in conquering maternal and child illness and deaths, breakthroughs that promised both tangible benefits to all children in the nation and a whole new perspective on childhood.

It should be noted that federal policy during this period concentrated on white children; black families lived primarily in the rural Southeast, out of the typical sphere of activities of the Progressives and out of the minds and thoughts of most of the socially conscious policy shapers. In fact, during the first *three* decades of the twentieth century, the attention of advocates for federal children's policies concentrated on children in large cities and in the rural Midwestern and Western areas. Very rarely described was the specific situations of black children who, the nation was later to learn, were living under the extreme hardships of Jim Crow laws, sharecropping, hunger, and exploitation.[2]

As the twentieth century opened there were vast gradations in the degree to which different groups of American children were protected against hardship. However, at least one condition of nearly all American children was patently undesirable: So much life was lost, both at birth and during the early years. In Massachusetts in 1900 there were about 160 infant deaths for every 1,000 live births, or almost 1 out of every 5 (Snapper, 1976). Massachusetts children aged five to nine years died at the rate of about 6 every 1,000. Although this was a lower rate than the 10 out of every 1,000 that died in 1880, it was still significant for a prosperous New England state (Snapper, 1976, p. 27). In New York City, one-third of all people who died every year were children under five years of age (U.S. Public Health Service, 1976, p. 62). Infant and child deaths were particularly prevalent in the summer months when "summer complaint" (infant diarrhea) swept through crowded areas.[3] Some cities, however, were experimenting with new ways to combat child deaths successfully. Rochester, New York began an intensive campaign to investigate the dairies from which mothers obtained milk for their children. Reports of manure-soaked utensils and rotting milk prompted action: stables were cleaned, the milk was boiled, and stations dispensing clean milk were established. Mothers bringing their children to these stations learned from trained nurses both how to respond to infant diseases and the most recent medical information on the prevention of diseases. Results were dramatic:

In the eight years before the establishment of municipal milk stations, the total number of deaths in Rochester of children under five years of age from all causes during the months of July and August was 1,744. The comparable figure for the eight years after the founding of milk stations was 864. [U.S. Public Health Service, 1976, p. 73]

City and state action to advance these very real gains for children and their families was hindered because no central coordinator existed to trace and publish data or to find, evaluate, and make available the promising approaches that local communities used to combat child death. Nationwide data on maternal and infant mortality were nonexistent; some states did not even mandate the registration of births or collect data about birth outcomes. Growing local demand for a national entity to perform these functions found national cohesiveness in 1909 in the highly visible White House Conference on Children and Youth convened by Theodore Roosevelt.

During these first three decades, another issue was working its way toward nationwide consciousness and a call for federal activity: child labor. Since about the mid-nineteenth century, local activists had campaigned against the horrors of child exploitation by industries who employed young children, often at hard labor for 12-hour days and under dangerous conditions. They had met with uneven degrees of success. Discouraged by the snail's pace of state-by-state activity, these child advocates turned toward the federal government and the possibility of a federal law that at one stroke could outlaw this horrendous activity in all states. In 1904 the National Child Labor Committee was formed. Just two years later, in 1906, the first federal law barring child labor was introduced in the Congress.

In 1912 the twin concerns of child mortality and child labor, along with increasing concern about delinquent and homeless children, provoked the establishment of the first federal "policy" for children and their families. It was the will of Congress, said the legislation, that a Children's Bureau be organized within the federal government to *investigate and report upon* all matters pertaining to the welfare of young children and child life among all classes of our people and shall especially investigate the questions of infant mortality, the birthrate, orphanages, juvenile courts, desertion, dangerous occupations, accidents and diseases of children, employment, legislation affecting children in the several states and territories.[4] [Emphasis added]

Thus, production of *knowledge* for the use of Congress and the public became the first American federal policy theme in matters affecting children. The absence of a mandate either to provide help or to prohibit exploitation of children is notable.

The Children's Bureau nonetheless vigorously set about initiating studies, demanding state and local registration of all births, and collecting data from every available source. By 1920, national data were being made available on infant and child mortality, data that were ominous in their proportions for a country thoroughly immersed in beliefs about its progressiveness. In the 35 states in the registration area in 1920, maternal mortality numbered over 16,000 (Lawrence, 1976, p. 21). The death rate for infants in 1920 hovered around 1 in 10 live births (Snapper, 1976, p. 26). Tuberculosis, diphtheria, polio myelitis, and measles together claimed the lives of 24,222 children in 34 states in 1920. Child deaths vastly increased during epidemics. During the epidemic of 1918, for example, influenza and pneumonia alone accounted for 77,800 child deaths in 30 states (Lawrence, 1976, p. 25). About this time, another shocking fact captured public attention. Fully one-third of all the eligible men called by the World War I military draft could not pass the physical examination (Lawrence, 1976, p. 25). This fact, not collected by the

Children's Bureau but put to good use by those pediatric professional organizations, child advocates, mothers' clubs, and emerging labor unions who supported the work of the Children's Bureau, was pieced together with the child and maternal mortality data, and became a rallying point for a new federal policy role: help. Specifically, the Sheppard–Towner bill was introduced in Congress in 1918 to set up and fund a joint federal–state program of maternal and child health clinics, making available new resources and knowledge capable of preventing maternal and child death to a greater extent than ever before. It was an entirely new federal policy posture, and, as might be expected, vigorous opposition emerged in the Congress. One senator decried the bill as "radical, socialistic and Bolshevistic" (quoted in U.S. Public Health Service, 1976, p. 81). Other opposing senators made good political use of the fact that the Children's Bureau was traditionally headed by unmarried women: "It seems to be the established doctrine of this Bureau," said Senator James Reed of Missouri, "that the only people capable of caring for babies and mothers of babies are ladies who never had babies [laughter]" (quoted in U.S. Public Health Service, 1976, p. 81). "Official meddling" was denounced as an obstacle to "mother love." All these themes – although unsuccessful in preventing passage of Sheppard–Towner – were to reemerge later in the development of federal policy for children. So also was the theme sounded by then Senator (later Vice-President) Alben Barkley in expressing his support for Sheppard–Towner. He believed, he said, that Congress could and ought to "provide for the general welfare" by helping to ensure that those who have just been born have an "equal chance with every other child in the world" (quoted in U.S. Public Health Service, 1976, p. 82). After passage of the act the Children's Bureau, with customary vigor, commenced the establishment of federally funded clinics. Between 1924 and 1929, almost 1,600 permanent local child health and prenatal centers were established (U.S. Public Health Service, 1976, pp. 83–88). Many of these provided programs that were comprehensive, popular, and innovative in their staffing of child health stations with nonmedical female personnel who worked well with mothers and children. In fact, they were a little too innovative for the tastes of the established medical profession, who, alarmed by this possible threat to physician usage, organized a successful campaign to prevent renewal of Sheppard–Towner in 1929 (Rothman, 1978). This policy theme – that of the organized opposition of professional groups to federally funded help that fails to acknowledge the primacy of the profession in delivering such help – reemerges later in the century.

In like manner, the other major policy issue prompting the establishment of the Children's Bureau, child labor, also evolved from an issue needing fact-finding investigations and reports to an issue requiring federal policy activity: protective regulation. The 1900 census revealed that almost three-quarters of a million children were employed by industry.[5] From 1906 to 1916, intense and tenacious lobbying by the opponents of child labor finally brought the issue to the point of congressional decision. The Owen–Keating Act, passed in 1916, prohibited the interstate and foreign shipment and sale of any produce made by an industry in which children were employed. In part, persuasive testimony that states were not doing an effective job of eliminating even the most abusive conditions for children finally convinced federal policy makers who had been anxious to avoid a federal role in this area that something had to be done. However, like Sheppard–Towner, the Owen–Keating Act was short-lived. Just two years after its enactment, in 1918, the Supreme Court struck down the act as unconstitutional. Undaunted, child advocates tried again, and in 1919 a tax on employers of children was written into Title XII of "An Act to Provide Revenue and for Other Purposes." Three years later, in 1922, this law, too, was held unconstitutional. Girding their loins, the opponents of child labor reentered the fray, and, two years later, in 1924, a constitutional amendment to ban child labor was introduced in both the House and Senate. Manufacturers denounced the amendment as "Russian in origin," a socialist scheme, and an abridgement of parental rights. A pro-child labor National Committee for the Protection of the Child, Family, School, and Church was formed. The amendment was never adopted. Until the terrible unemployment of the Great Depression made the employment of children a more universally undesirable activity, a permanent federal policy could not be established. Of the major policy roles described in this chapter, federal protective regulation remains to this day the most controversial.

During this period when the federal production of new knowledge and new public awareness led to bold if short-lived experiments with a new federal role in combating both maternal and child deaths and child labor, the investigations and reports of the Children's Bureau in the areas of child welfare helped bring about new public policies for children at the state level.[6] Legal protection for children and parents involved in adoption was enacted; state-funded institutions and shelters for abused and neglected children continued to grow; and, most significant, a new movement for state-funded mother's pensions – permitting widowed, divorced, or abandoned mothers to stay home and raise their children – was spreading throughout the states. In 1911 Illinois instituted the first mother's pension law. By 1919, 39 states had enacted similar measures (Lynn, 1980). From

1910 to 1929 states were moving rapidly into the development and funding of public policies that addressed the thorny and complex questions of the homeless child, the child subjected to parental violence or neglect, and the role of local and state government in the protection of both children and impoverished female heads of households. On a state-by-state basis, these measures were very uneven in terms of their authorized levels of protection and adequate coverage (Abbott, 1938; Dobelstein, 1980). This unevenness troubled child advocates, who felt children suffered unnecessarily in the less progressive states.

Furthermore, in most states there was (as is always the case in public policy) a great difference between statutory authorization of financial assistance to widowed, divorced, and abandoned mothers and the actual appropriation of funds needed to deliver that assistance to those legally entitled to it. In the absence of federal funding, each state must rely on its tax base to fund state programs. Thus affluent states are far better able to fully finance state programs than poorer states, even if the authorized coverage happens to be rather similar across states. This problem hindered the development of effective mothers' pension in many states and frustrated the efforts of child advocates just as much as the problem of the uneven coverage of the 45 different authorizing laws.

However, by the 1930s almost all of the states had an overriding problem: The Great Depression meant that everywhere, state funds were insufficient to do what state law required. In fact, state funds were becoming insufficient to meet even the most desperate human needs in a rapidly worsening national situation.

Federal policy, 1930 to 1959

The devastation wrought by the Great Depression on children and families was solidly documented by the Children's Bureau ("Six decades . . . ," 1972, p. 4). Those ravages were most acute, of course, for female-headed families, and the child advocates of the 1930s continued to press for increased assistance to widows and abandoned mothers. This pressure coincided with the universal pressure brought to bear on most federal domestic policy of this period: the need for massive fiscal relief to states, local governments, and individuals.

Local governments were bankrupt. Voluntary efforts ceased as people simply had less to share (Dobelstein, 1980, pp. 79–80). Estimates of the unemployed ranged as high as 13 million, almost one in four workers. Farms were being plowed under by families unable to gainfully sell their products. In the face of such suffering by so many families, the heretofore obdurate opponents of increased federal activity were just not as persuasive as the architects of the New Deal. Children and their families were dealt in, quietly. Surprising though it may be to today's student of "welfare," the passage of Title IV of the 1935 Social Security Act, Aid to Dependent Children (ADC), later to become Aid to Families with Dependent Children (AFDC), evoked very little opposition. Even the sponsors of the minority report opposing other provisions of the act expressed their support for federal fiscal assistance to dependent children (Library of Congress, 1968, p. ii.). In part, this was due to the spread of mothers' pensions in state policy. (By 1935, 45 states had enacted laws providing for such measures.) But the desperation of state governments for more funds to support needy citizens – through ways other than the controversial "public relief" programs – may have had some role in the easy passage of this new law. When the chairman of the House Ways and Means Committee rose to speak for ADC, he said:

Many of the children on the relief rolls are in families where there is no breadwinner, where the only head is a young mother who is needed to care for her children. There can be no question that for families of this kind, provision through ordinary public relief is socially undesirable.

Enlightened public opinion has long recognized that the most desirable type of public aid for such families is in the form commonly known as mothers' pensions – that is, aid to dependent children to maintain them in their own homes under their mothers' care. Forty-five States have laws providing for mothers' pensions but many of these States, for lack of funds, have been unable to care for more than a fraction of the families eligible to receive such assistance. Federal aid will permit the mothers' pension type of care to become nationally operative.[7]

Enunciating a theme that has been echoed to the present day, Title IV of the Social Security Act began: "For the purpose of enabling each State to furnish financial assistance, as far as practicable under the conditions in such State, to needy dependent children. . . ."[8] The federal government thus asumed a firm new policy posture vis-à-vis children and families – that of provider of financial assistance – but only by *enabling states* to become providers of financial assistance. The program began in 1936 with about half a million recipients (Library of Congress, 1968, p. LRS-2).

The statistics of the 1930s on the two primary federal concerns of the preceding decades – infant mortality and child labor – continued to support the need for federal policy activity. In 1935, some 120,000 infants did not survive their first year. The infant mortality rate hovered around 1 in every 20 babies (Lawrence, 1976, p. 22). The census report for 1930 revealed that almost 30,000 children still labored in industrial settings (Abbott, 1938, p. 267). With continued advocacy from both the Children's Bureau and from many public and private organizations, the two objectives that had been high on the Progressive agenda, federal provision of maternal and child health services and federal regulation of child labor, were successively enacted into law in 1935 and 1937, respectively. In the climate of the 1930s and 1940s, these laws, once so controversial, survived as viable federal policies.

As with Title IV, so also Title V (Maternal and Child Health Services) of the Social Security Act emphasized the *enablement* of states. Tentatively, a new federal policy was also included in Title V: federally funded services for homeless or delinquent children. The drafters of this law were cautious: "For the purpose of enabling the United States through the Children's Bureau, to *cooperate* with State public-welfare agencies in establishing, extending and strengthening, especially in *predominantly rural areas,* public-welfare services . . . for the protection and care of homeless, dependent and neglected children, and children in danger of becoming delinquent . . . "[9] (emphasis added). In contrast to the Aid to Dependent Children program, whose early funding was $58 million, Child Welfare Services began with an initial appropriation of $1.5 million (Library of Congress, 1968).

During the 1930s, this emphasis on the state as primary policy source and the federal government as enabler and cooperative partner was, as analysts have pointed out, an essential ingredient in allaying the fears of state governments and the many adherents of "states' rights" (Steiner, 1976, pp. 4–9). Fiscal relief was a strong attraction, of course, to the states' righters. But the design of the federal policy role, particularly as it is expressed in Titles IV and V of the Social Security Act, aided the states with more than just money. For the past 30 (and, in some states, 50 to 60) years the provision of publicly funded services to children and their families had been the province chiefly of local government – cities, towns, and counties. Thousands of approaches to these issues had developed locally, but in the absence of legislative oversight or similar means of ensuring accountability, abuses flourished. Says Andrew Dobelstein, writing in *Politics, Economics, and Public Welfare* (1980, p. 79):

Social, financial and political corruption was most rampant in local welfare programs. Relief in New York was distributed by the political precinct officers. Almshouses and county homes had become deathtraps plagued by filth and disease. Local officials exploited those who worked for relief by keeping small commissions for themselves. Everywhere children were exploited. Thus social reformers sought *state* welfare policies as a means to correct abuses. [Emphasis added]

Titles IV and V, in requiring state plans and state oversight of administration of these new federal programs, strengthened the power of governors and state officials in dealing with local units.

In a few years of intense activity in the early to mid-1930s, the federal government added to the federal role of producer of new knowledge two new policy perspectives that have since become strongly held elements of federal policy: (1) the belief that Washington could and should provide financial assistance to children and their families; and (2) the belief that Washington could and should provide services to children and their families, or at least fund those services, as long as both were done primarily through the states. It bears noting that the federal role of providing services to mothers and children – which in 1929 seemed to be dealt a firm rejection with the defeat of Sheppard–Towner – became just six years later a strongly held provision in a major federal law, the Social Security Act.

Two other roles – provider of jobs for the unemployed as child-care workers, exemplified by the 1,900 nursery schools sponsored by 1936 under the Works Project Administration, and provider of children's services as auxiliaries designed to support some other critical federal objective (such as the rapid production of war material), exemplified by the child-care centers funded under the Lanham Act in the 1940s – became intermittent features of federal policies (Ross, 1979, pp. 33–36; Steinfels, 1973, pp. 66–73).

Federal policy, 1960 to 1979

As the nation entered the 1960s, a major federal policy issue was emerging with respect to the nation's program of Aid to Families with Dependent Children: how to limit the growth of the program and the expenditures associated with it. This policy concern, however, collided with a very different policy concern that also captured public attention in the 1960s: response to the excruciating conditions of poverty affecting tens of millions of American children. Reconciling these two competing objectives – curtailment of AFDC and compassionate, immediate response to impoverished children – became a central task of the Great Society.

By June 1958, 23 years after ADC had been enacted, more than 2.7 million individuals were receiving this form of public assistance, up from the one-half million who were first covered in 1936. Annual expenditures were now more than $800 million, in contrast to the $58 million spent in 1937. Numbers in the "absent-from-home" category – children on public assistance whose fathers were alive but absent – had quadrupled in the decade between 1940 and 1950 (Library of Congress, 1968). As the program expanded, the federal perspective on providing cash assistance to needy children and their families changed markedly from compassion for young mothers and their offspring to alarm at the program's growth and concern that this federal policy might be "making it easier" for fathers to abandon their families and for unmarried women to have babies – a highly undesirable situation in the eyes of most Americans. Thus, a major concern of the next two decades became a search for alternative ways to reduce dependence (or dependents) on public assistance, to reduce the expense to the public, or both.

Additionally, as the postwar migration of minorities, especially blacks – who for more than three centuries had been denied equal opportunities for educational and economic development – brought millions of people from the rural areas of the South and Southwest into the Northern cities, the numbers of nonwhite recipients of public assistance grew. During the 1960s, as blacks and other minorities challenged white supremacy and protested minority exclusion from public policies that had aided others, Congress increasingly became the focal point for the great civil rights struggles of that decade. "Federal action" versus "states' rights" debates took on strongly racial overtones, and hostility toward the growth of AFDC seemed to go hand in hand with a sentiment among whites that blacks and Hispanics were being conceded "too much."

During the 1960s two major policy proposals aimed at curtailment of AFDC were forwarded: (1) funding of services that would encourage and support mothers seeking to produce income for their families through employment, and (2) enforcement of the financial obligations of fathers to their children. These proposals competed with other, expansionary efforts to increase the coverage of the AFDC program, make public assistance available to two-parent families where fathers were unemployed, and ensure equitable payment levels. Over time, in policies governing AFDC, curtailment emerged as the primary objective.

President Kennedy's proposal for opportunities to facilitate maternal employment was successfully enacted in 1962. Secretary of Health, Education, and Welfare Abraham Ribicoff called for waging "war on dependency. . . . The byword of our new program is prevention – and where it is too late – rehabilitation, a fresh start."[10]

The ensuing 1962 amendments to the Social Security Act funded, at a higher federal matching rate than the standard rate for AFDC payments, public employment and training programs, day care for children, and other services. Senator Kerr of Oklahoma praised this new approach as extending "hope of a future in which children helped by public assistance will grow up to be self-supporting, responsible adults, . . . hope for reuniting families parted by desertion and despair."[11] These measures of work, training, and the provision of child-care services were strengthened in the 1967 amendments.

The second proposal designed to reduce public spending on AFDC – federal enforcement of the absent father's child-support obligations – received only tentative endorsements in the early 1960s. By 1967, however, states were *required* (note the nonpermissive language here – quite a departure from the "enabling" mode) to establish procedures for determining the paternity of an AFDC child, for locating absent fathers, and for collecting child support from them. By 1975, child support had become a controversial major federal program, authorized to procure federal tax data to help determine a father's whereabouts and, if he is a federal employee, to garnish his wages if need be.

Thus, the two AFDC approaches that evolved during the 1960s and continued to be major policy themes in the 1970s were basically attempts to reduce the obligation of government to provide financial support to needy children.

At the same time that such restrictions were being legislated and implemented, however, startling new knowledge about children was forcefully brought to the attention of U.S. policy makers. The new facts divided into two major streams:

1. *Extraordinary sensitivity in the perinatal and early childhood developmental stages.* Scholars, psychologists, pediatricians, and other professionals established that conditions antecedent to birth and in the first five years of life shape adult development far more intensively than was previously thought. Furthermore, they contended that conditions detrimental to development, especially intellectual development – faulty nutrition, dangerous childbirth, insufficient stimulation of infant intelligence, childhood disease – are correctible. Popular interest in the scholarly works documenting these findings was to some degree stimulated by the Kennedy family's commitment to preventing mental retardation, which afflicted a Kennedy sister. But this new perspective on early childhood as a time of immense possibilities for "optimizing development" captured attention in all areas of the population, especially among newly prosperous American parents eager to advance their children's prospects for success in life. For those who had followed the interests of impoverished children, the new findings pointed to important possibilities for strengthening federal policy activity.

2. *The extent of suffering among needy American children.* A middle-class populace, concerned about growth in programs like AFDC and newly awakened to the concept of sensitive childhood, was suddenly paying attention to the shocking facts of poverty in the United States and its ravaging effects on innocent children. New surveys showed that almost 17 million children in 1959 lived in households where the total

income was barely sufficient to sustain existence (Social Security Adm., 1967). In 1960, some 10 million children lived in houses that lacked a proper toilet, bath, or hot water; 4 million lived in houses that census enumerators called dangerous (Schorr, 1966). On Indian reservations and in the rural South, children were so badly malnourished that cases were reported of kwashiorkor, a form of malnutrition common in African and Latin American countries (to which a compassionate American public committed aid), but thought to be nonexistent in prosperous America. Whereas white babies now nearly all survived childhood and the first years of life, nonwhite babies died at the same rate in 1960 – about 1 in 20 – that had prevailed for white infants during the Great Depression. America began to face these facts during a decade when television, radio, and newspapers documented, almost every day, that nonwhite children in some states were denied even the most fundamental civil rights and that nonwhites nationwide were taking to the streets and would sacrifice their lives, if need be, to abolish these inequalities.

As Americans watched on their televisions, state and local police unleashed attack dogs on peacefully demonstrating adults and children; in a church in Birmingham, Alabama, three little black girls were murdered by a bomb explosion. In 1967, escorted by a young civil rights lawyer, Marian Wright (now Marian Wright Edelman, founder of the Children's Defense Fund), Senator Robert Kennedy (N.Y.) visited the homes of children in the Mississippi Delta, witnessed firsthand the near-starvation of these children, and emerged shaken, with tears in his eyes, determined to alleviate the suffering (Kotz, 1969).

In the Northern cities, rebellions of angry minorities during the summer of 1967 rocked the urban economy as stores, banks, and other businesses were burned and looted. In April 1968, as word spread of Martin Luther King's assassination, inner cities across the nation erupted in fiery outbursts of anger. Billions of dollars of damage resulted. The nation's economic health was threatened by the spontaneous uprisings of people who would simply bear no more.

In the 1960s, the policy climate surrounding issues related to children and their families shared many characteristics with the climate that produced the Children's Bureau and the first child labor and child health laws: an energetic and (until 1967) popular chief executive who took a strong personal interest in children's issues, from mental retardation to elementary education; a grassroots movement among the disadvantaged themselves, who refused to accept unfair or injurious practices, coupled with heightened awareness among the educated young and their educators; the startling dedication of young middle-class men and women who risked their lives to enter the civil rights fray and put aside potentially lucrative careers in the private sector to join the ranks of antipoverty volunteers; and finally, the explosive new knowledge that poverty existed in acute forms in the United States and that something should and could be done about it.

During a decade when expansion of direct financial assistance to poor parents and children ran counter to the curtailment trend in the AFDC program – and furthermore was considered a failed policy at "breaking the cycle of poverty" – the new knowledge about early child development presented feasible policy responses to the appalling new awareness of poverty in America. Scholars were writing about something that held the promise of combating poverty: immediate and continuing correction of the childhood conditions that choked off later school and employment success. Damaging childbirth, poor nutrition, crowded housing, poor schools, and too little health care (especially preventive health care) limited opportunities for effective early education. These were conditions that *could* be changed, and with them, the unequal opportunities for a good start in life that made, in the words of President Johnson (1979, pp. 67–69) "poverty's children" become "poverty's captives." Thus one policy stance that emerged in the 1960s argued that the federal government should become far more activist both in producing knowledge about childhood and in producing help, just as it was becoming far more activist in ensuring voting and other civil rights of all citizens. Furthermore, it was argued, in carrying out this new role the federal government should be less willing simply to rely on the "good intentions" of the states and should provide more oversight of federally funded programs.

Of course, the strong states' rights tradition in America became a countervailing influence to this new push. The compromise that emerged between these two forces involved a far greater flow of resources from the federal government, but a mixture of approaches to delivering those goods and services, with some flowing through state and local government and others going directly to local community groups. Between 1965 and 1975, major legislation authorizing comprehensive child development services (Head Start), health care (Medicaid; Early and Periodic Screening; Diagnosis and Treatment), food and nutritional services (Food Stamps; Child Care Feeding Program; Women, Infants, and Children [WIC] Supplemental Feeding Program), social services such as child day care (Title XX of the Social Security Act), and compensatory education (Title I of the Elementary and Secondary Education Act) was enacted for needy children and their families. Older programs for children under existing laws were expanded: more targeted perinatal and child health care under Title V of the Social Security Act and broader programs of school breakfast and lunch under the National School Lunch Act. As the chill on domestic spending occasioned by the Vietnam War became a virtual freeze, however, many of the high hopes held by the authors of these programs for needy children were reluctantly abandoned. Head Start, for example, was never able to serve more than one in five children eligible for the program.[12] Title I educational programs in 1977 reached only slightly more than half of their eligible population (Chisholm, 1977). By 1975 President Ford, in an effort to reduce post-Vietnam and oil embargo inflation, was urging cutbacks in spending in nonentitlement programs. Nevertheless, the concept of direct federal responsibility for improving the lives of children and their families had been established, most notably in a popular program that by 1980 was being described in bipartisan political circles, by both conservatives and liberals as well as a blue ribbon commission established by President Carter, as one of the most effective programs in government: Head Start.

The 1970s renewed many older concerns about direct federal provision of help to children and families. Bouts of disquieting inflation provoked fears among Americans about the effect of apparently runaway federal expenditures on shrinking disposable family incomes. Expenditures for Medicaid and Medicare escalated enormously during the decade. Some analysts argued that these forms of help in fact worsened the well-being of some recipients by promoting expensive and sometimes grossly substandard institutional care in preference to home-based alternatives, and by inadvertently pushing up the cost of medical care for everyone. Policy analysts began to document undesirable, unanticipated consequences, carried like seeds in policy proposals that originally appeared to be reasonably benign. Hesitation in the policy community ensued.[13] President Carter, in his 1980 budget message to Congress, described one of the four principles guiding his budget decisions: "Government action must be limited to those areas where its intervention is more likely to solve problems than to compound them" (1980a). Finally, a "New Right" emerged – networks of citizens strongly committed to a halt or at least a sharp decrease in federal policy activity and strongly opposed in particular to federal programs for children and families.

From 1970 to 1979 there were, to be sure, numerous improvements made in existing policies: Social services were "unhinged" – at least in theory – from welfare status by the transformation of Title IVA services into Title XX of the Social Security Act. Early and periodic health screening for children came gradually to greater emphasis within the Medicaid program. In addition, major new laws were enacted – a special nutrition program, the Special Supplemental Food Program for Women, Infants, and Children (WIC) in 1972, and the landmark Education for All Handicapped Children Act in 1975. Two smaller federal programs also emerged: a National Center on Child Abuse and Neglect (slightly expanded in 1978 to emphasize federal response to the problem of sexual abuse of children) and a small effort (never reaching more than $3 million annual funding) aimed at providing data collection and counseling to parents whose babies died of sudden infant death syndrome. (This latter program was folded into a block grant during the Reagan administration.)

Three times a policy proposal for funding comprehensive child development programs failed to be enacted: once due to presidential veto and twice to combined congressional and administration antipathy and divisiveness among the program's advocates. Hostility toward an activist federal role defeated both successful implementation of revised protective standards for federally funded day care and passage of the Child Health Assurance Act. Federal efforts to assure minimum public assistance benefits to mothers and children on AFDC also failed. As the decade closed, however, a significant new program of federal assistance to parents adopting children with special needs, together with major reforms of the delivery system for the nation's billion-dollar financing of foster care – the Adoption Assistance and Child Welfare Act of 1980 – was passed and signed by President Carter. As had been promised, the president requested, and Congress approved, almost a tripling of the modest federal funds available to prevent long-term placement of children in foster care – a major objective of this new law.

Conclusion: themes that help, themes that hinder

Given the tradition of caution that has always enveloped federal policies regarding children and their families, today's policy makers – as well as aspirants to the policy process – do well to attend to those features of policy proposals that hinder the successful transformation of proposals into actual policy and to those that facilitate it. The lessons of the past suggest that the following policy elements hinder transformation of proposals into policy:

1. *Apparent intrusion on parental authority.* From the early defeat of child labor legislation to the stalemate over comprehensive child development legislation, *apparent* federal disregard of parents' rights renders a policy proposal vulnerable to defeat.

2. *Unresolved federal–state–local conflicts over responsibilities and power.* Disputes over traditional responsibilities and prerogatives among

various government levels inevitably serve as "red flags" to successful enactment of policies. Widespread concern for fiscal relief or equal opportunity can override the conflicts, of course. But the degree of friction involved in (a) deciding which competing governmental unit should do what and (b) maintaining complex delivery systems through three or four layers of government can make policy makers, especially those dependent on public goodwill, quite chary of proposals that appear to thread a program through too many levels. When a variety of agencies within those levels are embroiled in disputes over different pieces of the proposed program – and stay embroiled – federal policy makers, sensing trouble ahead, will feel a familiar instinct to "bail out."

On the other hand, an emphasis on block grants as a solution to avoid friction also has its "red flag" features. In federally funded block grants, for example, Congress pays the bill without ever getting a receipt, so to speak. Consequently it becomes difficult to tell taxpayers what they are "buying," and thus difficult to win broad public support for the program's appropriations.

3. *Too few facts, too little results.* Policy proposals that cannot be justified with explanatory facts and programs that fail to report desired effects have always been highly vulnerable, but more so in the climate of intense budget scrutiny prevailing today. Had there been no data about maternal and infant mortality, for example, the early proposals for the Children's Bureau might have been far more easily dismissed as the rantings of overemotional women. And had there been no subsequent evidence of a decrease in those mortality figures in response to legislated efforts, the early federal emphasis on maternal and child health care – now a billion-dollar commitment – would have shriveled.

In contrast, the evolution of the federal role vis-à-vis children and families shows that the following features of a policy proposal facilitate its success:

1. *New scientific knowledge made increasingly available to the public.* Basing a policy proposal on scientific advances that appear to promise real benefits or document real harm increases its chances for serious consideration. The fight against infant death, the federal vaccination programs in the 1950s, and the development and maintenance of Head Start began as policy proposals based on scientific advances. It is most important to emphasize scientific breakthroughs that demonstrate not only that harm is occurring, but that corrective technology likely to be successful is at hand.[14]

2. *Redress of state or local failure.* Proving that inadequacies and problems have *long* existed without effective action by state or local units –

and further that such failure to act exposes children to continuing harm, or to the risk of harm – will draw careful attention from some, if not all, federal policy makers. If state or local officials make this case themselves, the impact is even greater. In the 1960s, the persistent exposure of state failure to respond to hunger in impoverished children finally brought billions of dollars worth of programs into being. Some observers felt the turning point in that campaign came when a silver-haired senator from South Carolina testified that, indeed, his state had not responded adequately (Kotz, 1969).

3. *Promise of cost savings.* Throughout the development of the federal policy perspective on children and their families, most advocates for a given policy proposal have argued the merits of early prevention and its attendant short-term and long-term cost savings. Where they have been able to prove this assertion, their proposals have been well received. Of late, in a political climate urging extraordinary fiscal restraint, the cost-saving elements of a proposal have become virtually central to its successful enactment. Between 1976 and 1980, four programs for young children were, in comparative terms, substantially and deliberately expanded:[15] WIC (high-protein supplemental foods for mothers and babies), adoption assistance and services to prevent long-term foster care placement, childhood immunization, and Head Start. Supporters of all four programs were able to present a persuasive case that without this expansion, more costly expenditures would have resulted. Other proposals – no matter how meritorious in other respects – failed to win the same support.[16]

4. *Respect for the primacy of parents in the lives of most young children.* Three of the hard-won federal laws enacted during the 1970s – when comprehensive child development legislation was repeatedly attacked for "undermining" parents – deliberately emphasized parents. First, the Education for All Handicapped Children Act specifies that parents have the right of approval or diapproval over their children's individualized educational plans. Second, the Adoption Assistance and Child Welfare Act provides special funds for states that assume preventive measures before family breakup – protections that both biological parents and their children can look to as safeguards against undue removal of children from their families into the custody of the state. This law also emphasizes – once reunification of the biological family is no longer possible – the importance of the child's right to be adopted and reared by permanent, loving parents. In addition, the Child Abuse Prevention and Treatment Act (renewed in 1978 as the Child Abuse Prevention, and Treatment and Adoption Reform Act) directs special attention to parent self-help groups in the program of grants authorized under this law. Finally, many ob-

servers feel that the primary role accorded parents in the Head Start Program has been a major element in the widening base of policy maker support for Head Start.

Finally, although not an inherent element of a policy proposal, the persistence of a well-organized network of advocates is absolutely essential. In 1929 the supporters of maternal and child health services in the early decades of the century saw their efforts apparently summarily defeated after years of work and even after tangible successes. But they never quite gave up. Six years later, in 1935, a similar policy won approval and has endured. Head Start appeared to be almost a failed policy in the early 1970s after the publication of the Westinghouse Study. But Head Start has a national network of supporters, many of them parents of Head Start children. And nine years and several more accurate studies later, Head Start was given its own special day in the White House and hailed by a president of the United States as "one of the most beautiful things about America" (Carter, 1980b). In the four years from 1977 to 1981, the Head Start budget was almost doubled at a time when many nonindexed, nonentitlement programs barely kept even. Conversely, the persistence of those who fear any kind of federal "day-care bill" has for 10 years successfully prevented the enactment of a federal program specifically for day care.

Those whose policy interests center on the "unlucky child," whether they argue for or against federal policy involvement, will find, as others have before them, that the caution and protraction that characterize federal policy makers require, in turn, considerable commitment and persistence.

Notes

1 This is not always so. Both federal Aid to Dependent Children and the Early and Periodic Screening, Diagnosis, and Treatment (EPSDT) child health program, for example, were quietly legislated with virtually no opposition. Subsequently, policy decisions guiding their implementation were attended by controversy, but the initial enactment was quite peaceful.
2 I am indebted to the insightful comments of Dr. Faye Coleman, here and in other sections of this chapter, on an earlier draft.
3 See also Josephine Baker, *Fighting for Life* (New York: MacMillan, 1938) for vivid descriptions of maternal and child suffering and death in the urban slums.
4 37 U.S., *Statutes* 79 (1912).
5 Statement of Senator Beveridge, *Congressional Record*, 59th Cong., 2d sess., 1907, 41, pt. 2, excerpted in Grace Abbott, *The Child and the State* (Chicago: University of Chicago Press, 1938). This whole section is informed by the excellent coverage of the child labor issue given by Ms. Abbott, who was chief of the U.S. Children's Bureau from

1921 to 1938. See especially, Vol. 1, *Legal Status in the Family, Apprenticeship, and Child Labor*, pt. 4, "Child Labor in the U.S.," pp. 259–632.

6 Of course, state and local spokespersons for children and youth had a primary influence on these changes in state law. But armed with information collected by the Children's Bureau, they were often able to prod a state toward better adoption or child abuse laws by citing, for instance, the progress other states had made. See Abbott, *The Child and the State*, for example.

7 Statement of Rep. Daughton of North Carolina, Chairman, House Ways and Means Committee, in the *Congressional Record*, House, April 11, 1935, p. 5476, cited in Library of Congress (1908).

8 Social Security Act, 49 U.S., *Statutes at Large*, 78th Cong., 1st sess., chap. 531 (August 14, 1935), Title IV, sec. 401.

9 49 U.S., *Statutes* 633 (1935), Title V, pt. 3.

10 U.S. Congress, House, Committee on Ways and Means, *Hearings on H.R. 10032: Public Welfare Amendments of 1962*, 87th Cong., 2d sess., p. 165.

11 *Congressional Record*, Senate, July 3, 1962, pp. 11769–11770.

12 Testimony of officials of the Department of Health and Human Services in hearings before a subcommittee of the House Committee on Appropriations, 96th Cong., 2d sess., Department of Labor, Health, Education, and Welfare, and Related Agencies, *Appropriations for 1981*, pt. 5.

13 "Policy community" is intended here to mean (1) decision makers within all three branches of government; (2) activists and advocates for children and families; and (3) policy analysts in both research and academic worlds.

14 I am indebted to Gil Steiner of the Brookings Institution for his patient and persistent elucidation of these aspects of the policy process for me. However, Mr. Steiner should bear no responsibility for any of the thoughts presented here.

15 In contrast to the expansion of the Food Stamp program that is triggered automatically by inflation and, additionally, is greatly influenced by unemployment, which stimulates eligibility for the stamps.

16 The Child Health Assurance Act came close, but the attachment of antiabortion amendments, considered undesirable in a Medicaid authorizing statute, in conjunction with the eventual price tag, defeated this bill. In my opinion, although vigorous cost-saving arguments were made, their persuasiveness was hindered by a continued paucity of data showing all the *longitudinal* cost savings associated with early preventive health care.

References

Abbott, G. *The child and the state*. Chicago: University of Chicago Press, 1938.

Carter, J. E. The budget message of the President. In *The budget of the United States government, fiscal year 1980*. Washington, D.C.: U.S. Government Printing Office, 1980. (a)

Carter, J. E. Remarks on the occasion of the 15th anniversary celebration of Head Start, March 12, 1980. (Personal copy of the text of the president's speech) (b)

Children's Defense Fund. *America's children and their families: Basic facts*. Washington, D.C., 1982.

Chisholm, S. Remarks before the Conference of the National Coalition of ESEA, Title I Parents, October 8, 1977.

Dobelstein, A. *Politics, economics and public welfare*. Englewood Cliffs, N.J.: Prentice-Hall, 1980.

Johnson, L. B. Remarks on project Head Start. In E. Zigler & J. Valentine (Eds.), *Project Head Start*. New York: Free Press, 1979.

Kotz, N. *Let them eat promises: The politics of hunger in America*. Englewood Cliffs, N.J.: Prentice-Hall, 1969.

Lawrence, P. The health record of the American people. In *Health in America, 1776–1976*. Washington, D.C.: Department of Health, Education, and Welfare, 1976.

Library of Congress Legislative Reference Service. *Aid to Families with Dependent Children*. Unpublished manuscript, 1968.

Lynn, L. *The state and human services: Organizational change in a political context*. Cambridge: MIT Press, 1980.

Morris, E. *The rise of Theodore Roosevelt*. New York: Coward, McCann and Geoghegan, 1979.

Ross, C. Early skirmishes with poverty. In E. Zigler & J. Valentine (Eds.), *Project Head Start*. New York: Free Press, 1979.

Rothman, S. *Woman's proper place: A history of changing ideals and practices, 1870 to the present*. New York: Basic Books, 1978.

Schorr, A. Program for the social orphans: The next step in social security. *New York Times Magazine*, March 13, 1966, p. 32.

Six decades of action for children. *Children Today*, March–April 1972, *1*, 4.

Snapper, K. The American legacy. In E. Grotberg (Ed.), *Two hundred years of children*. Washington, D.C.: Government Printing Office, 1976.

Social Security Administration. *Research and statistics notes*. December 6, 1967.

Steiner, G. *The children's cause*. Washington, D.C.: Brookings Institution, 1976.

Steinfels, M. *Who's minding the children?* New York: Simon & Schuster, 1973.

United States Public Health Service. Two hundred years of child health. In E. Grotberg (Ed.), *Two hundred years of children*. Washington, D.C.: U.S. Government Printing Office, 1976.

Part II

Conceptualizing policy development

3   Competing perspectives on social policy

Theodore R. Marmor

This chapter addresses topics that are important to those interested in children and American social policy, but is not primarily about children's policies and their politics. Rather, the essay is about competing perspectives on the politics of American public policy. The first section examines the subject matter of politics. It is followed by a review of the dominant approaches taken by political scientists in trying to understand American political life. The third section presents three conceptual frameworks used by analysts in their investigations of American politics. In the fourth section, the workings of American politics are explored, focusing on influences on political outcomes. The chapter concludes with a presentation of conflicts that characterize American politics, emphasizing the peculiar features of redistributive, regulative, and distributive political struggles. Together, these sections review the literature on American politics so that those interested in politics affecting children can place those concerns in the appropriate intellectual setting.

The case for proceeding this way rests on the premise that neither the subject of child policies nor the modes of investigating their politics is distinctive. Government affects children through such diverse means as subsidy and command regulation, redistribution and pork barrel policies, taxation, and the direct provision of services. Moreover, children's lives are affected by policies for children, policies toward families, and policies of general relevance that bear on the fate of America's children. Hence, the subject cannot be narrowly circumscribed, and the methods appropriate to its investigation range over the full spectrum used in studying American politics. The result is an essay on the implications of political analyses of American politics for those especially interested in children.

There are, nonetheless, some conclusions worth highlighting about the character of political struggles over children. The political advocates of children have historically been weaker than those representing labor or

35

America's aged. Child advocates have not bound together social altruism and economic self-interest in the mix that characterizes other, more successful political lobbying groups (Steiner, 1976). That children are not the focus of a durable congressional standing committee both reflects this weakness and aggravates it. The result is a double liability: There are relatively weak institutional mechanisms, first, for producing legislative changes when congressional sponsors are enlisted and coalitions develop, and second, for overseeing agency action on children's programs once they are implemented.

Though the suggestion that Americans are a child-loving people is arguable, the view that the public is responsible for some children in some circumstances is widespread. The consensus could change, however, with important political implications. Over the next decade or two, the very problems that incite gravest concern – the use of drugs, alcohol, and cigarettes by children and adolescents; teenage sex, pregnancy, incidence of venereal disease, and abortion; juvenile crime; and uncertain relations between children and stepparents or single parents – could change the distribution and character of American attitudes toward child policies. Coupled with the blurring boundary between childhood and adulthood, the environment of child policy could substantially shift. One result might be sufficient public hostility or resignation to cause a renunciation of some forms of public responsibility toward children.

Contemporary approaches in political science

Political science is the study of how men are governed. Standard definitions of the focus of study range from the "authoritative allocation of values" (Easton, 1953) to Lasswell's "who gets what, when and how." Social choices concerning the distribution of material and symbolic benefits and burdens within society are central concerns.

The life of politics

The narrowest (and most common) approach in political science concentrates on conflict and decision making in government – who gets what and how in the public arena. Conceptually, analysts using this approach emphasize the direct influences on government (inputs), how governmental institutions convert (process) those influences into decisions or actions (outputs), and the effects of those actions (outcomes). The outputs and outcomes become part of the influences on government (feedback) completing the circuit. This approach has produced a substantial literature on public opinion, on the role of parties and voting, and on other forms of political participation. American political science has particularly emphasized the importance of organized interest groups in politics, not just in elections or in passing (or blocking) legislation, but also in the administrative implementation of programs. American political scientists have also argued that the internal organization and processes of government itself have a profound effect on what decisions are made and what actions are taken. There are innumerable studies of governmental structure, legislative arrangements and rules, public administration and bureaucratic behavior, and the judicial process. Finding out what the government is actually doing, however, is not at all easy. A major task of political science, accordingly, has been to identify and clarify what, in fact, the government does. Since the 1960s, political scientists have increasingly studied the impact of government programs. This approach in political science – the current mainstream – is concerned with what one might term the "life of politics," or the activities in the governmental or public sphere.

The politics of life

A broader (but rarer) approach in political science examines the "politics of life" by studying conflict and collective, authoritative decision making in general, not just governmental settings. This approach recognizes that politics takes place everywhere: in hospitals, in universities, and in relations between private organizations. This approach concentrates on organizations, nongovernmental as well as governmental, and on any situations where collective choices affect who gets what. It deals with micropolitics.

Social structure, political culture, and ideology

Finally, the broadest approach to political science begins with social structure, political culture, and ideology. This perspective highlights the context within which the life of politics and the politics of life take place. The values and social arrangements of every society create systematic biases that favor some interests, promote certain types of action, and affect whether some issues and policies get on the political agenda at all. This broadest approach is usually found in studies that include cross-cultural and cross-national comparisons. Such comparative studies can be very valuable in suggesting new policy alternatives, probable consequences of choices, and the limits of effective choice (Altenstetter, 1974; Heidenheimer, 1973).

Of course, many important issues do not reach the level of collective choice but are settled by what have been called "nondecisions" (Bachrach & Baratz, 1962). Nondecisions involve issues either not decided by the public or not seriously considered in the public realm. The relation between Social Security and health insurance during the Depression of the 1930s illustrates a nondecision. In 1935 President Roosevelt decided to exclude national health insurance from his Social Security proposals because he feared vitriolic and powerful opposition. There was virtually no serious congressional conflict over health insurance at that time – the issue simply did not get on the legislative agenda due to anticipation of political opposition. Politics may well be the "art of the possible," but it is important to understand what makes something possible and how and why that changes.

There are also innumerable instances of policies that are not even seriously considered by decision makers. Such issues are outside the contemporary politics of life or the life of governmental politics, yet they are often very important. They are important not only because the biases of a system are revealed in what is *not* done just as much as by what *is* done (who gets what and how also requires studying who does *not* get what and how). They also are significant because such issues may later become politically salient. To understand how, when, and why such changes take place over time is a neglected, but important, subject of political and sociological analysis.

The social system places limits not only on what is seriously considered but also on what can be accomplished. The structural approach in political science locates children's policies and programs (or those of any other sector) within the larger society, focuses on the incentives for the pressures toward coherence and compatibility with the society, and assesses the impact of society on the behavior of those policies and programs. Consider a society with a barter economy that contemplates a national child-care program that charges fees payable in *cash*. Such a policy is simply incompatible with the social system; it cannot work. The example is simplistic, but it does draw attention to the fact that every society has some limits, and that these limits are vitally important in the formation and implementation of social policies. A more realistic example would be the limits of egalitarian policies in a society based on individual material incentives. The basic problem of the poor in the United States is obviously that they do not have enough money. But massive redistributive cash transfers in an economic system based on wage labor would undermine work incentives. Even public services – education, public housing, food stamps, medical care, and so on – provided at "too high" a level might diminish work incentives. This is not to say such a limit is approached in the United States today, but simply to point out there *is* a limit, a ballpark within which social welfare policy is played out. This ballpark, of course, can and does change; for example, every industrialized nation has developed some form of welfare state over the last 50 years. The structural approach in political science tries to understand, explain, and predict such basic societal changes (Wilensky, 1975).

The social structure not only sets the boundaries within which social behavior occurs, it also directly affects that behavior. The structure of incentives, constraints, and possibilities in a society channels behavior in predictable directions. For example, the undersupply of physicians serving poor or isolated areas is part of larger social processes. Merely increasing the number of physicians will do little to bring medical care to these areas, since the existing incentives and other social and medical opportunities would continue to channel most physicians elsewhere.

Again, the societal context does change over time. A political analyst needs to be concerned not only with feasible short-run solutions to meet immediate problems, but also with how those solutions will interact with and possibly alter basic social processes and structures.

The changing societal context is a critical and often neglected point that should, in other settings, receive fuller elaboration. Here only two concerns must be emphasized. One is the way considerations of short-run political feasibility can unduly narrow the range of public policies considered. Reformers change agendas as well as particular decisions; a good example is how in the field of allied health personnel there has been constant pressure on the boundaries of practices reserved only for licensed physicians. At any one point in the past two decades, one might well have concluded that changes in how children receive care would be dominated by physicians. Changing social and political conditions have altered those constraints. The second point is that programs change the environment in which future possibilities are considered. The failure to consider how Medicaid would affect state budgets has, in some respects, transformed the ameliorative orientation of that program. The key objective for the late 1960s regarding Medicaid was to provide poor people – particularly mothers and children – with decent medical care. The continuation of serious medical inflation – in part fueled by Medicare and Medicaid – has made cost containment the central question for the 1980s.

A pragmatic perspective

Political science obviously covers a vast topic area, ranging from conflict over minor day-to-day collective decision making to major government programs and ultimately to the broadest considerations of social structure and values. There are disadvantages to this broad sweep of subject matter. Any field that can range from office politics to broad Marxist theories of historical development must of necessity often appear (and sometimes be) unfocused or contradictory. But there are also major advantages to be gained from this wide scope.

In the first place, everyone faces the politics of life in the course of daily work. We all are embroiled in issues of conflict and power both with other organizations (Elling, 1963) and within our own (Perrow, 1963). While effectiveness in such situations is to some extent an art – and in any case can only be truly mastered through experience – political science can help to make one sensitive to typical inter- and intraorganizational political problems and processes. Just being alert to the fact that most problems are partly political is a major step. Perhaps most important, by indicating what is typical and why, political science can help find ways to achieve the atypical results that are often desired.

On the next level, with the increased (and increasing) government involvement in many fields of service to children, particularly child health, those professionally involved in the field obviously find themselves affected even more significantly by government. They may often want or need to become involved in the life of politics to get their desired ends, and political science may help them be more efficient and efficacious in governmental settings. More importantly, they will need to be familiar enough with the public sphere to be prepared for the ways in which it can and will affect them. In short, they will need to be able to predict governmental behavior and impact.

Finally, it should be remembered that precisely because of its wide scope, political science is a consumer – and at its best, a synthesizer – of the full range of social sciences. As Aristotle said, it is the queen of the sciences. It is concerned not merely with governmental affairs or material benefits, but with the distribution of all types of social benefits and burdens. To pick just one example, a sensitive study of the development of Title V of the Social Security Act, a section pertaining to maternal and child health, would include a variety of topics: sociological analysis of the changing role of the family and the local and charitable institutions that have ministered to its needs; psychological discussion of children's needs and the reactions of the rest of the population; historical understanding of the evolutionary changes that led to the current situation; economic analysis of the supply, demand, and distribution of services under alternative programs; organizational analysis of the various proponents and public and private bureaucracies that have administered or been involved in the program; and a discussion of the political struggle – the stakes and personalities that have been involved in decision making and implementation. A good political analysis of American government must use all these approaches.

The American governmental system

Power in the American system is often described as "separated." This is inaccurate – it is really shared. The executive, legislative, and judicial branches do not have distinct arenas in which to exercise legitimate power as much as they have overlapping jurisdictions. Much of what we call "policy" develops *after* there has been a legislative decision. With the bureaucracy so large and influential, it has become in some ways a fourth branch of government (Allison, 1975).

The budget-making process illustrates the sharing of power among the branches. Although the Constitution gives Congress the "power of the purse," the budget is actually formed through a long, complicated, interorganizational process: Executive agencies make requests for what they need, want, or hope to get; these are modified by the president's Office of Management and Budget (OMB) before the budget message is sent to Congress; the various committees again change the budget (the Senate and House may have to compromise on an amount); then Congress sends the appropriation back to the president, who may veto it (and may have already threatened to veto it to get a figure more to his liking); the courts may force the president to spend money if he impounds it, or may forbid certain expenditures; and, finally, the bureaucracy administers – and often alters – the actual program expenditures. Thus, the executive, legislature, judiciary, and bureaucracy are all intermingled in ways that frustrate neat separation.

The federal nature of the American system also produces a substantial degree of shared, overlapping authority. Though federal, state, and local governments are often viewed as hierarchical and separate, as in a layer cake, it is more accurate to regard this governmental form as a marble cake, mixed and swirled together (Grodzins, 1966). This is partly because federal legislatures have local constituencies that affect their behavior whereas many federal officials have strong regional ties. More importantly, most programs are a complex mix of federal, state, and local action. The federal government provides categorical grants for a vast number of specific projects and sets standards that the states and localities to some degree meet. Many "federal" programs – like neighborhood health centers – are administered exclusively by local agencies and are altered significantly to fit the political and social features of the localities.

Conversely, even a basically "local" governmental activity like elementary education is strongly influenced by federal grants and regulations.

This sharing of and struggling over authority – both horizontally among the branches and vertically among the units of the federal system – means that most government activity is influenced by complex interactions among the components of the system. The many different federal, state, and local agencies that have overlapping responsibilities and programs in a functional area vastly increase the complexity. It is virtually impossible to learn the specific characteristics of all of these units. There are 50 states, 3,000 counties, and tens of thousands of local governments and special districts; among these various units, legal structures, governmental programs, and political settings vary immensely (Stevens & Stevens, 1974).

Political science can be most useful not by providing a detailed description of governmental institutions and processes, but by providing analytic models and explanatory paradigms that can be applied to both governmental and nongovernmental situations.

The perspectives of political analysis

Graham Allison (1971) has persuasively argued that analysts – and practitioners – tend to use one or more of three conceptual models in thinking about what the government and other political actors do. The models are typically implicit, but each focuses attention – often unconsciously – on different aspects of a situation and directs the user's attention to different problems and facts. The models are not theories of how or why events occur as much as conceptual "lenses" that direct one where to look and what to look for. Since observers see different things from different perspectives, it is important to be aware of these distinguishable models – or lenses – and their use. The three models (termed "rational actor," "political bargaining," and "organizational process") are all used to seek answers to the question, "Why did [will] the government [school] planning agency [commission] . . . etc. take a particular action?" But each uses different units of analysis and causal connections, and so each picks up important but dissimilar angles on the total picture. These models apply to private actors, too, but for convenience only a governmental example will be considered here.

Rational actor

The rational actor model examines governmental action as the product of a single policy-making center's rational choice. It assumes that government acts as a single unit faced with problems that it purposefully tries to solve. Someone using this model would focus on the goals and objectives of "the government," look at possible alternative means to achieve those ends, analyze the probable consequences of each alternative, and then identify the optimal solution as the predicted action (or explain an action as being a solution to the problems the government faced). A statement like "the Hill–Burton Hospital Construction Program was instituted because there was a shortage of hospital beds in the United States" is a good example of this mode of analysis. A problem is identified (a shortage of beds), and government action is explained as a rational response to that problem.

Political bargaining

This model treats government policy as a political result – not necessarily rational – of bargaining between various individual and group actors, each with their own interests, stakes, resources, and political skills. The political bargaining model recognizes that "the government" and attendant groups trying to affect policy are made up of many different agencies, groups, and individuals, and that they almost never share exactly the same goals and priorities. The analysis focuses on the players or actors in various positions and the rules of the game that order the process. Actors have their own parochial perceptions and priorities, for it is recognized that peoples' jobs affect their viewpoints: "Where you stand depends on where you sit." This is true both horizontally (the secretary of Health and Human Services [HHS] has different concerns than the secretary of Housing and Urban Development [HUD] and vertically (the president has different stakes and different perspectives on policy issues than the secretary of HHS). Thus, there is not one set of problems but many, with the players bargaining, compromising, competing, and forming coalitions with others in an attempt to accomplish their respective goals. The result of all this maneuvering is a function of how politically skillful the players are, what kind of resources (money, time, staff help, information, access to or personal ties with other players, official authority, etc.) they can command, and how important the stakes at issue are to them. The result may easily be one nobody set out to produce. Using the political bargaining model, Hill–Burton is viewed as the product of many different forces: the hospitals wanting money, but only for nonprofit hospitals; the Senate sponsors wanting political recognition; states struggling over the formula to apportion money; planners and state health officials wanting their part of the largesse from Washington as well as some control over it.

Organizational process

This model interprets governmental action as primarily the output of large organizations. What we call government action is mostly what goes on in large bureaucracies like the Social Security Administration and Internal Revenue Service. The personnel of such organizations must have rules, repertoires, and standard operating procedures (SOPs) to deal in an orderly manner with the vast number of cases they face. Such SOPs no doubt contribute to the organization's ability to function smoothly and perform its normal tasks. They are systematic and can be analyzed rigorously with fair predictability. Simultaneously, they are not particularly innovative nor adaptable to new circumstances or changed goals.

A central assumption of this model is that large organizations change slowly and incrementally. Most organizational behavior fits into previously established repertoires that constrain options open to government. However innovative a plan may be, it is usually implemented by a bureaucracy that will continue to do things as they were done in the past, at least in the short run. This is one reason new agencies are so often created to administer new programs. An effective decision maker must be aware that bureaucracies are blunt instruments and, when making decisions, must take into account the way in which a program will be administered. Finally, in complex programs involving more than one agency, problems of coordination become immense. Each agency will follow its own SOPs and deal with its own piece of the action, often leaving no one monitoring the overall result.

The organizational process model, then, notes a triple restriction on governmental behavior. First, information, definitions of problems, and suggested solutions often come to a top decision maker from within a bureaucracy, and so are shaped by the way a bureaucracy typically processes such policy tasks. Moreover, the bureaucracy in performing its normal functions has often helped to create the very problem the decision maker faces, and its behavior has foreclosed certain options and possibilities. A decision maker's choices and options are thus narrowed and defined in somewhat systematic ways by the bureaucracy. Second, there is a gap between "choice" at the top and what will actually be done by an organization. The effective decision maker's real options are, as a result, still further limited. Any program that calls for radically new behavior from an existing organization will not be implemented effectively unless very careful attention and substantial resources are spent on altering SOPs and monitoring performance. Finally, the decision maker is faced with a problem of coordination between different branches of the organization.

The interpretation of the Hill–Burton program from an organizational perspective highlights factors that are downplayed by the other approaches. The organizational analyst emphasizes that the problem of inadequate health care for many Americans, particularly in rural areas, was redefined as inadequate medical facilities and, in particular, a shortage of hospital beds. One would then stress that Hill–Burton was not entirely new but similar to other categorical grants to states according to formula. In evaluating the program, it would not be surprising to find that because, at first, the critical shortage was in rural areas, bureaucratic rules were established to channel funds there. Even when central cities had the most pressing need for modernized hospitals (partly through the very success of the program), the bureaucratic rules continued to channel funds to the rural areas (until a congressional amendment in 1964). Directed by the model to look for gaps between "policy decisions" at the top and actual organizational behavior, the analyst would find that although hospitals receiving Hill–Burton funds were supposed to devote 5% of their resources to charity cases, this provision was simply not enforced. Finally, an analyst using this model would look for evidence of poor coordination and might find the Small Business Administration giving loans to new proprietary hospitals (that, of course, were not included in the Hill–Burton plan) for construction right down the street from established hospitals receiving Hill–Burton funds (Lave & Lave, 1974).

Again, it should be emphasized that these models apply to nongovernmental behavior as well. The actions of a large community health center can be seen as the rational adaptation to the problems it faces, or as the result of the procedures and bureaucratic rules of various departments within the center, or as the outcome of bargaining or adjustment between different units (Perrow, 1963).

These conceptual models emphasize that what one sees depends in part on what one looks at and what one looks for. These lenses are employed intuitively and shape the perceptions of most participants. The central task is to use them systematically and consciously. Using only one lens will usually give an incomplete and inaccurate picture. Some combination of all three models is usually necessary to understand an organization's behavior. Most importantly, neglecting a model will usually mean that some crucial aspects of the situation will be ignored, for it is hard to see what one does not look at. In this context, the organizational process model should be emphasized since there is a tendency to assume that once a decision is made – whether through struggle and compromise or some "rational" choice – the issue is resolved. Use of the organizational process model at least ensures that the problems and distortions of implementation will be anticipated.

The workings of American politics: who benefits, who loses

In this section the workings of American politics are presented. The question of who benefits and who loses is addressed through the major claims made about the most influential factors in the outcomes of American political life.

In attempting to understand who gets what how, political scientists have produced several different broad theories about the relationship between political systems and their social setting. Various political science paradigms locate power in different places and regard government action as dominated by different actors and processes benefiting different interests. Although these paradigmatic accounts are not mutually exclusive, they do rest on different assumptions about government and society and, in particular, about the basic factors shaping American patterns of public policy.

Popular rule through elections

The first paradigm emphasizes the role of elections in public policy; it focuses on the undeniable fact that the American electorate has the ultimate formal power to select and discard many of the top government officials. Since these leaders themselves choose a considerable proportion of the nonelected officials, it can be argued that government is ultimately accountable and responsive to the needs and desires of the citizens. Government policies are thus understood as expressing the "will of the people."

Any simplistic democratic theory about American governance is invalidated by the fact that average citizens are not involved in – or even aware of – most government programs. Voting for a candidate cannot be a substantial policy statement on each of the many issues of the day, especially when candidates are ambiguous about their positions. Respected public opinion surveys of the American population show that politics is not a very salient concern to them and that the general public is uninformed about most political issues, personalities, and facts (Campbell et al., 1964). Between a quarter and a third of the adult American population *never* engages in any political activity at all, whereas another quarter does nothing besides vote every two years. Perhaps 10% of the population can be considered aware of, and deeply involved in, political activity.

Those who do vote or are active, it should be noted, tend to be wealthier, with views that are not representative of the whole population (Verba & Nie, 1972). It is still possible that the general public influences the tone or direction of government policy (if not the specifics) by voting against officials when there is a prolonged national crisis. Many voters firmly identify themselves as either Democrats or Republicans, and that identification has historically been the strongest determinant of whom they vote for (stronger than issues or personalities). To the extent that parties formulate different programs, the public, though unaware of specific political issues, may exercise some choice and control over policy by voting for the party whose basic stance they prefer. Still, it is certain that government policies are not a direct expression of popular views and that what government does (and will do) cannot be explained (or predicted) simply by public opinion and the electoral will of the citizenry.

Interest groups

The group process model, probably the dominant paradigm in political science, claims that organized groups and large organizations, not individual citizens, are the vital force driving American politics and that it is these organizations that raise issues, lobby for positions, help select officials, and influence the administration of government programs (Banfield, 1961; Dahl, 1961). The vital importance of organizations stems from their possession of the resources – time, information, and expertise – necessary for effectiveness in the political process. One version of this approach holds that organizations produce the democracy that the electoral system does not because, for example, even though individual workers or doctors are not politically active, the union or the American Medical Association (AMA) represents their position and promotes their interests. But the majority of doctors are not members of the AMA, and many that are do not agree with its political positions (Colombotos, 1975). There are also problems in assuming that an individual's interest and opinions are autonomous. It is known that changes in public opinion often follow events or official statements; it may be government action that causes public opinion, not vice versa (Edelman, 1964). A great deal of an interest group's political effort is expended on convincing its own members, so it is possible that union organizations create labor opinion as much as they express it. Regardless, the paradigm centers on the influence of interest groups, not their democratic nature.

"Pressure" on government officials is one of the least used and least effective means of influence despite the common usage of the term *pres-*

sure group to describe organizational participants in the political process. Interest groups are not in a good position to pressure an official except in rare circumstances. Very few can control enough votes to threaten a recalcitrant official with electoral defeat, nor is money consistently adequate to impose their will. The influence of interest groups comes, therefore, in part from the good relations they maintain with government officials. For example, congressmen must make decisions about so many issues that they simply cannot keep up with them all. Interest groups can usefully provide information, write speeches, even help draft bills for friendly congressmen. Interest groups usually work at activating and helping their supporters rather than trying to convert their opponents.

It is very hard for a congressman (or any official) to know what his constituents or the public are thinking. If those an official sees most often are violently opposed to some policy, the official is likely to have doubts about it, too. Government officials, like the rest of us, want a work setting that is pleasant, nonconflictive, and secure. They would rather avoid decisions that offend major groups with whom they must work or that generate political controversy. But this pattern of trying to control their environment through conciliation leads to a status quo orientation and implies a pattern of policies that typically benefits, or at least does not harm, the most active interest groups. It is good, mutually beneficial relations and extensive contacts that comprise the typical basis of an interest group's influence. Yet because the influence of an interest group rests on its good relations with officials, the power is problematic. Much of the AMA's reputed power and ability to block Medicare rested upon the large number of congressmen who agreed with the AMA and were themselves opposed to a major new government health insurance program (Marmor, 1973). When the 1964 Johnson landslide put new congressmen with different beliefs into office, the "power" of the AMA was revealed in a different light. The AMA was unable to pressure new congressmen into opposing Medicare. Obviously, many interest groups influence policy, but their influence is facilitated by a political culture and ideology that looks with favor on such groups and on private power, and not primarily by pressure.

Even if organized groups seldom have the political power to force a favorable outcome, they nonetheless are deeply involved and influential in the political process. All interests are not, however, equally likely to be well organized, and hence different groups have unequal access to political influence. First, it requires money to organize and engage in political activity, so there is a bias in favor of wealthy organizations. In his classic study of interest politics, Schattschneider (1960, p. 31) concluded that "the business or upper class bias of the pressure system shows up every-where." There is also a bias against large groups with relatively diffuse interests and small stakes, especially groups whose interests involve goods that are available essentially to all or none – clean air, conservation, and so on – so that the beneficiaries cannot be adequately charged.

American political culture

A variant of the group process model emphasizes the distinctiveness of American political culture (Hartz, 1955). Americans tend to distrust power, particularly governmental power and compulsion, and to prefer voluntarism and self-rule in small homogeneous groups with limited purposes. But the problem of compulsion and dominance is not overcome by voluntarism; it is just overlooked. The distrust and avoidance of governmental power typically leads to the capture of public authority by private groups (McConnell, 1970). In many states, for example, it is the doctors themselves who establish the standards for licensing physicians; agricultural policy is made by congressional committees composed of members of agricultural districts in collaboration with representatives of the Farm Bureau. Examples of public authority wielded by private groups could be extended indefinitely. There is an implicit American assumption that self-rule in small groups fosters greater freedom. Self-rule is a cherished American belief, but when hospitals make hospital policy and wheat farmers make wheat policy, their particular interests get well represented at the expense of other, less well-organized constituencies. The importance of this self-rule ideology is both expressed in and reinforced by the federal nature of American politics. Programs initiated and financed largely by the national government are often run and implemented (or not) by state and local interests, to the detriment of larger groups.

The American distrust of power produces a general opposition to increases in the scope of government authority. The American government's efforts in social welfare have been much more limited than in other industrialized democracies and tend to be decentralized and piecemeal (Heidenheimer, 1973). American politics have been characterized as incremental, with programs growing only slowly through time. Lindblom (1959) argues that policies are more the result of accretion than of broad policy decisions; they are not as much made as evolved. Wildavsky (1974) found this same incrementalism in the budgetary process, arguing that programs typically receive the same funding as they did in previous years, with only marginal changes. Lindblom in particular asserts that incremental policy making is desirable in a pluralist democracy because it ensures mutual adjustment and restrains authoritatively imposed policies in situations of uncertainty and value conflict.

Elite rule

Elite theory is the most common paradigm used to respond to the issue of who really influences policy. Its advocates stress that there are relatively few large and immensely powerful institutions in this country, and that these institutions are controlled by a few men in the top positions. C. Wright Mills (1959) has most forcefully presented this view, arguing that there is a power elite in the commanding positions of society who control vast resources and make decisions that dominate the country. Mills argues that the few hundred who run the key institutions – the president of the United States; the heads of General Motors, Exxon, CBS; the joint chiefs of staff; and the like – in effect run the country. He argues that although others certainly make some decisions, the really important decisions that shape the direction of the country are made by this small group. Although most political scientists are skeptical of Mills's extreme formulation, there is no denying the immense importance of a relatively few public and private institutions.

Most of the debate in political science over the role of elites has centered on community power studies. Elitists have argued that there are only a few powerful people who dominate each community or city. Pluralists agree that there is an iron law of oligarchy, that relatively few actors are directly involved in public decision making; but they disagree with the elite theorists on the size of this oligarchy, its homogeneity, and its openness to citizen pressures. Obviously, not all of the 6 million people in Chicago will actually participate in decision making; the real question is how responsive and accountable are the few who do participate in decision making. Robert Dahl (1961) in his classic study of New Haven argued that different leaders were influential on different issues (i.e., there was not one power elite, but different sets of influentials in school policy, urban renewal, etc.), that the actual decision makers were responsive to and influenced by a larger public (partly through anticipated reactions, especially of election results), and that it was possible for newcomers to become influential and affect decisions. Dahl also argued that these influentials were not restricted to the rich but extended to middle- and even lower-income groups. This debate is still unresolved among political scientists, partly because different cities have different power structures, but mostly because methodological and ideological issues seem to dominate the arguments.

Marxism

A Marxist variant of elite theory asserts that the key decision makers are either wealthy themselves or make decisions for the benefit of the capitalist class. More generally, Marxists see government in capitalist countries as serving the interests of capitalism, sometimes muting conflict but perpetuating the dominance of the propertied. This dominance is maintained in part by ameliorative programs for the lower classes that reduce the most disruptive consequences of capitalism without eliminating its basically unequal class structure. Thus, old people are not thrown out of hospitals into the street just because they have no money, unemployed workers are "bought off" by subsistence allowances, and so on. Other government programs socialize costs, so that the government pays for the education or health programs required by capitalism for greater productivity and profits (Miliband, 1969; Navarro, 1975; O'Connor, 1973).

At its strongest, this paradigm attempts to explain why the needs of capital development have led all industrial democracies to some form of welfare state and why the trend seems inevitably in this direction. In this connection, it is deemed noteworthy that education is not simply an individual right but a social duty. The young are required by law to attend school because society needs educated citizens. Some of the arguments in favor of national health insurance also follow in this tradition, stressing the social more than the individual benefits of improved health.

Public finance

It is interesting to compare Marxist paradigms with traditional public finance theory. There are striking similarities – except, of course, for the evaluation. Public finance theorists argue that the state should provide certain key services that cannot be – or are not – provided efficiently by the private sector. Defense and environmental protection are obvious examples, but so are education and training programs: An individual firm cannot provide these programs because workers are mobile, and citizens may not provide them for themselves because of the expense. Because such services in the end benefit all of society, the government should step in to augment or correct the private sector (Musgrave, 1959).

Statist theory

A small but growing body of literature is concerned with "corporatist" or "statist" theory. This school includes works that see the state itself and the top government functionaries as the source of most decisions and the most powerful influence on public policy. In reaction to the greatly increased role of the government, particularly at the federal level, and the shift in power from the legislature to the executive, several theorists have pointed out that the government now has far more resources at its command and much wider influence than does any other sector. The secretary of defense, after all, is the head of a larger enterprise than is the chairman of General Motors, and many government officials control more resources than do the individuals or nongovernmental organizations with whom they deal. Much public policy originates with these officials, reflecting their own view of the public interest or meeting their personal or organizational needs. Although statist theory was developed in studies of authoritarian governments, it is increasingly recognized as relevant to the United States and other democratic countries (Lowi, 1969; Navarro, 1975).

Political struggles: some characteristic types

What does political science specifically have to say about government behavior in programs for children? As mentioned earlier, there is no single "politics of children's policies"; rather, the character of the politics depends on the particular policy. Lowi (1964) has argued that different types of policy issues exhibit different types of political processes, with different actors, styles, locations of conflict, and typical outcomes. Disputes in any single substantive area would exhibit very different characteristics depending on whether the dispute fell into what we term the redistributive, regulative, or distributive arena of American politics.

Redistributive politics

Redistributive programs affect broad groups such as economic classes and large demographic units of the population. A proposal or program can fit into this arena even though, objectively, it is not (or will not be) redistributive in impact. What matters, for example, is not so much whether Medicare actually redistributes medical care income as much as the fact that it is depicted as redistributive and "socialistic." Participants' perception of the issue determines the nature of the political process. In the field of children's policy, redistributive politics confront issues like the proper role of government in organizing, financing, and distributing services for children. The question of the scope of government involvement in the field is the fundamental theme (Steiner, 1976). Although redistributive programs are often described as government "takeovers" or restriction of private initiative, they are not zero-sum games. Increased government involvement can and often does mean increased private authority, too.

Certain patterns of political conflict – site, contestants, argument – are common to redistributive policies regardless of the substantive field. Large national organizations tend to be opposed to one another; sides are relatively stable over time; disputes tend to be ideological in nature; and political struggle is centralized, usually in the federal legislature. The Medicare fight, the struggles over national health insurance, the long dispute about federal aid to education, and the debate concerning Social Security are typical examples of redistributive political struggles.

The scope of conflict (or who is involved) has been called the "most important strategy of politics" (Schattschneider, 1960, p. 31). Obviously, the arena of dispute has a major impact on what kinds of policies emerge and whom they benefit. Redistributive political conflict also takes place at the state and local levels. But because of the larger constituency, it is more salient and more common at the national level. McConnell (1970) argued that the larger the constituency actively involved in conflict, the closer the result will be to the interests of the mass public. Small constituencies, in this view, make it easier for private power to appropriate public authority for their own interests; federal programs, according to McConnell, tend to favor private interest less and to be more progressive than state programs. Resolutions of national redistributive conflicts do appear to distribute benefits to groups that normally benefit less from American politics (and American society). Yet clear decisions about redistributive conflicts are relatively rare. Because of the stable cleavage patterns involved in redistributive politics, it usually requires an unusual or dramatic event for political resolution. Thus, the Depression clearly helped produce the New Deal social welfare legislation, and the Johnson landslide in 1964 created the conditions for the immediate passage of Medicaid, Medicare, and federal aid to education. The stable cleavages associated with redistributive politics constitute reason for the oft-noted periodic nature of American politics – periods of relative stability followed by periods of major program innovation.

Regulative politics

When decisions about the proper scope and role of government are finally made, new conflicts emerge over the administration and financing of the programs and over the effects of such programs on the industry involved. Most political controversies over finance and administration conform to the pattern that Lowi (1964) terms "regulative politics." Regulative politics do not involve broad social groups but rather a sector, industry, or organized set of producers or consumers. The smaller groups involved in regulative politics are not class-based. The conflict is less ideological, and it tends to center in the executive branch. Regulative politics are not confined to what are officially called regulatory commissions or agencies, but they occur whenever decisions are made that change the burdens or benefits of an industry or sector.

Typically, producer groups, with relatively better organization, more resources, and greater stakes in the outcome, dominate the struggles in the regulative arena. This creates a situation of "unbalanced interests" where the producer groups have vital stakes for which to fight. Because they have the resources, the producer groups can usually get much of what they want.

The regulative policy arena is often characterized by what Edelman (1964, p. 38) has called symbolic politics. He defines this as "the rhetoric to one side and the decision to the other." For example, in the midst of popular demand to control rising medical service costs, a regulative commission might well be created to review rate increases. This satisfies the public that "something is being done," but the commission actually may have little control over rates or may not even end up aiding the industry. The political market of unbalanced interests means that while the public may receive symbolic benefits, the producers usually get most of the material benefits.

Distributive politics

The distributive policy arena, Lowi's third, involves issues that can be disaggregated into small units and decisions that can be made without general rules that apply to a whole sector or industry. Questions about the supply of services – where to build a new clinic, how to divide up a program budget among different localities or functions – typically fall into this arena. The key is that the beneficiaries are separated from those who bear the burdens, and the decisions are discrete and can be made with little obvious relation to other decisions. This is not to say that there are no relations, for with finite resources a special grant to one Head Start program means that another program will get less. But what is important is that the decision can be made on a case-by-case basis, the parties may never have to face each other, one group winning does not obviously point to another group losing, and there do not have to be rules that apply to all. An overall policy emerges, of course, but it is the aggregate of a large number of discrete decisions, not a consciously planned and coherent policy. Decisions are often arrived at through logrolling, in which there is a little something for everyone directly involved. Actors in this area tend to be individuals, committees, and planning commissions rather than classes, national organizations, or large groups of producers or consumers. Struggle is usually nonideological, and results depend on the specific circumstances of each case.

When such issues are decided at the local level, the outcome will depend on the local power structure, the salience of the issue, and the attitudes and skills of the individuals involved. Outcomes in this arena will vary by community and may change with time, but in general the dominant local elites and notables will win.

This chapter has dealt with what political science and its findings have said about the social policy world. In this discussion of various approaches to political life, examples have been culled from many disciplines and programs. Further discussion of different perspectives on social welfare programs and the effects that such perspectives have on policy evaluation is not possible in this context but may be found elsewhere.[1] What is crucial to underscore is that policy analysts and policy makers bring sharply different perspectives to the policy process, often mixing philosophical and empirical issues. What the welfare state was meant to accomplish has been and always will be contentious. That a coherent social policy for children has not emerged should surprise no one.

Note

[1] For a fuller discussion on perspectives of the welfare state, its purposes, the character of the programs, and its evaluation, the reader is guided to Theodore Marmor's "The North American Welfare State: Social Science and Evaluation," in Charles Anderson and Robert Solo (Eds.), *Value Judgement in Income Distribution* (New York: Praeger, 1981).

References

Allison, G. *Essence of decision: Examining the Cuban missile crisis.* Boston: Little, Brown, 1971.

Allison, G. Implementation analysis. In R. Zeckhauser (Ed.), *Benefit–cost and policy analysis.* Chicago: Aldine, 1975.

Altenstetter, C. Medical interests and the public interest: West Germany and the USA. *International Journal of Health Services*, 1974, *4*, 29–48.

Bachrach, P., & Baratz, M. Two faces of power. *American Political Science Review*, 1962, *59*, 947–952.

Banfield, E. *Political influence.* New York: Knopf, 1961.

Campbell, A., Converse, P. E., Miller, W. E., & Stokes, D. E. *The American voter.* New York: Wiley, 1964.

Colombotos, J. Physicians view national health insurance. *Medical Care,* 1975, *13*(5), 369–396.

Dahl, R. *Who governs?* New Haven: Yale University Press, 1961.

Easton, D. *The political system.* New York: Alfred Knopf, 1953.

Edelman, M. *The symbolic uses of politics.* Urbana: University of Illinois Press, 1964.

Elling, R. The hospital-support game in urban centers. In E. Freidson (Ed.), *The hospital in modern society.* Glencoe, Ill: Free Press, 1963.

Grodzins, M. *The American system.* Chicago: Rand McNally, 1966.

Hartz, L. *The liberal tradition in America.* New York: Harcourt, Brace and World, 1955.

Heidenheimer, A. The politics of public education, health, and welfare in the U.S.A. and Western Europe. *British Journal of Political Science,* 1973, *3,* 315–340.

Lave, J., & Lave, L. *The hospital construction act.* Washington, D.C.: American Enterprise Institute, 1974.

Lindblom, C. E. The science of muddling through. *Public Administration Review,* 1959, *19,* 79–88.

Lowi, T. American business public policy, case studies, and political theory. *World Politics,* 1964, *16,* 677–715.

Lowi, T. *The end of liberalism.* New York: Norton, 1969.

Marmor, T. R. *The politics of medicare.* Chicago: Aldine, 1973.

McConnell, G. *Private power and American democracy.* New York: Knopf, 1970.

Miliband, R. *The state of capitalist society.* New York: Basic Books, 1969.

Mills, C. W. *The power elite.* New York: Oxford University Press, 1959.

Musgrave, R. *The theory of public finance.* New York: McGraw-Hill, 1959.

Navarro, V. Health and corporate society. *Social Policy,* 1975, *5,* 41–49.

O'Connor, J. *The fiscal crisis of the state.* New York: St. Martin's Press, 1973.

Perrow, C. Goals and power structures: A historical case study. In E. Freidson (Ed.), *The hospital in modern society.* Glencoe, Ill.: Free Press, 1963.

Schattschneider, E. *The semi-sovereign people.* New York: Holt, Rinehart and Winston, 1960.

Steiner, G. *The children's cause.* Washington, D.C.: Brookings Institution, 1976.

Stevens, R. B., & Stevens, R. *Welfare medicine in America: A case study of medicaid.* New York: Free Press, 1974.

Verba, S., & Nie, N. *Participation in America.* New York: Harper & Row, 1972.

Wildavsky, A. *The politics of the budgetary process* (2nd ed.). Boston: Little, Brown, 1974.

Wilensky, H. *The welfare state and equality.* Berkeley: University of California Press, 1975.

4 The policy process as a perspective for understanding

Garry D. Brewer

The United States has no comprehensive policy to guide its hundreds of programs for children. Instead, there is a highly fragmented, ad hoc, complicated, and chaotic hodgepodge incapable of measuring up to the large and expanding set of problems that press for attention and resolution. Matters are clearly out of control, an opinion shared by former Secretary of Health, Education, and Welfare (HEW), Elliot Richardson:

There is, in my opinion, a developing crisis – still largely hidden – facing the human service sector of our society, a crisis which may challenge the fundamental capability of our society to govern itself. It is a crisis of performance – our institutions are failing to live up to our expectations. It is a crisis of control – in many fundamental respects the human service system is developing beyond the scope of Executive control . . . or of Congressional control . . . or of consumer control . . . or of public control. [Richardson, 1973, pp. 1–2]

If this assessment is even partly accurate – and events of the last decade seem to sustain it – there is a large requirement to begin diagnosing the problem in the interest of its prompt resolution. The following brief discussion begins this difficult task by presenting the elements of a general policy or decision process and then setting these off against several of the key intellectual and institutional features of policy making for children.

Policy as process

It is helpful to conceive of problems as having a "life," during which time they emerge, are defined and estimated as to their potentialities, are confronted with strategic statements (policies) and tactical measures (programs) that are meant to reduce or resolve their unwanted consequences, and in time end, stabilize, or worsen as the result of both corrective acts and changes in the problem setting itself (Brewer, 1974; Brewer & deLeon, 1983).

57

Initiation

The earliest phase of the process begins when a problem is recognized. Once this occurs, many possible means to alleviate, mitigate, or resolve it may be explored (Wilensky, 1967). It should be expected that many of the initially proposed "solutions" will be ill defined, inappropriate, or infeasible. This phase is marked by efforts to appreciate the full complexity of the problem, at least in its coarse outlines, and the beginning of data collection efforts thought to be needed to sketch out the form and texture of the situation (Lasswell, 1971, chap. 2). If successful, this phase stimulates enough creativity to enable unrefined and tentative answers to flow from an evolving and sharpening definition of "What's the problem?"

Estimation

Estimation generally continues work begun during initiation: Systematic investigation of a problem and thoughtful assessment of options and alternatives are featured tasks. Specifically, estimation concerns the accurate determination of all likely costs and benefits (considered in monetary and many other terms) that are expected to flow from decisions taken during the subsequent, or selection, stage of the overall process (Mishan, 1973). Consideration is given both to the probable consequences of positive action and to those expected to result from inaction, whether intentional or not (Quade, 1975). Estimation efforts aim to reduce uncertainties about possible choices to the greatest extent possible, given time, intellectual, and other constraints (Rivlin, 1971).

For some problems, the move from initiation to estimation is clear-cut: Formal ties are instituted with specialized individuals and experienced institutions. Sometimes the move is made only slowly or hardly at all: Many problems fail to capture public attention; fail to displace other, more salient ones; or remain unattended until some precipitate event forces the matter into the full glare of attention. The problem of inhumane conditions and treatment in the Willowbrook, New York mental institution had existed unattended for many years until brought to light in a sensational television documentary and book (Rivera, 1972). The "event," in this case, was a "media event" that served to focus public and official attention on severely needed changes.

In any case, estimation is usefully imagined as a separate phase of the policy process – a phase having many important aspects and functions and distinct participants. Estimation also has understandable implications for all other phases, the nature and quality of decisions made, and the specific outcomes eventually realized (Myrdal, 1971).

Selection

The third phase is most easily seen as the "political" step. Someone, usually the policy or decision maker, must select from the "invented" and "estimated" options. This individual (or collectivity) strikes a balance between the analyst's calculations and the multiple, changing, and conflicting goals of those having a stake in the problem and the society at large (Dahl & Lindblom, 1976; Vickers, 1968). The resolution, embodied in the option actually selected and the programs enacted in its behalf, is the primary business of the politician, who "has to balance the myriad forces as he sees best, and the citizens judge him only to a limited extent by his accordance with their preconceived ideas. Rather, a great political leader is judged like a great composer; one looks to see what he has created" (Lewis, 1967, p. 207). What is heard in the realm of children's policy is cacophony or, at best, an occasional jingle. The field has yet to produce a Beethoven.

Implementation

Implementation refers to the execution of the selected option. Until recently, this phase of the process had received only passing intellectual attention (Pressman & Wildavsky, 1973). In part this shortcoming stemmed from the mistaken impression that merely passing a law was equivalent to putting a law into practice (Rabinovitz, Pressman, & Rein, 1976). As many reflective and astute bureaucrats know perfectly well, the writers of rules and the issuers of guidelines can, and often do, play a critical political role in carrying out legislative intentions and decisions (Bardach, 1977). As with all phases of the overall process, we need to think more systematically about implementation so as to integrate it (Hargrove, 1975). Certainly one must understand implementation mechanisms before government (and other) performance can be evaluated and improved, the next step in the sequence.

Evaluation

Initiation and estimation are primarily forward-looking activities. Selection stresses the urgency of the present, as does implementation. Evaluation, basically backward-looking, is concerned with inquiries into system performance and individual responsibility and specializes in figuring out how well problems are being dealt with and resolved (Weiss, 1972). Typical topics and questions reflected in the idea of evaluation include the following: What officials, policies, and programs were successful or unsuccessful in resolving a given problem? How can one assess and measure performance (Chapple & Sayles, 1961)? What criteria were used to make those determinations (Suchman, 1967)? Who made the assessment, and what motivated the assessor and those commissioning the evaluation (Clark, 1975; Hyman & Wright, 1971)? Evaluation is an essential input to the next and final phase of the process, termination.

Termination

Termination is necessary when policies and programs have become dysfunctional, redundant, outmoded, unnecessary, and so forth. From the conceptual point of view, it is not a well-developed phase (Cameron, 1978); however, one should not rate its importance by the lack of understanding of it – as has been startlingly illustrated by recent taxpayer initiatives and by a growing concern in the federal legislature for "sunset laws," "zero-based budgets," "deregulation," and the like (Levine, 1980). How, for instance, can a policy or program be adjusted or terminated without having had a thorough evaluation? If the closing of Massachusetts's public training schools proved nothing else, it was that termination without evaluation could be accomplished, but at great cost to those involved (Behn, 1976). Who suffers from this termination, which is often cloaked in bureaucratic euphemisms such as "deinstitutionalization"? In the case of those turned out of the Agnews State Hospital in California, suffering was not simply limited to the released patients, but to many in the communities where these souls sought solace (Wolpert & Wolpert, 1976). What provisions of redress have to be considered? What personal costs are involved in termination? Can they be met? What can be learned from termination that will inform the initiation of new policies and programs in the same or related fields? In the case of major changes in California's foster-care programs, for example, short-term successes in creating private group-care homes appear to have attenuated rapidly in the face of accelerating costs; the problem of what to do with those in need of foster care did not "go away" by replacing public services with private ones (California Department of Social Services, 1980). The list of relevant questions is long (Brewer, 1978), but neither these questions nor the fact that termination is linked intimately to the other steps in the policy process should be ignored (Bardach, 1976).

An overview of the model

The value of the conception of policy as a sequential process lies mainly in its utility; it is a useful device to help one orient problems to the individual and institutional settings in which they occur. The process view has other general benefits for those who adopt and take advantage of it. For instance, initiation and estimation together refer to preventive activities that conceivably take place before someone reaches decisions about "what to do." These two phases allow problems to be recognized and hence engender creative thinking, crude hypothesis testing, and prototypical designing. As circumstances move beyond initial recognition, preventive acts change somewhat to emphasize more scientific and analytic explorations of the likely consequences of decision options. Besides analysis, estimation involves the development of policy and programmatic specification and details. Estimation responds to the questions: "What are we trying to accomplish?" and "How are we going to go about doing it?" The overriding value of preventive efforts lies in the increased prospect for timely sensing of problems and efficiently allocating resources for their solution.

Selection and implementation concern more active policy modes. Selection allows politics to operate: Compromises are struck and debate and attention settle on more realistic, feasible, and desirable options. Implementation is the "doing" phase: Rules, regulations, and guidelines are developed; program structures, including the precise allocation of budgets, are formulated and put into action; and expected performance standards are established (Downs, 1976).

Evaluation and termination are more reactive or remedial in character. Means to compare actual and expected performance are instituted, and the assignment of responsibility and imposition of sanctions for both outstanding and substandard performance are made. Based on such realistic comparisons, including a determination of whether a problem has been resolved to some acceptable degree, termination in whole or part may be indicated – a reaction to the changed circumstances resulting from the natural evolution and dynamics of a given problem, its response to policy and program interventions, or other, competing demands on the resources expended in the problem's behalf. Termination also has a capacity for generating new problems that, in time, may require the entire process to begin anew.

Children's policy and the process: a larger view

The preventive steps of initiation and estimation have taken a back seat to more active ones and have therefore contributed to the "crisis" atmosphere noted earlier by Richardson. For instance, detailed estimates of the scope and likely expense related to the 1975 Education for All Handicapped Children Act (Public Law 94–142) were only initially undertaken five years after the legislation was enacted and various complex rules and regulations for its implementation had been mandated to the states.[1] Little wonder that so much confusion and disagreement exist as to program objectives, execution means, and performance standards. In the well-intended effort to secure and reaffirm certain educational rights to a large number of this nation's children, many critical longer-term consequences were scarcely considered. Not the least of these is the emerging and sharp doubt cast on the legitimacy of federal education officials and, in turn, the entire system of government that they represent and symbolize.

It is also evident that a comprehensive and holistic approach, wherein the full complexity of children's needs is considered and then matched against present and future programs and services, has not gained official favor, nor has it taken hold in the analytic and scientific communities. At approximately the same time that decisions were being made to provide the extremely costly special educational programs wrought by P.L. 94–142, a comprehensive evaluation of *all* handicapped children's programs and services was reporting that there was "only some $50 million specifically targeted for prevention activities for children; in other words, about 1 percent is targeted for prevention and 99 percent for service after the child is handicapped" (Brewer & Kakalik, 1979, p. 101). (Of that 99 percent, more than half was already for special education.) This same report noted nearly comparable imbalance for programs meant to identify children with actual or potentially handicapping conditions, despite the well-known fact that early identification and appropriate treatment often result in a reduction in the individual's deficit and hence in the total amount, intensity, and cost of services required throughout later life (Brewer & Kakalik, 1979, chap. 7).

Initiation and estimation, in short, are sporadic and disconnected from the sources of power and wealth that could and should be galvanized to make creative and useful decisions on behalf of children. Great deficiencies exist in the data describing important characteristics of children in this country, not the least of which is a reliable, generally-agreed-to set of incidence figures to indicate children with special needs. Common reliance on "rules of thumb," such as fixing 3% as the percentage of the total child population that is mentally impaired, is simply inadequate for making responsible estimates of social policies and programs. Not only does it fail to yield a respectable sense of the total magnitude of the problem of mental impairment,[2] it does little to indicate varying degrees of impairment, different services and resources required throughout the children's lives, or readily observed variations in the concentration and composition of the total population throughout the country (Conley, 1973). Estimation has been neglected. In a situation where many centers of research and analysis are needed and where continuity of work is imperative (Hobbs, 1975, pp. 275–283), we are confronted with one-shot studies, ad hoc analyses of dubious merit, spotty coverage of faddish topics, and exasperation in having to start over from scratch to rediscover old truths forgotten in the disorderly turnover of bureaucratic sponsors and in the ineffective use of studies commissioned, completed, and then set on a shelf never to be read again.[3] The general field of policy research and analysis is a complicated one; however, it is fair to say that there is not enough of it, and what does exist is seldom orchestrated to advantage or well connected to decision-making and implementation activities.

Decision making affecting children's lives has evolved piecemeal and without benefit of much compelling or thoughtful analysis (Berke & Kirst, 1972; Hobbs, 1975; Riessman, 1972; Spiegel, 1971). Decisions have been reached, when made at all, in a crisis atmosphere of last-resort measures taken to placate special interests;[4] they have tended to be short-sighted and unmindful of longer-range consequences (Brewer & Kakalik, 1979, chap. 15); and they have been little concerned with the complex needs of the total child (e.g., categorical aid programs that "act" as if only a bureaucratically defined and sanctioned part of a child's needs warranted attention). Much of this can be grasped, if not readily corrected, by realizing that the overall process has not been understood or institutionalized. Comparable problems with implementation exist, too.

Implementation has been left to a bewildering array of offices and agencies at all levels of government, and the results have been far from satisfactory. With respect to any defined population of exceptional children (e.g., gifted and talented, learning-disabled, sensorially impaired, malnourished, or abused), no one really knows or knows very well the whole array of programs and services that exist and to which these individuals are entitled. In the words of Hobbs, "In Washington, programs for exceptional children are lodged in a myriad of agencies on authorization of hundreds of separate pieces of legislation that defy complete understanding and make coordination of effort extremely difficult" (1975, p. 185). For example, the challenging task of making an inventory of existing programs for exceptional children has not been done. Lacking such basic information, no agency or individual can know how a new policy or program proposal is likely to relate to, complement, or conflict with those already in place. No parent or family, in the present situation, can be expected to know what is available, what their child needs and could benefit from, and to what they are entitled. As it stands, the system currently providing services to the nation's exceptional children is so complex and disorganized that it defies efficient and effective operations (Brewer & Kakalik, 1979, chap. 8).

This is not to say that the federal government should be held solely accountable for these deficiencies. Nor is it to say that future efforts should concentrate attention and effort at the federal level. Rather, a full flowering of policy and program activities in a variety of governmental and other institutional settings is long overdue. Lacking such developments, the present chaotic system edges ever closer to a full-blown crisis (Brody, 1980, p. C-1). At the moment it is a system that features expedient political choices made without fundamental information about children's full needs. Quieting vocal parochial interests that dominate many key decisions is not the same as developing an intelligible or intelligent policy for children. It is a system that fails to learn from its own mistakes. And it is a system that is headed for even more monumental difficulties if many concerned scholars, analysts, and officials do not begin to face these facts responsibly. For instance, it is inconceivable that one could propose terminations of existing programs without there having been full and comprehensive evaluations of their relative merits. A "10% across the board" reduction strategy may very well spread the political pain of termination, but it does little to recognize the real difference in quality and need that mark respective programs. A 10% reduction in a vital program certainly has different consequences than a similar reduction in one filled with fat. Lacking sensitive and sensible evaluation, however, this essential distinction gets lost very quickly and easily falls victim to the political meat ax. This theoretical point was sharply underscored by Secretary of Education T. H. Bell, who noted very early that the Reagan administration was going to cut back on numerous educational programs. But how this was to be accomplished and what outcomes were to be expected – in addition to cost cutting – were not determined, or, in Bell's words, "We don't yet know how we're going to do it, but we're going to reduce the dollar demands" (cited in Fiske, 1981, p. A-1).

Any one of the individual phases of the policy process could be singled out for more detailed attention, especially concerning the information, resources, demands, and institutions that are operating or that could be devised to improve prevailing practices. Such in-depth studies have value in their own right and offer opportunities to explore many important connections among the individual phases. Our purposes here, however, are more modest, and only a few of the more obvious weaknesses of the initiation and estimation phases of the process are detailed.

Severe weaknesses in the process

General goals sought

Although one may differ with the precise statement of goals to be sought through improved initiation and estimation, the following examples from Richardson (1973) help focus the discussion and provide points of departure for the balance of the chapter. Richardson provides a remarkably clear and concise treatment of changes needed in initiation and estimation:

> *Increasing comprehensiveness:* In planning and programming, our perspective must be comprehensive. . . . Integration must replace fragmentation. [P. 10]
>
> *Increasing participation:* Effective management . . . is crucially dependent upon: . . . the processes which define the relationships among people – the means openly and equitably to ensure the orderly and timely participation in the decision-making process by all affected parties. [P. 13]
>
> *Increasing awareness of intended and unintended consequences:* [Improving management] means developing informed and sensitive appreciation of the consequences of intended action. [P. 13]
>
> *Institutional reform:* Institutional reform can . . . contribute to the conservation of limited resources. It can seek to assure that the agencies, organizations, and skills that are capable of making some contribution to the protection and development of human resources are properly deployed. [P. 21]

Attainment of the goal of comprehensiveness has been thwarted for many of the general reasons noted earlier. Its accomplishment, through better, ongoing, and relatively holistic problem-identifying and problem-solving activities, would do much to bring perspective and proportion to the totality of children's needs and the policies and programs we have created in their behalf.

The desire to increase and broaden participation is, of course, consonant with general democratic principles meant to include all who have an interest and stake in a given problem. Development of early warning (initiation) and related follow-up analytic capacities (estimation) would do much to reduce a current situation of crisis decision making – where problems are allowed to go unattended until conditions become severe enough to warrant action, but where such action is taken quickly and without benefit of wide consideration of interests and alternative means for achieving relief or remediation. Improved initiation and estimation have the desirable properties of giving one time to create alternatives and to imagine how each will alter individual circumstances. Participation is necessarily curtailed when choices are demanded instantly.

Similarly, precipitate action taken in the absence of forethought carries with it an unwanted and unnecessary burden of uncertainty about what will actually happen in the aftermath. Although no analysis will ever totally reduce uncertainty, some prior thought is usually better than little or none.

Of course, institutional reform is one means to improve deficient practices. A major focus for such reform is one that emphasizes the creative requirements for improved initiation and estimation.

Initiation

Much decision-making activity in the general area of children's policy appears to have occurred without benefit of suitable or adequate data and information.

Every child is exceptional in some way.[5] But how exceptional and in what ways must a child be exceptional before society deems it desirable to provide special services? No one would disagree with the premise that a severely retarded or deaf–blind child is exceptional, but when children have mild degrees of exceptionality the choice of whether or not to provide special services is more difficult. A fundamental truth is that sufficient funds are not available, and are not likely to be available in the near future, to provide every conceivable service to every individual child. Decisions must thus be made on definitions of who will be provided special services. Obviously these definitions will affect the number of children eligible for special services and the funding levels reasonably likely to be available, and the likely costs and benefits from providing or refusing to provide special services will affect society's definition of exceptional children. All of this has serious implications for the collection of stable, reliable, and meaningful primary data on the size, composition, and spatial distribution of our child population (i.e., demographic information of the most fundamental sort). Such data are essential to efficient decision making and management and to effective understanding of many social problems. Demographic information is the most basic element of any social or policy analysis, and yet it is repeatedly found to be inappropriate, outmoded, or simply not available. Because the definitional matter has been left to political whim, accurate and consistent portrayals of our children's evolving status and needs have been extremely rare.

Definitions in the field of child policy have routinely changed over time and have varied from one jurisdiction to another. For example, definitions of those children eligible for special education services have shifted in recent decades from exclusion to inclusion of the more severely handicapped, the very mildly handicapped, and some children below the age of five years. Such changes reflect political considerations, not scientific ones. They furthermore make evaluation of cumulative improvements or impacts on the population in question difficult if not impossible (Sarason & Doris, 1979, chaps. 15 & 17).

In addition to changes in differences with time and place, nearly all definitions of exceptional children are nonspecific in the sense that they permit a great deal of latitude on the part of local agencies and personnel to decide who actually are exceptional children. Because definitions are not necessarily comparable across jurisdictions, an individual child might be "handicapped" if he or she lived in one location but "normal" if he or she lived elsewhere. Or a child might be categorized as having one type of handicap in one location and another type in another location, even if both locations had the same set of possible categories of handicapping conditions (Hobbs, 1975).

The fact that the definitions of service needs also change through time and from place to place further complicates the matter of trying to figure out "What is the problem, and for whom?" For instance, the definition of service need for moderately retarded children in many jurisdictions used to be 24-hour-a-day residential care in a mental institution, with little attempt to provide specific educational services to help them develop toward their maximum potential. Today the prevailing notion, which is by no means invariable, is to provide special education and training services to develop the child's potential and allow him or her to function in the least restrictive environment possible.

Resolution of the definition issue is primarily a matter of making a value judgment and being precise in articulating that judgment. Most existing definitions appear to be purposefully vague, perhaps as a result of compromises made to attain political consensus or perhaps as a result of unwillingness to say precisely and unequivocally to any organization or group of lobbying parents that their children's needs are of low priority and will not be met. Resolution of the definition issue is a vital research matter. The dearth of data available on the populations of interest and on the costs and effects of serving or not serving exceptional children with various characteristics makes it difficult to make responsible judgments on the definition issue and on the realistic needs of our children. Unfortunately, current definitions are not closely related to service needs, and data on incidence rates of exceptionalities in the general child population are appallingly lacking (Brewer & Kakalik, 1979, chap. 5; Craig, 1976; Craig & McEachron, 1975; Rossmiller, Hale, & Frohreich, 1970).

Responsible problem identification or initiation proceeds by determining the relevant actors and their interactions and by discovering how the problem can be bounded, analyzed, and understood. The identification and assessment of actors comprise an overtly judgmental activity that continues throughout the entire policy process. However, the analyst has a responsibility to define who is likely to be affected by a particular problem and the alternatives generated for its solution; lacking such information, no one can judge the importance or priority of the problem (Quade, 1968). The result is policy making without adequate information; if one is unable to ask appropriate questions, there is no reason to expect there to be many reasonable answers. A common error at this step has been to define children's problems in parochial, narrow terms emphasized by a particular interest group; most children's issues are in fact broad in scope and contain numerous important interdependencies, as we shall see in a later illustration of planning for deaf–blind children.

Bounding the problem requires that the analyst reduce the problem to manageable proportions; the analyst has only limited time and information, and choices must be made. In a very few cases, the whole problem may be dealt with directly. More often, the problem must be decomposed into a number of smaller and more manageable parts. Misspecification appears to have happened in many specific instances of children's legislation: Only a small piece of the problem was treated directly within the policies and programs created to "solve" it. In many cases, the "solution" only made matters worse. Pouring many additional billions of dollars into special education, as has been done, without considering related aspects associated with prevention and identification services is a very clear instance of problem misspecification.

In any event, adequate problem identification, the primary function of initiation, has been seriously hampered by poor or nonexistent data. Two extreme "solutions" to the data problem exist: ignoring it by concentrating mainly on theoretical relationships imagined to exist governing social action, or picking selectively from "data" whose sources, validity, and interrelationships are not well established, so as to sustain politically or ideologically driven preferences (Coleman, 1966). Neither course is recommended. But what to do?

Thinking about this question and then trying to resolve it call attention to several fundamental difficulties that confront one interested in responsible policy analysis or estimation.

Estimation

A simple solution is not to do policy analysis at all, and hence to rational-ize away the importance, priority, or solvability of the specific problem at hand. Such a choice, of course, reaffirms the status quo. A more satisfac-tory solution is not to ignore one's professional responsibility. Advice based on poor data, the most common situation, may be less than ade-quate, but it may also be the best advice available under the circum-stances. A decision maker should know – be informed – about data and analytic shortcomings of this and other sorts. The adequacy, expediency, and erroneousness of data collection and use are all relative concepts, to be judged with respect to realistic conditions. Could someone else have done better . . . under the given circumstances? All data and analyses are more or less erroneous or inadequate, and these qualities apply to both policy and basic research. These properties, too, are not properly con-sidered as absolutes (since all data are erroneous, one should not do analysis); rather one needs to determine the degree of error and the amount of inadequacy tolerable, given time and other circumstances (Bardach, 1974).

This is not to say that data are entirely lacking; often they are not. Rather, the actual problem appears to be one where estimation is both ill developed and disconnected from selection and other subsequent phases of the policy process.

Many of these general points are illustrated in specific detail by our society's response to an exceptionally large population of handicapped children who were born during a major outbreak of rubella in the mid-1960s. Estimates vary, but something on the order of 30,000 to 40,000 handicapped children were born during the 1963–1965 period of epidemic rubella in this country (Calvert, 1969). Many of this group were severely disabled (e.g., multiple handicapping conditions, deafness, and blind-ness). This much-larger-than-average cohort of handicapped contains children who are all presently entering late teenage and early adulthood. This fact has created major problems for the service system in responding to the children's needs as they progressed from needing medical and preschool services to needing very special types of education, vocational, residential, and other services more directly related to their advancing years.

While the total number of deaf–blind children identified in this cohort is small – somewhere between 4,500 and 5,500 have been discovered (Dantona, 1974) – their obvious plight and demands for services are extra-ordinary. These children, perhaps more than any other category of exceptional children, require services that are more specialized and usually more expensive. Furthermore, because these services are not normally in high demand and are hence scarce, better planning (estimation) is needed. The response of the total system to this very special group of children has not been exemplary.

The rubella cohort, and more specifically the deaf–blind component of it, produced a large, disequilibrating shock to the system. Because the system is not integrated, but rather composed of a number of fragments, response was piecemeal, with first one fragment and then another eventually sensing and then becoming overloaded by this group. Many segments of the system did not sense the heavier load sufficiently in advance to allow the development of added service capacity, such as trained personnel. At an early age, the medical system was confronted by these children, and "made do" as best it could (Sever, 1969). The existence and special demands of the population were evidently not communicated to those responsible for its education, a judgment supported in a stinging indictment by Doctor and Davis (1972). One of the points they made was that the generally different character of the population was not appreciated. The learning problems demonstrated by this population were far different from those the system had learned to cope with 10 to 15 years earlier in terms of the polio-afflicted cohort. The polio cohort, unlike the rubella cohort, was more like a normal or nonhandicapped cohort in terms of its educational needs. In mid-1981, officials of Gallaudet College, a federally supported college for the deaf in Washington, D.C., began making alarmed public statements about their need to more than double the enrollment. Why? Because 1964 + 17 = 1981. The rubella cohort had arrived. But "unannounced"? Hardly.

The right question, which did not get asked, is "What needed to be done in anticipation of the known but as yet unrealized needs for service represented by this cohort?" The question, which exemplifies a main purpose of estimation, is what adjustments were needed to change the level of services to accommodate those coming along? The question, in present circumstances where the cohort has already passed through, is what further adjustments are being planned to change the level of services currently being delivered? (That is, should there be increasing attention to finding more children and serving those with less severe handicapping conditions, or to decreasing the level of services back to a steady state reflecting the expected number of seriously impaired children who will in future require services?)

For instance, some component of service demand will doubtless be chronic, and one might work to provide full coverage to all children in that component who can be found. Another component of service demand will probably be recurring, as in the case of another epidemic (a possibility given the dearth of sustained rubella prevention services currently being delivered) or some unknown horror that might render a portion of an unborn cohort deaf and blind. Finally, some component of today's demand, generated by the 1963–1965 rubella cohort, is genuinely regarded as "nonrecurring," and once that proportion has been served, resources no longer needed can be reallocated. For instance, in the Gallaudet College case, a reasonable expectation is that today's demand to double enrollments will fade by about 1985. If correct, what does this imply for interim service strategies and resource allocations at Gallaudet?

Unfortunately, these rather obvious adjustments may not take place and there is little evidence that they have. The system appears to have learned little from these experiences about matters of system responsiveness and control – lessons that could very well stand in good stead for some future, unknown disaster of comparable magnitude.

We need to concentrate on estimation: means to increase lead time or advanced planning and preparation for future service needs. Short or no-lead-time situations are undesirable for several reasons – many of which relate directly to Richardson's and the author's objectives for improvement. Unanticipated problems tend to produce solutions outdated before they are implemented (e.g., solutions to yesterday's problems or solutions that require far more resources than would have been necessary had there been adequate preparation). With increased lead time, those responsible for a system may work out better, more appropriate, or less costly solutions in advance. Resource allocation decisions take time; with insufficient lead time, resources are more likely than not to be inefficiently and ineffectively allocated – poor allocations based on poor or nonexistent feedback or information about the actual situation.

Estimation has many other facets, many of which are less practical and immediate than the few discussed so far. For instance, there is an ever-present need to conduct estimation from a variety of observational standpoints and intellectual perspectives. Estimation proceeds by simplification: the breaking down of a problem into parts and the ordering of these in accordance with the dictates of the theories and methods used. This is reasonably well known; however, the consequences of such simplification are less well known. The methods employed and the theories invoked involve the projection of order on a problem, which, in turn, presupposes an answer to it. For instance, when a physician confronts the horror of child abuse or negligence, the intertwined effects of role and training cause attention to be directed to immediate health needs, with time and other resources being expended to make the child well and to reduce suffering. In the same circumstances, a judge or lawyer would care far less for the immediate well-being of the child, but would focus on matters of legal assistance, custody, and long-term care. A psychiatrist, as distinguished from a general practitioner, would respond to the psychological environment that contributed to the abuse and would be driven to make therapeutic recommendations to lessen the deep-seated, stress-provoking conditions that lead to abuse (Goldstein, Freud, & Solnit, 1979). Each specialized perspective, in this example as well as other examples posing complex problems, carries with it ethical baggage founded on individual personality traits, past experiences, training, and many other factors. Such baggage, or presumptions, help the estimation specialist get oriented to a new situation by providing cues and guidance to some of its aspects while weighting others less. Outcomes, in the sense of determining what is "right," "best," or "most appropriate" to do, are understandably biased as a result. The need for numerous multidisciplinary estimation activities is pronounced. Unfortunately, there are precious few in existence.

There are no "answers"

Estimation presents some extraordinarily difficult and essential tasks. The most striking realization may be that there are no "answers" whose truth can be proved and whose efficacy can be foretold. Rather, one hopes that analysis will enhance understanding of problems by creating opportunities to exploit many perspectives and by using diverse criteria to represent the hopes and expectations of those whose lives will be touched by pending decisions (Lasswell, 1971, chap. 2). There are no best or correct answers, only numerous real and imaginable possibilities whose ultimate significance can only be comprehended in the aftermath of experience (Boulding, 1961).

The decision-making setting is ever-changing and is truly knowable only through experience. Estimation precedes this experience; it is synthetic and hence nearly always errs. The point is to appreciate the inevitable mistakes by working hard to minimize them: by taking a broader view; by working self-consciously with both part and whole of a problem, including the values and perspectives of those who have a stake and interest in the matter; and by using a variety of analytic methods and disciplined perspectives. These essential aspects of estimation suggest attitudes and procedures substantially different from those usually encountered – if encountered at all.[6] Recommended are a strong dose of humility and many overt measures to anticipate, search out, and correct inevitable errors of prior formulation of alternatives and possible errors in future decision and execution (Kaplan, 1963).

Prospects

It is somewhat reassuring to realize that many of the difficulties inherent in a full appreciation and understanding of the policy process as it touches the lives of children are beginning to surface and to demand attention and clarification. This book is partial testimony here. Much more is needed. The creation of many permanent centers devoted to the study of children's problems would be helpful; only a handful exist. Likewise, serious fundamental efforts to take a comprehensive view, including the provision of basic human and program data, seem well worthwhile; very little exists here. However, one must stress not only the incredible tasks of conceptualization, institution building, and analysis that face those who care deeply about children, but also the enormity of the stakes at issue. As compared with the resources expended for many other problems facing our society, the sum expended on the formulation, analysis, and execution of children's policies and programs is paltry indeed. As compared with the stakes – our children *are* the future – the diffuse attention and scant resources being devoted to improvement of the quality of our children's lives is negligible.[7] The time is long overdue when all best efforts should be bent toward the formulation and implementation of comprehensive national and international policies and programs – efforts that may only begin after the full complexity of the policy-making process is appreciated and that may succeed when that complexity is in time mastered.

Notes

1 Two separate estimation activities, both undertaken well after the fact of decision, exist and begin to shed important light on aspects of the Education for All Handicapped Children Act. The fiscal dimensions and implications of P.L. 94–142 were assessed by Dr. James S. Kakalik and several of his colleagues at the Rand Corporation (Kakalik et al., 1981). The broader social and more practical implications of the law have been probed by a multidisciplinary group under the direction of Drs. Jay Chambers and William Hartman of the School of Education, Stanford University (Chambers & Hartman, 1983). Taken together, there is little doubt left after reading these studies that no one really knew what P.L. 94–142 involved. It is a clear case of policy making without information.

2 Necessary distinctions between mental illness and mental retardation are often not made, and this lack of distinction sometimes carries over into programs more or less intended to benefit both general categories but that in actuality do little for either (Hobbs, 1975, chap. 3).

3 These are sweeping charges; however, the author's experience with the aforementioned handicapped children's study gives them weight. Only some six months after this $500,000-plus study had been completed, it was discovered that its existence was simply unknown to the officials who had assumed responsibility for the work (Brewer & Kakalik, 1979, p. 595).

4 Of all those classified as handicapped, for instance, the blind alone profit from special tax treatment that allows them an exemption because of this disability. Comparable consideration is not afforded the deaf, the physically impaired, or any other equally handicapped group.

5 The arguments in this section are elaborated and documented fully in Brewer & Kakalik (1979, pp. 74–97).

6 Not the least in importance is the human-centered, not thing- or institution-centered, basis for estimation and other treatments of the policy process. A key informant is Harry Stack Sullivan (1971).

7 The cost of a single engine for the U.S. Army's new M-1 main battle tank is on the order of $225,000, and, with a production run of some 7,058 tanks, the total expenditure for engines will be approximately $1.6 billion, not allowing for cost overruns or inflation (AVCO, 1981). By comparison, in fiscal year 1976, the total annual government expenditures for all types of services to handicapped children and youth were in the range of $7 billion, of which no less than $4.7 billion were for special education (Brewer & Kakalik, 1979, pp. 10–13). In other words, the *total* provision of health, welfare, vocational, mental health, and retardation services for all this nation's handicapped children and youth, approximately $2.3 billion in a representative recent year, is only somewhat more than the projected expenditure for tank engines – not the entire tank, just the engines. (FY 1976 is cited because it is the last year for which even approximate total comprehensive expenditure data have been assembled and totaled.)

References

AVCO: An unworried supplier. *New York Times,* January 30, 1981, pp. D-1, D-3.

Bardach, E. Gathering data for policy research. *Urban Analysis,* 1974, *2,* 117–144.

Bardach, E. Policy termination as a political process. *Policy Sciences,* 1976, *7,* 123–131.

Bardach, E. *The implementation game.* Cambridge: MIT Press, 1977.

Behn, R. Closing the Massachusetts public training schools. *Policy Sciences,* 1976, *7,* 151–171.

Berke, J. S., & Kirst, M. W. *Federal aid to education: Who benefits, who governs?* Lexington, Mass.: Heath, 1972.

Boulding, K. *The image.* Ann Arbor, Mich.: Ann Arbor Press Paperbacks, 1961.

Brewer, G. D. The policy sciences emerge: To nurture and structure a discipline. *Policy Sciences,* 1974, *5,* 239–244.

Brewer, G. D. Termination: Hard questions, harder choices. *Public Administration Review,* 1978, *38,* 338–344.

Brewer, G. D., & deLeon, P. *The foundations of policy analysis.* Homewood, Ill.: Dorsey Press, 1983.

Brewer, G. D., & Kakalik, J. S. *Handicapped children: Strategies for improving services.* New York: McGraw-Hill, 1979.

Brody, J. E. Health care for children assailed as chaotic. *New York Times.* December 2, 1980, pp. C-1, C-2.

California Department of Social Services. *Policy review of California foster care placements and payment systems.* Sacramento, Calif., May 1980.

Calvert, D. R. *Report on rubella and handicapped children.* Washington, D.C.: Department of Health, Education, and Welfare, May 1969.

Cameron, J. Ideology and policy termination. *Public Policy,* 1978, *26,* 533–570.

Chambers, J., & Hartman, W. (Eds.). *Special education policies: Their history, implementation, and finance.* Philadelphia: Temple University Press, 1983.

Chapple, E. D., & Sayles, L. R. *The measure of management.* New York: Macmillan, 1961.

Clark, R. F. Program evaluation and the commissioning entity. *Policy Sciences,* 1975, *7,* 11–16.

Coleman, J. S. *Equality of educational opportunity.* Washington, D.C.: U. S. Government Printing Office, 1966.

Conley, R. *The economics of mental retardation.* Baltimore: Johns Hopkins University Press, 1973.

Craig, P. A. Counting handicapped children: A federal imperative. *Journal of Education Finance,* 1976, *1*(3), 318–333.

Craig, P. A., & McEachron, N. *The development and analysis of base line data for the estimation of incidence of the handicapped school-age population.* Menlo Park, Calif.: Stanford Research Institute, 1975.

Dahl, R. A., & Lindblom, C. E. *Politics, economics, and welfare.* Chicago: University of Chicago Press, 1976.

Dantona, R. Demographic data and status of services for deaf–blind children in the United States. In C. E. Sherrick (Ed.), *1980 is now.* Los Angeles: John Tracy Clinic, 1974, pp. 25–33.

Doctor, P. V., & Davis, F. E. Educational impact: The 1964–1965 rubella epidemic in the United States. *American Annals for the Deaf,* 1972, *117,* 11–13.

Downs, G. W., Jr., *Bureaucracy, innovation, and public policy.* Lexington, Mass.: Heath, 1976.

Fiske, E. B. Education secretary plans cutback in student aid. *New York Times,* January 29, 1981, pp. A-1, A-20.

Goldstein, J., Freud, A., & Solnit, A. *Before the best interests of the child.* New York: Free Press, 1979.

Hargrove, E. *The missing link: The study of the implementation of social policy.* Washington, D.C.: Urban Institute, 1975.

Hobbs, N. *The futures of children: Categories, labels, and their consequences.* San Francisco: Jossey-Bass, 1975.

Hyman, H., & Wright, C. R. Evaluating social action programs. In F. Caro (Ed.), *Readings in evaluation research.* New York: Russell Sage Foundation, 1971, pp. 185–220.

Kakalik, J., Furry, W., Thomas, M., & Carney, M. *The cost of special education.* Publication N-1792-ED. Santa Monica, Calif.: Rand Corporation, November 1981.

Kaplan, A. *American ethics and public policy.* New York: Oxford University Press, 1963.

Lasswell, H. D. *A pre-view of policy sciences.* New York: American Elsevier, 1971.

Levine, C. H. (Ed.). *Managing fiscal stress: The crisis in the public sector.* Chatham, N.J.: Chatham House, 1980.

Lewis, W. A. Planning public expenditures. In M. F. Millikan (Ed.), *National economic planning.* New York: National Bureau of Economic Research, 1967, pp. 201–227.

Mishan, E. J. *Economics for social decisions: Elements of cost–benefit analysis.* New York: Praeger, 1973.

Myrdal, G. *Objectivity in social research.* New York: Pantheon, 1971.

Pressman, J. L., & Wildavsky, A. B. *Implementation.* Berkeley: University of California Press, 1973.

Quade, E. S. Pitfalls and limitations. In E. S. Quade & W. I. Boucher (Eds.), *Systems analysis and policy planning.* New York: American Elsevier, 1968.

Quade, E. S. *Analysis for public decisions.* New York: Elsevier, 1975.

Rabinovitz, F., Pressman, J. L., & Rein, M. Guidelines: A plethora of forms, authors, and functions. *Policy Sciences,* 1976, *7,* 399–416.

Richardson, E. L. *Responsibility and responsiveness: A Report on the HEW potential for the seventies* (Vol. 2). Washington, D.C.: Department of Health, Education, and Welfare, January 18, 1973.

Riessman, F. *The culturally deprived child.* New York: Harper & Row, 1972.

Rivera, G. *Willowbrook.* New York: Vintage, 1972.

Rivlin, A. M. *Systematic thinking for social action.* Washington, D.C.: Brookings Institution, 1971.

Rossmiller, R. A., Hale, J. A., & Frohreich, L. E. *Educational programs for exceptional children: Resource configurations and costs.* Madison: University of Wisconsin, Department of Educational Administration, 1970.

Sarason, S. B., & Doris, J. *Educational handicap, public policy, and social history.* New York: Free Press, 1979.

Sever, J. L. *Perinatal infections affecting the developing fetus and newborn: The prevention of mental retardation through control of infectious diseases* (Publication No. 1692). Washington, D.C.: U.S. Department of Health, Education, and Welfare, 1969.

Spiegel, H. B. C. Citizen participation in federal programs. *Journal of Voluntary Action Research,* 1971, Monograph no. 1.

Suchman, E. *Evaluative research.* New York: Russell Sage Foundation, 1967.

Sullivan, H. S. *The fusion of psychiatry and social science.* New York: Norton, 1971.

Vickers, G. *Value systems and social process.* New York: Basic Books, 1968.

Weiss, C. *Evaluative research: Methods for assessing program effectiveness.* Englewood Cliffs, N.J.: Prentice-Hall, 1972.

Wilensky, H. L. *Organizational intelligence.* New York: Basic Books, 1967.

Wolpert, J., & Wolpert, E. The relocation of released mental hospital patients into residential communities. *Policy Sciences,* 1976, *7,* 31–51.

Part III

Constructing social policy at the federal and state levels

5   The legislative policy process

Pamela Ebert-Flattau

Adams to Jefferson: "By Jove, Tom, I think you've got it. But what's
this bit about the pursuit of happineff?"
   The Georgetowner, 1979

Nestled on a hilltop overlooking the vast expanse of once-virgin marsh-
land that skirts the Potomac River, the U.S. Capitol has echoed with the
ideas of the great and near-great in whose trust the Constitution has
placed the lawmaking powers of our country:

All legislative powers herein granted shall be vested in a Congress of the United
States which shall consist of a Senate and a House of Representatives. [Art. 1,
sec. 1]

Whereas the chief function of Congress is to make laws, it also has the
power to raise taxes, appropriate federal funds, propose amendments to
the Constitution, approve treaties, and impeach (House) or try (Senate)
certain federal officials for wrongful conduct.

The Congress must assemble at least once every two years, at noon on
the third day of January, unless by law they appoint a different day. A
Congress lasts for two years, commencing in January of the year following the biennial election of its members, typically an odd-numbered year.
For example, the 97th Congress convened in January 1981. The first year
of a Congress is referred to as the "first session" and the second year as
the "second session."

The structure of Congress

The Congress is a bicameral legislature with coequal houses. Each house
determines its own rules and proceedings.

79

The House of Representatives

The House of Representatives has 435 members. The federal census determines each state's portion of the 435 seats, with one representative for every 500,000 people. However, even those states with fewer than a half-million residents have a representative in Congress. A representative must be at least 25 years of age, have been a citizen of the United States for seven years, and, when elected, be a resident of the state in which he or she is chosen. As Michigan's Democratic Senator Don Riegle (1976) summed it up when he was a member of the House of Representatives:

Doing this job means wanting to go to work for 500,000 people. It means listening to them, understanding their worries and needs, studying the issues and then expressing your own best judgments on how to act in their behalf.

The House originates all bills that raise revenue and, by tradition, all bills that appropriate funds to run the government.

The chief officer of the House is the Speaker. Prior to the convening of each Congress, the members of each political party represented in Congress meet in caucus and nominate one of its members for Speaker. When Congress convenes, the first order of business is to elect a Speaker, and, in what is often the only display of party solidarity that year, the majority party inevitably elects their nominee. The Speaker is the leader of his or her party in Congress, but is expected to preside over the House in an impartial and unbiased manner. The Speaker has broad powers over the functioning of the House, including the power to assign bills to the various committees, to make committee appointments, to schedule floor debates, and to preside over those debates. Other leaders in the House are elected by their party caucuses. They include the majority leader, who serves as the Speaker's chief lieutenant and handles partisan affairs; the majority whip, who is third in command and polls members of the party on pending legislation, informs them of bills and schedules, and summons them to the floor for crucial votes; the minority leader, who is the highest-ranking member of the minority party and lines up opposition to legislation proposed by the majority party; and the minority whip, whose duties are similar to those of the counterpart in the majority party.

The Constitution requires that House members be elected every two years. Some professional congressional observers believe that this factor more than any other is responsible for the distinct differences in legislative style evident in the operations of the House and the Senate (members of the latter house serve six-year terms).

The Senate

There are 100 members of the Senate, 2 from each state regardless of the size of the state's population. A senator must be at least 30 years of age, have been a citizen of the United States for 9 years, and, when elected, be a resident of the state from which he or she is chosen. The term of office is six years, with elections so arranged that the terms of both senators from the same state do not terminate in the same year and that only one-third of the Senate stands for election at any one time. Because of these staggered terms, the Senate is known as the "continuing body" and does not reorganize itself after each general election as does the House.

A substantial reorganization occurred following the general elections of 1980. For the first time in over 20 years the Republican party gained control of the Senate, and so Republicans were chosen to serve as Senate majority leader, majority whip, and chairpersons of the various committees and subcommittees.

The Senate has certain advantages over the House of Representatives: With only 100 members, there is greater flexibility in its rules of procedure; the longer terms permit freedom from the pressures and uncertainties of frequent campaigning experienced by members of the House; because the Senate has the unique prerogative to review and ratify treaties, it has some special leverage with the president; and its power to confirm or reject presidential nominations gives the Senate a special voice in executive decision making.

The vice-president of the United States presides over the Senate (under the title of president of the Senate) but belongs to no standing committees and has minimal powers. The senior member of the majority party is usually elected president pro tempore, presiding over the Senate in the vice-president's absence.

The Senate is led by officers much the same as the House: The majority leader is the chief Senate officer in terms of power, determining the Senate's legislative schedule and often leading the majority side in legislative debate; the majority whip fills in during the majority leader's absence from the Senate floor; the minority leader represents the opposition party and often confers with the majority leader to obtain prior agreement on legislative scheduling, parliamentary tactics, and the like; and the minority whip assists the minority leader in fulfilling these tasks.

The path to legislation

Although it is possible to describe the process by which a bill becomes law, one can never capture adequately the forces that shape the bill as it winds its way through the legislative labyrinth. Perhaps Woodrow Wilson said it best: "Once begin the dance of legislation and you must struggle through its mazes as best you can to the breathless end – if any end there be" (quoted in Redman, 1973).

Sources of legislation

Ideas for legislation originate from many and diverse quarters:[1] The congressperson may wish to fulfill a campaign pledge or to satisfy a personal interest; constituents – either as individuals or as representatives of unions, associations, or other corporate bodies – may transmit proposals for legislation, a right guaranteed by the First Amendment to the Constitution; the president may transmit a draft of a proposed legislative initiative to the Speaker of the House and the president of the Senate in the form of an "executive communication"; or congressional committees may draft legislation after conducting studies and hearings, which may cover periods as long as several years.

The bill

The most common form used for most legislation is the bill. In the 97th Congress that convened in 1979, some 13,200 bills and resolutions were introduced. Only 375 were signed into law. Bills may originate in either the House or the Senate, with one notable exception. Article 1, section 7 of the Constitution provides that all bills raising revenue shall originate in the House of Representatives. A bill originating in the House is designated by the letters "H.R." followed by a number that it retains throughout all its parliamentary stages. A Senate bill is designated by the letter "S." followed by a number.

A bill must state in precise legal language what it does and does not do. Hence, bill drafting requires a degree of technical skill not possessed by the average citizen. Most members of Congress call upon hired specialists to write legislation. After a senator or representative conceives the idea for a bill, the proposal is sketched out in rough draft and sent to the legislative counsel's office for transformation into legal language. Both the House and the Senate have their own legislative drafting staffs. The executive departments and agencies also hire lawyers to draft bills that are sent over to Congress, as do many private associations and labor unions. Once a bill has been found not to conflict with existing federal statutes and has been reworked in appropriate legal language, it is ready for presentation to the House or the Senate.

Introduction of a bill

In the House, a sponsoring member may introduce a bill whenever the House is in session by simply dropping the typed bill into a wooden basket or "hopper" hanging on the clerk's desk below the Speaker's rostrum. The member is not required to ask permission to introduce the measure or to make any statement at the time of introduction. The procedure is more formal in the Senate. At the time reserved for such purposes, the senator who wishes to introduce a measure rises and states that a bill is being offered for introduction. The bill is then sent by page to the secretary's desk. No more than 25 members may cosponsor a bill in the House, whereas unlimited sponsorship is permitted in the Senate. Occasionally a member may insert the words "by request" after his or her name to indicate that cosponsorship is in compliance with the suggestion of some other member.

In the House it is no longer customary to read a bill – even by title – at the time of introduction. The title is entered in the journal and printed in the *Congressional Record.* In the Senate the bill is read by title for the first and second reading. If no objection has been made to the introduction of the bill, senators often obtain consent to have the bill printed in the *Congressional Record,* along with their formal statement of introduction, at the time of the introduction.

Upon filing, the bill is assigned a number and is referred by the Speaker of the House or by the president of the Senate to the appropriate committee for legislative action. The bill is also sent to the Government Printing Office where it is printed the same night in its introduced form. Printed copies are available the next morning from the Documents Room of the appropriate House. Anyone can obtain a free copy of a bill simply by specifying the number (H.R. 30 or S. 401, for example) and enclosing a self-addressed label in a written request to the Superintendent of Documents:

House Document Room	Senate Document Room
H-226 Capitol	S-325 Capitol
Washington, D.C. 20515	Washington, D.C. 20510

The committee process

The committee to which a bill is assigned often determines the ultimate fate of the bill. Assigning the bill to the appropriate committee can be a difficult process. Consider, for example, the bill that proposed regulating the size of apple barrels (Bacon, 1969). The Committee on Interstate and Foreign Commerce wanted the bill because the barrels were to be transported across state lines; the Agriculture Committee sought jurisdiction because the bill would affect apple growers; and the Committee on Coinage, Weights, and Measures (no longer existent) wanted the bill because it involved a change in the form of measurement. The Speaker finally sent the measure to the last committee, although it was within his rights to send it to any one of the three.

In the 95th Congress (1977–1978), the Senate modified its committee system so that the number of standing committees was reduced from 31 to 15. Each senator is now limited to membership on three committees and may chair no more than a total of four committees or subcommittees. These changes were designed to provide senators with sufficient opportunity to carry out the work required of committee members while discharging their duties as members of the full Senate. Early in the 96th Congress (1979–1980) the House established a Committee on Committees with the similar goal of streamlining its committee system. The result was 22 standing House committees and a total of 142 subcommittees. Clearly, it is not surprising to find a great deal of overlap among jurisdictions.

The most important phase of the congressional process is the action by committees. The committee is the place where bills are given most intensive consideration and where people outside the Congress are given th. opportunity to be heard. The chairperson of a committee often assigns the bill to a subcommittee specializing in the area of the legislation. One of the first actions to be taken by the subcommittee is to send a copy of the bill to the executive departments or agencies concerned with the subject matter of the bill. These departments determine whether the bill is consistent with the program of the president. A report is eventually submitted by the department via the president's Office of Management and Budget. These reports are given serious consideration by the committee but are in no way binding on their deliberations.

If a bill is of sufficient importance, public hearings are scheduled. Public announcement of hearings may be found in the "Daily Digest" portion of the *Congressional Record*. Personal notice, usually in the form of a letter, but possibly in the form of a subpoena, is sent to individuals, organizations, and government departments and agencies that would be affected by the bill. Any interested parties may ask to be heard.[2] However, minor witnesses may be requested to submit written statements for the hearing records rather than testifying orally. Hearings are usually open to the public. Committees and subcommittees require that witnesses who are to appear before them file written statements in advance, largely to permit development of questions to be asked during the course of cross-examination. A typewritten transcript of the testimony taken at a public hearing is available for inspection at the committee's office, and may be printed later in the form of a bound volume suitable for distribution. After hearings are completed, the subcommittee will usually consider the bill in a session known as the "mark-up." The views of both sides are studied in detail and a vote taken of subcommittee members to determine whether the bill should be reported favorably to the full committee (with or without amendments), reported unfavorably, or reported for tabling. Any subcommittee member may propose amendments to the measure during the mark-up, and such amendments are voted on during this session. An amendment rejected in the mark-up may be offered again when the bill comes to the floor of the house chamber for debate.

If the subcommittee has conducted full, balanced hearings and has reported the bill favorably, the full committee may decide to move directly to executive session for further mark-up. If, instead, hearings are scheduled, the format is much the same as that for subcommittee hearings. Hearings scheduled by the full committee tend, however, to be broader than those held by subcommittees. For example, a full committee hearing may focus on several related bills rather than just one. Following hearings are publication of the hearing record, mark-up sessions, and full committee report. Once it has been decided that legislation is desirable, the bill is reported out of the committee and automatically placed on the legislative calendar for floor action in the committee's appropriate house.

House action

As soon as a bill is favorably reported by the House, it is assigned a calendar number on one of two principal calendars: the Union Calendar for bills that raise revenues or appropriate money or property, or the House Calendar for most other bills. Some bills remain on the calendar for the entire legislative session without being called up on the floor for debate, whereas others are on the calendar for a very short period of time.

Any member may ask for a bill to be placed on a third calendar – the Consent Calendar – if the member believes it is noncontroversial and has a good chance of unanimous approval. On the first and third Monday of each month the Speaker directs the clerk to call the bills that have been on the Consent Calendar for three days. If no objection is heard to the bill, the bill is considered passed. A single objection blocks the bill from further action that day. When it is brought up again two weeks later, it takes three objectors to prevent passage of the bill. Two weeks later, if it is blocked again, it is dropped from the Consent Calendar but remains on the regular calendar.

A bill reported out by committee and assigned to a calendar typically still must clear the Committee on Rules before it reaches the House floor. The Rules Committee was established to determine which bills deserve to proceed and what ground rules will be used for debate. A bill that has been cleared by the Rules Committee is thus accompanied by a resolution that specifies the rules for debating the bill. The resolution itself is debated for up to 1 hour before the bill itself is brought up. Rules vary, but some typical ones include a rule that says a bill will be debated for 2 hours after which the bill is open to amendments; a rule (say, for a controversial bill) that says it may have from 8 to 10 hours for general debate; a closed rule that permits amendments only from the sponsoring committee; and open rules that permit unlimited amendments. On the first and third Monday of each month the Speaker may entertain a motion to suspend the operation of rules to dispose of low-priority, fairly noncontroversial legislation. Debate is limited to 20 minutes for both those supporting the bill and those opposed.

Another means for the House to dispense with legislation quickly is Calendar Wednesday. On each Wednesday the clerk calls the names of the standing committees in alphabetical order. When called, a committee may raise for consideration any bill reported by the committee on the previous day and pending on either the House or the Union Calendar. Not more than two hours of general debate is permitted on each such measure. The affirmative vote of a simple majority of the members present is sufficient to pass the bill. Another tactic to expedite legislation is for the House of Representatives to reconstitute itself as the Committee of the Whole House on the State of the Union – thus making all members of the House members of this single committee. This parliamentary procedure enables the House to act on legislation with a quorum of only 100 members instead of the usual 218. The Speaker leaves the chair after appointing a presiding chairman, and the silver mace that is the symbol of the House is removed from its pedestal, thus indicating the convening of the Committee of the Whole. At the conclusion of a bill's consideration, the Committee of the Whole rises and reports the bill to the House. The House then votes immediately on whatever amendments have been reported by the Committee of the Whole. Roll call votes are taken on every amendment. This gives the minority one last opportunity to influence the content of the bill. A motion may be made to recommit the bill to the standing committee that reported it. If the motion is defeated, there is another motion that the bill, as amended, be adopted. In the Committee of the Whole, voting is conducted by voice vote, division (standing to be counted), or electronic teller.

Once a bill has passed the House, a copy is printed on blue paper with all the amendments in place. This "engrossed bill" is delivered in a formal Senate ceremony while that body is actually sitting, thereby requesting concurrence of the Senate.

Senate action

Once the Senate has received the engrossed bill passed by the House, the bill is referred to the appropriate standing committee for consideration. The standing committee gives the bill the same kind of detailed consideration as it received in committee in the House, and may report it or table it.

The voting rules of the Senate are much less complicated than those of the House. When a bill is reported, the senator reporting the bill may ask unanimous consent for immediate consideration of the bill. If the bill is uncontroversial, it may pass with little or no debate. If there is any objection, it is placed for later consideration on the calendar. (There is only one calendar of bills in the Senate.) Because there is no committee comparable to the House Committee on Rules, any bill may be called up for vote at any time. The scheduling responsibility belongs to the Senate majority leader. The Senate permits the debate and emendation of legislation at the same time, unlike the House where debate is separated from periods for amendments. Furthermore, the length of time for debate is unlimited in the Senate. This has led to the use of the debate period for "filibustering." Strom Thurmond established the record for filibustering when he spoke against a civil rights bill for 24 hours and 18 minutes on August 29, 1957. Although this technique may be the work of a single dissident, groups of senators have also been known to band together to obstruct the passage of a bill. A filibuster may be stopped by invoking "cloture," wherein two-thirds of the members present may stop a filibuster by bringing a bill to a vote.

As in the House, in the Senate there are three methods for voting: voice vote, division, and roll call. Since a roll call takes only about 10 minutes in the Senate, it is used more frequently than in the House. A simple majority is necessary to pass a measure. The original engrossed House bill, together with any engrossed Senate amendments, is returned to the House with a message from the Senate. Of course, the Senate may also initiate bills that, upon passage, are also sent with messages to the House for their consideration.

Conference committees

Bills may be quite different when they emerge from the two houses and as a result need reconciliation. In those instances, a conference committee, composed of an equal number of members from both houses, meets to iron out the differences in the legislation. Conferees are expected to negotiate only within areas of difference, although this rule has been violated on occasion (Bacon, 1969). When conferees have reached agreement, the new bill, in the form of a conference report, is presented for approval first to the house where it originated and subsequently to the other body. A conference report can only be approved or rejected; it cannot be amended. Once approved by both houses, it becomes an "enrolled bill" and is sent to the White House for signature of the president.

Presidential action

The president has 10 days in which to sign a bill. If he approves and signs it, it becomes law. If he does not approve it, he can veto it and send it back to the originating house. A two-thirds majority of each house is needed to override a veto, at which time it becomes law despite the veto. If the president does not wish to sign the bill or to veto it, and the Congress adjourns before the 10-day period elapses, the bill does not become law. This is known as a "pocket veto."

A bill that becomes law is assigned the letters "P.L." (Public Law) and given a number (e.g., P.L. 97–142); the first two digits indicate the number of the Congress in which the law was enacted. Copies of the law are available by number from the Document Room of either house.

A glossary of terms

It is useful to understand the federal legislative policy process. It is also important, however, to understand the language of legislators.

Appropriations. Money set aside for a specific use. The U.S. Constitution indicates that no money shall be drawn from the Treasury but in consequence of appropriations made by law. Appropriations are determined annually by Congress for the following fiscal year for every program or activity funded by the federal government. Appropriations committees have been established in the House and Senate to recommend these spending levels to Congress.

Appropriations cycle. The yearly review and approval by Congress of spending levels for the following fiscal year. Appropriations committee hearings begin in February and often continue through May and June. After the Appropriations committees complete their hearings, mark-up begins. In July, these committees report their bills to the floor of their respective houses and conference committee considerations begin. Congress completes all action on spending legislation by mid-September of each year.

Assignment process – bill. The decision by the Speaker of the House or the majority leader of the Senate that determines which committee in their respective houses will handle a bill after its introduction. The assignment process often decides the fate of the bill. Should it go to a disinterested or unsympathetic committee, it is unlikely to emerge again in that Congress.

Assignment process – committee. Appointment of a member of Congress to various House or Senate committees. Initial committee assignments are determined by special partisan committees in each house who recommend candidates to their majority or minority leaders. Members generally seek appointments to committees related to their personal interests. But many members actively seek assignment to such powerful committees as the Appropriations committees, the Budget committees, the Senate Finance Committee, or the House Ways and Means Committee.

Authorization. The act of sanctioning federal support of a program or activity. In addition to specifying what a program is intended to do and who will do it, authorizing legislation often contains a section that provides for a fixed level of funding to meet program costs. Although such funds may be authorized, no money may be spent unless it has been appropriated from the Treasury through a separate legislative process. More often than not, authorization levels are far more generous than the levels of funding ultimately appropriated. Unlike the clearly labeled Appropriations committees that handle the spending process, authorizing legislation is handled by the House and the Senate through committees named for the subject matter over which they have jurisdiction, such as Agriculture, Nutrition, Housing, or Science.

Authorization cycle. The review and approval (or abolishment) by Congress of programs or activities sanctioned by the federal government. Programs and activities may be authorized to operate for periods from one year to five years or more. At the time of its expiration, the program or activity is considered by Congress for reauthorization. Authorization hearings begin in February and continue through March and April. However, congressional authorizing committees must submit anticipated legislative authorizations to the Congressional Budget Office and to the House or Senate Budget Committee, so that anticipated levels of outlay can be worked into the proposed congressional budget. Authorizing committees of the House and Senate must report new authorizing legislation during May and June. Congress begins floor action during July, and it may continue through August. Conference committees will also be convened during these months to iron out any differences between the House and Senate on authorizing legislation.

Briefing. A meeting in which a member of Congress receives information pertinent to consideration of legislative action. A briefing may be conducted by a member of the senator's or representative's staff, a representative of the Congressional Research Service, a lobbyist from a national organization, a specialist from a federal agency, or a concerned constituent. Briefings tend to be much like their name: They usually last no longer than 15 or 20 minutes. Often briefings may be conducted in the elevator by staff as the member of Congress is hurrying to the floor of the chamber to vote.

Briefing memo. The most valuable, but most difficult, document to draft for use by a congressperson. Restricted to one page, the briefing memo typically takes the form "Background," "Issue," or "Recommended Action."

Caucus. A group of legislators of the same political party or faction who meet to decide on policies and/or candidates. In the Congress there is a Congresswomen's Caucus, for instance, as well as the Congressional Black Caucus. Besides these formal groups, however, the word *caucus* refers to any gathering of a group of congresspersons with a common concern.

Chamber. Assembly room for debate and voting. The House of Representatives meets in this chamber in the south wing of the Capitol. The Senate conducts its business in a smaller chamber located in the north wing of the Capitol.

Cloakroom. An anteroom to the House or Senate chamber. In the old days, this was literally the place where members would hang their cloaks. Today the cloakroom is a place where a beehive of last-minute discussion occurs prior to votes taken in either the House or the Senate. Legislative information on current floor activity may be obtained by telephoning Democratic or Republican cloakrooms in the House or Senate. In the Senate, the telephone number for the Democratic cloakroom is (202) 224-8541, and the number for the Republican cloakroom is (202) 224-8601. In the House, the numbers for the Democratic and Republican cloakrooms are respectively (202) 225-7400 and (202)

225-7430. Updated electronic recordings provide the caller with information relative to votes and amendments on legislation under consideration in that chamber.

Concurrent resolutions. A matter affecting the operations of both houses of Congress is usually initiated in the form of a concurrent resolution. These are not customarily matters of a legislative character but are merely expressions of fact, principle, opinion, or purpose of the two houses.

Congressional Budget and Impoundment Control Act of 1974. Commonly called the Congressional Budget Act, this act revolutionized the congressional budget process. It established new Budget committees in the House and Senate and a Congressional Budget Office to improve Congress's informational and analytic resources with respect to the budgetary process. The act designated a timetable and new procedures for various phases of the congressional budget process and provided for a new fiscal year (which now begins October 1 and concludes September 30). Improvements in budget terminology and information to be included in the president's budget submissions were also spelled out by the act. The Congressional Budget Act was the result of a two-year study by Congress of procedures for improving congressional control of budget outlay and receipt.

Congressional Budget Office (CBO). A nonpartisan agency designed to provide Congress with information needed to make informed decisions about budget policy and national priorities. The CBO monitors the economy and estimates the impact on the economy of government actions, improves the flow and quality of budget information, and analyzes the costs and effects of alternative budget choices.

Congressional Record. The proceedings of the House and Senate are printed and published daily in the *Congressional Record*. The *Record* may be obtained by mail for $104.00 for six months, $208.00 per year, or $1.00 per copy payable in advance. A check or money order made payable to the Superintendent of Documents may be sent directly to the Government Printing Office, Washington, D.C. 20402.

Congressional Research Service (CRS). The Congressional Research Service was established in 1914 to provide members of Congress, committees, and staff with information in an objective, nonpartisan, and scholarly manner. Services include analysis of issues before Congress, legal research and analysis, consultation with members of Congress, assistance with statements and speech drafts, and general reference assistance. More than 200,000 requests are responded to annually, 61% within a day of receipt. CRS is a component of the Library of Congress.

Congressional staff. The 100 senators are served by about 7,000 professional and clerical assistants, the 439 representatives in the House by 11,000 assistants. This magnitude of congressional bureaucracy is related in part to the enormous demands for help from constituents. A representative may receive an average of 1,200 to 1,500 letters a week on simple issues. When an issue is highly controversial, a member of Congress may receive more than 50,000 communications a week from impassioned voters. In recent years, the writing of the nation's laws has for all practical matters passed from the legislators to their staffs. Staffs frame the questions for their bosses' consideration, schedule committee hearings, select witnesses, and meet with lobbyists and interested constituents to discuss legislation. In a recent issue of *Fortune* magazine, Juan Cameron (1979) referred to this body as "the shadow congress."

District work periods. A regularly scheduled period when the Senate or House is not in session. These are usually scheduled in mid-March and mid-August and permit busy lawmakers to return to their home districts or to take extended business/pleasure trips. In even-numbered years Congress prepares to adjourn in October in anticipation of biennial elections. In odd-numbered years the legislative calendar often runs through November.

Federal Register. A document published daily that includes federal agency regulations, proposed regulations, and other legal documents of the executive branch. It is mailed to subscribers for $300.00 per year, payable in advance. Individual copies are $1.50. A check or money order made payable to the Superintendent of Documents should be sent to the Government Printing Office, Washington, D.C. 20402.

Fiscal year. The period from October 1 to September 30.

Floor. A parliamentary term referring to the right to speak from one's place in an assembly. The term is also applied to the room in which the desks of the senators or representatives are located, as in "the floor of the House" or "the floor of the Senate."

Gallery. The balcony in which the public may observe the workings of the House or Senate when they are in session.

General Accounting Office (GAO). Headed by the comptroller general of the United States, the General Accounting Office reviews and evaluates existing government programs. This includes general review, evaluation, analysis, and audit functions. The GAO may respond to requests by Congress to conduct an investigation of a program or may recommend to Congress programs that need such evaluation.

Introductory remarks. Any senator or representative may read into or have printed in the *Congressional Record* remarks made at the time of a bill's introduction. These introductory remarks often contain statistics or other descriptive illustrations of need for the legislation. The scientist who has conducted a national survey or has other information pertinent to the remarks of the bill's sponsor may find his or her facts or figures incorporated in the congressperson's introductory remarks.

Joint resolution. Joint resolutions may originate in either the House or Senate (not jointly in both houses). There is little practical difference between bills and joint resolutions, although the latter are not as numerous as bills. Joint resolutions may represent amendments to the Constitution, which must be approved by two-thirds of each house and then sent to the states for their ratification.

Lobby. To exert influence on a member of Congress to vote for or introduce legislation desired by the interest group.[4] The interests of science, for example, are most often represented by a single, visible lobby organization. However, this does not disallow efforts by individual scientists to lobby members of Congress whose votes, say, are necessary for the passage of legislation important to the interests of science. Lobbying is a skill cultivated with experience.

Mark-up. Line-by-line, highly technical consideration of a bill by a subcommittee or committee after hearings are completed. During the mark-up, views of both proponents and opponents of the legislation are studied in detail, legislative language is perfected, and a vote is taken of subcommittee or committee members to determine whether the bill should be reported favorably, reported unfavorably, or tabled. Amendments to the legislation by subcommittee or committee members are also considered during the mark-up.

Office of Technology Assessment (OTA). An advisory arm of the Congress whose basic function is to help legislators anticipate the consequences of technological changes. OTA consists of a nonpartisan congressional board comprised of six senators and six representatives. Assisted by a professional staff, OTA responds to the requests for studies suggested by the board.

Oversight. The act of reviewing and monitoring federal programs and policies. Oversight responsibilities typically belong to standing committees in various jurisdictional areas in the House and Senate. As part of their oversight responsibilities, committees or subcommittees may conduct "oversight hearings."

Report out. The final action taken by a subcommittee or committee on a legislative measure. A subcommittee reports out a bill favorably, unfavorably, or for tabling to its parent committee. Similarly, a committee reports out a bill for consideration by its legislative body.

Rescission. Literally, taking away – as in the president rescinding appropriations approved by the Congress.

Simple resolution. A matter concerning the operation of either house is initiated by a simple resolution. It is considered only by the body in which it is introduced and, upon adoption, is published in the *Congressional Record.*

Standing committees. Often called permanent committees, these are established to treat legislation within a carefully defined area of jurisdiction.

State delegation. The total number of representatives and senators elected from a state.

Table. A parliamentary motion to remove a bill from consideration indefinitely. A bill or legislative proposal may be tabled by a subcommittee or committee for the remainder of a congressional session.

Testify. To make a formal statement in a committee or subcommittee hearing in favor of or in opposition to a legislative measure. Individuals appear as witnesses in person, having filed a written statement in advance. Pursuant to the presentation of their testimony, witnesses are cross-examined by members of the committee or subcommittee holding the hearing.

Veto. Once a bill has been approved by both houses, it becomes "an enrolled bill" and is sent to the White House for the signature of the president. The president has 10 days in which to a sign a bill. If he does not approve it, he can veto it and send it back to the originating house. A two-thirds majority of each house is needed to override a veto, at which time it becomes law despite the president's veto.

Notes

This chapter is adapted from *A Legislative Guide* prepared for distribution by the Association for the Advancement of Psychology (Washington, D.C., 1980). The *Guide* serves as an introduction to the legislative policy process. It was developed as a result of the author's experience as an American Association for the Advancement of Science – American Psychological Association Congressional Science Fellow in 1974–1975, and is intended to be something of an update of lengthier texts on the topic, such as Zinn's *How Our Laws Are Made.* Its inclusion herein is designed to provide the reader with an overview of essential elements of the federal legislative process.

1 For alternate perspectives on the origins of legislation, see Green (1975).
2 The experiences of some scientists in influencing congressional policy can be found in Feller (1974), Ratchford (1974), and Saks (1978).
3 For a fuller treatment of this aspect of policy making, see Zinn (1972).
4 For an explication of changes in the concerns of psychologists as an interest group over the years, see Bevan (1976) and Ebert-Flattau (1980). A discussion of the interface between science and public policy can be found in Caplan, Morrison, and Stambaugh (1975), Daddario (1974), Goodwin (1975), Stratton (1966), and Wiesner (1965).

References

Bacon, D. C. *Congress and you.* Washington, D.C.: American Association of University Women, 1969.

Bevan, W. The sound of the wind that's blowing. *American Psychologist, 1976, 31,* 481–491.

Cameron, J. The shadow congress the public doesn't know. *Fortune,* 1979, *99*(1), 38–42.

Caplan, N., Morrison, A., & Stambaugh, R. *The use of social science knowledge in policy decisions at the national level.* Ann Arbor, Mich.: Institute for Social Research, 1975.

Daddario, E. Science policy: Relationships are the key. *Daedalus,* 1974, *103*(3), 135–142.

Ebert-Flattau, P. Federal legislation of concern to research/academic scientists. *American Psychologist,* 1980, *35,* 852–853.

Feller, I. The role of expert information in legislative decision making. Paper presented at the Annual Meeting of the American Psychological Association, New Orleans, August, 1974.

The Georgetowner. (Washington, D.C.), 1979, *25*(6).

Goodwin, L. *Can science help resolve national problems?* New York: Free Press, 1975.

Green, M. J. *Who runs congress?* Toronto: Bantam, 1975.

Ratchford, J. T. How scientists advise the Congress. *Physics Today,* 1974, *27,* 38–41.

Redman, E. *The dance of legislation.* New York: Simon & Schuster, 1973.

Riegle, D. *O Congress.* New York: Popular Library, 1976.

Saks, M. Social psychological contributions to a legislative subcommittee on organ and tissue transplants. *American Psychologist,* 1978, *33,* 680–690.

Stratton, J. *Science and the educated man.* Cambridge: MIT Press, 1966.

Wiesner, J. *Where science and politics meet.* New York: McGraw-Hill, 1965.

Zinn, C. D. *How our laws are made.* Washington, D.C.: U.S. Government Printing Office, 1972.

6   The role of state government in child and family policy

J. Lawrence Aber

Prevailing notions regarding the proper role of state government toward children and families have undergone a series of revisions over the last century and are still topics of considerable controversy. The debate over the creation of a federal Children's Bureau, and federal and state constitutional histories, provide some insight into the changing conceptions of the state role.

Before the second half of the nineteenth century, government at any level – federal, state, or local – played no appreciable role in child and family policy. The foci of child and family policy, services to needy children and families, were the near-exclusive domain of religious organizations and private philanthropic groups. This state of affairs was encouraged by churches, through their interpretation of the constitutional doctrine of separation of church and state. In the second half of the nineteenth century, in response to repeated failures of the private system in coping with the need to assimilate large numbers of immigrant families into the major cities of the East coast, some municipal governments began to provide publicly financed services to destitute, abandoned, and handicapped children (Bremner, 1971, pp. 751–755).

During the first decade of the twentieth century, a major debate emerged over federal and state roles in child and family policy. The debate centered on legislation to create a Children's Bureau within the federal Department of the Interior that would provide the sort of vital statistics and scientific data needed to convince state governments to mount progressive policies toward children, especially in the areas of child labor and child health (Bremner, 1971, pp. 757–758). States rights advocates lined up firmly in opposition to the legislation. They argued that the federal government has no constitutional authority to pass legislation designed to influence the child and family policies of state governments (Bremner, 1971, pp. 768–769). In their view, this class of legislation entailed a federal presumption of a state right. In addition, they believed that states could accomplish, better than the federal government could, the task of implementing locally sensitive legislation regarding children. States rights advocates were joined in opposition to the Children's Bureau by family rights advocates who believed that the precedent of federal government inquiry into private family life and child rearing was dangerous at best, socialistic at worst (Bremner, 1971, pp. 764–767). The advocates for a Children's Bureau rebutted these ideas by arguing that children are an invaluable national resource. They felt that the state of the nation's children is of more compelling national interest than other objects of federal information-gathering activity, such as the problems created by the boll weevil in the South.

A parallel debate concerned the need for national uniformity in standards for state child welfare systems. Because of the constitutional limits to federal activity, advocates of uniform standards as a method to upgrade the quality of state systems quickly adopted the strategy of using regulations accompanying federal grants-in-aid programs to states to implement their goals. With the creation of the Children's Bureau in 1912 and the enactment of the Sheppard–Towner Act in 1920 (creating a federal public health grants-in-aid program), the advocates for a meaningful federal role in child and family policy won the day on both the information-gathering and standards-setting issues.

The concept of a legitimate national interest over and above state-defined interests in such issues as children's health, education, and welfare gathered increased credibility during four major phases of federal activity in twentieth-century America. The first phase encompassed the first task that the Children's Bureau set for itself: the passage of national child labor laws despite the resistance of many states and local authorities (Bremner, 1971, pp. 601–749). A second phase developed out of the relief efforts championed by the Children's Bureau for families during the Great Depression, and culminated in the ADC (Aid to Dependent Children) provisions of the New Deal's Social Security Act of 1935 (Bremner, 1971, pp. 793–796). Third, the litigation articulating and protecting the constitutional rights of minority children to equal educational opportunity ushered in the major federal initiatives in civil rights of the 1950s and 1960s. A final phase of federal activity in the 1970s involved the federal legislation extending the concept of civil rights to handicapped children as well as minority children (*Harvard Educational Review*, 1974, pp. 53–73).

Each of these movements in a sense casts the federal government in the role of "progressive" champion of children's rights and casts state government as a reactionary defender of the status quo, protecting the parochial interests of the state. Even today, arguing for an increase in power for

state governments in areas where federal and state responsibilities overlap appears to be inextricably linked to reactionary policies toward children and families. President Reagan's new "states rights" philosophy in
the provision of health, education, and social services through a transformation of numerous small categorical grant programs run by the federal
government to a few large block grant programs administered by state
governments is also a vehicle for enacting severe cuts in the federal funds
available to serve needy children and their families.

Misconceptions regarding the states' role in the creation of child and
family policy abound. Prevailing notions of the federal government as
progressive versus state governments as reactionary are both inaccurate
and unfortunate. The top-down-only theory of policy creation and implementation still prevails, even when a bottom-up-too theory would not
only serve to encourage greater experimentation in policy and programs
but, most importantly, may be a more accurate description of the present
state of policy affairs. Any theory that leads activists for children to
believe that the only or the most important battlefront for child and
family policy is on the federal level distracts vital attention from a policy
arena that is also crucially important if real advances for children are to
be secured in the next decade – at the state level. This chapter examines
the states' role in policy making by focusing on policy making in Massachusetts between 1970 and 1980.

Major child and family policy trends, 1970–1980

Historical trends in a state's policy toward children and families are a
reflection of many social, demographic, economic, and political factors that
influence the attitudes and moods of the populace and its elected representatives. In the 1970s, child and family policy in Massachusetts began by
reflecting the prevailing mood that more could and should be done by state
government for the commonwealth's neediest children and that the very
nature of state government, its priorities, institutions, and decision-making
processes needed to be reformed if state government was not to meet the
challenge of improving the quantity and quality of child and family services.
Several major trends were evidenced during the decade.

*Expansion in the delivery of services and growth in expectations in
the role of government*

Perhaps the most striking feature of child and family policy in Massachusetts during this decade was the tremendous growth in the demand for

and provision of state-financed services. For instance, when Chapter 766, the state precursor to the Education for All Handicapped Children Act, was passed in 1973, 74,000 children were enrolled in special education programs across the state. By 1980, these numbers had grown to 154,000 (Commonwealth of Massachusetts, 1980a, p. 23-2). Similarly, 45,857 families received Aid to Families with Dependent Children (AFDC) in 1969 (Commonwealth of Massachusetts, 1980a, pp. 18-6–18-7). This figure had swelled to 121,500 by 1980. Most dramatically, prior to passage of the 1973 National Child Abuse Prevention and Treatment Act, 2,000 children were reported to state authorities as abused/neglected in 1970. In 1980, the state received nearly 20,000 reports of maltreatment, a 1,000% increase in a decade. These increases are not isolated incidents. Other services as varied as day care and child mental health services also experienced great growth during this same time period.

The increase in each service turned on a unique combination of factors. Increased enrollment in special education programs was fueled by state legislation that adopted a very modern civil rights perspective on the centuries-old special education problem (Sarason & Doris, 1979). By statutorily mandating that local educational authorities rather than state authorities pay for that education (even though the fiscal role of state government was to pledge aid to localities in their efforts), legislation legitimated lobbying by concerned parents and school administrators for more programs under auspices of special education. Rarely mentioned, but quite important in creating increases in special education, is the fact that school enrollments began to decline in the 1970s after the exodus of the baby-boom generation. Special education legislation made continued growth of local school budgets possible even in the face of declining enrollments. At the same time, the market for teachers began to contract even as higher education was still training large numbers of teachers. The special education movement, with its pledge to reduce teacher/student ratios for the neediest children, was regarded by some as a "full-employment act" for teachers.

The astronomical growth in child abuse reports offers still another example that divergent factors precipitate an increase in and demand for services. Although some early observers prematurely argued that America had experienced a dramatic increase in the actual incidence and prevalence of child maltreatment, the best explanation of the increase in reports lies in the activities of the National Center on Child Abuse and Neglect. The center, in developing regulations to implement the National Child Abuse Prevention and Treatment Act, required states to adopt "mandated reporter" laws if they wished to receive federal funds for child abuse services. The precise nature of the "mandated reporter" laws varies from state to state, but they all require professionals who work with children to report cases of suspected maltreatment to state authorities. Failure to report leads to civil penalties in most states and criminal penalties in some states.

Clearly, no single or simple explanation of the growth of child and family services in Massachusetts during the decade of the 1970s will suffice. What is important to highlight, even from such a close vantage point as the first years of the 1980s, is that for a period of time during the 1970s a strong consensus existed among citizens and elected and appointed officials in Massachusetts that their state government could and should do more for its more troubled children and families.

Changes in the mode of service delivery

Accompanying growth in services were profound changes in the methods and mechanisms by which services were delivered. The most visible and widely publicized changes came in the delivery of mental health–mental retardation and juvenile delinquency services. Massachusetts entered the decade of the 1960s still very dependent upon large state institutions to provide care for mentally ill, retarded, and seriously delinquent youth. In 1967, the Youth Services Board and Commissioner of Youth Services, Jerome Miller, mounted a series of initiatives that completely transformed the face of the Youth Services program in the state. Later depicted as "radical correctional reform," Miller's actions included the sudden closure of the state's training schools for delinquent youth and the development of the most comprehensive network of community-based juvenile delinquency treatment and prevention services in the country (Ohlin, Coates, & Miller, 1974). A decade later, despite repeated attempts by opponents of the community-based approach to youth services to build new institutions, Massachusetts was still posting the lowest rate of incarceration of delinquent youth of any state in the country, a testimony to the enduring quality of Miller's reform efforts (Backman, 1979).

The Massachusetts Department of Mental Health's (DMH) deinstitutionalization efforts began a few years later and proceeded at a slower pace but nonetheless rank among the nation's most ambitious. Whereas deinstitutionalization of youth services was initially accomplished largely through the charismatic leadership of a single state executive, Miller, DMH's efforts to deinstitutionalize state hospitals and state schools for the retarded originally gathered strength among a broad consensus of mental health professionals and administrators in the state. The movement to community-based services in mental health received an additional boost from a series of class action suits charging inhumane treatment of mental patients and retardates in Massachusetts's institutions. In the consent decrees settling these court cases, the state proposed developing smaller, community-based facilities rather than investing large sums of money in refurbishing and restaffing large institutions.

The move throughout the 1970s from institution to community involved two additional and related trends in the modes and mechanisms of state service delivery: decentralization and a shift from public to private provision of services. First, in order to support a community-based system of services, the Department of Mental Health (and now the Department of Youth Services, Department of Social Services, and others) found it was necessary to decentralize many routine functions previously performed by its large central office bureaucracies. Even functions always thought to be most effectively performed at the statewide level – for instance, service delivery to low-incidence "special" populations or monitoring and evaluation – became more decentralized than ever before. DMH decentralization was established through two strategic maneuvers: decentralizing discretionary fiscal power to area directors and establishing local boards that advised the area directors. These strategies proved to be important components of the decentralization efforts.

The second main change in the mode of service delivery was the shift from public to private provision of services. In order to respond to the rapid changes in demand for services without being hamstrung by an antiquated civil service system, the state encouraged the development of small, entrepreneurial human service organizations that would provide community-based services under a contract with the state. A secondary advantage to the private contracting approach has been an enhancement of the state's ability to adopt a monitoring and evaluation posture toward publicly financed services for children and families. Because contracts are time-specific and subject to renewal (compared to the more-difficult-to-change nature of civil service employees and capital investments in state-owned properties), the state can reward higher-quality providers while allowing the lower-quality providers to wither on the vine.

New political and economic constraints on child and family policy

Policy makers in the executive branch of state government work in a system that places numerous constraints on their efforts on behalf of needy children and families. Successful policy making requires careful attention to the precise nature of each of these constraints. The difference between a noble idea and a sound action lies in the policy maker's ability to pursue his or her policy goals by pushing these constraints to their farthest limits but stopping short of the twin pitfalls of subverting the democratic process and isolating oneself by failing to respect the rights of other interest groups in the policy-making process.

Whereas some constraints change very little from age to age, others change a great deal. The decade of the 1970s marked the emergence of important constraints on executive branch policy makers.

One such increasingly powerful constraint on child and family policy is the ability of state revenues to pay for state policies and programs. The 1970s was a period of tremendous growth in child and family services and programs in Massachusetts that necessitated a comparable growth in state revenues to pay for these programs. The state constitution requires that revenue sources cover state expenditures – which presently stand at approximately $6 billion annually – or the commonwealth must borrow money to meet the ensuing deficit and plan to pay off the loans through future budgets. From this perspective, the annual budget process can be viewed as a joint attempt by the legislature and the administration to finance a selected number of government actions in order to balance the state's need for certain services with the state's ability to raise or borrow the funds required to pay for the services. When revenues will not cover expenditures, the government can choose among three strategies to counteract a potential deficit: tax increases, borrowing, or service cuts. Conversely, when revenues are likely to exceed expenditures, borrowing is unnecessary (except for major capital outlays) and tax cuts and/or service increases are viable policies for that fiscal year.

Since the mid-1970s the state has faced the problem of budget deficits more often than the luxury of budget surpluses. The realization that state revenues are limited has rapidly become the major preoccupation of policy makers and child and family service advocates alike. State taxes seem to have reached the limits of political tolerance. In such a climate, Massachusetts's generosity in the provision of basic services (it is the fifth most generous state in AFDC payments and eligibility criteria) and its level of enlightenment in social policies (its progressive experiments in deinstitutionalization and special education) have come to be identified by certain groups (for instance, the Massachusetts Taxpayers Association) as the major factors contributing to the state's high rate of taxation.

At the local level, property taxes in Massachusetts (which finance local educational programs, including the increases since 1973 in community-based special education programs) are among the highest in the nation. The combination of high state and high local taxes led to the state's new nickname "Taxachusetts." More important for its impact on child and family policy, the recent history of property tax increases led to passage in November 1980 of a referendum called "Proposition 2½," which limited the annual rate of local property taxes to 2½% of assessed value. Local municipal governments anticipated cuts in their budgets averaging nearly 40%. The largest share of these cuts was absorbed by schools. And, as usual, the proposal cuts into the school budgets of the poorest communities more deeply than the prosperous communities because the poor communities have to tax their less valuable property at higher rates to provide adequate funds for educational services.

For a host of complicated political and economic reasons, the pendulum that swung in favor of expanded programs for children and families in the 1970s has now begun to swing the other way. In the 1980s, at every level of government – local, state, and federal – the need for services, and in some cases still the demand for services, now seems to be outdistancing the fiscal resources that the public and its elected and appointed officials are willing to devote to services.

Massachusetts could and perhaps should have been prepared for this reversal because the state had endured what is now referred to as "the fiscal crisis of 1975." The crisis that appeared then as a circumscribed, time-limited problem now appears to presage a more enduring trend.

During the campaign for governor in 1974, the incumbent liberal Republican differed very little from his liberal Democratic opponent on key child and family issues. Both candidates favored a number of costly but socially progressive policies, including increased state aid to local municipalities to reimburse educational costs, increased day-care services, and cost-of-living increases to AFDC recipients. Upon taking office in 1975, the new governor discovered that his predecessor had bent to the pressures of campaign sloganeering and had wildly underestimated the potential state deficit for the coming fiscal year. As mentioned above, unlike the federal budget, the state budget must be balanced. If the state overspends revenues, it sometimes has to borrow; and if it can't borrow, it goes bankrupt. To finance a projected $530 million deficit, the governor wanted to float a $450 million bond issue. The recent near-bankruptcy of New York City's government, however, made the bond market very suspicious of local or state governments who could or would not contain costs in the spiraling educational and human services portions of their budgets.

Consequently, to establish solvency the new administration instituted a program of cuts in the budgets of state agencies. Curiously, the necessity for cuts and the level of the cuts, 10%, were less controversial in and out of government than the nature of the cuts: across the board equally from all agencies with no prior exceptions to the rule! Conceived as a politically necessary strategy to reduce charges of favoritism and to increase compliance, the policy rebounded to cause tremendous hardship and chaos in the human services. Because human service agencies accounted for 40% of the state budget, they collectively had to make 40% of the budget cuts. This level of budget cutting severely hampered a number of important policy initiatives mounted by previous administrations and endorsed by the new administration.

The best-documented example of the impact of these across-the-board budget cuts on newly emergent policy initiatives lay in the effects of the budget cuts on staffing patterns of state institutions for the mentally ill and retarded. The Department of Mental Health, which runs the state's institutions for the mentally ill and retarded, is the commonwealth's largest single employer, paying the salaries of nearly half of Massachusetts's 120,000 state employees. The administration pushed a state hiring freeze as a method to reduce costs in all state agencies. But state schools and state hospitals were already operating at bare-bones levels due to the gradual shift of personnel to community-based programs to support the deinstitutionalization movement that began in the late 1960s. Dangerously understaffed institutions were unable to hire new staff when old staff departed. The Massachusetts Advocacy Center, a private, nonprofit advocacy group, documented the human costs exacted by the hiring freeze (Massachusetts Advocacy Center, 1978). The rates of seclusions (locking patients in isolation rooms) and chemical and physical restraints (drugging or tying up patients), otherwise only treatments of last resort for extreme violence and disruption in a state institution, skyrocketed due to the lack of staff to implement less extreme forms of management.

In similar fashion, the new governor was forced to abandon or delay other parts of his liberal agenda in favor of a drastic curtailment in state spending in order to create the confidence among financial institutions required for the commonwealth to enter the bond market and borrow money successfully.

The fiscal crisis of 1975 had other profound effects on the human service delivery system in general and child and family services in particular. The newly emerging system of private provision of services was dealt a blow by the sudden contraction of funds. Due to cash flow problems, small privately operated, publicly funded community programs either had to merge with larger programs, thus reducing the unique nature of the smaller programs, or fold altogether.

Perhaps most important, the sudden and arbitrary nature of the budget cuts served to create a climate of chaos and unpredictability in human services policy and program planning at precisely the time such planning desperately required stability and predictability to nurture the just-blossoming relationship between the public and private sector on which hinged so many of its most progressive social policies toward children and families. Deinstitutionalization, special education, group care for delinquent and dependent youth, day care, and protective services all were counting on the growth of service agencies in the private sector with which they could contract, rather than mount an in-government response that would depend on civil service employment. The advantages of scale and experimentation anticipated by policy makers in relying on the private sector were negated by the private sector's hesitation to hitch their wagon to such an unpredictable horse as the government.

By 1980 the state still had no capacity for integrating intermediate and long-term fiscal planning with trends in demand for service. Consequently, the possibility that another fiscal crisis could produce dangerously arbitrary cuts in service should serve as a spur to state government to begin to limit growth in expenditures for services in a more thoughtful, humane fashion.

Beyond the glaring issue of the appropriate level of cuts in the growth rate of state expenditures lies the more politically and technically complex issue of precisely how an agreed-upon level of cuts is to be achieved. In the human services area, including child and family services, this is no easy question. The inability of state revenues to pay for policies and programs acts as a major constraint on child and family policy makers in a very complicated manner.

Policy makers in the executive branch of government face a number of new constraints due to intergovernmental relations. One such constraint on child and family policy in Massachusetts is the changing nature of the fiscal relationships between the state government and federal and local governments.

Federal funds comprise 22% to 23% of the state revenues annually. In fiscal year 1981, the federal government sent Massachusetts $1.05 billion in reimbursements, $596 million in grants, and $36 million in revenue sharing (Commonwealth of Massachusetts, 1980a, pp. 2-17–2-21). While ranking tenth in population, Massachusetts ranks eighth in both total federal aid and federal aid per capita. This favorable inflow of federal resources was an advantage in the 1970s and could be credited in part to the influence of House Speaker Thomas P. O'Neill with the Carter administration. But President Reagan's cuts in federal aid to states and local governments hurt Massachusetts more than other states that rely less heavily on federal aid.

The largest reimbursement programs in Massachusetts–Medicaid and AFDC–are entitlement programs and cannot be modified or eliminated without congressional approval. But the new Republican majority in the Senate coupled with a majority coalition of Republicans and conservative Democrats in the House provided the president with sufficient support in the 97th Congress to make the most dramatic changes in domestic programs since the New Deal. Massachusetts's fiscal solvency during the decade of the 1980s may prove to hinge on the decisions made in Washington during the first years of Mr. Reagan's administration.

Just as the federal government reimburses state governments for a percentage of the costs of certain federally mandated child and family programs (e.g., AFDC, Medicaid, Child Welfare), so too state governments partially reimburse local municipalities for certain state-mandated children's programs (Commonwealth of Massachusetts, 1980a, pp. 2-32–2-37). Unless policy initiatives in related areas are coordinated and unless the implementation mechanisms of a policy are clearly anticipated, state aid for local programs can have effects that are the opposite of those intended. A notable example of the paradoxical effects of state on local governments in Massachusetts is state aid to 350 cities and towns to provide educational services for special-needs children under an innovative special education law known as Chapter 766. In 1973, to increase the likelihood of passage of the bill by reducing opponents' concerns over future costs, the legislation stipulated that state aid for special education be taken off the top of the general pool of state funds for local aid for education. Because the state budget was growing and local aid funds were relatively plentiful, this compromise with opponents of the bill seemed like a wise political decision at the time. But a major flaw in the strategy was somehow overlooked.

In order to pursue another related social policy, namely to decrease the inequality of educational opportunity between the rich and poor communities in Massachusetts, state aid for general education is distributed using a formula favoring poor communities. Consequently, by reducing the amount of state funds available to be distributed by this progressive formula favoring poorer communities, the designers of the compromise legislation on special education inadvertently exacerbated the problem in that the 70 poorest communities in the state must tax their residents at a much higher rate to provide comparable educational services than the 70 richest communities. A social policy designed to provide equal educational opportunity for special-needs students paradoxically reduced equality of educational opportunity for students in poor communities because of the way the fiscal relationship between state and local government was redefined.

Because of state promises made prior to the fiscal crisis of 1975 for massive state aid to local educational authorities to implement Chapter 766, and because state aid under Chapter 766 was nearly the same in 1981 as it was the year after its implementation in 1974 (approximately $20 billion a year), some citizens considered the new special education law to be almost totally responsible for the dramatic increases in their local property taxes. These public sentiments helped set the stage for Proposition 2½, the tax-limiting referendum issue that now threatens to wipe out many of the gains made by the commonwealth in providing educational services to children with special needs.

In a sense, the state came full circle. A model piece of "progressive legislation" to provide children with special-needs equal educational opportunities in the least restrictive settings possible helped create the conditions in which children in poor communities as well as children with special needs were among the first to suffer. A chilling parallel can be drawn between the effect of the fiscal crises in 1975 on state-funded human service programs and the effect of Proposition 2½ on local special educational programs. The failure to anticipate the fiscal consequences of progressive legislation may create the conditions under which those most in need of help are actually hurt. These events should not be viewed as historical anomalies but as possible precursors of things to come. The president's plans to eliminate federal categorical programs in health, human services, and education and to replace them with block grant programs to the states will redefine the nature of the fiscal relationship not only between federal and state government, but also between state and local government. State government must become increasingly adept at the technical and political tasks of creating mechanisms for the equitable distribution of resources to local areas.

Reform of decision-making structures and processes:
increased demands for accountability

Scholars and critics of government policy are fond of making the distinction between substantive and procedural reforms. Substantive reforms entail changes in the "what" of government policy – what new laws are enacted, what new programs are funded, and so on, to address pressing social problems. Procedural reforms represent changes in the "how" of government policy – how to include more consumer and citizen input into the policy-making process, how to debate policy decisions in a more equitable, informed fashion on the road to addressing pressing social problems.

A very important development in child and family policy during the decade of the 1970s was the growth in the belief among progressive elements in the child and family policy arena of Massachusetts that the surest, most enduring road to substantive reforms was the enactment of procedural reforms in the state's decision-making structures and processes. The goal of these procedural reforms was to increase government accountability for child and family services and government responsivity to child and family needs. The reforms most important to the progressives were embodied in legislation to create an Office for Children (OFC) in the Executive Office of Human Services (Massachusetts General Laws, Chapter 28-A). The statutory mandates and activities of the OFC provide a concise summary of the hopes and accomplishments of the procedural reformers.

The role of local Councils for Children. For decades in Massachusetts access to the real decision-making process of state government was restricted to "insiders." Although the "insiders" changed over time, they always included the political professionals, their organizations, and those upon whom the organizations depended for campaign help–union interests, local ward organizers, and so forth. It is not surprising that state policy consistently ignored the needs of the state's most troubled children and families. Children don't vote, and troubled families rarely contribute to campaign chests. If the state's decisions about child and family policy were to be reformed, then advocates for children needed a voice in the decision-making process.

Who should the advocates be: citizens, parents, professionals, service providers? Elected or appointed? Local or statewide? And what kind of voice should they have in the policy arena: advisory, investigatory, approval? These questions were among the most important issues addressed in the legislation that created the Office for Children in the executive branch of government and the 40 semiautonomous Councils for Children (one in each of the local service areas across the state).

To avoid the perceived pitfalls of the DMH area boards, councils were designed as locally elected bodies and were mandated to include at least 51% nonprofessional citizens and consumers of services (parents of children receiving state-funded services) and no more than 49% professionals and providers of services. These provisions were deemed necessary to guarantee the community representativeness of the councils as well as autonomy and independence from public officials and providers, who were considered part of the system. Rather than simply possessing advisory capacity, similar to DMH area boards, the local councils were authorized to monitor and evaluate local, publicly funded services for children, conduct annual assessments of the service needs of children in the local area, and review and approve all proposals by private organizations to state agencies to provide services to the area's children. In short, local citizen-based councils were authorized by law to collect and use invaluable information. The statutory authority and responsibility to collect this information was thought to empower citizens in the political decision-making processes.

Local councils, armed with information about services to children in their areas, lobby public officials at three different levels of influence: (1) local area service administrators; (2) locally elected state officials; and (3) in concert with similar information gathered by other councils, at a statewide level through the efforts of the director of OFC. Because each council represents a geographically defined service area common to all human service agencies, council members are able to develop enduring relationships with public and private agency executives and administrators. Therefore, information from needs assessments, monitoring and evaluation activities, and proposal review are most frequently used by councils to influence the programs and policy decisions of local program administrators.

Not all local issues can be addressed through administrative action. Some require legislative action – either budgetary or statutory. Each local council covers the districts of two to four state representatives and one to two state senators. In a sense, each council has its own legislative delegation to approach and lobby on issues vital to the area's children and families because no local politician can afford to ignore the inquiries of an active group of 20 to 100 local citizens.

The efforts of local councils focus largely on groups of children in need and on issues of class advocacy. But the reformers who created OFC knew that local citizens are most often moved to action not by abstractions like "service gaps for abused/neglected children" or "equity for special-needs children" but because of their outrage that "Johnnie Jones isn't receiving protective services" or that "Suzie Smith doesn't meet the stringent eligibility criteria for special education services even though her needs are tangible and acute." Often the interests of citizens are captivated by the plight of one child who seems to be falling between the cracks of the state service system. Thus, as an organizing tool as well as a protection against "pie in the sky" class advocacy, the early leaders of OFC turned their statutory mandate to provide information and referral services for needy children into an individual-child-focused advocacy program called "Help for Children." Each council hired one or two paid child advocates (depending on the population of the area) who received inquiries from parents or children's service professionals about children in the local area who were not receiving the state services to which they were entitled. Child advocates serve as brokers among interested and responsible parties, usually state agencies and local school authorities with overlapping responsibility to serve a child in need. If a case can't be resolved on the local level, OFC advocates convene regional and central office representatives from the various state agencies to resolve program and policy disputes that prevent a child from receiving necessary services. In other words, unresolved cases of individual children become policy issues!

The role of the Office for Children. If the local Councils for Children operated in isolation, their political effectiveness would be drastically reduced. Thus, a major responsibility entrusted by the enabling legislation to the director of the Office for Children and the director's staff was the coordination of local council efforts. OFC analysts developed common prototypes to be used by all local councils for needs assessments, monitoring and evaluation reports, and reporting "Help for Children" cases. By employing common prototypes, the local councils placed the OFC in a position to pool local efforts and develop a state-level picture of children's service needs and a coordinated set of budgetary proposals to meet those needs. The tension between local area independence and initiative and statewide leadership and coordination always remained but was viewed by most OFC administrators and councils as a healthy tension that kept the organization honest and effective.

To forge local council efforts into a statewide effort, the enabling legislation granted the OFC central office more than the authority and ability to coordinate the information gathered by the local councils. It also gave OFC the authority to gather its own information about children's programs and policies from the central offices of all the state agencies providing children's services. Both the local councils and the central office provisions of the statute creating OFC were based on the premise that information is power in the child and family policy arena. And just as the local council authority to gather information empowered local citizens, so too the sweeping authority of the OFC director to request any child-related information from another state agency empowered the executive branch agency. The director's information-gathering authority led to many creative and influential policy analyses. But nowhere was the information-gathering authority used more creatively and powerfully by the OFC central office than in the annual preparation and dissemination of a document called the Children's Budget (Commonwealth of Massachusetts, 1980b).

The Children's Budget. The Children's Budget, published at various critical stages during the budget process and distributed to all local Councils for Children and any other interested parties, provided a step-by-step analysis of the fiscal proposals related to child and family services of all the state agencies and executive and legislative offices involved in the budget process. Thus, the Children's Budget began with a line-item–by–line-item analysis of the budget proposals made by the commissioners of each child-serving state agency and continued through each step of the budget process: the proposals of the secretaries of human services and of elder affairs to the secretary of administration and finance (A&F), those of A&F to the governor, of the governor to the legislature (in the form of House Bill No. 1), the governor's annual budget message, to (Massachusetts) House Ways and Means Committee and floor action, onto the Senate Ways and Means Committee and floor action, to the results of the House/Senate conference committee appointed by the House Speaker and Senate president to resolve differences, and finally to the final appropriations passed by the entire legislature and signed into law by the governor. In recent years, as debates over the budget have carried over into the expenditures phase of the budget cycle, the Children's Budget has even included an analysis of the departments' expenditures of appropriations.

The preparation of the Children's Budget has itself created major changes in budgetary procedures and in allocations for children's services. Many agencies were required to break out child expenditures from adult expenditures in line-items in their budget in order to comply with OFC's request for information. Discounting AFDC and educational funds, the proportion of the human services budget uniquely devoted to children's services has grown from approximately 5% to 20% over the first half-dozen years that the Children's Budget has been published. Most observers attribute much of this growth to the lobbying efforts of local councils for Children. Children, who make up one-third of the state's population, are now receiving a more equitable share of the human services pie.

Licensing. The final major responsibility of the director and OFC central office staff lay in licensing day-care and residential programs for children and youths. Prior to the creation of OFC, each state agency licensed and inspected its own programs as well as programs run under contract by private organizations. This practice came to be viewed as a serious conflict of interest for the state agencies. The day-care and residential programs had the state trapped by a seller's market. The shortage of day-care and residential placements across the state served as a disincentive to the agencies to perform their licensing function in a rigorous fashion. It was hoped that OFC would bring greater independence to the licensing function and therefore greater protection to the children. But OFC's boss, the secretary of human services, was also the boss of the direct service agencies. This meant that many licensing quarrels took on the character of a family argument rather than the quasi-judicial character of the process that the designers of OFC had in mind.

Present status of the reforms embodied in the creation of OFC. Underlying the creation of the Office for Children are clear notions borrowed from political philosophy about how in-government child advocates could mount procedural reforms in state government decision making about child and family policy. Children, like all other political causes, need a *constituency.* Child advocates need to be viewed by other actors in the policy-making process as the leaders of a group with some form of political power. Ideally, the constituency would be broad and locally based but capable of coordinated statewide action. The advocates for children need to possess *legitimacy.* In other words, the advocates must be viewed by other participants in the policy-making process as the legitimate spokespersons for children. Locally elected bodies with non-professional citizens as the majority (and therefore controlling) faction were considered to be the groups with the greatest potential claim to legitimacy. Finally, child advocates required both *authority* and *ability* to act on behalf of the interests of the commonwealth's neediest children. An advisory role would not suffice: Advocates needed statutory mandates of consequence (authority) and the executive branch support and staff to pursue the mandates (ability) if they were to participate in an effective way and compete with other organized interests in the policy-making process.

By most objective indices, these underlying political–philosophical tenets and their implementation through legislation and practice were a marked success during the 1970s. Thousands of citizens joined and participated in Councils for Children. Their efforts resulted in the proposal, appropriation, and expenditure of millions of new dollars of services to the state's neediest children. And most importantly from the point of view of enduring procedural reform, the growth in services was prompted by a statutorily mandated citizen-based mechanism to develop and provide the public with more information about child and family programs and policy than had ever been available before.

However, the strengths of OFC during the 1970s may entail its weaknesses in the 1980s. OFC developed in a climate where the populace and its elected representatives expected state government to do more for needy children and families. During the administrations of liberal governors Sargent and Dukakis, OFC and local Councils for Children became adept at identifying and documenting gaps in services and mounting lobbying efforts to close the gaps during the annual budget debates. But what happens to such an organization whose raison d'être is increasing services to children when the public attitude toward the proper role of government shifts dramatically and the state elects a conservative governor whose campaign themes are to (1) get government off the backs and out of the lives of private citizens and businesses; and (2) cut taxes, if necessary, by reducing government expenditures? Can an organization (perhaps more accurately described as a movement) that gained its life and strength through demonstrating that government can generate the political will, administrative skill, and fiscal resources to do *more* for children suddenly learn to be satisfied by doing *better* for children (by shifting from quantity to quality of services as its standard)? Can it learn the even more difficult task of exercising its legitimate voice in the policy-making process by helping to choose the least harmful, least painful ways of doing less for children (Polsky, 1981)?

If the answer to the above questions are no, what will become of the organization? Does such a turn of events prove the intrinsic inadequacy, or fallibility, or vulnerability of a within-government model for an advocacy agency? Despite OFC's close and informal relationship with the most important policy makers in state government (e.g., the secretary of human services, department commissioners, etc.) by virtue of its position within the Executive Office of Human Services and despite its ability to gather and disseminate extremely important information on child and family policy, is an agency like OFC just too dependent upon the support of the state's chief executive to offer the prospect of the enduring procedural reforms that its architects hoped for?

Only time will tell. What is clear is that the administration of the new conservative governor correctly perceived OFC and its Councils for Children as the major lobbyists for continued growth in government services to children. Consequently, the secretary of human services introduced legislation on behalf of the administration both in 1980 and 1981 sessions to dismantle OFC. The councils rose to the challenge in 1980, lobbied the legislature, and gained a reprieve. The status of future efforts remains in doubt. No matter which way the issue is decided, however, the fate of OFC and its efforts can be viewed as the prolog to a national debate on the fate of child and family policy of the 1980s. All the elements of the national debate are anticipated by the debate in Massachusetts.

The limits of the reforms of the 1970s

Massachusetts was in the vanguard of substantive and procedural reform in child and family policy in the 1970s in areas as broad-ranging as special education, juvenile justice, mental health and retardation, and child advocacy. At the same time, its budget expanded to pay for these reforms. Small wonder, then, that two years before Ronald Reagan was elected and began his dismantling of New Deal and Great Society legislation at the federal level, Edward King was elected governor of Massachusetts and began his overhaul of a decade of reforms of state government policies and practices concerning children and families. The electorate agitated for cuts in government expenditures and cuts in income, property, and corporate taxes as the opening moves in the 1980s' battle over inflation. They elected executives who espouse these goals as the top priorities of their administrations.

These goals also coincide with a desire to realign the distribution of power and responsibility among the various levels of government. Ronald Reagan hopes to soften the shock of cuts in federal social programs by increasing states' power in deciding how to use federal funds. The mechanism chosen to accomplish this shift in power is the abolition of categorical programs and their replacement with block grants. But before the Reagan administration initiated its newly defined federalism, Massachusetts experienced a comparable shift, in this case from state to local power. Through decentralization of central office functions to local area offices, especially budget functions, and later in the 1970s through the pledge to return more state revenues to cities and towns through no-strings-attached forms of local aid, Massachusetts had begun devolution before comparable federal initiatives.

There are other striking parallels between state-level trends during the turn of the decade in Massachusetts and the policies of the Reagan administration. Since 1979 Massachusetts has attempted to tighten eligibility criteria for certain high-growth services that represent a major drain on state revenues (e.g., AFDC) just as the Reagan administration has proposed changes in eligibility criteria for federally administered programs (e.g., Social Security benefits).

As Councils for Children have been asked to help state government decide which good causes would be underfunded, the new rules under which Congress operates set spending ceilings for all programs under a committee's jurisdiction. This pits various constituencies against one another during the budgetary debates (poor children vs. minority children vs. handicapped children for education funds; abused children vs. homeless children vs. children of working mothers for social service funds; etc.) The national debate over which problems necessarily and legitimately transcend state boundaries and call for a federal response if they are to be addressed effectively (e.g., a national welfare policy sufficiently coordinated across states to actively discourage migration of the poor from state to state in search of better benefits packages) follows a similar debate over state government's role in enhancing equality among Massachusetts's municipalities in resources to provide public education. Finally, at both the national and the state level now, the clearest and most forceful voices of citizens in the policy arena emanate not from child advocates or advocates for other social programs or progressive social causes, but instead from groups such as taxpayers' associations, conservative political action committees, and the Moral Majority, who collectively wish to reduce the role federal and state governments play in influencing family life.

Note

The material on which this chapter is based stems from three major sources: *the study of public documents* – for instance, the budget proposals and narratives of the Senate Ways and Means Committee for fiscal year 1981; *the author's own experiences* as an advocate for children as Special Assistant to the Director, Massachusetts Office for Children (1976–1978); and *interviews with major policy makers* from the executive and legislative branches of Massachusetts state government during the administration of Governor Michael Dukakis (1975–1979). The interviews were conducted from October 1980 to January 1981. The author wishes to express his gratitude and appreciation to each of these public servants who took time from their busy schedules to share their understanding of child and family policy making in state government. Of course, the author is solely responsible for the accuracy of information and the balance of interpretations of Massachusetts state policy presented in this chapter.

Finally, the author wishes to thank Professors Seymour Sarason and Edward Zigler of Yale University and Ms. Joyce Strom, formerly Director of the Massachusetts Office for Children, for the unfailing guidance and support necessary to transform a student–practitioner of clinical–developmental psychology into a workable scholar–activist in social policy on behalf of children and families.

Interviews

Senator Chester Atkins, Chairman, Senate Ways and Means Committee
Senator Jack Backman, Chairman, Joint Committee on Human Services and Elder Affairs

Mr. Jack Calhoun, former Commissioner, Department of Youth Services (at time of interview: Commissioner, Administration for Children, Youth and Families, U.S. Department of Health and Human Services)

Governor Michael Dukakis, former Governor, Commonwealth of Massachusetts

Mr. Gerald Goldman, former Director, Policy Unit, Massachusetts Office for Children

Representative Philip Johnston, Chairman, Special Legislative Committee on Children in Need of Services

Mr. Patrick Moscoratolo, former Director, Office of Federal/State Relations, and Aide to Massachusetts Lieutenant Governor Thomas O'Neill

Mr. Jerald Stevens, former Commissioner, Department of Public Welfare, and former Secretary, Executive Office of Human Services (presently Vice President for Finance and Administration, Yale University)

Ms. Joyce Strom, former Director, Massachusetts Office for Children (at time of interview: Associate Commissioner, Administration for Children, Youth and Families, Department of Health and Human Services)

References

Backman, J. Testimony of State Senator Jack Backman before the Subcommittee on Child and Human Development of the Committee on Labor and Human Resources, United States Senate, January 24, 1979, Washington, D.C.

Bremner, R. H. *Children and youth in America: a documentary history* (Vol. 2). Cambridge: Harvard University Press, 1971.

Commonwealth of Massachusetts. *Senate Bill No. 2200*. Boston: Senate Ways and Means Committee, 1980. (a)

Commonwealth of Massachusetts. *The children's budget*. Boston: Massachusetts Office for Children, 1980. (b)

The Editors, Harvard Educational Review. An interview with Marion Wright Edelman. *Harvard Educational Review,* 1974, *44*(1) 53–73.

Massachusetts Advocacy Center. *Frozen means you don't move: The impact of budget cuts on people in Massachusetts institutions*. Boston, 1978.

Ohlin, L., Coates, R., & Miller, A. Radical correctional reform: A case study of the Massachusetts youth correctional system. *Harvard Educational Review,* 1974, *44*(1) 74–111.

Polsky, A. New York City: Managing without democracy. *Democracy,* 1981, *1*(3).

Sarason, S. B., & Doris, J. *Educational handicap, public policy, and social history*. New York: Free Press, 1979.

7   The case of intergovernmental relations: values and effects

John E. Hansan

Before the Depression of the 1930s, there was very little federal government intervention in human services. State and local governments provided the few existing public services, usually in the form of protective services or cash assistance, and then only for the most vulnerable or seriously handicapped citizens. Since that time, the role and influence of government at all levels has grown enormously. Today, a complex intergovernmental hierarchy, with the federal government at the top, is the single most influential factor in the development of social policy and the financing of human services. Increased governmental intervention in human services has fostered a proliferation of programs and delivery systems that reflect the pluralistic and democratic nature of our intergovernmental system. Public services therefore are no longer limited to servicing the most needy. Publicly funded programs now benefit a very large proportion of our population, including children, the elderly, minorities, and the handicapped.

Most local communities have a complex but disconnected array of publicly funded services designed to meet particular social needs or enhance the capacities of different population groups. As the costs for maintaining public services have grown, a corresponding interest in reducing costs has developed. As the number of duplicative programs and services increases, there is also greater public interest in program coordination and integration of services. Recently, it has become evident that the public feels the role of the federal government in connection with human services should be changed or at least curtailed drastically. The public wants tax relief, even if it means a large reduction in the level of public support for social programs. Such expressions of public concern reflect a growing awareness that existing systems of organizing, financing, and providing human services may be either totally out of control or too complex to manage effectively.

117

Using human services as the field of investigation, this chapter explores the effects of two important factors that have strongly influenced the development of American social policies. The first factor is the American value system and its beliefs, attitudes, and norms. The second factor is the history and structure of the uniquely American system of intergovernmental relations. Together, these two factors have helped shape our public response to social needs and problems. Certainly in a period of significant change in human service policy, it is important to understand how social values and intergovernmental relations influenced organizations in the past and how they are likely to affect reorganization.

American social values

According to Robert Morris, professor emeritus at Brandeis University, "the central character of American social policies has a direction and a continuity. It is shaped by a few basic attitudes or social norms shared by most citizens as well as by their public officials" (Morris, 1979, p. 19). This societal policy is the sum total of laws, habits, mores, and practices. Societal policy, according to Morris, represents "the accumulation of values and normative standards which a society builds up over time. . . . They are an unwritten blend of what a people think their society ought to be, what they wish to do collectively for the good of all, and how they prefer to act to achieve such ends" (p. 16).

Since the mid-1960s there has been an enormous amount of federal activity directed at helping people. Starting with the Great Society programs and the War on Poverty, a wide range of opportunity programs were designed to bring into the mainstream of American society the poor, minorities, and others who could benefit from educational opportunities, jobs, job training, or personal social services. Federal funds were used to expand coverage and increase benefits of income maintenance programs such as Social Security, Medicare, food stamps, and public assistance for the needy, aged, disabled, and blind.

The 1980 elections may have signaled the reversal of what is considered by many to be liberal altruism. Voter initiatives to control taxes clearly indicate that the public wants elected officials to restrain government spending, even if it means some needy persons or worthwhile programs are left wanting. As the costs of human services rise and inflation reduces the value of earned income, taxpayers are asserting themselves more vigorously to slow the growth of government expenditures. This has been evident at the state and federal levels. Voters in many states have acted to limit the power of elected officials to raise and spend taxes. At the national level, voters in 1980 elected a president and a Congress pledged to a balanced federal budget, even if it means higher unemployment and the withdrawal of federal funds from social welfare programs. The press for reduced government spending is an example of the tension between the nation's collective social values and what elected public officials perceive to be the will of the public. Since social values are not shared uniformly by a majority of the citizens at any given time, it is necessary for elected officials to attempt to represent the priorities and preferences of the people who voted them into office.

In contrast to the need for legislators to represent their constituents' values, there is in the public domain a series of implicit social values that undergird American policies. More specifically, Morris (1979) describes five societal values or preferences that guide the direction of our social welfare programs at the present time.

1. *Preference for private or marketplace decision making.* This refers to our belief that the best solutions to problems come through the interaction of decisions made by individuals to suit their own needs; this value is represented in our preference for a free market economy and the idea that individuals have control over their own lives and can pull themselves up by their own bootstraps. This value gives support to the use of tax credits for child care rather than direct federal subsidy of child-care centers.

The preference for private decision making also supports pluralism in the United States and in the federal system of government, where power is fragmented among many different influential actors. Americans appear to prefer "muddling through" decision making in contrast to planning or decision making where control is vested in a single powerful office or individual.

2. *Belief in government aid to the weak and helpless.* When the marketplace does not serve all individuals' needs equally, the need for government to act on behalf of the "weak and helpless" is recognized. The "weak and helpless" include the aged, orphans, the handicapped, and others in serious trouble not of their own making. Governmental aid to those who are not considered weak or helpless is one area causing public concern today. Many are concerned that governmental responsibility has been substituted for the help and care previously provided by families, churches, community groups, and other informal support systems. In the area of childrens' policies such concerns are reflected in debates about the role of government financing or subsidizing child-care services for working parents, or the propriety of middle-class families with handicapped children receiving cash assistance from the Supplemental Security Income (SSI) program.

3. *Continued belief in the saving virtues of work.* Americans have historically reflected a belief in the notion that through hard work an individual can meet his or her personal needs. This value has fostered the growth of government support of work programs, job training, and supportive services needed to help individuals become employable (e.g., basic education, vocational rehabilitation, day care, etc.). The social values we hold about work also support and shape our basic governmental social insurance program – Social Security and unemployment insurance – insofar as individual eligibility and benefits are determined by work history and wages earned. Vulnerable citizens then are defined as those who are not able to work: the elderly, the handicapped, the ill, and so forth. Able-bodied poor people are believed to be poor because they are lazy and do not work.

4. *Continued optimistic view of progress through science.* Collectively, Americans believe a better world can be achieved through science and technology, solving or abolishing, in the process, all of our social problems. Elected officials in turn express this collective belief by seldom, if ever, making long-range plans to deal with significant social problems such as poverty, delinquency, child abuse, or child health. As a consequence of this optimistic view of progress through science and technology, our legislative and fiscal responses to social problems are usually time-limited and subject to frequent review, cancellation, or gradual withdrawal of public funds.

5. *Preference for shared responsibility.* Americans prefer shifting responsibility or distributing the costs of government action to the farthest point possible. This value is reflected in the tendency to prefer to pay a small insurance premium in anticipation of a very large cost. It is also reflected in the tendency to believe that actions of the federal government financed through withholding taxes are somehow less direct or expensive than the same actions by local government when financed through a property or sales tax.

Though public policy is usually framed by these prevalent social norms, it does not follow that social norms do not change over time. They do change, but the change is usually very slow, almost imperceptible. More abrupt change usually results from the effects of a catastrophe or social upheaval that reorders the society. For example, the economic conditions that precipitated the Great Depression of the 1930s changed the role of the federal government and the public's attitude toward government intrusion into private decision making. However, even as the role and scope of governmental action have increased over time, these basic values have acted to shape the nature of specific public policies adopted by elected officials.

It is no longer necessary to defend the necessity for government to act to protect or aid some portion of the population. Americans have come to expect a considerable degree of government involvement in many aspects of society, and the majority continue to pay the taxes necessary to support these activities. The areas of difference or controversy center around such questions as: What are the role and responsibility of the federal government in assuring minimum standards or availability of services? What is the proper role for local government in the provision of publicly funded services? What is the efficacy of voluntary agencies using public funds? How much of the gross national product should be dedicated to human services?

The development of our intergovernmental system: the influence of social values

Our intergovernmental system and our fundamental attitudes toward government support for human services, shaped early in this country's history, are predicated on a system of values and beliefs. Early American settlers and succeeding waves of immigrants were, for the most part, fleeing a central, unitary church or a central, unitary government. For these reasons, Americans long resisted the development of a strong central government and the intrusion of government into private actions. When it was necessary to form a national government, a Constitution was written that prevented any one branch or level of government from becoming too powerful. The powers of the federal government were initially limited to defense, interstate commerce, and setting tariffs. Most other powers were reserved for the states. The nature and power of local government was a matter for each state to decide. As a result, the role and responsibility of local government differ widely among the states.

Our early American societal values about social welfare were heavily influenced by English traditions, including the Elizabethan Poor Laws and notions about the moral virtue of work. Among other things, the Elizabethan Poor Laws established the principle that local governments should tax citizens to raise funds to assist those who could not care for themselves. The Poor Laws also classified the poor into different categories: the worthy poor, which included the frail elderly, orphans, and the handicapped; and the less worthy poor, which included the able-bodied unemployed, vagrants, and others who appeared able to work.

The elevation of the concept of work to the status of a moral virtue was a necessary adjunct to the Industrial Revolution and served the need for a surplus of low-cost labor to supply the manpower for an emerging factory system economy. The development of a work ethic and laissez-faire capitalism were greatly aided by the teachings and writings of Adam Smith, Thomas Malthus, and Herbert Spencer. Together, these men were influential in stressing the value of personal and economic independence, which in turn tended to lessen the value of and societal concern for individuals unable to work. Taken together, these traditions and values helped shape early American society's strong reliance on personal freedom and economic independence, support for a free market capitalism, and rejection of government intrusion in private decision making.

Before the Great Depression, these societal values largely shaped the human service programs that developed in the United States in response to social need. Most local communities were served by a number of religious and voluntary charities. Local government provided poor relief, emergency aid, shelters, hospitals, and child welfare services. State government financed and operated prisons, mental hospitals, and similar institutions that could not be supported by a single town or city. A number of states intitiated pensions for single mothers and the elderly, who were often unable to work for wages.

The economic conditions resulting from the Great Depression of the 1930s caused large-scale unemployment and widespread poverty. Existing programs of public relief and private charity proved inadequate to cope with the consequent flood of requests for help. The public realized that only the federal government had the resources necessary to assist state and local governments with the financial burden of public relief and establish national programs to prevent the total loss of income for wage earners during periods of unemployment.

The Social Security Act of 1935, designed to ensure some protection for all wage earners and their families against the loss of income due to retirement or temporary unemployment, was an outgrowth of the Great Depression. The act authorized establishment of unemployment compensation and old age insurance programs. Both of these programs were based on the assumption that the main source of family income was from wages and, therefore, when something happened to prevent the wage earner from working, there should be a level of income insured by the national government. In 1939 protection was extended to survivors of a covered wage earner, and in 1956 the program was expanded to include the disabled. For those persons who were not then eligible or likely to become eligible for benefits under the wage-related social insurances, the Social Security Act also authorized federal financial participation in a new system of state-administered public relief programs. The categories of public assistance for which federal funds were authorized originally were:

Old Age Assistance, Aid to the Blind, and Aid to Dependent Children. Aid to the Permanently and Totally Disabled was authorized in 1950.

It should be noted that these state-administered public relief programs created in 1935 conformed to existing patterns of federal–state responsibility for human services. Under the law, states were responsible for deciding whether or not to establish programs and for setting the terms of eligibility and the level of benefits. States also decided how to organize the relief programs and whether or not to involve city or county government in the administration or financing of the programs. The major role of the federal government was simply to pay a portion of the costs of benefits to clients and to share in the administrative costs incurred by the states. This pattern of federal–state cooperation accounts for why, even today, there is so much difference among states in relation to the organization and benefits of Aid to Families with Dependent Children (AFDC) and Medicaid. Although there have been a number of important changes in the public welfare programs over the years, they essentially exist as a state–federal partnership.

The next significant era of change in federal–state relations occurred in 1964 when Congress passed the Economic Opportunity Act and the administration declared a War on Poverty. These actions began an era of national social planning that significantly changed federal–state relations. The War on Poverty was possible because the United States was entering a period of unprecedented prosperity that created what Robert Harris of the Urban Institute has described as a "fiscal dividend," a surplus of federal revenues that could be used for social purposes. For the first time Americans as a nation were not constrained by scarce resources and they found it possible to act on their good intentions of helping the disadvantaged (Harris, 1979, p. 20).

The federal surplus of the 1960s developed from the revenues of a progressive income tax, low unemployment, high productivity, and a stable or slow-growing inflation factor. With this surplus the Congress and the administration found it possible to enact yearly tax cuts *and* finance a host of social programs. Federal policy makers used social opportunity programs – not cash assistance or public jobs – to fight poverty. To a large extent this decision and the programs created by the War on Poverty reflected prevailing societal values – attitudes about why the poor are poor. During the Depression, when unemployment was high and poverty widespread, the government created jobs for all able-bodied unemployed and expanded public relief programs for persons who could not work. Public jobs and public relief were seen as appropriate ways to eliminate the poverty of so many citizens. In 1964 and 1965, poverty was a condition limited primarily to racial minorities, welfare families, and the elderly. In the public's view, these people were not poor because of the economy or lack of jobs. Rather, they were "flawed" populations and needed to be trained, educated, motivated, or otherwise assisted to take advantage of existing opportunities. The Economic Opportunity Act of 1964 created community action programs, Volunteers in Service to America (VISTA), Neighborhood Youth Corps, Job Corps, and other programs. Within a few years, local community action programs had initiated Head Start, legal services, Foster Grandparents, parent–child centers, and a wide range of additional opportunity programs. In 1965, the 89th Congress enacted a host of other Great Society initiatives, most notably Medicare, Medicaid, the Older Americans Act, the Vocational Rehabilitation Act, the Elementary and Secondary Education Act, and Model Cities. This pattern continued during the next several years as Congress appropriated more and more federal funds for various other social problems and conditions.

Only a small number of the Great Society programs were federal programs actually administered from the national level. The vast majority of these new programs were designed to be managed and delivered at the local level. In order to entice state and local governments to accept these nationally designed programs, the authorizing legislation usually provided for generous matching formulas under which the federal government agreed to finance 75%, 80%, or 90% of the costs. To obtain their fair share of these massive amounts of federal funds, state and local governments established new departments, commissions, and other types of administrative or supervisory agencies. Nearly always, these Great Society categorical grant programs provided funds only after certain conditions were met. With few exceptions, state and local governments bought into the federal game, attracted by the prospect of favorable matching rates and the notion that participation would relieve them from having to use scarce state or local funds to meet pressing social needs.

One effect of accepting so much federal financing has been the proliferation of categorical service programs at the local level, programs that are largely outside the control of state and local elected officials. Another result has been the unplanned commitment of large amounts of state and local discretionary funds for use as the local match, leaving state and local officials in the position of having to budget ever-larger amounts of their constituencies' scarce resources for programs over which they have little or no direct control. In other words, since the mid-1960s the power to initiate and finance social programs has been almost exclusively at the national level, particularly in the Congress, which has the responsibility for determining the size and nature of the federal budget. This has occurred even though the programs are situated and administered locally.

It is estimated there are now approximately 450 federal categorical grant programs. For fiscal year (FY) 1975, the Advisory Commission on Intergovernmental Relations (ACIR)[1] reported that a total of $37.5 billion was channeled to state and local governments through these types of programs (ACIR, 1978, p. 4). The President's Reorganization Project in 1978 identified 100 different human services programs administered by 10 federal agencies and costing $23.5 billion annually (President's Reorganization Project, 1978, p. 1). The Reorganization Project identified 30 programs intended to assist individuals and families in meeting the needs of everyday living and help them obtain access to other resources. These programs were administered by seven different federal agencies involved solely with social services. For FY 1978, $9 billion in federal funds were provided for social services.

The effects of this proliferation of federally funded and controlled programs on the states and the federal system have been judged differently by different authorities and advocates. Some have viewed the effects as positive and contributing to the strength of the federal system, ensuring common standards of service, more equality of opportunity among states, and greater concern for vulnerable populations unable to compete effectively at state and local levels. For others, the proliferation of federal categorical programs has meant the loss of traditional state and local control over essential human services with excessive duplication and overlapping of programs or services designed for similar populations or problem areas. Also, the nature of federally funded programs administered at state or local levels creates the need for regulation and a means for ensuring that the funds are used properly. This in turn results in the creation of very large bureaucratic offices or agencies at all levels of government, thereby adding to administrative costs.

In June of 1978, ACIR published a summary of 13 studies of the intergovernmental grant system. The report described the congressional role in the development of categorical programs:

Yet, at bottom, Congress – and the categorical grant system – mirror the American political process as a whole, with its many points of access and power, its loosely structured political parties, its fluctuating sources of policy initiatives and leadership, its difficulty in sustaining a long-range planning effort, and its tendency to react to, and act upon, specific problems rather than move toward comprehensive national goals and explicit policy objectives.

The problems of program numbers is not so much that of duplication and overlap, in the sense of two or more grants authorizing aid for identical activities, but excessive specificity, with clusters of several grants for servicing, planning, training, and demonstration in the same narrow program area. This applies particularly to project grants. Often a single social problem has been attacked from many different directions, with programs distinguished by the particular activities they support, the clientele group they serve, the manner in which services are delivered, or the places on which they focus. [ACIR, p. 6]

The role of the federal agencies was also critically assessed by the ACIR:

The attempts to improve coordination among programs have demonstrated that federal agencies have few incentives to standardize, simplify, or "target" their activities. Their primary concern (shared by most Congressional committees which oversee them, as well as most interest groups) is to be able to account for and make effective use of each specific grant program they administer. [ACIR, p. 6]

Since 1970, a number of efforts have been made to relieve the structural and administrative problems that have accompanied the growth of federal categorical programs. President Nixon proposed a national plan for a guaranteed family income and initiated general federal revenue sharing with the states. President Ford was successful in consolidating a number of different programs into special revenue-sharing programs. President Carter established a Presidential Task Force on Reorganization to examine the relevant issues. His task force identified nine problem areas needing attention from the federal government:

1. Imprecise federal policy goals and objectives for human services
2. Unclear assignments of responsibility for service delivery
3. Lack of effective citizen involvement and empowerment in the delivery of human services
4. Uncoordinated delivery systems
5. Complicated and burdensome program administrative requirements
6. Inadequate access to, and information on, available services
7. Weak federal enforcement, monitoring, and evaluation of policies and programs
8. Absence of adequate federal supportive services to improve human services programs
9. Poor coordination among federal agencies [President's Reorganization Project, pp. 10–15]

Most recently, President Reagan took steps to drastically reduce the involvement of the federal government in human services. Citing the public's desire to control federal spending and lower taxes, President Reagan acted to reduce the level of federal financial support for a wide range of health and social welfare programs. In addition, the Reagan administration was successful in completely eliminating some programs while combining many others into block grants, thereby devolving to the states policy and program control of existing programs.

Intergovernmental relations in the future

The success of the Reagan administration in reducing federal support for human service programs will have severe and far-reaching effects on intergovernmental relations and social programs at the state and local levels. In the short range, many citizens in need of services or benefits will be unable to obtain what they require to be independent or productive. People who are now hurting will hurt even more. Some preventable problems will become acute or chronic, requiring even more time and resources in the future for repair, restoration, or rehabilitation.

It is very unlikely that state and local governments will be able to make up immediately, or ever, for the loss of federal funds. Certainly it is even less likely that private contributions from the business community, churches, or the United Way will be large enough to cover the difference. Therefore, it is anticipated that many existing agencies, programs, and services will be completely eliminated. Most others will be reduced in size, and eligibility criteria will be tightened so that only the most needy are served. Important services such as research, demonstration, program evaluation, and training programs will be severely curtailed. There will be intense competition for available funds. Along with these problems, many others will certainly arise.

It is also possible that the devolution of federal power to state and local officials will provide some new opportunities. The challenge to local citizens, consumers, providers, professionals, and public officials is to exploit the new reality and use the opportunities it presents to lessen the impact of budget cuts and plan for establishing more rational priority-setting mechanisms and delivery systems at state and local levels.

If the period of federal support for human services has ended, it also means that there is an end to the national, central programming that has characterized human services since 1964. As federal funds are reduced, national policy makers will be less able to insist on program conformity and the volume of reports and audits that add to administrative costs. There should be more opportunity for local initiatives and greater involvement of citizens and consumers.

The fact that there is no longer an excess of federal funds represents the end of an era, and so a shift in the distribution of power should be witnessed. The power of national planners will be reduced, and the potential exists to increase the power of state and local officials to influence the organization and delivery of human services. Local citizens, consumers, providers, and professionals will need to organize around common interests and work to influence the decision-making process of state and local officials. Those who are interested in and committed to improving the effectiveness of human service programs need to take advantage of these new opportunities. They need to be prepared to offer workable alternatives to what exists. They need to be prepared to be generalists and work for simplification of existing arrangements. In some instances, they may need to be advocates for the coordination and integration of others' special interests. They will need to act to guarantee that state and local policies include provisions that ensure individual protection and concern for the most vulnerable.

The challenge to state and local officials will center on their ability to take advantage of these new conditions. Will they be able to fill the void and move to make needed changes in existing human service arrangements? For example, will it be possible for state and local officials to establish program priorities that result in the elimination of some low-priority services? Will it be possible for state and local officials to move to reorganize some existing programs, consolidate other programs, and develop centrally controlled and financed core services for others? Will state and local officials have the courage to raise more taxes to support needed programs and services?

The 1980s could be a period of program consolidation and sorting of program responsibility. It could be a period during which certain programs and functions such as jobs, income maintenance, and health care financing are transferred entirely to the federal government. Although the prospects for this scenario in the immediate future may appear dim, the fact remains that the federal government is presently supporting a broad array of national programs in these areas. It would be a relatively small step for the federal government to assume total financial responsibility for Aid to Families with Dependent Children (AFDC), Medicaid, food stamps, and public jobs. Not only would such an action relieve the states of a large financial burden, but it would also permit the establishment of truly "national" standards and benefits for the most basic services a government should provide for needy citizens: the opportunity to work for the able-bodied and cash assistance for all citizens who are unable to compete in the workplace. Large amounts of state and local tax funds are presently required for these basic social welfare programs. If the federal government could be persuaded to assume the full costs, the available state and local funds could be used to finance programs and services in the area of child development, mental health, housing, social services, and programs for special populations such as children, frail elderly, and the physically and mentally handicapped. Whether or not such improvements can be made in the existing human service system depends largely on the ability of citizens, human service providers, and public officials at all levels of government to work together. Human services are too costly and too important to be the exclusive responsibility of any single group. A network of support that includes providers, public officials, and the special populations who need and use the services available must be built. Most importantly, a value system must be developed that supports the notion that the purpose of government, at all levels, is to enable citizens to develop to their full potential and to ensure that everyone has adequate amounts of food, clothing, shelter, education, and health care.

Note

1 ACIR was created by the Congress in 1959 to monitor the operation of the U.S. federal system and to recommend improvements. It is a permanent nonpartisan body composed of 26 persons: 9 represent the federal government, 14 represent state and local government, and 3 represent the public.

References

Advisory Commission on Intergovernmental Relations. *Summary and concluding observations: The intergovernmental grant system – an assessment and proposed policies* (GPO 723-164/1016). Washington, D.C.: U.S. Government Printing Office, June 1978.

Harris, R. *Trends in human services: Factors that will shape the future.* Paper presented at the 106th Annual Forum of the National Conference on Social Welfare, Philadelphia, May 14, 1979.

Morris, R. *Social policy and the American welfare state.* New York: Harper & Row, 1979.

President's Reorganization Project. *Human services study (Staff working paper).* Washington, D.C.: U.S. Government Printing Office, 1978.

8   Federal–state–local relations and the policy process

Carol Mershon Connor

"Federalism" refers to the distribution of authority among national, state, and local levels of government. In a book about specific policies and political processes in the United States, a chapter on structural arrangements may seem out of place. Yet governmental structures and relations among them reflect past political struggles and policies and shape future ones.

Power may be distributed and redistributed among levels of government in a federal system by constitutional provisions, judicial decisions, legislation, and transfers of funds from one level of government to another. Recently, changes in fiscal relations among levels of government have shaped policy in important and subtle ways. For example, in the past several decades, state and local governments in the United States have become more dependent upon federal funding. In the 1960s, federal grants took the form of categorical aid. In the 1970s, new forms of aid – general revenue sharing and block grants – gave more discretion to state and local officials in the expenditure of federal monies.[1] Do these developments indicate a shift in power away from the national government and toward state and local governments? Who advocated such a shift? Was the shift unintended? What effects have followed from it?

This chapter explores these themes. Its first section provides the context for understanding changes in the structure of American government during the 1960s and 1970s. It surveys statesmen's ideas about federalism and links these to the history of intergovernmental relations in the United States. The second section analyzes how issues regarding the sharing of funds – and power – among levels of government were placed on the political agenda in the 1960s. The third section investigates how lobbying and legislation altered the system of federal funding in the 1970s. Both the second and third sections illustrate their discussions with examples from social policy for children and their families. The fourth section

130

concludes the chapter by assessing current developments in federal–state–local relations in light of past ones.

Context: conceptions of federalism

The origins of the American federal system lie in the colonial and revolutionary experience. Division of governmental authority between the English crown and the American colonies paved the way for a sharing of power between the new national government of the United States and thirteen state governments, and between the states and local units of government. The Articles of Confederation, which went into effect in 1781, left the states free to act independently of a weak national government. Delegates to the Philadelphia Constitutional Convention of 1787 sought to modify the Articles while maintaining the ideal of limited government. After three months of debate, they agreed upon three branches of government – the two houses of Congress, the presidency, and the Supreme Court – which would check and balance one another in the exercise of their powers. The framers of the Constitution also created multiple levels of government. However, they never explicitly discussed federalism. Thus, the Constitution failed to define the relationships between national, state, and local governments:

> While there is no doubt that the framers visualized two levels of government, each exercising power over the nation's affairs at the same time, they failed to make clear what should be the precise relationship between them or how either level might relate to local and private sources of power. Neither in Article IV, where a few necessary points of federal–state and interstate but not other intergovernmental relations were dealt with, nor in Article VI, section 2, the so-called "supremacy" clause, . . . did they deal with specifics, and nowhere else in the document did they address themselves to questions of federalism at all. [Leach, 1970, p. 8]

The precise meaning of federalism has remained open to debate throughout American history. From the Revolution to the mid-twentieth century, four main conceptions of federalism developed, largely through decisions of the Supreme Court (Leach, 1970, chaps. 1 & 2).

Nation-centered federalism

Alexander Hamilton vigorously upheld the primacy of national government in his writings in the *Federalist Papers* and through his actions as George Washington's secretary of the Treasury. John Marshall, as chief justice of the United States, later contended in the Supreme Court's decision in *McCulloch* v. *Maryland* (1819) that the national government

is the government of all; its powers are delegated by all; it represents all, and acts for all. . . . The nation, on those subjects on which it can act, must necessarily bind its component parts. But this question is not left to mere reason; the people have, in express terms, decided it by saying, "this constitution, and the laws of the United States, which shall be made in pursuance thereof, . . . shall be the su-preme law of the land."[2]

State-centered federalism

Such leaders as Thomas Jefferson, James Madison, John C. Calhoun, and John Taylor argued that the national government wielded authority only as an agent of the states. As John Taylor asserted:

In the creation of the federal government, the states exercised the highest act of sovereignty, and they may, if they please, repeat the proof of their sovereignty, by its annihilation. But the union possesses no innate sovereignty, like the states; it was not self constituted, it is conventional, and of course subordinate to the sovereignties by which it was formed. [Quoted in Mason & Leach, 1959, p. 224]

Many Southerners used the defense of states' rights to rationalize differ-ences between the South and other states of the Union. They fought the Civil War against the advocates of nation-centered federalism.

Dual federalism

Even before the Civil War, the Supreme Court under Chief Justice Roger B. Taney had begun to articulate the notion that national and state gov-ernments formed two distinct centers of power. The Court's decision in *Ableman* v. *Booth* (1858) defined dual federalism: "The powers of the general government, and of the state, although both exist and are exer-cised within the same territorial limits, are yet separate and distinct sover-eignties, acting separately and independently of each other, within their respective spheres." After the Civil War, dual federalism underpinned arguments for a laissez-faire economy. Invoking dual federalism, businessmen avoided government regulation, presidents vetoed federal aid legislation, and the Supreme Court ruled against legislative efforts to institute social and economic controls.[3]

Cooperative federalism

The fourth conception of federalism developed as a result of the landmark legislation of Franklin D. Roosevelt's presidency. Before Roosevelt's New

Deal, national and state governments had practiced collaboration, even though political leaders had preached competition among governments. Different forms of intergovernmental cooperation had predominated in different eras: the joint stock company from 1789 to the mid-nineteenth century, land grants from the national to subnational governments during the latter part of the nineteenth century, and cash grants after 1913 (Elazar, 1967). The Roosevelt years marked a turning point in American politics. Faced with the Great Depression, Roosevelt legitimized government activism and increased intergovernmental cooperation. The period of cooperative federalism began. For the first time, national leaders assumed wide responsibilities for the functioning of the American economy. The variegated programs packaged as the New Deal "stood for the centralization of government authority and the nationalization of political action as ways of furthering national economic and social development" (Beer, 1979, p. 9). The federal government initiated programs to be administered at the national level and, by enlarging its grants to state and local governments, assisted these governments in achieving their policy objectives.

From the late 1930s until the late 1960s, the New Deal formed the basis for political debate in the United States and organized "liberals" and "conservatives" into two cohesive teams. Liberals believed in the efficacy of government, particularly the national government, in solving the country's economic and social problems. Conservatives, in contrast, warned that government could infringe upon individual liberty and self-reliance, and preferred state and local government action to national government intervention. Among themselves, liberals took similar positions on a range of political issues; the same held true for conservatives. "To know that a politician or aspiring politician was a New Dealer, or alternatively an anti–New Dealer, was to be able to predict his stands on a wide variety of seemingly discrete political issues: public housing, public power, social security, progressive taxation, the role of labor unions, and so on" (King, 1979, pp. 371–372).[4]

Fiscal influences on intergovernmental relations: the 1960s

Before the 1960s, constitutional provisions, Supreme Court rulings, and legislation had shaped the sharing of power among levels of government. Legislation enacted during the 1960s set in motion another influence upon the distribution of authority: the transfer of funds. Federal funding emerged as a controversial issue on the political agenda.

The legislation of the early 1960s departed from New Deal norms. President John Kennedy launched the War on Poverty in 1963:

The legislation of the first two Kennedy years had derived from the broad premises of the great Rooseveltian initiatives: its concerns were minimum wages,
social security, public works, housing, food stamps, regional economic development. In method and purpose, however, the War on Poverty broke fundamentally with New Deal precedents. Moreover, its new departures were later embodied in the most characteristic programs of the Great Society. [Beer, 1979, p.
16]

Soon after his election, President Lyndon Johnson mobilized members of
Congress to establish programs in the areas of medical care, urban renewal, transportation, welfare, environmental protection, civil rights, and
education.

Education programs illustrated three distinctive features of the policies
of the early 1960s: nationwide goals, fiscal centralization, and program
decentralization. National leaders announced goals to be pursued at all
levels of government. Johnson called for a comprehensive effort to help
disadvantaged youth and labeled it education. "The answer for all our
national problems," he declared, "comes to a single word. That word is
education" (quoted in Breneman & Nelson, 1980, p. 208). With federal
guidance, schools were to become instruments in the campaign to eliminate poverty, reduce unemployment, and ensure equal opportunity. In
many policy areas, including education, the federal government detailed
new programs to attain specific national objectives.

Federal goals in a policy area brought increases in federal funding and
thus fiscal centralization. Congress passed the first general aid-to-educa-
tion bill in the United States, the Elementary and Secondary Education
Act (ESEA), in 1965. Title I, "the heart of the bill where most of the
money was concentrated," based grants to local educational agencies on
the number of students from low-income families in each public school
district (Jeffrey, 1978, p. 76). Local areas could use federal funds under
Title I for school enrichment projects if the projects focused upon the
needs of educationally deprived children from poor areas. Although the
other titles of the ESEA did not use Title I's poverty formula, they too
aimed at improving educational quality by distributing categorical grants.[5]
As a result of the ESEA and other legislation, federal spending on education and training increased from $569 million (.7% of federal outlays) in
1960 to $23.3 billion (5.2%) in 1978 (Breneman & Nelson, 1980, p. 208).
Taken as a whole, federal grants-in-aid to state and local governments
grew from $3 billion in 1955, to $7 billion in 1960, to $24 billion in 1970,
and to $91 billion in 1980 (U.S. Office of Management and Budget
[OMB], 1981, p. 252). In education and other policy areas, "the federal
government obviously has become the major 'bank' for state and local

activities. . . . Federal grants have come to dominate state and local revenue systems" (Anton, 1979, pp. 17–18).

Fiscal centralization did not lead to program centralization. The federal government funded new services with categorical grants, but state and local governments exercised the power to deliver services or to divert federal funds to other uses. After conducting audits in 41 states, the Department of Health, Education, and Welfare's Audit Agency reported in 1971 that few states carried out their administrative or supervisory duties under Title I of the ESEA. Indeed, it found "naivete, inexperience, confusion, despair, and even clear violations of the law" in the states' expenditure of Title I monies (Jeffrey, 1978, p. 121). Early evaluations of local implementation of Title I also showed dispersal of power and disappointment of national purpose. These evaluations

not only were unable to document the program's effectiveness, but also were unable to establish whether or not there was even a program in place at the local level. Title I funds, it seems, had simply disappeared into the quagmire of local school systems, leaving only an occasional trace of something that could reasonably be called a compensatory education program. [Elmore, 1976, p. 102]

The federal government attempted to control decentralized program implementation by attaching application, accounting, and reporting requirements to its categorical aid. As suggested by the early record of Title I, its efforts met with mixed success.[6]

With this combination of features, the programs of the early 1960s made federal funding into a political issue. As state and local governments received federal dollars and were required to administer federal programs, they hired more employees. Between 1955 and 1974, while private sector employment rose by 39% and federal government employment rose by 19%, the number of state–local employees increased by 125% (Anton, 1979, p. 40). State and local officials, larger in number, grew stronger in organization. The National Governors' Association, National Association of Counties, U.S. Conference of Mayors, and other associations of elected and appointed subnational officials expanded their staffs and budgets in the 1960s. Moreover, these organizations began to lobby for state and local interests in national policy making.[7] At first, the government interest groups focused on specific programs, assuming "a subordinate or at best coordinate position with other interested groups in maintaining, modifying, and enlarging existing programs" (Beer, 1976, p. 164). As the 1960s unfolded, the organizations of state and local officials moved to a position of prominence and criticized the system of federal funding. After competing among themselves for categorical grants, many governors, county executives, and mayors found grounds for cooperation. They decried the complicated procedures and lack of coordination in categorical aid programs, protested federal attempts to control program administration, and argued for the adoption of revenue sharing and block grants.

New forms of federal aid: the 1970s

The idea of revenue sharing had attracted interest before the rise of state and local actors. Republican Representative Melvin Laird of Wisconsin had proposed general-purpose aid in 1958 as a substitute for the system of categorical grants. In 1964, Walter Heller, while chairman of President Johnson's Council of Economic Advisers, had endorsed revenue sharing as a way to supplement existing categorical aid and to absorb expected surpluses in the federal budget. However, Johnson rejected the idea, and Great Society programs and the Vietnam War consumed the forecasted federal surpluses (Myers, 1975).

In the late 1960s, support for block grants and revenue sharing grew. Backed by intense lobbying from state officials, Republicans in 1968 secured the approval of block grants in law enforcement by winning Southern Democratic votes for the measure. This was "the first major new bill adopting the state-oriented block grant approach to pass Congress" (Dommel, 1974, p. 70). Over 70 revenue-sharing proposals appeared in the 90th Congress (1966–1968), almost all with Republican authors. Most Democrats opposed revenue sharing. Revenue sharing was languishing in the House Ways and Means Committee when Richard Nixon embraced the concept in his 1968 presidential campaign. President Nixon presented a revenue-sharing plan in August 1969 as the centerpiece of a "new federalism." However, the Democratic House leadership ignored the Nixon bill. At issue was the distribution formula for revenue sharing. In awarding general-purpose funds to state and local governments, the federal government could follow criteria of need, distributing most funds to low-income governments; follow criteria of merit, distributing most funds to high-taxing governments; or simply distribute funds evenly among the population (Beer, 1976, pp. 132–144).

The enactment of revenue sharing

A series of compromises culminated in the enactment of revenue sharing in October 1972. The associations of state and local officials worked to organize a campaign in favor of a second Nixon bill of February 1971. "Between late fall [1970] and January 1971, a durable alliance was consummated between the White House and the government interest groups over revenue sharing which, in spite of obvious partisan tensions and periodic cleavages within and between the groups, persisted through revenue sharing's passage" (Haider, 1974, p. 67). The groups' lobbying resulted in five congressional initiatives. The House Ways and Means Committee considered three revenue-sharing proposals, the last of which passed the House in June 1972. The Senate Finance Committee voted out still another version of revenue sharing. In October 1972 the House–Senate Conference Committee decided upon the final compromise. Whereas the original Nixon proposal stressed merit criteria, the State and Local Fiscal Assistance Act of 1972 combined need and merit criteria.

The House vote of June 1972 and the Conference Committee compromise hold particular interest. The House vote revealed the decline of party loyalties. In their campaign for revenue sharing, government interest groups for the first time united their efforts and applied pressure for passage of major legislation. Weakened party loyalties gave the margin of victory to state and local officials. Analysis of the critical House vote indicates that Republicans split into groups of moderately conservative (for revenue sharing) and very conservative (against it). The votes of Democrats divided along traditional ideological lines, between Northern and Southern factions, but serious cleavages also appeared within each Democratic faction. In the end, "Eastern Republicans, Northern Democrats, rank and file Democrats, members from states favored by the pending bill, the more liberal and the less conservative from both parties – the detritus of a half-decade of party decomposition – provided the political material most malleable to pressure" (Beer, 1976, p. 191).

The successful compromise of 1972 signaled trends toward decentralization. The lobbying of state and local actors produced an extremely complicated distribution formula that, by mixing offsetting criteria, followed neither: It tended toward an equal per capita allocation.[8] Excluding no level of government, the 1972 act spread revenues widely and evenly among states, counties, and cities. Revenue sharing proved to be "decentralizing in a distinctive way. . . . [It tended] to increase the supply of public goods by subnational governments, while maintaining and enhancing the existing territorial fragmentation of power among these governments, with little regard for merit or for need" (Beer, 1976, p. 195).

Block grant legislation

Similar pressures from state and local actors and similar congressional voting patterns led to the passage of block grant legislation soon after the adoption of revenue sharing (Hargrove & Dean, 1980). In 1971, President Nixon had put forward "special revenue sharing" as a companion to the projected general revenue sharing. Altering Nixon's proposal to permit some federal control of state–local expenditures, Congress established block grants for employment and training (the Comprehensive Employment and Training Act of 1973), for community development (the Housing and Community Act of 1974), and for such social services as day care, foster care of children, and drug counseling (Title XX of the Social Security Act, 1974).

The operation of the social services block grant showed that this form of aid furthered decentralization in the 1970s. The Title XX amendments were written in part to remedy the deficiencies of earlier legislation: They specified guidelines for the states' expenditure of federal monies made available under 1967 amendments to the Social Security Act. Title XX, in merging previously separate categorical programs, also meant to transfer to recipient governments the authority to plan programs (not just to implement them), to open the planning process to local needs, and to reduce federal involvement in program planning and implementation. Title XX shared these goals with other block grants. It also shared with them a pattern of outcomes:

(1) It has proved difficult to create, as intended, institutional arrangements at the grass-roots level that allow programs to be planned in a comprehensive way. (2) The search for accountability to local publics has resulted primarily in responsiveness to organized groups – whether service providers, specific clientele, or other government bureaucracies. (3) Federal officials have had difficulty transferring their procedural authority to local governments, but at the same time have been slow to develop new substantive roles as advisers to local governments in methods of service delivery. [Hargrove & Dean, 1980, p. 142]

The pattern resembled that of revenue sharing: Decentralization of planning brought fragmentation of power. When receiving block grants, state and local governments had greater opportunity to dilute the equalizing, redistributive effect of social policies, and did so.

Together, the introduction of revenue sharing and block grants marked the weakening of past political alignments. The design of antipoverty and Great Society programs had broken with New Deal precedents. As the 1970s unfolded, disillusionment with those programs broke down New Deal coalitions. Newly strong state and local officials succeeded in altering the system of federal funding because their efforts coincided with a retreat from traditional liberalism and a decline in political party organization. Many liberals moved to "moderate" stances, some converted to "neoconservatism," and still others defied ideological labeling (Steinfels,

1979). Most conservatives became more so, and a radical right appeared. As noted, the political parties' role in organizing members' votes in Congress diminished during the 1970s; so also did the parties' roles in defining the electorate's choices and controlling presidential politics (Ranney, 1979). Party "outsiders," not party regulars, won presidential nominations and the presidency itself in 1976 and again in 1980.

Retrospect and prospect

Ronald Reagan's election did not reverse the decline of party organizations and New Deal coalitions. The Republican party emerged from the 1980 elections with the presidency and, for the first time in 22 years, a majority in the Senate. Yet as before, candidate personalities and single issues dominated electoral politics, not disciplined party organizations. Traditional liberalism remained in disarray, its attempted solutions to social problems discredited. More political leaders and voters moved rightward, further blurring the traditional definition of conservatism. "The politics of the 1930s and 1940s resembled a nineteenth-century battlefield, with two opposing armies arrayed against each other in more or less close formation; politics today is an altogether messier affair, with large numbers of small detachments engaged over a vast territory, and with individuals and groups changing sides" (King, 1979, p. 372). This observation, accurate before Reagan's election, acquired more force after it.

Reagan's policies in office may open a new stage in American federalism. As in the Great Society period, the federal government under Reagan has depended upon decentralized program implementation. Reagan has continued to stress decentralized program planning: Echoing the presidents of the 1970s, he has proposed to consolidate federal aid programs into block grants.[10] Reagan has started a new trend by decentralizing program *funding*. He has sought to decentralize funding in two ways: by reducing the amount of federal aid given to states and localities, and by reassigning the responsibility for financing programs.

First, Reagan has reduced program funding. Federal grants to subnational governments, by all measures, rose continuously during the 1950s and 1960s. Federal grants in percentage terms (as a percentage of total federal outlays, of domestic federal outlays, and of state and local expenditures) first dipped in the mid-1970s, and fluctuated thereafter. Measured in dollar amounts, and excluding payments to individuals, federal grants to states and localities decreased slightly for the first time in fiscal year 1981 (U.S. OMB, 1979, p. 225; 1981, p. 252; 1982, p. 17).[11] Federal grants in both percentage terms and dollar amounts (excluding payments to individuals) dropped sharply in Reagan's 1982 and 1983 budgets, and were scheduled to fall further in subsequent budgets (U.S. OMB, 1982, p. 17). State and local officials, still prominent, have protested but not prevented a cut in aid.

Second, Reagan has attempted to place the responsibility for funding many programs upon states and localities. In his State of the Union address of January 1982, Reagan presented the blueprint for a "new federalism." At one stroke, this plan would have exchanged a federal takeover of Medicaid for state takeover of welfare (the food stamp and Aid to Families with Dependent Children programs), transferred dozens of federal aid programs to states, set up a temporary trust fund for states, and designated a transitional period after which the states would assume the full burden of financing the transferred programs. In the face of opposition from both Congress and state and local officials, Reagan revised the plan in the spring of 1982. In August 1982, he postponed submission of details of the plan to Congress until 1983; and administration officials admitted that Reagan might pursue a more gradual strategy in 1983. It appears that Reagan has marshaled enough support to carry out the first but not the second phase of funding decentralization.

"The taxing power of government must be used to provide revenues for legitimate government purposes. It must not be used to regulate the economy or to bring about social change," Reagan stated flatly in his budget speech of February 1981. "And while we will reduce some subsidies to regional and local governments, we will at the same time convert a number of categorical grant programs into block grants" (Reagan, 1981, p. B-8). In Reagan's view, "block grants are only the intermediate steps. I dream of the day when the federal government can substitute for those the turning back to local and state governments of the tax sources we ourselves have preempted here at the federal level" (quoted in Stanfield, 1982, p. 369).

The U.S. Constitution established a federal system. The distribution of authority among its components was later shaped by judicial decisions, legislation, and, after the mid-twentieth century, transfers of funds. During the 1960s, the national government awarded categorical grants to officials in state and local governments for the implementation of antipoverty and Great Society programs. In the 1970s, these officials successfully lobbied for revenue sharing and block grants, forms of federal aid that allowed states and localities more discretion in implementing and planning programs.

To the extent that he turns rhetoric into reality, Reagan will redefine the purpose of national government and redistribute authority in the

American federal system. For the sharing of funds continues to mold the sharing of power among levels of government in American federalism.

Notes

1 A *categorical grant* consists of national funds awarded to state and local governments for attainment of a specific objective in a program area. It carries two sorts of requirements: The recipient government must usually match a portion of the grant and must follow federal application, accounting, and reporting procedures. *Revenue sharing* refers to general-assistance grants from the national to subnational governments, awarded with none of these "strings" attached. *Block grants* to state and local governments place more conditions upon their use than do revenue-sharing grants, but fewer than do categorical grants. They merge existing categorical programs into one grant, or they fund a broad new program.

2 *McCulloch* v. *Maryland,* 4 Wheaton 316 (1819). Other important national decisions of the Supreme Court were *Marbury* v. *Madison,* 1 Cranch 137 (1803), and *Cohen* v. *Virginia,* 6 Wheaton 264 (1821).

   Compare Nos. 9 and 16 of *The Federalist Papers* (Garden City, N.Y.: Anchor, 1966), written by Hamilton, with Nos. 39, 40, and 45, written by Madison.

3 *Ableman* v. *Booth,* 21 Howard 506 (1858). See also *Hammer* v. *Dagenhart,* 247 U.S. 251 (1918), where the Court struck down national legislation forbidding the transportation across state lines of goods produced by child labor.

4 Not all political scientists agree that the New Deal set the terms of American political debate. Theodore Lowi (1969, chaps. 1–3) disputes the liberal–conservative dichotomy.

5 Aid under Title II of the ESEA furnished public and private schools with library books and other materials. Title III set up supplementary experimental educational centers, and Title IV supported regional centers of educational research. Title V allocated monies to state education agencies. Titles added to the ESEA since 1965 (for example, Title VI in 1966, Education of Handicapped Children) extended financial assistance to children with disadvantages other than poverty.

6 State and local leaders often frustrated the redistributive intent of antipoverty and Great Society legislation because they tended to pursue economic prosperity in their jurisdictions at the expense of economic equality. In any federal system, lower levels of government cannot control external socioeconomic forces and so concentrate upon protecting their economic base. The national government can control those forces and so can redistribute wealth through social policy. Thus, in the American system, "the primary role of the central government has been to finance the redistributive activities of states and localities. . . . When given the opportunity to participate in redistributive Great Society programs, local governments . . . have every incentive to accept the monies (for their short-term positive effect on local economies) but then to modify any redistributive impact they might have" (Peterson, 1980, pp. 278, 281).

7 Six of the seven major state and local associations were founded before World War II. In the mid-1960s, these groups experienced increases in staffs, budgets, and lobbying. For example, the National Governors' Association established a Washington office in 1966 and obtained an independent research facility in 1974. The National Association of Counties (NACO) more than doubled its representation from 1963 to 1973 (from 400 to 820 counties, or 60% of the U.S. population); and, while two Washington lawyers managed (part-time) NACO in 1957, the organization in 1973 had a staff of 100. Early in the Kennedy administration, the U.S. Conference of Mayors operated with a staff of 3

and a budget of $100,000; its lobbying activity grew as its budget rose to $175,000 in 1964 and to $338,000 in 1968 (Beer, 1976, pp. 163–171).

8 The act of 1972 provided the following: Each state's share would be computed twice, once according to the five-factor distribution formula approved by the House, and once according to the three-factor Senate formula; each state would receive the larger of the resulting sums, but all shares might be reduced proportionately so as to fit the national total authorized for revenue sharing; local units would obtain two-thirds of each state allocation.

9 Other block grants followed those of 1973–1974. In response to the 1976 recession, a block grant in local public works was introduced. Grants for elderly assistance and vocational rehabilitation were consolidated during the Carter administration.

Thus, in 1976, revenue sharing constituted 12.1% of federal grants to state and local governments, block grants 10.6%, and categorical grants 77.3%. In 1978, the figures stood at 12.3% for revenue sharing, 14.8% for block grants, and 72.9% for categoricals. Reflecting the phasing out of the antirecessionary general-purpose and block grants, the figures in 1980 were 9.4% for revenue sharing, 11.2% for block grants, and 79.4% for categorical grants (U.S. OMB, 1981, p. 255).

10 In 1981, Reagan advocated the consolidation of 88 categorical programs into five block grants. Congress merged 57 programs into nine block grants for health, education, community and social services, community development, and energy assistance. Congress imposed more constraints on state use of the funds than Reagan had planned; but these new block grants still gave the states more discretion in planning and spending the money than did the block grants created before 1981.

In 1982, Congress enacted block grants for job training to replace CETA, which expired in September 1982.

11 Payments to individuals are defined as federal budget outlays whose benefits constitute income transfers to individuals or families. The category comprises Medicaid, assistance payments, housing assistance, food stamps, and nutrition programs for children and the elderly.

Measured in dollar amounts, and *including* payments to individuals, federal grants to states and localities were estimated to have decreased for the first time in fiscal year 1982 (U.S. OMB, 1982, p. 17).

In sum, federal aid to states and localities is declining when measured as a percentage of total federal outlays, a percentage of domestic federal outlays, or a percentage of state and local expenditures. It is also declining when measured in dollars and excluding payments to individuals. According to a fifth measure (dollars, including payments to individuals), federal aid is probably beginning to decline.

References

Anton, T. J. Federal assistance programs: The politics of system transformation. In D. Ashford (Ed.), *National resources and urban policy*. New York: Methuen, 1979.

Beer, S. H. The adoption of revenue sharing: A case study of public sector politics. *Public Policy*, 1976, *24*, 127–195.

Beer, S. H. In search of a new public philosophy. In A. King (Ed.), *The new American political system*. Washington, D.C.: American Enterprise Institute, 1979.

Breneman, D. W., & Nelson, S. C. Education and training. In J. Pechman (Ed.), *Setting national priorities, 1980*. Washington, D.C.: Brookings Institution, 1980.

Dommel, P. R. *The politics of revenue sharing*. Bloomington: Indiana University Press, 1974.

Elazar, D. J. Federal–state collaboration in the nineteenth century United States. In A. Wildavsky (Ed.), *American federalism in perspective*. Boston: Little, Brown, 1967.

Elmore, R. F. Follow through planned variation. In W. Williams and R. F. Elmore (Eds.), *Social program implementation*. New York: Academic Press, 1976.

Epstein, L. D. The old states in a new system. In A. King (Ed.), *The new American political system*. Washington D.C.: American Enterprise Institute, 1979.

Fairfield, R. P. (Ed.). *The federalist papers* (2nd ed.). Garden City, N.Y.: Anchor, 1966.

Haider, D. H. *When governments come to Washington: Governors, mayors, and intergovernmental lobbying*. New York: Free Press, 1974.

Hargrove, E. C., & Dean, G. Federal authority and grass-roots accountability: The case of CETA. *Policy Analysis*, 1980, *6*(2), 127–149.

Jeffrey, J. R. *Education for children of the poor: A study of the origins and implementation of the Elementary and Secondary Education Act of 1965*. Columbus: Ohio State University Press, 1978.

King, A. The American polity in the late 1970s: Building coalitions in the sand. In A. King (Ed.), *The new American political system*. Washington, D.C.: American Enterprise Institute, 1979.

Leach, R. H. *American federalism*. New York: Norton, 1970.

Lowi, T. J. *The end of liberalism: Ideology, policy, and the crisis of public authority*. New York: Norton, 1969.

Mason, A. T., & Leach, R. H. *In quest of freedom: American political thought and practice*. Englewood Cliffs, N.J.: Prentice-Hall, 1959.

Myers, W. S. A legislative history of revenue sharing. *Annals of the American Academy of Political Science*, 1975, *419*, 1–11.

Peterson, P. E. Federalism and the Great Society. In V. T. Covello (Ed.), *Poverty and public policy: An evaluation of social science research*. Cambridge, Mass.: Schenkman, 1980.

Ranney, A. The political parties: Reform and decline. In A. King (Ed.), *The new American political system*. Washington, D.C.: American Enterprise Institute, 1979.

Reagan, R. State of the Union message on economic recovery (transcript). *New York Times*, February 19, 1981, p. B-8.

Stanfield, R. L. "Turning back" sixty-one programs: A radical shift of power. *National Journal*, 1982, *14*, 369–374.

Steinfels, P. *The neoconservatives: The men who are changing America's politics*. New York: Simon & Schuster, 1979.

United States Office of Management and Budget. *Special analyses, budget of the United States government, 1980*. Washington, D.C.: U.S. Government Printing Office, 1979.

United States Office of Management and Budget. *Special analyses, budget of the United States government, 1982*. Washington, D.C.: U.S. Government Printing Office, 1981.

United States Office of Management and Budget. *Special analysis H, budget of the United States government, 1983*. Washington, D.C.: U.S. Government Printing Office, 1982.

9   A federalist paper: the current debate

Stephen B. Heintz

Five weeks after the inauguration of Ronald Reagan in 1981, the nation's governors met in Washington for their annual winter meeting. The governors gathered in the wake of a startling national election. A former member of their ranks, espousing a consistently conservative ideology, had captured the presidency, carried a Republican majority into the Senate, and substantially eroded the margin of Democratic control in the House of Representatives.

Mr. Reagan had long favored a fundamental realignment of the relationship between the states and the federal government. During the campaign, he offered a "new federalism" to guide the restoration of a more appropriate balance to American intergovernmental relations. This realignment was to include a "sorting out" of the proper roles of each of the three levels of government, the deregulation of the federal–state relationship, and a significant reduction of the federal presence in domestic policy. Political analysts proclaimed the election of 1980 the dawn of a new age, a political revolution of a magnitude equal to the New Deal. The breadth of the president's victory gave every appearance of being a popular mandate for the reconstruction of the federal–state relationship he proposed.

Many governors of both political parties have shared a similar desire to recast the roles of the state and federal governments. Indeed, the National Governors' Association, under the leadership of Georgia Governor George Busbee, had embarked during 1980 on a major federalism project. The governors sought a less restricted relationship with the federal government, one that would allow states greater discretion in the administration of federally supported programs. Thus there was little doubt about the likely outcome of a vote taken at the governors' postelection meeting on a resolution broadly supporting the president's recently announced Economic Recovery Program and the initial phase of his proposed new federalism. Only the governors of Connecticut and Maine dissented.

It is doubtful that when they cast their votes, the two dissenting governors were thinking of the *Federalist Papers* or contemplating the musings of Tocqueville or Lord Acton on the workings of American democracy. They responded by instinct, in the face of enormous peer pressure and against the seeming tide of current events. The two governors questioned the pragmatic, not the philosophic, implications of the new federalism. Would the states of Connecticut and Maine be able to accept the burdens imposed by the president's plan?

There are, in fact, legitimate philosophic as well as pragmatic concerns to be raised about the new federalism. The basic philosophic premises of the new federalism are debatable. In addition, the very real effects of the president's program may threaten rather than enhance the ability of state governments to meet the needs of their citizens. This chapter examines both areas of concern by focusing on the new block grants, a cornerstone of the new federalism, and one state's initial response.

Philosophical issues

In a literal sense there is no such thing as the *new* federalism. There is only the federalism of the Constitution, our understanding of which has changed markedly over the past 200 years. President Reagan's new federalism is a new understanding, a new interpretation of the nature of the Republic itself and the Constitution on which it is constantly being built.

In many respects it is the Constitution's inherent ambiguities that have sustained the union throughout the challenges of history. James Madison described this dynamic ambiguity as follows:

In its foundation it is federal, not national; in the sources from which the ordinary powers of the government are drawn, it is partly federal, and partly national; in the operation of these powers, it is national, not federal; in the extent of them again, it is federal, not national; and finally in the authoritative mode of introducing amendments, it is neither wholly federal, nor wholly national. [Madison, 1961a, p. 246]

As Madison indicates, the federalism of the Constitution is not clearly defined: The boundary between the legitimate powers of the national and state governments is obscure, and purposely so.

The *Federalist Papers* explicitly recognized that controversies regarding the division between state and federal authority and responsibilities were inevitable. The Founding Fathers never intended in drafting the Constitution to do more than to establish, with only some detail, the broad parameters of American federalism. The Constitution specifically enumerates certain powers of the federal government: taxation, minting of currency, maintaining military forces, declaring war, regulating foreign and interstate commerce, and so forth. In addition, the "elastic clause" (art. I, sect. 8, clause 18) grants Congress the power "to make all laws which shall be necessary and proper for carrying into execution" these enumerated powers. It is upon this clause that much of the growth of the federal government has rested.

Interpretations of the Tenth Amendment to the Constitution have provided the framework for scholars and politicians who argue that considerable latitude is reserved for the states in the exercise of their authority: "The powers not delegated to the United States by the Constitution, nor prohibited by it to the States, are reserved to the States respectively, or to the people." It is the tension between the "elastic clause" and the Tenth Amendment that joins the issue of federalism.

Our political and judicial heritage has been shaped by our understanding that the Constitution and American federalism are growing, evolving ideas. Notions of federalism are much like religious faith: They are shaped as much by interpretation and experience as they are by the documents that lend them literal support. As Woodrow Wilson noted:

The question of the relation of the states to the federal government is the cardinal question of our Constitutional system. It cannot be settled by the opinion of any one generation, because it is a question of growth, and each successive stage of our political and economic development gives it a new aspect, makes it a new question. [Wilson, 1908, p. 173]

The *Federalist Papers* reflect the strength of the Constitution that is derived from its evolutionary nature. Published during 1787 and 1788 in an effort to persuade reluctant states to ratify the Constitution, the *Federalist Papers* were written by three men (Hamilton, Madison, and Jay) with profoundly different viewpoints on the nature of federalism. The varied interpretations of these three statesmen, and the scholars and politicians who have followed, are all sustained by the document around which the ongoing debate regarding American domestic policy has been framed.

More recently, twentieth-century debate has largely been framed by the events of the Great Depression and the response of the New Deal. While rarely explicitly addressing the issue of federalism, Franklin Roosevelt offered an implicit interpretation that signified a new era in the balance of state and federal roles. By thrusting the federal government broadly into a wide variety of economic and social issues, Roosevelt established a federal dominance that persists to the present. Roosevelt clearly viewed the shattering of the American economy as a national crisis demanding a national response superseding the capacities of the individual states. The New Deal inauguarated a Democratic approach to federal domestic policy, which was modified, but maintained, by the Fair Deal, the New Frontier, and the Great Society.

In a political sense, President Reagan has proffered the nation's second "new federalism." Richard Nixon proposed the first during the early years of his presidency. Nixon proposed a partnership between the levels of government in order that services be provided with greater efficiency and effectiveness. Five months into his administration, President Nixon outlined the nucleus of his views:

If there is anything we know, it is that the federal government cannot solve all the nation's problems by itself; yet there has been an overshift of jurisdiction and responsibility to the federal government. We must kindle a new partnership between government and people, and among the various levels of government. [Quoted in Mars, 1970, p. 435]

To finance the partnership, Nixon proposed and Congress enacted the Revenue Sharing Act of 1969, which redistributed federal revenues to the states and localities for their use to support an extensive array of eligible programs. In his first State of the Union address, Nixon put forward a series of domestic reform proposals and formalized his view of federalism. "The time has come," the president argued,

to assess and reform all of our institutions of government at the Federal, state and local level. It is time for a New Federalism, in which after 190 years of power flowing from the people and state and local governments to Washington, it will flow from Washington back to the states and the people. [Nixon, 1970, p. 4]

Nixonian new federalism envisioned reforms designed to maximize efficiency in the management of programs established to fulfill the mutual interests of the national and state governments. But the new federalism did not take hold. The 1970s continued to be a period of major federal initiatives in domestic policy: welfare, education, transportation, environmental protection, and so on. Other than revenue sharing, the domestic legacy of the Nixon years was the maintenance of federal supremacy. In fact, unlike the debate of the early 1980s, the key constitutional issues of the early Nixon years related to the separation of powers between the executive and legislative branches and not the separation of responsibilities in intergovernmental relations (Evans & Novak, 1971). Consequently, Nixon's federalism had little impact because categorical programs continued to grow and philosophical issues of federalism were never fully addressed.

Ronald Reagan's new federalism is substantially more than a rephrasing of Richard Nixon's earlier program. It has become the ideological base for almost every aspect of the president's domestic policies. There are essentially three broad philosophical elements of the new federalism. First, and primary, is the belief that the Washington bureaucracy has simply grown too big, too pervasive, too authoritarian, and too distant from the people it is intended to serve. A second and corollary element is the premise that most domestic policy issues are more appropriately addressed within the jurisdiction of state and local governments. The new federalism would reduce the scope and authority of the federal government by transferring major responsibilities to state capitols and city halls. Finally, the underlying dogma of the president's program is the conservative ideological tenet that American governments per se are too deeply involved in American life. The new federalists place greater reliance on the marketplace and on economic competition than on government.

The new federalism is predicted on a strict construction of the Constitution and an emphasis on the Tenth Amendment. Reagan's view is that the federal government exists as a creation of the states, only to perform those functions that no state can accomplish alone. In this view, the states are seen as the basic foundation of the Constitution: The nation thus becomes an afterthought. Carried to its logical extreme, the parts would swallow the whole.

The fundamental flaw of the philosophy of new federalism is its premise that the powers of the states are unlimited and their sovereignty full. The individual states that originally entered the union were never fully sovereign. As Alexis de Tocqueville noted, "the confederated states had long been accustomed to form a portion of one empire before they had won their independence; they had not contracted the habit of governing themselves completely" (Tocqueville, 1835). The colonies had not demanded independence individually; they won sovereignty collectively.

American federalism begins with the nation. The phrasing of the Preamble to the Constitution reads, "We the people of the United States . . . ," not we the states of Connecticut, New York, Virginia, and so forth. Although the enumerated powers of the national government are limited, its sovereignty is full within its sphere of action. The reserved – but undefined – powers of the states are unlimited, but their sovereignty remains less than full, ultimately subordinate to the supremacy of the nation. American federalism as embodied in the Constitution is the continuous reconciliation of dual sovereignties, federal and state, in a harmonious relationship. Not only does the federal government exist to perform those functions no state can perform individually, but it exists to perform those functions better performed collectively.

The dominant national interest in the view of the new federalists is national defense. Regulation of the economy and interstate and foreign commerce are also considered federal responsibilities in initial concepts of "sorting out." Other vital areas, including welfare, education, and transportation, are viewed as more appropriately within the purview of the states. The new federalists challenge the growth – which commenced with the New Deal and progressed through the 1970s – of the federal presence in these areas as federal preemption and an encroachment of states' rights under the Tenth Amendment. State sovereignty becomes the ultimate principle to be served by the national government. James Madison offers the most incisive criticism of this view:

It is too early for politicians to presume on our forgetting that the public good, the real welfare of the great body of the people, is the supreme object to be pursued; and that no form of government whatever has any other value, than as it may be fitted for the attainment of this object. . . . In like manner, as far as the sovereignty of the states cannot be reconciled to the happiness of the people, the voice of every good citizen must be, let the former be sacrificed to the latter. [Madison, 1961b, p. 289]

Neither the Constitution nor American federalism is static. Their value has grown with the history of our nation. The new federalism reflects the view that the Constitution allows for little evolution in the relationships between the levels of government. President Reagan has stated that the goal of his new federalism is to take the nation back "as far as the Constitution" (Reagan, 1981, p. 11). To interpret the Constitution so finely is to deny the document its essential strength and its continuing relevance to an evolving United States.

The new federalists convey the impression that their views are a return to the federalism of the Constitution. Yet their views are simply an interpretation of federalism as they would like it to be. The new federalism is not inherently a constitutional issue; it is a political issue in that it offers a philosophical base upon which the Reagan administration hopes to gather support for fundamental pragmatic revisions in American social and economic life.

Pragmatic issues

The need for reform

Philosophical differences aside, few scholars, politicians, or public administrators would deny that the present condition of American federalism requires reform. The trend of the past 50 years has been one of an evolving "unrestrained intergovernmentalism" (Advisory Commission on Intergovernmental Relations [ACIR], 1981a, p. 1). The rate of growth in federal grants-in-aid to state and local governments is but one measure of the dramatic expansion of the federal presence in domestic affairs.

The federal government entered new arenas as Congress established programs in the fields of elementary and secondary education, health care, law enforcement, mass transit, and many others. Each program carries its own regulatory requirements and administrative provisions, and each supports its own element of governmental bureaucracy.

The result has been an inefficient system, a dysfunctional federalism (ACIR, 1981b, p. 7) in which priorities are set in Washington for programs administered at the state and local level. Program goals often overlap and are occasionally conflicting or even contradictory.

Local officials frequently are granted little discretion in the administration of programs, with the result that local priority needs may not be served by closely related federally funded programs. The elements of social policy have thus become fragmented and the administration of social programs inefficient and even ineffective. Finally, this fragmented, cumbersome, and costly federal system is firmly entrenched and sustained by an "iron triangle" of executive branch agencies, legislative committees, and special interest groups, all protecting narrow, parochial concerns. Penetrating this triangle requires a realignment of political forces focused on a rational and comprehensive approach to social issues.

Although the entry of the federal government into many diverse areas of social policy marked a recognition that legitimate national interests are at stake, the effect has often been shaped by a resort to the doctrine of federal preemption. The "supremacy clause" of the Constitution and indeed the idea of nation mandate that federal law be supreme, but preemption need not entail the obliteration of legitimate state or local interests.

Elements of Ronald Reagan's new federalism

President Reagan's approach to federalism reform as articulated in his 1982 State of the Union message and exhibited in his federal budget recommendations for fiscal years 1982 and 1983 includes four basic features: substantial budget reductions, the deregulation of intergovernmental relations, program and revenue "turnbacks," and consolidations of federal categorical aid programs into block grants.

It has become increasingly clear that the Reagan administration views federalism reform as a vehicle for accomplishing a key element of its economic policy: stemming the growth of the federal budget. Of the approximately $50 billion of budget reductions requested by the president in his 1982 budget, over 30% were in programs of aid to state and local governments. Indeed, in real (inflation-adjusted) terms, federal financial assistance to states and localities was approximately 26% less in 1982 than it was in 1981, and 37% less than in 1980. Funds were slashed in every program area, from local education and welfare to sewer construction and rail transportation improvements. Many state and local governments, also crippled by economic conditions, have simply been unable to supplant lost federal dollars with local revenues, and the net effect has been a significant reduction in services.

"Unrestrained intergovernmentalism" has been managed in large part through unrestrained regulation. The hundreds of categorical aid programs are controlled by thousands of pages of regulations. Many of the regulations have been imposed to ensure that programs fulfill congressional intent. Others protect civil rights and establish service parameters: eligibility, levels of service, frequency of service, and so on. But many regulations often complicate the management of programs, requiring detailed but marginally useful reporting, mandating audit procedures that duplicate existing mechanisms, and so forth. President Reagan has initiated a major regulations review process with two key goals: reducing government interference in the market and curtailing the "red tape" and bureaucracy associated with the intergovernmental relationship. In both cases, deregulation is intended to enhance competition and efficiency while it reduces excessive administrative burdens. Although there is validity in both elements, unrestrained deregulation may promote social and economic inequity and permit an increase in the negative effects of commerce – for example, environmental deterioration.

A vital component of any federalism reform effort must be the "sorting out" of responsibilities appropriate to each level of government. Sorting-out schemes should address the questions of what are legitimate national interests, legitimate state interests, and, perhaps most importantly, legitimate concurrent interests? The new federalism includes several salient proposals for a "swapping" of responsibilities between the federal and state governments and for "turnbacks" of both federal programs and revenue sources to the 50 states. In his 1982 State of the Union message, President Reagan offered his view of the necessity for a realignment of functions: "A maze of interlocking jurisdictions and levels of government confronts average citizens in trying to solve even the simplest of problems. They do not know where to turn for answers, who to hold accountable, who to praise, who to blame, who to vote for or against" (Reagan, 1982, p. 6).

The president proposed "the return of some \$47 billion in Federal programs to state and local governments, together with the means to finance them and a transition period of nearly ten years to avoid unnecessary disruption" (Reagan, 1982, p. 6). At the end of the 10-year period, the federal government would no longer be involved in major areas of domestic policy, eliminating over 100 categorical grant programs and reducing federal taxes to allow states to capture revenues, previously flowing to Washington, to finance programs reverted to the local level.

Finally, and of primary concern to this analysis, the new federalism is dependent on the consolidation of still other categorical programs into block grants that are intended to permit state and local grantees to address their own priority needs within a framework of greater administrative and programmatic flexibility. In his 1982 budget and Economic Recovery Program, President Reagan proposed seven block grants, consolidating some 97 grant-in-aid programs and reducing funding levels as much as 30%. The seven proposed grants consolidated programs in a wide array of areas including social services of the Social Security Act of 1974 (Title XX), day care, health care, community development, and elementary and secondary education. In the budget reform plan the administration set forth the following rationale for block grants:

The widely acknowledged benefits of block grants are that they allow the reduction of overhead because there are fewer people processing papers, and that they permit state and local officials to allocate funds to the most urgent areas of need. Thus a block grant program funded at a lower level can provide as many benefits for the state and local recipients as a higher level of funding for a multiplicity of narrow categorical grants. [Office of the White House Press Secretary, 1981, p. 24]

Passage of block grant legislation during the 1981 session of Congress signaled the first success of the new federalism, and the experience of states during the initial year of the grants offers an opportunity to assess the pragmatic effects of the president's program.

The block grants are but one mechanism that the administration intends to employ in its effort to reverse the trend of federal primacy in the formulation and execution of social policy. The administration plans to reduce gradually the levels of block grant funding over a brief period of years with total administrative and financial responsibility for the programs ultimately transferred to the states. At the time of total transfer, state and local officials would have to choose either to continue the programs with funding from local sources or to eliminate the services. Implicit in this stratagem is the premise that vast areas of social policy are not legitimate national interests, but the responsibility of state capitols and city halls. The concept of legitimate concurrent interests is rejected in that it is antithetical to the fundamental premise of dual and equal sovereignties.

Among the results of this aspect of the new federalism will be the development of 50 separate social service systems severely constrained by local revenue-raising capacity. Rather than the decentralization of power for the stimulation of a healthy competition among states that the administration envisions, the transfer of responsibilities may lead to a balkanization of America, a twentieth-century return to the Articles of Confederation that the colonists abandoned. Issues of welfare, child and family policy, and education, for example, would be primarily matters of local concern with little regard for the aggregate national effect. In the president's view, a citizen dissatisfied by the level of services in one state would be able to exercise "the right . . . to vote with his feet." As the president has stated: "If the state is badly managed, the people will either do one of two things: they will either use their power at the polls to redress that, or they'll go someplace else" (Reagan, 1981, p. 5). The new federalism is rugged individualism carried to an extreme: millions of people stripped of loyalties asking 50 jealous competitive sovereignties, "What can you do for me?" John Jay could well have been commenting on this brand of federalism when he noted: "This country and this people seem to have been made for each other; and it appears as if it was the design of Providence that an inheritance so proper and convenient for a band of brethren, united to each other by the strongest ties, should *never* be split into a number of unsocial, jealous and alien sovereignties" (Jay, 1961, p. 38).

Poverty would no longer be considered a national problem, but only a problem for those states with large populations of underprivileged families. Wealthy states would be able to absorb the burdens less painfully than those states with diminished revenue-raising capacity. But it is precisely the less wealthy states that often have the populations most at risk. The abdication of federal responsibility for income maintenance programs as proposed by the Reagan administration ignores the fact that many of the causes of poverty are the result of national economic conditions far beyond the ability of the states to control.

The new block grants: one state's response

Regardless of the philosophical and political disputes in the debate over the new federalism, state governments have had to develop pragmatic responses to the reality of block grants and the shift in intergovernmental relations.

With passage of the Omnibus Budget Reconciliation Act of 1981, Congress enacted nine block grants, combining 57 existing categorical programs. Although the configuration, number, and scope of the block grants differed from the president's original proposals, Congress did enforce reductions in funding of as much as 30%, as the administration had requested. The nine block grants are as follows: Alcohol, Drug Abuse, and Mental Health Services; Community Development–Small Cities; Community Services; Education; Low-Income Energy Assistance; Maternal and Child Health Services; Preventive Health and Health Services; Primary Health Care; and Social Services. The specific provisions of the authorizing legislation do not afford the states the measure of increased flexibility they have sought nor even the level proposed by the president. The block grants do confer, however, significant additional responsibilities on state and local governments. Judging from the experience of the state of Connecticut, and the reactions of a number of governors and other state and local officials, the response has been a mixture of hope and fear: hope that the block grants represent a true cornerstone in a new effort to match national policy objectives with local priority needs, and fear that they mark a new variation in a fiscal shell game.

Upon his return from the National Governors' Association winter meeting in February of 1981, Governor William A. O'Neill of Connecticut organized a multifaceted effort to assess and respond to the president's program. Like many of his colleagues, the governor assigned the issue of block grants to an Interagency Task Force on Block Grants comprised of the commissioners of each of the state agencies having responsibility in the program areas likely to be transformed by the consolidated grants. The governor charged the task force with the responsibility to design a process that would ensure the equitable and effective administration of the block grant programs. Equally important, the governor asked the task force to explore innovative mechanisms to fully utilize the increased measure of flexibility offered by the grants in the setting of program priorities. In effect, the governor initiated an analysis of the legitimate state and concurrent interests at stake.

The funding proposed by the administration for the block grants would be far short of levels that states could absorb without severely impairing the delivery of services. In addition, the separate categorical programs to be supplanted directly funded a variety of local service providers that would now be dependent on the state government for a share of the available funds. Municipal officials, community leaders, and representatives of client groups and nonprofit service providers approached the Connecticut task force with grave concerns about the future of essential services. In order that their concerns be equitably addressed, the task force expanded its membership to include the participation of representatives of many affected or concerned community and municipal organizations. The involvement of local government officials, antipoverty workers, human services advocates, nonprofit service providers, and community and private sector foundations legitimized the efforts and recommendations of the task force.

Since the configuration of the proposed block grant programs changed from week to week as the legislation progressed through Congress, Governor O'Neill's task force directed its efforts to three key issues that would obtain under any final block grant legislation. First, the group identified the demographic data required to support systematic priority setting. Concurrently, a subcommittee defined alternative allocation procedures that could be employed to distribute the limited funds to various competing programs and services. Lastly, the members devised a number of meaningful channels for public participation in the process of determining priorities and allocating funds.

The demographic inquiry of the Connecticut task force sought to describe the recipients of services eligible for block grant funds and to develop projections of population changes over a 10-year period that might affect the mix of program needs. Through informal survey instruments the demographic analysis attempted to identify current service populations, to relate services to population characteristics, and to determine the interrelationships among populations and services that would affect the aggregate need for services. The task force concluded that sufficient compatible data to provide a complete picture of the entire human service network in the state did not exist. Although data were maintained for a broad spectrum of services and programs, mechanisms to permit integration of the data elements were inadequate. The analysis did demonstrate that a significant number of people receive services from more than one program and stressed the need for data on program and population overlap so that the coordination of service delivery and benefits could be planned. Finally, the analysis indicated a significant increase over the next 10 years in the dependent segment of the population, especially among the very young and the elderly, concurrent with a static wage-earning segment. In Connecticut, at least, it is apparent that the need for services, and therefore the cost, is likely to grow, while the base of taxpayers supporting them will not keep pace.

In reviewing alternative allocation models, the Connecticut task force acknowledged existing structures for determining priorities: the mandates of existing state and federal law and constitutional guarantees, priorities established through planning procedures, and priorities set by current practice. The confluence of these factors coupled with demographic data would guide the allocation of block grant funds to eligible agencies and services. To provide for maximum integration of state and federally funded programs, the task force recommended that any allocation methods employed be compatible with the established state budget formulation process. To ensure the careful setting of priorities, the task force offered serveral variations on the standard budget process designed to provide greater flexibility to those state agencies most intimately involved with the eligible programs, local service providers, and clients.

Chief among the variations presented in the task force's final report were a "surrogate lead agency" model and a "negotiated" model (State of Connecticut, 1981). Under the former, lead responsibility for establishing program priorities within a particular block would be assigned to the state agency most generally related to the program area. This model is best suited to those block grants that relate to or directly affect only programs within the purview of a single agency. The Maternal and Child Health Services block grant, for example, would thus be assigned to the state's Department of Health Services. The lead agency would be charged with the responsibility of consulting with local service providers, municipal officials, and representatives of client and advocacy groups in the preparation of a recommended allocation plan. The proposal would then be submitted to the central budget and policy office for review against other programs and priorities; finally, it would be sent to the governor for approval. The lead agency model draws on the expertise and experience of the single agency most affected by the program consolidations implemented by the block grant. In addition, accountability is clearly focused on a single, accessible administrative entity.

For more complex block grants that would combine categorical programs previously administered by a number of state agencies as well as municipal and other local agencies, the task force proposed the development of a process of negotiation in which a consensus of affected parties would be reached in planning funding allocations. The task force recommended an adaptation of the "Negotiated Investments Strategy" devised as a mechanism for the coordinated implementation of intergovernmental urban policy by the Charles F. Kettering Foundation of Dayton, Ohio. A negotiated approach to block grant allocations would bring to a bargaining table administrators of each of the state agencies with jurisdiction of programs eligible for funding. To protect local interests, representative negotiating teams comprised of municipal officials and administrators of nonprofit service providers would also participate. Negotiations would progress during a series of sessions focusing respectively on ground rules, common data elements, program priorities, target populations, and shares of available funding. A professional, impartial mediator would manage the negotiations process to assure equity, to help resolve conflicts, and to maintain an orderly schedule. A written agreement would result.

The Connecticut task force determined that the Social Services block grant, which combines and replaces the three essential programs of Title XX (social services, day care, and training), could be best allocated through a negotiated process. Some 15 state agencies had participated in the Title XX program, as had numerous municipalities and local non-profit agencies. Congress reduced funding for eligible services by approximately 30%, thus inducing intense competition among the service providers and the need for a systematic review of program priorities. Recognizing the lead time required to develop an effective process, the Connecticut task force proposed that the negotiated approach be implemented for fiscal 1984 funds. For 1982 and 1983 a "straight-line" allocation distributed proportionately reduced funds to each of the previously participating agencies.

In recommending the negotiated approach, the task force recognized the potential pitfalls of an untried innovative process. However, as noted in the task force report, the approach offers several unique advantages. First, administrators would be forced to balance the priorities of their own programs and agencies with those of competing claims. All participants enter the process realizing that the end result must be a binding consensual agreement. Enhanced coordination of programs may result from a process that inherently requires improved interagency and intergovernmental communications. Finally, it empowers those who have a stake in the outcome to be part of the decision.

Recognizing the increased competition for the reduced levels of funding provided by the block grants, the Connecticut task force set forth a number of recommendations to ensure maximum opportunity for public access to and participation in allocation decisions. In addition to formal public hearings on draft allocation plans, the task force proposed that hearings be held during the priority-setting phase of the allocation process. Lead agencies with assigned responsibility for particular block grants would be urged to conduct consultations with appropriate local officials prior to the preparation of draft allocation plans. For block grants to be allocated through negotiations, the negotiations would be preceded by public hearings on service priorities, and the formal negotiation sessions would be conducted in public.

Formal negotiations on the allocation of the Social Services Block Grant were conducted in Connecticut during the fall of 1982. Three five-member teams represented the interests of the state human services agencies, municipal governments, and community-based nonprofit service providers. A professional impartial mediator directed the seven-day-long public negotiating sessions over 10 weeks.

At the conclusion, the participants signed and transmitted to the governor a document containing agreements on uniform service definitions, criteria for the evaluation and selection of competing service providers, and an allocation of funds in accordance with service priorities. Participants in the process generally agreed that the negotiations provided a unique opportunity for representatives of municipal and nonprofit agencies to be involved in the state's decision-making process. As stated by the lead negotiator for the municipal team, "There's no question in my mind that this is a quantum improvement. It's a major achievement, a major improvement in doing the public business" (Cogen, quoted in Bernstein, 1982). Critical to the success of the process was the governor's sponsorship and agreement in advance to accept the results.

The legislative branch of state government is also a key stakeholder in the process of block grant allocation. In recent years, legislatures across the country have sought increased oversight of the administration of state-managed federally funded programs and services. With the transfer of additional responsibilities to state executives, a majority of legislatures have initiated procedures to share in the decision making. In Connecticut, as the task force addressed executive branch concerns, the General Assembly adopted a bill requiring legislative review and approval of the governor's allocation plans. Because the Connecticut General Assembly meets in session for only a portion of the year, and state applications for block grant funding are required to be submitted to Washington when the legislature may not be in session, the legislation enacted provides for review, modification, and approval by two standing committees: Appropriations and the appropriate subject matter committee (e.g., Public Health for the Maternal and Child Health Services block grant). The two committees have 30 days to complete their review; if they take no action within that time, the governor's proposal stands.

Certain executive and legislative jealousies exist in the control of block grants. Despite the reductions in funding, significant sums are at issue. The allocation of funds is inherently a political as well as programmatic function, and the allocation of budget cuts is intensely political. Notwithstanding the tensions, the opportunity and need for genuine partnership exists. In the determination of legitimate state interests under the new federalism, neither branch can be isolated from the process.

In concluding this review of one state's response to the new block grants, several points should be noted. State administrators, in accepting the responsibilities conferred, are acutely conscious of one fact: In allocating block grant funds, state governments are allocating burdens, not benefits, and cuts in funding, not additional support. As Arizona Governor Bruce Babbitt noted, "Block grants are now a tactical weapon to cut the federal budgets while deputizing the governors to hand out the bad news" (Babbitt, 1981, p. A-12). In the view of state officials, the reductions in funding far exceed the potential savings that may accrue from reduced administrative costs. Thus although the federal government has cut taxes and budgets, fiscally constrained states must choose between increasing taxes or reducing services.

Although the block grants do remove some of the strings traditionally attached to federal categorical programs, they fall far short of providing the states with the administrative and program latitude that would enable the tailoring of programs to meet particular local needs. Certain administrative requirements are common to all of the block grants. In addition, each one bears limitations imposed by Congress. The Alcohol, Drug Abuse, and Mental Health Services block grant offers a good example. In the first year of the grant (1982), states were required to allocate the total grant between mental health and substance abuse programs in the same proportion as before the block grant. In addition, states must use 35% of the funds allocated for substance abuse programs for drug programs and 35% for alcohol abuse programs, and of these amounts at least 20% must be used for programs to enhance the prevention of substance abuse.

Additionally, the initial block grants fail to offer meaningful consolidation of categorical programs. For example, a full range of federal social services programs are not consolidated within the Social Services block grant. The intergovernmental program maze persists. Several of the new blocks combine only two or three of the categorical grants-in-aid. Much broader program consolidations are required if the goals associated with block grants are to be realized.

The block grants enacted during the 1981 session of Congress offer an initial step, if an uncertain one, toward a more rational and productive intergovernmental relationship. The concerns identified by state administrators, like those in Connecticut, do not challenge the concept of block grants, but rather they challenge the context of the new federalism in which they have been established and the defects inherent in their specific design.

Conclusions

Ronald Reagan's new federalism is perhaps the boldest blueprint for change in the structure of American federalism to be offered in the last 50 years. The implications of his program for domestic policy and especially social services are profound. But whereas the president's proposals denote considerable change in the system, whether they constitute reform of the system is a debatable point. For it appears that the fundamental question that neither the new federalism nor the haphazard federalism of recent decades has successfully addressed remains this: How are legitimate concurrent federal–state interests to be reconciled? Neither federal abdication of responsibility nor federal domination is an appropriate answer.

The new federalism includes several elements that could contribute to true reform of the federal–state relationship. A "sorting out" of roles that recognizes poverty, income maintenance, and other nationally pervasive social problems as being in the federal interest would contribute to true reform. Reductions of excessive bureaucracy through deregulation without the reversal of long-standing national policy objectives would be an important element. And it is the concept of block grants that offers perhaps the best mechanism for defining the legitimate concurrent interests of the state and federal governments.

In earlier years, state governments varied greatly in their capacity and commitment to respond to key issues of social policy. Response at the state level to growing social problems was ineffective. Congress thus established the categorical programs as mechanisms to induce states to address a myriad of issues with federal funds and federal prescriptions. Since the early 1960s, however, state governments have modernized and their capacity today is substantial. Many states have initiated programs and services recognized by the national bureaucracy as models. State budgets have grown considerably to meet the needs of their citizens. State executive branches have been reorganized and have instituted modern management systems. State legislatures, once dominated by rural interests, now more fully reflect urban constituencies, the result of the Supreme Court dictum of "one man, one vote." In short, state governments are prepared to assume greater responsibility in partnership with the federal government, but not in its place.

Federal block grants could be a significant mechanism for productive reform of the federal system. The rationale is simple: The state governments are the best judge of how programs can be suitably adapted to meet their needs and priorities. But the limited revenue-raising capacity of states often restricts their ability to respond effectively. To be a meaningful element of reform, block grants must be broad in scope, adequately funded, and free from excessive federal requirements.

Block grants, to work effectively, should be the dominant grant-in-aid mechanism. Dozens of categorical programs should be consolidated, not just a few. Authorizing legislation should prescribe national policy objectives within which the states must employ the funds and be held accountable. But the program priorities and design are best left to the states working with local officials and program clients. The Connecticut experiment with negotiations as an allocation procedure offers just one example of innovation in the design of programs at the state level. Block grants that are viewed as only a transition to the withdrawal of the federal government from the development and management of social policy detract from rather than contribute to meaningful federalism reform.

This initial review of the first elements of Ronald Reagan's new federalism indicates two basic flaws. First is the fundamental premise that the national and state governments are dual and equal sovereignties. This premise supports the broad distinctions between legitimate federal interests and legitimate state interests, and minimizes those interests that are concurrent. The second is the application of the new federalism to budgetary policy. A restructuring of the intergovernmental relationship that reduces federal tax and expenditure burdens at the expense of state and local governments and the citizens they serve accomplishes no overall reform. Domestic social policy must be viewed as being as vital to our national strength as is military defense. Just as our federal system protects the collective defense of the 50 states, it must not leave their citizens defenseless against national social problems. The new federalism has encouraged a fundamentally healthy national debate that perhaps is long overdue. The outcome of this debate will likely shape the American future.

Note

The author wishes to acknowledge the research and editorial assistance of Robert W. Grant in the preparation of this chapter.

References

Advisory Commission on Intergovernmental Relations. *The federal role in the federal system: The dynamics of growth.* Vol. 2: *The condition of contemporary federalism: Conflicting theories and collapsing constraints.* Washington, D.C. 1981. (a)

Advisory Commission on Intergovernmental Relations. *The federal role in the federal system: The dynamics of growth. Vol. 10: An agenda for American federalism: Restoring confidence and competence.* Washington, D.C. 1981. (b)

Babbitt, B. The governors will fight. *Washington Post,* July 14, 1981, p. A-12.

Bernstein, L. Panel changes way state does business. *Hartford Courant,* December 13, 1982, p. B-1.

Evans, R., and Novak, R. *Nixon in the White House: The frustration of power.* New York: Random House, 1971.

Jay, J. Federalist paper #2 (1788). In A. Hamilton, J. Jay, & J. Madison, *The Federalist paper.* New York: New American Library, 1961.

Madison, J. Federalist papers #39 (1788). In A. Hamilton, J. Jay, & J. Madison, *The Federalist papers.* New York: New American Library, 1961. (a)

Madison, J. Federalist paper #45 (1788). In A. Hamilton, J. Jay, & J. Madison, *The Federalist papers.* New York: New American Library, 1961. (b)

Mars, D. Nixon's new federalism. *Nation,* April 13, 1970.

Nixon, R. *State of the Union address, January 11, 1970* (Document 91-226).Washington, D.C.: U.S. House of Representatives, 1970.

Office of the White House Press Secretary. Budget reform plan. In *Program for economic recovery.* Washington D.C., 1981.

Reagan, R. *Interview with the president on federalism, November 19, 1981.* Washington, D.C.: Office of the White House Press Secretary, 1981.

Reagan, R. *State of the Union address, January 26, 1982.* Washington, D.C.: Office of the White House Press Secretary, 1982.

State of Connecticut. *Report of the interagency task force on block grants.* Hartford: Office of Policy and Management, 1981.

Tocqueville, A. de. *Democracy in America* (Vol. 1 [1835]). The Henry Reeve text as revised by Francis Bowen; revised and edited by Phillips Bradley, New York: Knopf, 1945.

Wilson, W. *Constitutional government in the United States.* New York: Columbia University Press, 1908.

Part IV

Influencing the policy process

10   Advocacy movements in the century of the child

Catherine J. Ross

The idea of a coherent social policy for children and families has deep roots in philanthropic and local activities designed to regulate and aid the young. Highly articulated national movements to achieve better policies for children, however, have been a product of the late nineteenth and early twentieth centuries.

Two distinct approaches to advocacy placed the child at the center of movements of social reform: single-issue campaigns and intellectual crusades to transform public attitudes. Single-issue movements, as exemplified by the national struggle to end child labor, sought specific legislative protections for minors. Rhetorical campaigns, in contrast, used the child to symbolize the importance of far-reaching social change. In order to explore some of the patterns and problems that child advocates have faced over the years, this chapter will consider prominent examples of how both strategies functioned in the early twentieth century.

Organized efforts on behalf of children grew from several intellectual and social developments. The popular view of childhood in the Western world had undergone a transformation between the sixteenth and nineteenth centuries. Childhood came to be viewed sentimentally, as an innocent period that demanded special sheltering. Yet disagreements about the nature of childhood continued into the twentieth century. Modern science supported a romantic vision of childhood by highlighting its significance for adulthood. The Darwinian approach to evolution suggested that childhood played an even more crucial role in development than earlier theories indicated, as scholars quickly adapted Darwinian ideas to the study of child life. G. Stanley Hall, for example, suggested that each individual experienced stages in life patterned after the evolution of the species. If growth suffered in any one stage, the mature human being would be less than perfect. Hall played a major role in developing acceptance for modern theories. Besides his adaptation of Darwin, Hall invited

165

Sigmund Freud to the United States for his famous lectures at Clark University in 1909. Freud's own emphasis on childhood as providing the basis for later patterns of behavior reinforced the growing interest in childhood among social scientists. Simultaneously, the so-called progressive ideology gave direction to the efforts of social reformers to apply new popular and scientific insights to social realities. Reform activities reflected the dominant positivist belief that rational endeavor could change human behavior and resolve most social ills. The progressive movement, backed by a burgeoning rhetoric of conservation and national purpose, emphasized government regulation of industrial and private behavior. The ideals of conservation and regulation were easily applied to the problems of childhood.

A new vision of childhood, the messages of modern science, and the progressive ideology created an atmosphere conducive to organized activities on behalf of children. Those efforts found expression in a variety of political, literary, and philanthropic endeavors that we would label today as "child advocacy." The national movement to end child labor may be regarded as the first national child advocacy movement in the United States. It typifies an important strategy for achieving reform: the concentration of rhetoric and political activity on a carefully defined single issue.

Symbolic success: an end to child labor

For most families in the Western world, child labor had always been an accepted reality of economic life, supported for several centuries by ideological commitments to the importance of good work habits. With industrialization, the patterns of the workplace began to change. Those changes combined with new ideas about childhood to fuel a growing belief that labor deprived children of the education, health, and play necessary for their development into strong adults. In the United States, as in England and Western Europe, the campaign against child labor started slowly prior to the Civil War, when isolated state statutes required minimum education for young factory workers. But enforcement was totally inadequate, and well-orchestrated efforts for better and widespread legislation awaited the end of the century.

The campaign for child labor legislation – to provide for shorter hours, minimum ages, certificates of health, compulsory education, or to ban minors from especially dangerous jobs – began in earnest in the 1880s. At its first meeting in 1881, the American Federation of Labor (AFL) made the abolition of child labor a top priority. Couched in the language of social justice and emphasizing the debilitating effects of factory work, that group left no doubt that it was dismayed first and foremost by the depressing effects child labor had on adult wages in factories. The AFL was the only group to make a consistent connection between the necessity for parents to send their children to work and the low wages that resulted from the availability of a pool of child laborers. Labor leaders also predicted that child labor reform could be the opening wedge that gained acceptability for the labor movement among middle-class reformers. The AFL mounted a fact-finding and lobbying campaign in 1900 that prompted the establishment of local child labor committees in Alabama and Georgia (AFL, 1906, p. 3; Ashby-McFadyn, 1902, pp. 215–223).[1]

In the meantime, settlement workers and other urban reformers began organized lobbying efforts in the North. Hull House in Chicago, for example, proved pivotal for the child labor effort, as it did for other social reforms of the time. Settlement workers learned about the costs of child labor through their intimate contact with their impoverished neighbors. They were disturbed when the neighborhood children refused offers of candy at Christmastime until they learned that the youngsters worked in a local candy factory six days a week (Davis, 1967, p. 128 & chap. 7). Such incidents powerfully impressed reformers, including Florence Kelley, a social investigator who was later to spearhead the efforts of the National Consumer's League, and Julia Lathrop, who would become the first chief of the Children's Bureau. Kelley began a Hull House investigation of child labor conditions that the Progressive governor of Illinois later expanded into an official state study of Chicago sweatshops. The settlement workers used that study to draft, lobby for, and secure passage of the 1893 Illinois act that provided for inspection, eight-hour days, and a minimum age of 14 for factory work. But the courts overturned the law after two years. Eight years of constant battles followed before reformers achieved a similar piece of legislation.

Such state campaigns led, through personal contacts at the National Conference of Charities and Corrections, to the formation in 1904 of the National Child Labor Committee (NCLC), the first national advocacy group for children. That organization, composed of people who had been active in a variety of reform efforts, singled out child labor as a major social ill. It used the classical progressive methods of investigation, publicity, and lobbying to seek passage of a model bill in every state. Its experienced workers, some volunteer and some paid, knew from local experiences that legislation meant little without public support, adequate funding for inspection, and stringent enforcement. Above all, the committee achieved the major feat of educating the public about the circumstances under which thousands of children lived and toiled. Simultaneously, the efforts of many of the same individuals contributed to the first White House Conference on Children in 1909 and the formation of the federal Children's Bureau in 1912. The Children's Bureau played a major role in gathering information, publicizing it, and taking over tasks that had previously been performed by the National Child Labor Committee. Later, the bureau supervised enforcement of federal child labor provisions. Equally important, it symbolized the federal commitment to children.

Symbolic success notwithstanding, the battle for a federal child labor bill proceeded even more uncertainly than the parallel struggles in states like Illinois. Reformers themselves were uncertain about the legitimacy of a federal role at first, and accepted federal legislation as an objective only in desperation over intransigency at the state level and after the Senate had begun to act on its own. Senator Albert Beveridge introduced the first child labor bill in Congress in 1906 based on the interstate commerce clause of the Constitution; it failed to pass, but similar bills emerged in every session until a 1916 bill became law. The Supreme Court quickly overturned the law in response to a suit brought by a textile manufacturer.[2] A second attempt at federal legislation levied a tax on all goods that children helped to make; the Court overturned that, too. The National Child Labor Committee then tried to obtain approval of a constitutional amendment giving Congress the right to regulate child labor but failed.[3] Yet the very states that resisted federal regulation began to pass stronger local laws.[4]

The child labor issue ventilated many central and emotional arguments: Was the parent or the state ultimately to say what was best for children? Was factory work as an assistant to parents really much worse than farm work? Was regulation a socialist plot? Would reformers next move to say a child could not help on the cheerful family farm or work to support a widowed mother?

The final federal victory regarding child labor during the New Deal seemed almost anticlimactic. The National Industrial Recovery Act codes, which were quickly invalidated, banned most employment of children under 16 in industry.[5] But the section of the 1938 Fair Labor Standards Act that finally set constitutional age limits for child labor was barely debated, in part because of changes in attitude, and in part because of common agreement during the Depression that adults would work at even the worst jobs for the minimum wage being established.[6]

During World War II, the lack of clear consensus about child labor was indicated by the difficulties the Children's Bureau had in convincing other agencies of the federal government – let alone private industry – to abide by the law. Its officials, protégés of the settlement workers, felt it was necessary to waive many provisions in order to maintain the letter of the law regarding child labor intact for enforcement in the postwar period. As late as the 1940s, parents and children continued to perceive benefits in good hard work for teenagers and petitioned for special exemptions from child labor provisions. A 1943 National Opinion Research Center poll found that Americans of all social classes would allow their sons to deliver newspapers at 6 a.m.[7] The skeletal staff that remained at the NCLC was forced to conclude that "a large segment of public opinion tolerates restrictions on the employment of minors in depression periods when labor is plentiful, but does not really accept the basic premise underlying such legislation, namely that it is essential to the welfare of children and the well-being of the state" (National Child Labor Committee, 1944, n.p.).

These developments appear neat and structured. Volunteer effort led to government action, information gathering led to social awareness, state legislation complemented by a federal campaign brought those lagging behind into the ranks. These were important patterns, but there are some interesting anomalies in the story of child labor reform. On closer examination, the patterns seem almost *too* neat, like the perfect alibi of the guilty party in a detective story. Irregularities under the surface suggest some of the practical constraints on efforts to change values and behavior.

The most striking oddity is that by the time reform efforts began in earnest, children were already being phased out of precisely those modern industries the legislation was designed to regulate.[8] None of the efforts to regulate or eliminate child labor affected *all* children in *all* kinds of occupations. There were both pragmatic and philosophical reasons for that limitation, but the fact remains that although the majority of young workers were involved in agriculture, home industry, or street trades, the legislation addressed only industries such as factories, mines, and other endeavors using heavy equipment. The National Child Labor Committee scored its biggest victories in nonindustrialized states like Montana, where child labor laws did not affect economic realities. It made slower inroads in the Southern textile states, where children continued to work in the mills until the prosperity that accompanied government contracts during World War I encouraged higher wages for adults that created a more receptive atmosphere for state legislation limiting child labor.[9]

Child labor legislation certified changes already achieved through public opinion and behavior. The effective regulation of child labor paralleled a perceived decline in the efficacy of child labor in the industries affected by the new laws. During the 1903 campaign to end home industry for children, one professional lobbyist on the staff of the New York Child Labor Committee confronted that problem. He confessed to his colleagues that child labor in tenement homes had already decreased dramatically due to industrial changes. He discovered, for example, that the "machine manufacture of cigars has so greatly cheapened the factory costs that even home work, with its cheap child labor, is now more expensive" than factory production.[10] The inefficiency of child labor was apparent in all areas of home manufacture except the removal of basting threads, which had to be done by hand.

Despite its limitations, child labor legislation both ratified and symbolized a national commitment, voiced in the debates, to preserving the future strengths of the nation by treating children as a national resource to be nurtured into a healthy and intelligent maturity. That goal had clear economic and military, but also moral, significance.

Repeated legislative and legal battles led many child labor reformers to broaden their sweep. In the early years of the struggle, many observers accused working-class parents of exploiting their children. Gradually they came to see the connection the AFL had drawn between child labor, low wages, and the necessity for the whole family to work. As their campaign gained momentum, reformers were forced to view child labor as inseparable from other social problems.

The child as metaphor

A broader vision of the place of the child in social reform accompanied a more sophisticated critique of the social order. Felix Adler, founder of the Ethical Culture movement and chairman of the National Child Labor Committee, addressed the NCLC's third annual meeting on "The Attitude of Society toward the Child as an Index of Civilization." He stated that the modern "conception of an evolution" made modern man attach an idealistic value to the child as offering the "possibility of something finer, . . . something greater on this earth than had yet been." He meant this vision to include more than a democracy in which "everyone shall be well-fed and everyone well-clothed." In the tones of the pulpit, Adler indicated that economic security would not suffice. "Is that our highest and best work?" he asked. "Or does not our American democracy rather mean for us the development of a new type of civilization, of entirely new conceptions of life, of new contributions to art and science, and to social living" (Adler, 1907, p. 138). Adler forged a clear tie between a climate conducive to healthy child development and a social order that enhanced the lives of adults in an atmosphere of democratic sufficiency. He approached a second mode of child advocacy that, in contrast to the single-issue campaigns, used the child's vulnerability as the basis for a campaign to achieve sweeping reform. Advocacy for the child became a metaphor for advocacy of human potential and of social justice.

That strategy for child advocacy gained prominence at the turn of the century through the work of Ellen Key, a Swedish Christian social feminist. She summed up her argument in a now forgotten but once influential work entitled *The Century of the Child* (Key, 1909). That title in itself may give pause to some child advocates who had to fight to secure even the single *year* of the child observed in 1979. Key's book, which received great acclaim in the United States, opened with a vivid image of popular tableaux celebrating the 1900 New Year that depicted the infant century recoiling in terror from an overcrowded and militarized world:

The events at the turn of the century caused the new century to be represented as a small naked child, descending upon the earth, but drawing himself back in terror at the sight of a world bristling with weapons, a world in which for the opening century there was not an inch of free ground to set one's foot upon. . . . despite all the tremendous development of civilization in the century just passed, man had not yet succeeded in giving to the struggle for existence nobler forms. . . . nothing will be different in the mass except in so far as human nature itself is transformed. [Pp. 1–2]

Key proposed that the hope for the new century lay in the transformation of human nature through what she called "the holiness of generation." In her new world, all social arrangements and decisions would be based solely on an assessment of their impact on children. In examining how a society that recognized its responsibility to children would function, Key ranged over many topics. She held forth on the need for marriages based on love and affection, the choice to bear children, and ensuring prenatal health of mothers. Key argued for education attuned to the nature of each individual child. She attacked such evils as corporal punishment, child labor, unemployment, and "soul-deadening" industry. Finally, Key called on a benevolent state to provide universal education for parenthood and to regulate the power of parents over their children.

Key acknowledged that ideas about genetics influenced her to focus on the evolution of the race. She was also indebted to John Ruskin and other critics of the modern order. Like many social observers of her generation, she mingled an excitement about the unfolding potential of modernity with a nostalgia for a past and simpler age. To that end, she emphasized a return to home life, with full-time, well-trained mothers caring for children. She romanticized the past, as many authors continue to do today. But she proposed an idea that remains radical: that society recognize how important the work of parenting is through economic compensation that would elevate the task to a profession. Indeed, Key even suggested that paid mothers would give their children a better education than schools could provide.[11]

The kind of wide-ranging critique Key presented – tying a better world for children to a better world for adults and vice versa – can help to create receptivity for reform. But it proves hard to translate into concrete social policy or activism. Still, it may set a tone for long-term change. It may not be entirely coincidental that Sweden, Key's native country, now leads the Western world in legislation and programs designed to recognize the social importance of parenting.

Key considered herself a feminist, but her ideas on the importance of women's role as mothers made her the subject of bitter attacks by other Swedish feminists. Key believed that women should have the option to choose their special role as mothers freely – and be rewarded for it – although she herself neither bore children nor married. The Swedish Women's Rights party, in contrast, was working to assure women's social, political, and economic rights as human beings (Ellis, 1913, p. vi; Larsen, 1916, p. 356). Key resembled Jane Addams and other social feminists in America who were not concerned with issues of women's suffrage because they believed in the inherent moral superiority of women who could transform the world through their good works.

Women and children have been grouped together in social considerations for a long time because of "the maternal relation and . . . their common political disabilities," as one settlement worker, Mary Simkovitch, observed (quoted in Davis, 1967, p. 133). In the closing decades of the nineteenth century, legislation designed to recognize the special needs of both women and children stripped them, paradoxically, of what have since come to be regarded as rights. Children in the late nineteenth century were denied the right to enter saloons, gamble, see certain theatrical productions, choose how to spend their time, or carry weapons. Those restrictions were based on moral considerations. As some feminists and industry spokesmen pointed out at the time, there were similar implications in laws that regulated the working hours of women or children but not of men. Efforts to provide special protection also meant a special definition of the limits of citizenship (Ross, 1982).

Because of the long-popular connection of women and children, it seems no accident that the truly new theme of children's rights should have followed so closely on the heels of the women's rights and civil rights movements that began in the 1960s. The reassessment of paternalistic social welfare and the new emphasis on freedom and rights have been especially important in the courtroom, but have also had reflections elsewhere. One early example of that viewpoint, though an isolated and untheoretical one, is found in a 1922 account of child labor on farms. The author wryly accepted at face value the common argument that children should work on family farms because the family ran the farm as a mutually beneficial project. He concluded: "If a child is a partner in the work of the farm, he should share in the profits" and not just receive "board and keep" (National Child Labor Committee, 1922, p. 85). In fact, financial compensation for children's farm work was one of the major accomplishments of the early 4-H projects. A recognition of rights is a first step in achieving the difficult reconciliation of the popular view of the special needs of women and children with their inherent rights of citizenship and the realization of human potential.

Ellen Key's title, *The Century of the Child,* was inspired by an observation made in a play that was overoptimistic about the victories the women's movement had scored by the close of the nineteenth century: "The next century will be the century of the child, just as this century has been the women's century. When the child gets his rights, morality will be perfected" (quoted in Key, 1909, p. 45).[12] The century in question was *this* century – and it is four-fifths over.

The search for a new voice

The passage of time is not necessarily cause for discouragement. Reformers learned early that they would win victories only after long and repeated battles. It took from the 1881 meetings of the AFL until 1938 to achieve a constitutionally sound federal law on child labor. The course of that struggle demonstrated the importance of two equally significant arenas for reform effort: first, the arena of popular attitudes and actual behavior, and second, the arena of the public imperative or legal regulation of behavior. Those two arenas complemented and reinforced each other, and both responded to public interest campaigns. Experience in both arenas also demonstrated the importance of practical, expedient considerations in making change seem acceptable, as disparate motivations led different groups to seek similar ends.

Both the single-issue and the symbolic campaign ultimately proved inadequate in isolation from each other. The single-issue approach to child advocacy or other social reforms must be tied to a broader social vision; at the same time, idealistic or utopian visions have had little practical impact if they were not tied to a slate of concrete reforms. These structural dilemmas continue to plague reformers interested in the welfare of children. Perhaps one reason that Gilbert Steiner has concluded that "the children's policy most feasible – and most desirable – is one targeted on poor children, handicapped children, and children without permanent homes: unlucky children whose parents cannot provide them a start equal to that provided most children" is that such a program is consonant with a compelling dream of equal justice (Steiner, 1976, p. 255). Compared to the campaign to end child labor, such contemporary efforts are handicapped by the difficulty of convincing diverse powerful groups that the proposed agenda serves their own self-interest. On the other hand, Steiner argues that family policy has been emasculated by its infinite flexibility. "Politicians, family service practitioners, and some analysts are," Steiner charges, "less specific when they come to the substance of a national family policy [that would benefit children] than when they affirm or deny the need for one" (Steiner, 1981, p. 197). Partly as a consequence of this flabbiness, few specific issues have united advocates in recent years.

Proponents of several programs and bills have tried to make them into such focal points. Examples of ideas that have raised expectations for fostering a children's coalition include Head Start, the Comprehensive Child Development Act, and programs to stem child abuse. The case of Head Start illustrates successful lobbying to ensure the program's survival by reformers, professionals, and, most significantly, the parents of the children Head Start served. To the extent that lobbyists could convince officials that Head Start functions as a national laboratory and that a vote against funding for Head Start is a vote against children, they made Head Start a magnet for support (Valentine, Ross, & Zigler, 1979, pp. 509–514). The Comprehensive Child Development bill, sponsored by Walter Mondale and John Brademus and ultimately vetoed by President Richard Nixon in 1971, briefly promised to provide national direction and support services for child care by addressing the need many families in the United States feel for affordable day care. But instead of explaining the bill's importance to their colleagues and the public, many congressmen who supported the idea of a comprehensive child development program dissipated their energies in endless debates about the merits of specific legislative provisions. As a result, they failed to create popular understanding of the bill's broader purposes. Indeed, they lost the rhetorical momentum to the bill's opponents, as powerfully indicated by Nixon's veto message:

This legislation would be truly a long leap into the dark for the United States government and the American people. . . . this legislation would leap toward altering the family relationship . . . [and] would commit the vast moral authority of the National Government to the side of communal approaches to child rearing over against the family-centered approach [*sic*].[13]

Another cause – the child abuse umbrella – developed into an extensive framework. Definitions of child abuse and neglect have, however, become so all-embracing that they are practically useless for defining social policy (Ross & Zigler, 1980).

All of these campaigns underscore the historic importance of cooperation between the voluntary and public spheres. Private lobbyists, such as the Children's Defense Fund, resemble organizations like the National Child Labor Committee in providing a focused forum for monitoring and influencing public policy. They rely on historically tested methods of fact gathering, lobbying, and publicity, and refuse to define their activities as a passive response to government leadership. But powerful as their impact may be, like their predecessors today's advocates may find that events supersede or limit their effective advocacy.

The similarities between the child advocacy efforts of the early twentieth century and contemporary activities do not merely offer useful models. The echoes may also serve as warnings. To the extent that advocates for children adopt the premises and language of earlier reformers uncritically, they may limit the effectiveness of their own efforts. But understanding debts to the past may help child advocates to grasp the ambiguity often inherent in progress, to perceive their goals more clearly, and to achieve them more fully.

Notes

The author wishes to thank the Herman A. and Amelia S. Ehrmann Foundation for the generous support that made this work possible.

1 For other arguments given see "The Industrial Crime: Child Labor, A Symposium . . . ," *American Federationist*, May 1903, pp. 339–360.

2 Beveridge's bill, introduced in the 59th Cong., 2d sess., was S. 6562. The Supreme Court overturned the successful Keating–Owen bill of 1916 in *Hammer* v. *Dagenhart*, 247 U.S. 251 (1918).

3 On the progress of federal legislation to end child labor see Stephen B. Wood, *Constitutional Politics in the Progressive Era: Child Labor and the Law* (Chicago: University of Chicago Press, 1968).

4 For a detailed account of this coincidence see Elizabeth H. Davidson, *Child Labor Legislation in the Southern Textile States* (Chapel Hill: University of North Carolina Press, 1939).

5 48 Stat., 73rd Cong., 1st sess., ch. 90.

6 52 Stat., 75th Cong., 3rd sess., ch. 676.

7 Gertrude Folks Zimand to Beatrice McConnell, June 16, 1943, with a typescript of the National Child Labor Committee's analysis of the poll results, mss, Children's Bureau Records, at the Federal Records Center, Suitland, Md., R.G. 102, Accession No. 53-A-465.

8 On similar ironies in Great Britain see F. Musgrove, "Population Changes and the Status of the Young in England since the Eighteenth Century," *Sociological Review,* March 1963, pp. 69–93.

9 As adults sought children's jobs in mills and factories, an increasing proportion of children found employment in agriculture. On the activities of the NCLC see Walter I. Trattner, *Crusade for the Children: A History of the National Child Labor Committee and Child Labor Reform in America* (Chicago: Quadrangle Books, 1970).

10 Frederick S. Hall, "Child Labor in Home Manufacture," unpublished typescript, September 1903, Archives of New York Child Labor Committee, box 29, folder 24, at the New York State Library at Albany, Manuscript Division.

11 In chaps. 5 and 6 Key contrasted "The School of the Future" in the home to the existing system of "Soul Murder in the Schools."

12 Professor George Schoolfield of Yale University helped me locate the original play, *Lejonets Unge* (The lion's whelp), which appeared in 1896. It is attributed to "Harold Göte," which proved to be a pseudonym for Helga Friedeborg Steenhoff.

13 Richard M. Nixon, "Veto Message – Economic Opportunity Amendments of 1971" (S. 2007), 92nd Cong., 1st sess., Senate Doc. 92-48.

References

Adler, F. The attitude of society toward the child as an index of civilization. In *Child labor and the republic.* New York: National Child Labor Committee, 1907.

American Federation of Labor. *Report of the First Annual Session of the Federation of Organized Trades and Labor Unions of the United States and Canada, 1881.* Bloomington, Ill.: Pantagraph, 1906.

Ashby-McFadyn, I. Child life vs. dividends. *American Federationist,* May 1902, 215–223.

Davis, A. F. Spearheads for reform: The social settlements and the Progressive movement, 1890–1914. New York: Oxford University Press, 1967.

Ellis, H. Introduction. In L. Nystrom, *Ellen Key: Her life and work.* New York: Putnam's, 1913.

Key, E. *The century of the child.* New York: Putnam's, 1909.

Larsen, H. A. Four Scandinavian feminists. *Yale Review,* January 1916, 347–362.

National Child Labor Committee. *Rural child welfare.* New York: MacMillan, 1922.

National Child Labor Committee. *Child manpower: After three years of war.* New York, 1944.

Ross, C. J. Of children and liberty: An historian's view. *American Journal of Orthopsychiatry,* 1982, *52*(3), 470–480.

Ross, C. J., & Zigler, E. An agenda for action. In G. Gerbner, C. J. Ross, & E. Zigler (Eds.), *Child abuse: An agenda for action.* New York: Oxford University Press, 1980.

Steiner, G. *The children's cause.* Washington, D.C.: Brookings Institution, 1976.

Steiner, G. *The futility of family policy.* Washington, D.C.: Brookings Institution, 1981.

Valentine, J., Ross, C. J., & Zigler, E. Epilogue. In E. Zigler & J. Valentine (Eds.), *Project Head Start: A legacy of the War on Poverty.* New York: Free Press, 1979.

11   Social policy and advocacy

Ellen Hoffman

The most influential social policy advocates of the 1960s and 1970s worked primarily to expand and strengthen the role of the federal government in meeting the needs of groups whose needs are not otherwise met by society. The movement to increase the number of day-care slots and the quality of care by requiring compliance with federal standards, the expansion of federally supported food and jobs programs, and the creation of federal programs to ensure the education of disadvantaged and handicapped children are all examples of their agendas. The political representatives of these advocates held the balance of power in Congress and the White House for the majority of the 15-year period from 1965 to 1980.

The United States is still far from meeting even the basic survival needs of millions of poor children and families. But in those years we established programs, institutions, and legal rights essential to the support of millions of Americans unable to help themselves and essential to the elimination of the discrimination against those whose opportunities were limited by race, sex, or handicap.

Advocacy in transition

Toward the end of the 1970s, voices of a new breed of social policy advocates grew increasingly loud. The new social policy advocates included those whose primary goal was to force the retreat of the federal government from the legal and financial responsibilities to the poor, minorities, and handicapped that it had shouldered since the mid-1960s. These advocates opposed federally funded day-care centers, argued that food and jobs programs should be slashed because there was too much "waste, fraud, and abuse," and proposed that federally supported education programs be abandoned and replaced with tax credits that would allow parents "free choice" in the education of their children.

177

The 1980 election was a watershed in the history of American social policy because it strengthened and legitimized both the constituency and the ideology of a generation of social policy advocates whose main goal was the retreat of the federal government from a positive social role. After the 1980 election, the advocates of the 1960s and 1970s no longer held the balance of power in national politics. They could therefore also no longer discount the political forces for the agendas of what they had previously considered to be peripheral organizations and institutions – the American Enterprise Institute, the Heritage Foundation, the Moral Majority, and the like.

The meaning of November 4, 1980

The 1980 election brought into sharp focus changes in the makeup of the social advocacy community, in the balance of political power, and in the content of the nation's social policy agenda. A series of political conflicts and events that occurred in the 1970s spotlighted the emergence of these political forces, ideas, and institutions that were legitimized by the 1980 election results. During the 1971 lobbying effort for the Child Development Act, these forces played an important role in shaping the opinion that ultimately led to President Nixon's veto. Voices urging a veto on the grounds that federally funded day care would destroy the American family and lead to "Sovietization" of our children were relatively muted compared to those heard some years later – but they were heard in the White House by people who counted, and the veto message reflected their impact.

Four years later the message was similar, but it was sent by thousands of constituents who flooded Capitol Hill and the media with their anonymous and inaccurate attacks on the Child and Family Services Act of 1975,[1] a bill that subsequently never got beyond the congressional hearing stage. The dismantling of the Office of Economic Opportunity in 1973, the continuing campaign to restrict the role of Legal Services lawyers, and the battle for control of state delegations to the White House Conference on Families were all manifestations of the growing organizational and political skills of the advocates seeking retreat of the federal government from its social role.

The advocates of the 1960s and 1970s were civil rights organizations, unions, churches, public interest groups, consumer groups, and organizations of professionals in areas including education and social welfare. But as the 1980s approached, new players entered the social policy game. These included numerous local and state government entities (both individually and in the aggregate – some state, city, and county governments have their own representatives in Washington, as well as national confederations of governors, state education or welfare directors, etc., which also represent them). These new players tended to support increased federal funding but at the same time created a new antifederal rhetoric based on their objections to "interference" and "red tape." Another new set of forces with similar views included strong antifeminist women's organizations and a wide range of new mass-membership organizations and "think tanks."

These groups nurtured politicians who were elected to Congress, and during the 1970s they began to put their stamp on both the substantive and procedural work of that institution. Their agendas unfolded in a series of legislative proposals for sweeping social change: the Laxalt Family Protection Act; the Hatch constitutional amendment prohibiting laws, programs, or policies that make distinctions on the basis of race, color, or national origin (i.e., affirmative action efforts[2]); and consolidations of numerous domestic categorical programs. They mastered parliamentary tactics and used them with increasing success to stall congressional action on civil rights and government spending measures and to enact restrictions (e.g., antibusing, antiabortion, postponement of daycare standards) on the role of the government through the use of vehicles including appropriations bills and the budget process.

On the fundamental questions of governmental role and expenditure, these politicians increasingly won votes in Congress. After the 1980 election, they enjoyed the support, and sometimes the leadership, of the White House.

The ranks of the present opponents of the government's social role in the 1960s and 1970s are by no means only Republicans. Even before the election, they were strengthened by congressional Democrats who began to be more selective in their support of social programs and spending and who received ratings of around 50% on both liberal and conservative voting scales. After the 1980 election, these ranks were swelled by additional Democrats – particularly those in the House – who were confronted with facing the electorate in 1982. Having secured a shift in the balance of power on the national level, the new social policy advocates were pushing for enactment of their comprehensive, sophisticated, and highly developed social agenda.

The agenda of the new social policy advocates

Cutting the federal budget

It became evident shortly after the 1980 election that the focus of federal budget cutting would be social programs; there was strong sentiment in the administration and the Congress to increase defense spending. The massive cutbacks proposed by the administration even went far beyond the proposals and probably the expectations of most members of Congress, many of whom had been promising for years to bring the budget "under control." The presidential rhetoric promised "fairness" and the creation of a "social safety net" that would protect the "truly needy," but the impact of the proposed cuts fell with particular harshness on working families who were forced by social services cuts to abandon their jobs and return to the welfare rolls. Further, on closer examination, the proposed safety net offered more protection to Americans over the poverty line than to those earning less than the 1981 standard of $8,400 for a family of four. For example, of the $220 billion in the safety net, in 1981 some $150 billion went to Social Security recipients, one-third of whom receive more in other income than they receive from Social Security (*New York Times,* 1981).

Establishing block grants and consolidating federal programs

The trend toward making the budget process the primary vehicle of federal policy making was intensified when the president proposed the repeal of some 93 federal programs and their replacement with block grants to states and localities as part of his budget package. In the 96th Congress, during the last two years of the Carter administration, the Senate had gone on record in support of program consolidation in the areas of education and child nutrition and had approved a bill that would force speedy congressional action on future consolidation proposals.[3]

The Reagan proposals, however, went far beyond these tentative steps. They included destruction of the entire legal framework and operational structure of existing social programs in the interest of "saving" the money allegedly spent on duplicative administrative activities and paperwork. In education, the administration proposed to create a block grant to local education agencies and to cut the aggregate funding of programs to be subsumed in the block grant by more than 25%. If adopted as proposed, the result would have been the elimination of requirements that local agencies target federal spending on the education of either disadvantaged or handicapped children. In social services, the proposed consolidation would have wiped out existing statutes, including child welfare reform legislation enacted by Congress only eight months before the Reagan administration proposed to kill it. Specifically and desperately needed protections for the more than half-million children in the foster-care system – approved by Congress in June of 1980, after years of study in response to the clearly documented needs and failures of the states – would have been totally abandoned as a federal responsibility.[4]

Decentralizing authority to states, communities, and families

The purpose of the block grant proposals is to "return power" to forces and institutions outside Washington as much as it is to reduce the federal budget. Conservatives, liberals, and new and old social policy advocates alike could probably agree that in principle our institutions and decision making should be as close and responsive to the people to be served as possible. The current movement toward decentralization of authority would be spurred by "deregulation" and substitution of "certification" by state and local governments for current requirements for compliance with federal standards and procedures. Numerous legislative proposals designed to move in this direction have been introduced in the Congress.

Yet, as Marian Wright Edelman testified to the U.S. House of Representatives Budget Committee, "How short our memories are! The reason that the federal government is playing and must continue to play a role in providing homes to homeless children and in the education of children with special needs is that states and localities have failed in their responsibility to do so in the past" (Edelman, 1981).

The inadequacy of mechanisms on the local level for parent and community involvement and participation in the programs and the inadequate mechanisms for the accountability and monitoring of programs by local government only strengthen the concern about what will happen to those truly in need if federal funds are turned over to state and local authorities with "no strings attached."

As specifications for the block grants became public, so did the federal government's intent to retreat totally from support of certain social goals. Lack of "maintenance of effort" and "nonsupplanting" requirements would enable state and local governments to spend previously targeted funds with complete discretion, in effect turning the federal aid into a slush fund of fiscal relief.

Even in cases where the intention to completely withdraw federal support is not stated, there is great concern that the political identity and effectiveness of advocates for children will decline along with the funding. It is feared that the eventual result will be a powerless constituency, too weak to even preserve the current efforts.

Regulatory reform

"Regulatory reform" is a catchall phrase that encompasses a wide range of procedural changes in the workings and interrelationships of federal, state, and local governments. The common element in most of these proposals is an attempt to lighten or eliminate the "burden" imposed on governmental and private agencies and business by compliance with federal requirements. Proposals for achieving this include completely abolishing regulations for certain programs, requiring funding decisions to be made on the basis of "cost/benefit" analyses, and eliminating a range of "paperwork" requirements. The greatest danger to the integrity of social programs from these approaches is the tendency to reduce decision making and program administration to the lowest common denominator, creating an atmosphere in which simplistic, governmentwide procedures are applied to a wide range of different programs with little or no regard for the original purpose and the rationale for the unique characteristics of each.

Entrusting achievement of social goals to the "free market" and private enterprise

Another goal of the new social policy advocates is ostensibly designed to reduce the role and cost of "government bureaucracy" and replace it with an unregulated system in which the marketplace would automatically respond to social needs, presumably in a more efficient and cost-effective manner. Enactment of tuition tax credits for elementary and secondary school education is one example of this approach. Proponents of such proposals generally insist that endeavors supported by the tax system should be totally free of any federal requirements, including civil rights regulations, equal employment laws, and quality standards. Although implementation of the elementary and secondary education tax credit, for example, would cost American taxpayers billions of dollars, such programs are somehow not perceived as expenditures that add to the drain on the federal budget.

Strategies for "traditional" child advocates

The combination of newly found political power and the articulation of a massive new social agenda designed to reduce the role of government poses a series of difficult challenges to those who continue to believe that government must be the vehicle for social justice for the millions of Americans who cannot secure it through any other mechanism. What alternatives are available to these advocates?

Redefining the constituency

The constituency that produced the policies of the 1960s and 1970s must be redefined and strengthened if new outlets and leadership to work for the values reflected in those policies are to be found. The traditional constituency has become divided in the face of massive attacks on the budgets and legal underpinnings of so many programs and policies. For example, state and local administrators of federal programs – once assumed to be single-minded proponents of the expansion of these efforts – have emerged in many cases as vociferous critics of federal paperwork and regulatory requirements.

Governors were at first tantalized by promises of "flexibility" in federal block grants to the point where they would have accepted significant budget cuts. They seemed unconcerned about the horrendous political battles they would face on the state level as federal funds dwindled and they were forced to mediate among the old, the young, the handicapped, and the unemployed, all of whom would be competing for their share of substantially reduced federal pie. The press understood that it was the state and local officials empowered to distribute block grant funds who would have to confront these pressures on a daily basis (*Washington Post*, 1981). Later, as the national economy and state revenues declined, governors and other local and state officials became increasingly critical of the administration's new federalism proposals. A major reason Congress refused to enact any more than a small portion of the proposed program was the concern voiced by these officials. Even early on, a major poll taken shortly after President Reagan announced his budget cuts showed that although in the abstract Americans "supported" the president's program, when it came to specifics they advocated current or increased federal spending levels in health and education and programs for the poor.

Those who continue to believe that the majority of Americans want the federal government to maintain its commitment to meeting the basic needs of the poor, children, the elderly, and working families must work more closely and effectively with large groups such as the churches to mobilize their members on these issues. New allies must also be sought by approaching, informing, and convincing individual business leaders and corporate interests of the shortsightedness of policies that will reduce next year's budget but create an even more un-controllable bulge in unemployment and welfare expenditures in future years.

Maximizing the effectiveness of varied strategies

The ability of advocates to conduct these fights must be expanded in the different arenas in which they are decided: the courts, the federal admin-istrative agencies, the Congress, and the media. Dismantling the Legal Services Corporation, attacks on the authority of the courts, destruction of federal programs and protections through administrative fiat, "reduc-tion in force" of federal employees, deregulation, and campaigns to drum the public into encouraging these efforts constitute a multistrategy offen-sive on the part of the new advocates. Designed to produce victory in one arena even if failure occurs in the others, this strategy must be matched by the marshaling and organizing of resources. Traditional child advo-cates must eliminate duplicative efforts and make tough decisions about which organizations and interests can and should take on particular fights in various arenas.

These efforts must be pursued simultaneously on the local, state, and national levels. First, state and local organizing efforts must operate on at least two levels. They must stimulate parents, citizens groups, and the media to inform members of Congress about the effects of proposed budget cuts and block grants on the people who vote them into office. Second, business interests accustomed to approaching politicians to repre-sent their immediate financial interests must be educated to the relation-ship among social policy, the health and availability of their labor force, and the economy in general. Not only does the business community need to be educated, but it must be actively encouraged to broaden its own political agenda to address social policy issues.

Developing, experimenting with, and learning new techniques

The success of the social advocates – as is the case for any advocate – will depend on their mastery of the complex of processes that interact to create national social policy. Prime among these at the federal level is the budget process. Congress and the executive branch have different proce-dures for developing their budget proposals. On the one hand, budget development in the executive branch has for years been relatively inacces-sible to advocates. Compounding the difficulties, the Reagan administration further centralized the budget process by eliminating a large part of the agency role and turning decision making over to a small circle of officials in the Office of Management and Budget, an adjunct of the White House.

In Congress, the budget process is comparably challenging for the advocate. The Congressional Budget and Impoundment Act of 1974 created a new and complex, albeit much more public, system for congressional budget action. Establishment of this process significantly altered the entire legislative process in the Congress. Mastery of this process by advocates on the federal, state, and local levels is a "must" for any who wish to have an impact on federal policy decisions. Congress's decision to postpone implementation of the Federal Interagency Day Care Requirements (FIDCR) in 1980 is an example of how crucial substantive policy decisions can be made through the budget process. In that case, the postponement was effected through an abstruse technical budget process known as "reconciliation." The purpose of reconciliation is to cut spending. But the approximately $8 million saved by postponing the standards was hardly a major factor. More than $8 billion in cuts was sought at the time.

A second area which demands expertise is the federal tax system. President Reagan has said that "the taxing power of government . . . must not be used to regulate the economy or bring about social change. We've tried that and surely must be able to see that it doesn't work" (Reagan, 1981). The president's comments notwithstanding, the tax system is a social policy instrument with a fundamental role in distribution of income and establishment of incentives and disincentives for a tremendous range of decisions made by American families and institutions. It is important for us to understand how the system now works, as well as the implications of proposed changes with regard to day care, marriage taxes, education tax credits, and so forth in order to clarify to the public and policy makers alike the choices to be made through this system.

A third category to be mastered consists of the many skills related to community organizing. These skills include the use of the media, mass mailings, and other types of communication and mobilization of individuals and communities to take a role in the political process. The incredible lopsidedness of congressional mail in favor of President Reagan's 1981 budget proposals and the creation of a sophisticated public relations team to stimulate support of key local, state, and business interests demonstrate the types of strategies that the social advocates of children, the poor, and minorities must conceive and employ.

Getting off the defensive, rhetorically and substantively

Social policy advocates can and should continue to make strong, compelling arguments for the social programs and policies that help people who need help. But they must also recognize that across-the-board defense of all social programs and all social spending increasingly falls on deaf ears with the public and members of the Congress. The proponents of "less government" have created both a new rhetoric and a new social policy agenda. Everyone has some gripes with the government – its red tape, bureaucracy, inefficiency, and unresponsiveness. Many social programs were structured precisely to remedy these problems. Poor families who require government asistance to survive bear the brunt of these inefficiencies as they fill out endless forms and wait in seemingly endless lines at a series of different agencies to secure minimal benefits.

Social advocates must identify and build on areas of consensus both to improve the system for beneficiaries and to increase their own credibility with policy makers.

Nurturing new political leadership

Finally, advocates must nurture political leadership that will not only react but will also initiate and encourage compassionate social policies at all levels of government. They must establish criteria for policy judgments and begin to respond to across-the-board attacks by defending programs that do work and by proposing improvements in the ones that don't work or allowing them to die.

Advocates must be willing to propose alternative budget cuts and policy options rather than insisting on retention of all social programs at current or greater funding levels and in their present form.

Starting at the neighborhood level, social needs must be identified, citizens and politicians must be made aware of social conditions, and a constituency that will hold leaders responsible for meeting these needs must be created. Among the strongest congressional advocates of deregulation and the other social agendas discussed are former state and local officials, disillusioned and frustrated by their experiences with federal programs and officials. To counter these forces, the parents of the handicapped child and the local businessperson who has seen unemployment decline because of federal training efforts must be identified and encouraged to become more politically active.

All of the points made in this section really add up to a final and critical need for political leadership. The "less government" advocates have been supremely successful in building a constituency, mastering political skills, creating new techniques, and creating a successful rhetoric backed by a substantive agenda. Social advocates who do not subscribe to this rhetoric and the policies it implies must do the same. These agendas will be accomplished only if we resolve to commit ourselves to seeing them happen. For as Anthony E. Shorris said in a February 1981 *New York Times* article: "Policy is made . . . no matter who is interested. When an uninterested public avoids its responsibility or politicians hide the issues, choices are still made. . . . Until we face the difficult choices of a mature people in an economy with limited growth, our political system will become increasingly irrelevant and the more significant decisions will be made by default" (p. A-27).

Notes

1 Ironically, the Child Development Act was renamed the Child and Family Services Act in an attempt to characterize it as supportive of the rights of families to make key decisions affecting their children.
2 S. J. Res. 200, "The Equal Protection Amendment," introduced by Senator Orrin Hatch, 96th Cong.
3 *The Federal Assistance Reform Act,* S. 878 in the 96th Cong., introduced early in 1981 in the 97th Cong. as S. 45.
4 Congress accepted some, but not all, of the block grant proposals made by the Reagan administration in its first two years. Although the social services and child welfare services programs were not merged, social services was made into a block grant with virtually no procedural protections. Targeting of the Title I education program for disadvantaged children was diluted, although the program was not made into a block grant. The administration tried to reduce protections for education of handicapped children through regulatory changes but did not succeed in its first two years.

References

Edelman, M. W. *Testimony before the Budget Committee, House of Representatives,* February 24, 1981.
New York Times. Reagan's safety net proposal: Who will land and who will fall? March 17, 1981, pp. A-1, B-10.
Reagan, Ronald. *Address to the Congress: Program for economic recovery.* Washington, D.C., February 18, 1981.
Shorris, A. E. In politics "process" is up and policy down. *New York Times,* February 12, 1981, p. A-27.
Washington Post. Reagan program strongly backed: *The Washington Post* – ABC News poll. February 24, 1981, pp. A-1, A-5.

12   Development of childhood social indicators

Nicholas Zill II, Heidi Sigal, and Orville G. Brim, Jr.

"How are the children?" Social scientists concerned about the welfare and development of American children are responding to this question in new ways. During the 1970s, a body of information emerged known as "childhood social indicators." These indicators are statistical time series that measure changes (or constancies) in the conditions of children's lives and in the health, achievement, behavior, and well-being of children themselves. They are numbers that tell something significant about how today's children live and how we as a society are raising them.

Some childhood indicators – such as the birth rate, the infant mortality rate, or the proportion of 17-year-olds who are still enrolled in school – have a long and venerable history. Other child and family indicators – such as the proportion of U.S. elementary schoolchildren who report that their parents let them watch television whenever they want – have only recently been measured on a nationally representative basis. The systematic development of the child indicators knowledge base can provide a powerful tool for understanding the influence of social change on the well-being of children. These indicators can also be of assistance in charting policies to ameliorate current childhood problems and to facilitate optimal child development in the future. This chapter provides a brief introduction to the social indicators "movement," focusing on efforts to improve statistics on children.

The social indicators movement

Research on the statistical measurement of social change in the United States may be dated back to 1929, when President Hoover established a Committee on Recent Social Trends (President's Research Committee, 1933), or even earlier. However, social indicators emerged as an important field in the social sciences during the mid-1960s and early 1970s

188

(Parke & Peterson, 1981; Sheldon & Parke, 1975). The notion of constructing and monitoring "social indicators" was inspired in great measure by the success that economists had had in developing a national income accounting system and economic indicators such as the gross national product and the consumer price index. But the social indicators "movement" also represented a protest against the dominance of business interests and economic values in government statistics and political decision making (Biderman, 1979). Leaders of the movement argued that there is more to the good society than affluence or economic growth. Hence, one of the key functions of social indicators is "to measure what is omitted from the national income accounts, to assay the 'quality' of life and not merely the magnitude of market activity" (Duncan, 1974, p. 16).

The general intellectual background of the movement may be found in such classics as Bauer's *Social Indicators* (1966), Sheldon and Moore's *Indicators of Social Change* (1968), Gross's *Social Intelligence for America's Future* (1969), and Campbell and Converse's *Human Meaning of Social Change* (1972). Strategies for developing and maintaining a national data base of measures of social change were outlined by Mancur Olson in *Toward a Social Report* (U.S. Department of Health, Education, and Welfare, 1969; Olson, 1969), by Otis Dudley Duncan in *Toward Social Reporting: Next Steps* (1969), and by Eleanor Sheldon in "Social Reporting for the 1970s" (1971). A Center for Coordination of Research on Social Indicators was established in Washington, D.C. in 1973 by the Social Science Research Council (SSRC) with funds provided by the National Science Foundation. The principal functions of the center have been to encourage greater sophistication in the construction and interpretation of indicator data and to act as an information clearinghouse on indicators research.

The development of social indicators has been marked by both interdisciplinary and international collaboration. No single branch of science or single nation has a monopoly on useful quantitative methods for assessing the human condition. Social indicators research has made use of methods and concepts drawn from criminology, demography, economics, epidemiology, geography, history, market research, opinion polling, political science, social psychology, and, of course, sociology and statistics.

An example of international collaboration is the social indicator development program of the Organisation for Economic Cooperation and Development (OECD). Members of the program's advisory committee formulated a *List of Social Concerns Common to Most OECD Countries* (OECD, 1973) and have worked to establish comparable measures relevant to these concerns in their home countries (OECD, 1976). A recent

product of the OECD program is a report on child and family demographic developments in its member countries (OECD, 1979). Other
efforts at indicator development and social reporting from around the
world are described in the *Social Indicators Newsletter* (published by the
SSRC Center) and in *Social Indicators Research* (published by D. Reidel
since 1974), "an international interdisciplinary journal for quality of life
measurement."

The growth of the indicators field in the United States since the early
1970s can be seen in the expanding number of social reports that have
been produced both within and outside government. Some federal examples are the triennial chartbook *Social Indicators* (Office of Management and Budget, 1973; Bureau of the Census, 1977b, 1980a) and the
annual reports entitled *Health: United States* (U.S. Department of Health
and Human Services) and *The Condition of Education* (National Center
for Education Statistics). Social scientists at the Institute for Social Research of the University of Michigan have published several major studies
of the "sense of well-being" or the "subjective quality of life" experienced by U.S. citizens, based on nationwide interview surveys of the
adult population (Andrews & Withey, 1976; Campbell, 1981; Campbell,
Converse, & Rodgers, 1976; Veroff, Douvan, & Kulka, 1981). The
Michigan Survey Center has also conducted national studies of how
American adults use time. These studies make it possible to compare
daily time-use patterns in the United States with those in other countries
(Szalai, 1972) and to see how these patterns have changed since the 1960s
(Robinson, 1977).

The General Social Survey, a recurring national survey conducted by
the National Opinion Research Center (NORC) at the University of Chicago, is designed to produce indicator time series data on a wide variety
of beliefs, attitudes, values, and behaviors of the U.S. population (Davis,
Smith, & Stephenson, 1978). Data from each year's survey are distributed
rapidly to scholars around the country and are also analyzed and reported
by the project's staff. The availability of up-to-date national data along
with earlier "readings" on the same survey items has stimulated a host of
informative trend studies (Condran, 1979; Davis, 1975a, 1979b, 1981;
Smith, Taylor, & Mathiowetz, 1979). There are a number of continuing
surveys conducted directly by the federal government, such as the Current Population Survey, the Health Interview Survey, the Annual Housing Survey, and the National Crime Survey, that are also intended to
generate indicator series.

The progress of the social indicators endeavor at the national level has
been slowed somewhat during the Reagan era. At first, it was feared that

the drive to reduce federal budgets would disrupt the continuity or impair the quality of some important statistical series (Reinhold, 1981). As it turns out, most of the major federal statistical programs have been preserved, partly as a result of vigorous lobbying by the social science community. However, the frequency with which data are collected or the speed with which data are reported has been cut back in many instances.

Social indicators on children

The development of social indicators and social reports on children has been an increasing enterprise in recent years. The rapid pace of change in patterns of family life, coupled with uncertainty over what the changes might mean for children's development and well-being, have prompted a widespread interest in reliable new information on the condition of children and youth. The audience for such information is not restricted to child development experts and social scientists. It includes other professionals who must deal with family stress and its consequences, as well as officials and policy makers whose decisions affect children's lives. This constituency includes teachers, physicians, lawyers, psychotherapists, social workers, judges, corrections officials, legislators, public administrators, corporate executives, and, of course, parents and even children themselves.

Two indicators that illustrate the rapid pace at which family living conditions have changed are the proportion of children whose mothers work outside the home and the fraction of children who live with one parent only. From 1970 to 1981 the percentage of U.S. children under 18 whose mothers worked outside the home went from a minority of 39% to a majority of 54% (Bureau of Labor Statistics, 1981; Grossman, 1981). Over the same period, the fraction of children under 18 who were living in single-parent households went from 12% to 20% (Bureau of the Census, 1982c). It has been estimated that nearly half the children born in the 1970s and 1980s will spend some part of their childhood in a single-parent household. This is usually the result of parental separation or divorce or of birth out of wedlock (Glick, 1979).

Several major social reports on trends in family life in the United States, and their implications for children, have been published since the mid-1970s. The titles include Bane's *Here to Stay* (1976), Keniston's *All Our Children* (1977), Masnick and Bane's *The Nation's Families, 1960–1990* (1980), and Cherlin's *Marriage, Divorce, Remarriage* (1981).

Other trends that have aroused public concern are increases in adolescent homicide, suicide, and marijuana use (Kovar, 1979; National Insti-

tute on Drug Abuse, 1980; Rice & Danchik, 1979) and a long-term decline in the average scores achieved by college-bound high school students on the Scholastic Aptitude Test (SAT) (Wirtz & Howe, 1977; Austin & Garber, 1982).

Contrary to popular impressions, however, not all of the statistical
news concerning the younger generation is bad. Current trends in teenage
drug use appear to be leveling off or even reversing (Johnston, Bachman,
& O'Malley, 1981). The drop in SAT scores has apparently stopped
(College Entrance Examination Board, 1982), although today's students
are still performing well below the levels attained by high school students
in the early 1960s. There are even some childhood indicators that show
clear-cut signs of improvement. There has been a marked reduction in
infant mortality since the mid-1960s, for example (Kleinman & Kessel,
1980). The basic reading skills of elementary school pupils have been
getting better, especially among children from "disadvantaged" backgrounds (National Assessment of Educational Progress, 1981). And the
proportion of children whose mothers have at least a high school education has been increasing, most notably among black children (Glick,
1981).

In short, the condition of children in the United States is more complex
and multifaceted than it is usually portrayed. In order to do justice to this
complexity, more and better data are needed on *what* is happening to
American children. And more analysis is needed to establish *why* changes
are occurring. Researchers from a variety of academic backgrounds and
institutional affiliations have been working to compile the presently available statistical data on children, to improve the usefulness of this information, and to develop new kinds of childhood indicator data.

Data presently available

Statistics on children vary greatly in availability, quality, adequacy of
population coverage, geographic scope and detail, and continuity and
comparability over time. The best national trend data are basic statistics
on how many children there are in the nation and their distribution by
age, sex, ethnic group, and geographic location. These statistics come
from the population enumeration and estimation programs of the Bureau
of the Census (Bureau of the Census, *Current Population Reports,* Series
P-25).

Children's living conditions. The decennial census and the Current Population Survey also provide much of the available information about the

basic conditions of children's lives: the types of housing in which they live; whether their parents live together; how many brothers or sisters share the household with them; how many years of formal education their parents have had; whether their parents work and, if so, at what sorts of occupations; and the approximate amounts of their families' annual incomes. These data have been collected on an annual basis for more than 30 years (Bureau of the Census, *Current Population Reports,* Series P-20 and P-60).

Since 1980, the Census Bureau has collected annual data on the receipt of noncash benefits, such as food stamps, free or reduced-price school lunches, and Medicaid, by U.S. families, including those with children (Bureau of the Census, 1982b). The bureau has also carried out special studies on the child-care arrangements of working mothers (Lueck, Orr, & O'Connell, 1982) and on the receipt of child support payments by mothers with minor children from an absent father (Bureau of the Census, 1981). These data have not been collected on a regular basis, however.

Some aspects of census data on family living conditions have been tabulated and reported only on a "per family" basis and not in formats that use the child as the unit of analysis. The latter are more useful for studies focusing on children.

Until relatively recently, national statistics had little to tell about the *quality* of the family environments in which U.S. children are raised. What rules do children have to live by at home? What sorts of rewards and punishments do they receive? How do children spend their time when they are not behind their desks in school or in front of television sets? How much do they see of their parents? How many children are a source of pride and joy to their parents, and how many have parents who wish their children had never been born?

In the past, answers to questions like these had to be derived from a variety of small studies with samples of families and children that were not fully representative of the general population, using measures that were not precisely comparable from one study to the next (Bronfenbrenner, 1965). There are now some more definitive answers available, due to a handful of nationwide studies of children and youth that have examined young people's daily lives and inquired about various aspects of the parent–child relationship. However, there are as yet very few of the repeated national measurements that are necessary to ascertain how the quality of children's family environments is changing over time.

The quantity and quality of data on children's development and well-being depend on whether the focus is on the physical, intellectual, or social and emotional aspects of child development. Trends in the physical

health and growth of American children are most thoroughly documented. Data on trends in the social behavior and emotional well-being
of young people in the United States are least adequate.

Physical health. The vital statistics system has been gathering data on
births and deaths in the United States for more than half a century. These
data are obtained at the local level from birth certificates and death
certificates. After being compiled at the state level, information from
these certificates is transmitted to the U.S. National Center for Health
Statistics (NCHS), which then develops national estimates and publishes
a range of indicators for the nation and for smaller geographic areas.
Fundamental indicators of child health such as infant mortality rates, low
birth-weight ratios, life expectancy estimates, and the leading causes of
death in childhood are derived fom the vital statistics system (NCHS,
Vital and Health Statistics publication series, Series 1: *Programs and
Collection Procedures;* Series 20: *Data on Mortality;* and Series 21: *Data
on Natality, Marriage, and Divorce*).

Another major source of information on the health status of children
and their parents is the National Health Interview Survey, which has been
conducted annually by NCHS since 1957 (NCHS, 1975a). This survey
collects reports from parents on children's recent episodes of illness and
injury, on their visits to physicians and hospitals, and on chronic conditions, limitations to activity, financial expenses associated with obtaining
medical care, and so forth. It is the source of such indicators as the
average number of days per year children spend in bed or lose from
school due to illness and the percentage of children who have not seen a
doctor or a dentist in the last two years (NCHS, *Vital and Health Statistics,* Series 10).

In the National Health and Nutrition Examination Survey, probability
samples of the U.S. population (including both adults and children) receive physical examinations and medical testing in mobile vans that travel
around the country (NCHS, *Vital and Health Statistics,* Series 11). Several
different versions of this government survey have been conducted in the
last two decades (NCHS, 1967, 1969, 1973a). The program is the only
source of detailed national information on the changing health status of
American children that is based on actual medical examinations (NCHS,
1973b; Grossman et al., 1980).

Educational achievement. Changes over time in young people's educational achievements have not been measured for as long or as systematically as health trends. Data on school enrollment and educational attain-

ment (years of formal schooling completed) among members of the U.S. population have been collected in the decennial census and the Current Population Survey, so extensive trend data are available on these aspects of education. But actual tests of the knowledge and skills of American young people have not been administered on any regular, comparable basis, except for standardized testing programs in some local public school systems and the College Board tests, which do not apply to the entire student population.

As of 1969, however, the data base in this area expanded considerably, due to a federally sponsored assessment program that began in that year – the National Assessment of Educational progress (NAEP, 1974). The program is based on exercises in 10 different subject areas – reading, writing, mathematics, literature, science, social studies, citizenship, music, art, and career and occupational development – that are periodically administered to national probability samples of pupils at three different age levels (9-, 13-, and 17-year-olds) as well as to household samples of young adults and 17-year-old dropouts. Although NAEP has been criticized for failure to collect sufficient background information on students in the survey and for the lack of causal analysis and policy-relevant data in assessment reports, the project is succeeding in its principal objective of assessing changes over time in educational achievement in the United States.

Social behavior and emotional well-being. Until the 1970s, discussions of trends in these areas had to rely largely on institutional records, such as juvenile arrest statistics or data on the number of youth who were admitted to psychiatric facilities each year. Administrative statistics such as these have serious limitations as indicators of change: They are subject to distortion by changes in administrative definitions and practices; they provide little background information on the children who are counted as "cases"; and they reveal nothing about children who do not come into contact with particular agencies or services.

The data base on young people's behavior and subjective well-being grew substantially during the 1970s as a result of a variety of surveys sponsored by both public and private agencies. Many of these surveys dealt only with adolescents and focused on specific types of teenage behavior. Behaviors that have received particular attention are teenagers' smoking, drinking, and drug use (Bachman, Johnston, & O'Malley, 1981; Fishburne, Abelson, & Cisin, 1980; Johnston, Bachman, & O'Malley, 1981; Kovar, 1979), their sexual activity and use (or nonuse) of contraceptives (Zelnick & Kantner, 1977, 1980), and their delinquent behaviors

(Bachman et al., 1978; Gold & Reimer, 1975; Hindelang & McDermott, 1981; McDermott & Hindelang, 1981). A few studies have attempted a more comprehensive assessment of the attitudes, emotional adjustment, and behavior problems of adolescents or of preteenage children.

Statistical reports on the "state of the child"

Despite the limitations of existing trend data on children, there is much to be learned from a perusal of the statistical information that is available. A number of data books or "state of the child" reports have been compiled, especially at the national level (which is where the greatest abundance of reliable statistics may be found). Noteworthy reports have also been produced at the state, local, and even the international level. Although there is a good deal of overlap in the types of information these reports present, there is also considerable variation in the data series each report chooses to emphasize or ignore. Regrettably, no one report contains the whole range of child indicator data now available.

In observance of the International Year of the Child, the World Bank prepared a *World Atlas on the Child* (1979), bringing together basic demographic, child health, and education statistics from 185 countries. In the same year, the Population Reference Bureau published a *World's Children Data Sheet* (1979) covering 150 individual countries, a chartbook on *Children in the World* (McHale, McHale, & Streatfeild, 1979a), and an accompanying report on historical trends in the status of children in more developed regions of the world and the current needs of children in less developed regions (McHale, McHale, & Streatfeild, 1979b). The range of national statistics available on a worldwide basis is, of course, severely limited, and the accuracy of many of the figures is questionable. Nevertheless, these data books amply illustrate the very different prospects that face children growing up in different portions of the planet.

For the United States as a whole, several volumes have been released since the comprehensive chartbook *Profiles of Children* was prepared for the 1970 White House Conference on Children. Two editions of *The Status of Children* (Snapper et al., 1975; Snapper & Ohms, 1977) and a recent expanded compilation, *The Status of Children, Youth, and Families, 1979* (U.S. Department of Health and Human Services, 1980), have been produced under the sponsorship of the Administration for Children, Youth, and Families. The Bureau of the Census has published two editions of *Characteristics of American Children and Youth* (Bureau of the Census, 1978, 1982a), a limited compilation of indicator data derived from census and vital statistics systems. The Census Bureau also produced *American Families and Living Arrangements* (1980b), a chartbook prepared for the 1980 White House Conference on Families. The National Academy of Sciences report, *Toward a National Policy for Children and Families* (National Research Council, 1976), contains a chapter on trends in "The State of American Families and Children."

The annual statistical report entitled *The Condition of Education,* published by the National Center for Education Statistics, focuses on school staffing and financial data, pupil enrollment figures, educational attainment statistics, measures of academic achievement, and other education-related data. In addition, it frequently includes other social trend data (e.g., see pp. 4–25 in the 1977 edition) that provide a context for examining the achievement of the nation's schoolchildren and the performance of its educational establishment. The yearly volume of statistics, *Health: United States,* published by the U.S. Department of Health and Human Services, incudes data series pertinent to child health each year. It also contains special sections, such as the overview "Children and Youth: Health Status and Use of Health Services" (Kovar, 1978) in the 1978 edition, and an analysis, "The Recent Decline in Infant Mortality" (Kleinman & Kessel, 1980), in the 1980 edition. Two of the most comprehensive compilations of national data on children and youth recently published are the statistical profile prepared for the Report of the Select Panel for the Promotion of Child Health (Kovar, 1981) and a fact book prepared for the Children's Defense Fund (Simons, 1982).

At the state level, a number of childhood indicator reports have had public and private sponsorship. The states for which such reports have been produced include Arkansas (Arkansas Advocates for Children and Families, 1980), Illinois (Testa & Wulczyn, 1980), North Carolina (North Carolina Division of Policy Development, 1979), South Carolina (South Carolina Department of Social Services, 1977), Texas (Texas Department of Community Affairs, 1978), and Virginia (Virginia Division for Children, 1978). Reports on children in the South (Breen, 1981) and in the Appalachian region (Tracy & Pizzo, 1977) have also been issued. States in which new reporting efforts are under way include Massachusetts and New York.

To date, the description of children at the local level has received less attention. The Child Well-Being Study, directed by Harold C. Wallach at the Census Bureau, was an effort to develop indicators of child health and welfare using census figures, vital statistics, and administrative data that are available at the city, county, or district level (Bureau of the Census, 1977a). Rudimentary indicators of child well-being such as the median family income in an area, the proportion of children in female-headed families, the percentage of all local births that were premature or out of wedlock, and the proportion of the local child population receiving Aid to Families with Dependent Children or other welfare payments have been combined statistically and used to rank community districts in New York City and counties in New York State (Kogan & Jenkins, 1974) and counties in the states of Texas (Nesenholtz, 1976) and North Carolina (North Carolina Division of Policy Development, 1979).

A more comprehensive effort to describe the characteristics and life conditions of children in one locality is the production by the Foundation for Child Development of two volumes entitled *State of the Child: New York City* (Lash & Sigal, 1976; Lash, Sigal, & Dudzinski, 1980). Of course, the "locality" in question is hardly a typical one, having a population larger than that of many nations and local statistical systems that are better developed than those in most other jurisdictions. Nevertheless, the volumes do illustrate the range and variety of information on children's lives that is potentially available when federally collected census and survey data are combined with vital statistics and locally generated administrative data. A list of data tables from the family, health, and education chapters of the second New York City report is presented in the accompanying exhibit.

Social indicators versus needs assessments. It may be useful to make a distinction here between childhood social indicators and the "children's needs assessment" efforts that a number of states have undertaken (Education Commission of the States, 1976) in response to the "planning–programming–budgeting" requirements imposed on federally funded programs. The needs assessment approach emphasizes the measurement of childhood conditions and problems that are amenable to treatment or for which some program or service is available (or potentially available). The approach also assumes that there is general agreement as to what constitutes a "normal" or ideal value for the characteristic in question. Thus: "Need is usually determined by assessing two factors: (1) a standard or ideal program, service, health statistic or other indicator of the quality of life desired and (2) the present situation, an accurate assessment of the status quo. 'Need' is the difference between the two" (Education Commission of the States, 1976, p. 10).

In contrast, the social indicators approach seeks to measure significant child and family characteristics, whether or not those characteristics fall into the purview of some government program or service delivery system. Social indicators researchers are primarily concerned with describing and understanding social change. Government programs "are only a

Exhibit

CHILDREN IN FAMILIES

The structure of family life

Fewer families with children

Families with children under 18, by number of children per family, N.Y.C., 1960, 1970, 1976

Fewer children per family

Families with children under 18, by number of children and ethnicity of family head, N.Y.C. vs. U.S., 1976

Live births, by birth order, N.Y.C., 1970 vs. 1978

First births as percentage of all live births, by age of mother, N.Y.C., 1970 vs. 1978

More single-parent families

Families with children under 18, by family type, N.Y.C., 1960, 1970, 1976

Children under 18, by presence of parents, N.Y.C., 1960, 1970, 1976 and vs. U.S., 1976

Children under 18, by presence of parents and ethnicity, N.Y.C., 1976

Families and subfamilies, by presence and age of children under 18, family type, and marital status of female heads, N.Y.C., 1976

More out-of-wedlock births

Out-of-wedlock births, N.Y.C., 1958 to 1978

Total live births and births out of wedlock, by ethnicity and age of mother, N.Y.C., 1977

Teenage mothers

Teenage births as percent of total births by ethnicity, N.Y.C., 1960, 1965, 1970, 1975 to 1977

Teenage abortions

Live births and abortions, by method of payment and age of woman, N.Y.C., 1978

The economics of family life

Rising cost of maintaining a family

Itemized budget costs for a four-person family at three levels of living, New York–Northeastern New Jersey, autumn 1978

Change in itemized budget costs for a four-person family at three levels of living, New York–Northeastern New Jersey, spring 1967–autumn 1978

Family income

Median family income in 1975, by presence of children under 18, family type, and ethnicity of family head, N.Y.C., 1976

Exhibit (cont.)

Almost one child in four in poverty	Children under 18 in families with income below poverty level in 1975, by family type and ethnicity, N.Y.C., 1976
	Families with children under 18 with income below poverty level in 1975, by family type and ethnicity of head, N.Y.C., 1976
	Families with income below poverty level, 1969 vs. 1975, by family type and by presence and number of children under 18, N.Y.C., 1970 vs. 1976
Working mothers	Labor-force participation of mothers, by family type and age of children, N.Y.C., 1970 vs. 1976
	Labor-force participation of female family heads and wives, by ethnicity and presence and age of children under 18, N.Y.C., 1976
The child-care problem	Estimated number of children in preprimary programs, N.Y.C., 1969–70, 1974–75, 1976–77, 1978–79
Public assistance	Children receiving public assistance by type of aid, N.Y.C., 1970 to 1979
	Estimated child public assistance rates, N.Y.C., 1970, 1974 to 1978
	AFDC cases accepted during year, by presence and status of father, N.Y.C., 1975 vs. 1978

CHILDREN'S HEALTH

Life chances: the first year

Infant mortality	Infant mortality rates, N.Y.C., 1936 to 1978
	Reported cases of polio, scarlet fever, and whooping cough, N.Y.C., 1940 to 1978
	Infant mortality rates by ethnicity, N.Y.C., 1961 to 1977
Low birth weight	Low-weight births, N.Y.C., 1958 to 1978
Prenatal care	Month of first visit for prenatal care, N.Y.C., 1970 vs. 1977
	Month of first visit for prenatal care, by age of mother, N.Y.C., 1977

Childhood mortality, illness, and injury

Why some children die	Child deaths from accidents, N.Y.C., 1978
Poisonings	Cases of poisonings reported for persons under 15, by age and poisoning agent, N.Y.C., 1978

Exhibit (cont.)

	Lead-poisoning cases and bloods analyzed, N.Y.C., 1970 to 1978
	Lead-poisoning cases by Health Center District, N.Y.C., July 1970–December 1978
	Deaths in the 1–14 year age group, by chief causes, N.Y.C., 1978
Childhood diseases and immunization	Reported cases of selected communicable diseases for persons under 15, by age, N.Y.C., 1978

The impact of illness and the use of health services

Short-term disability	Restricted-activity and bed-disability days for persons under 17, N.Y.C., 1969–70, 1973–74, 1976–77
	Restricted-activity and bed-disability days for persons under 17, by age and income, N.Y.C., 1976–77
Ambulatory care	Doctor and dental visits for persons under 17, N.Y.C., 1976–77 vs. N.Y.C. 1969–70 and U.S. 1976–77
Dental visits	Dental visits for persons 6 to 16, by income, N.Y.C., 1976–77
Doctor visits	Doctor visits for persons under 17, by income, N.Y.C., 1976–77
	Doctor visits for persons under 17, by place of visit, N.Y.C., 1969–70 vs. 1976–77
Place of ambulatory care	Doctor visits for persons under 17, by income and place of visit, N.Y.C., 1976–77
	Doctor visits at office vs. at hospital for persons under 17, by income, race, and Spanish origin, N.Y.C., 1976–77
Health insurance and assistance	Health assistance or insurance coverage for persons under 18, by type of coverage and family income, N.Y.C., 1976
	Medicaid claims and payments for welfare-eligible children by selected service providers, N.Y.C., June 1, 1978–May 31, 1979

CHILDREN IN SCHOOL

Characteristics of school children

Fewer students	Children enrolled in public and nonpublic schools, N.Y.C., 1969–70 to 1978–79
	Students enrolled in public schools, by level, N.Y.C., 1969–70 to 1978–79
Ethnicity	Students enrolled in public and nonpublic schools, by ethnicity, N.Y.C. 1969–70 to 1978–79

Exhibit (cont.)

	Nonpublic school students as a percent of all students, by ethnicity, N.Y.C., 1969–70 to 1978–79
Many poor school children	Children eligible for free meals, N.Y.C., public schools, 1968–69, 1973–74 to 1978–79
Mobility	Transfers among public elementary and junior high schools, by district, N.Y.C., 1977–78
	Mobility rate, reading achievement, attendance, crime, and suspension rates for public elementary and junior high schools, by district, N.Y.C., 1977–78
Achievement	Reading achievement levels, by grade, N.Y.C. public schools, March 1978
	Sixth-graders reading below minimum competency, N.Y.C. public schools, 1970–71 to 1978–79
	Reading and mathematics competency levels in grades 3 and 6, N.Y.C. public schools, fall 1978

The school experience

Teachers and classroom conditions	Authorized teaching positions, teachers on October payroll, and pupil/teacher ratio, N.Y.C. public schools, 1970–71 to 1977–78
	Average class size by grade, N.Y.C. public schools, 1975–76 to 1978–79
	Classroom teachers by certification and degree status, experience, ethnicity, and age, N.Y.C. public schools, 1973–74 vs. 1978–79
	Ethnic distribution of students and teachers, N.Y.C. public schools, 1977–78
	Degree of English-language difficulty for students whose primary language was not English, by language of child, N.Y.C. public schools, spring 1979
Programs for children with special needs	Children enrolled in special schools and classes, by type of handicap, N.Y.C. public schools, 1970–71 to 1978–79
	Placement in special schools and classes, by ethnicity and type of handicap, N.Y.C. public schools, 1978–79
Absenteeism	Student attendance rates by school level, N.Y.C. public schools, 1970–71 to 1978–79
	Estimated absence rates, by school level and ethnicity, N.Y.C. public schools, 1977–78

Exhibit (cont.)

School crime and safety	Reported school crime incidents by school level, N.Y.C. public schools, 1973–74 to 1978–79
	Reported school crime, by type of incident and school level, N.Y.C. public schools, 1978–79
	Victims of reported school crime, by identity and school level, N.Y.C. public schools, 1978–79
	Perpetrators in reported school crime incidents, by identity and type of crime, N.Y.C. public schools, 1978–79
	School actions against student perpetrators in reported school crime, by type of incident, N.Y.C. public schools, 1978–79
Suspensions	Student suspensions by school level, N.Y.C. public schools, 1969–70, 1974–75, 1976–77 to 1978–79
	Student suspension rate, by ethnicity and school level, N.Y.C. public schools, September 1978–January 1979
	Student suspensions, by reason and ethnicity, N.Y.C. public high schools, September 1978–January 1979
Leaving school	
Dropouts	Dropouts from N.Y.C. public high schools, by reason, 1965–66 to 1977–78
	Graduates and dropouts from N.Y.C. public high schools, classes of 1966 to 1979
	Yearly enrollment for the class of 1979, by ethnicity, N.Y.C. public schools, 1976–77 to 1978–79
Uncertainty of graduation	Students scoring below minimum competency levels in reading and writing, 8th, 9th, and 10th grades, N.Y.C. public schools, April 1979
Scholastic Aptitude Test scores	Scholastic Aptitude Test, average scores, N.Y.C. vs. U.S., 1972–73 to 1978–79
	College Board Achievement Test, average scores by subject, N.Y.C. vs. U.S., 1978–79

Source: Lash, Sigal, & Dudzinski (1980).

part, frequently a very small part, of the complex of factors affecting
social change" (Duncan, 1969, p. 6). Moreover, a given indicator may
tap an important aspect of social change even though there is no consensus as to which direction of change is "good" or "bad" for the society.
For example, a measure of the proportion of children in a state or city
who receive regular religious instruction would not be appropriate for
inclusion in a "needs assessment" report. Government agencies in the
United States are constitutionally prohibited from establishing or in-
terfering with religious practices. Furthermore, there is strong disagreement as to what kind of religious training (if any) is an essential part of
children's upbringing. However, an examination of trends in the religious training of children would be very much in order in a volume of
childhood social indicators.

Surveys of children and youth

Efforts to develop new indicators on children and families have made
extensive use of the sample survey mechanism. Surveys of children or
adolescents are based on probability samples that may be drawn from the
entire country or from more limited geographic areas. The subject children may be obtained from a sample of households within selected neighborhoods or – for school-aged children – from a sample of schools. Well-
established sampling methods exist to ensure that the sample represents
the child population faithfully, provided that good cooperation can be
obtained from the families or schools that fall into the sample.

Information on the children and families in the sample may be collected by a variety of methods: through interviews or questionnaires
administered to parents, to teachers, or to children themselves; through
physical examination or psychological testing of the sample children;
through direct observation of the families' living conditions and interaction patterns; and through the use of birth certificates, school records,
medical records, arrest records, or other archival data. A wide age
range of children may be studied at a single point in time or a limited
age group may be followed and their development studied over a period
of years.

Advantages of surveys. Sample surveys have a number of advantages as a
means of generating social indicator information on children and families:

They provide statistics that may be generalized to the entire population, avoiding biases introduced by use of convenience samples such as
ones based only on those children who come into contact with some

agency or service. A probability sample has the advantage of placing the various elements of the population in proper relation to one another.

One of the major strategies that social indicator researchers have used to generate new trend data is to repeat survey items or entire studies that were done in the past (Davis, 1975b; Duncan, 1969, 1975; Duncan, Schuman, Duncan, 1973). By clearly specifying the sampling procedures, the researcher may facilitate such comparative studies at a future point in time or in different geographical areas.

Surveys in which interviews or questionnaires are administered to children or adolescents provide young people with an opportunity to speak for themselves. This makes it possible to find out about their hopes and fears, their interests and aspirations, and their perceptions and feelings about various aspects of their lives. They can also report on topics where parents and teachers are apt to be poorly informed, such as adolescents' sexual experiences or their experimentation with drugs.

Surveys of children make it possible to collect a broad range of information on each child and family. This permits the investigator to study the "whole child" by, for example, making estimates of how many children have multiple handicaps or overlapping problems. It also makes it possible to correlate various measures of children's living conditions with measures of children's development and well-being at the level of the individual child and family. For example, does the mother's employment status bear any relationship to the child's school performance? Such questions can be posed using multivariate analysis methods to control for some indirect or spurious sources of association. Thus, it is possible to examine the correlation between maternal employment and school performance while controlling for such related factors as marital status, parent education, and family income.

By obtaining survey information about the child from more than one source (e.g., from parents *and* from teachers), the researcher may examine the extent of agreement or disagreement between the sources. By combining multiple perspectives, the analyst may be able to compensate somewhat for the limitations of each source and build a more rounded and (one hopes) more accurate picture of the child.

When surveys are conducted or sponsored by universities or other private research agencies, they are able to collect information that government agencies may be unwilling or unable to gather (e.g., information about marital conflict, religious practices, criminal behavior, etc.).

Major survey programs. Examples of studies that have tried to assess the physical health, school performance, and psychological well-being of children in one locality, using information provided by both parents and teachers, are the Isle of Wight survey in England (Rutter, Tizard, & Whitmore, 1970), and the Woodlawn Mental Health Project in Chicago (Kellam et al., 1975). Studies in New York City (Langner et al., 1976) and in the Washington, D.C. area (Achenbach & Edelbrock, 1981) have surveyed child behavior problems using information provided by parents only. In Oakland, California, children's daily activity patterns outside school have been studied using information provided by both parents and children (Medrich et al., 1982).

On a nationwide level, there have been two major longitudinal studies of child development carried out in England, the Douglas Study (Douglas, 1964; Douglas & Blomfield, 1958; Douglas, Ross, & Simpson, 1968) and the National Children's Bureau Study (Davie, Butler, & Goldstein, 1972; Ferri, 1976; Fogelman, 1976; Wedge & Prosser, 1973), and a third is being prepared. In the United States, two cycles of the Health Examination Survey conducted during the 1960s focused specifically on children ages 6 to 11 (NCHS, 1967) and adolescents ages 12 to 17 (NCHS, 1969) and included extensive psychological testing (Edwards & Grossman, 1979) as well as the collection of behavior reports from parents and teachers (NCHS, 1971, 1972, 1973b, 1974, 1975b). Part of the national sample of children who were examined in the first survey were also studied several years later in the youth survey.

The Equality of Educational Opportunity Survey (Coleman et al., 1966; Mayeske et al., 1972) was a massive school-based study of 3rd-, 6th-, 9th-, and 12th-graders in the United States conducted in 1965. The principal purposes of the study were to measure the education achievement of black, Hispanic, and other minority-group students in comparison with that of the white majority and to provide an inventory of the facilities of schools attended by students from the different ethnic groups. Some data on children's perceptions and attitudes were collected in the test booklets (Mayeske et al., 1968; Mayeske, Okada, & Beaton, 1973). Although the sampling of schools and students obtained was large and diverse, it was not fully representative of the nation because of substantial nonresponse on the part of whole school systems. This illustrates one of the major drawbacks of a school-based sampling frame.

Since the early 1960s there have been at least seven national longitudinal studies in the United States that have followed young people from their high school years through their post–high school training and into their early adult careers (Bachman et al., 1969; Bachman, O'Malley, & Johnston, 1978; Flanagan et al., 1962, 1964; Flanagan & Cooley, 1966; NCES, 1977, 1981; Parnes et al., 1969). These studies have examined the relative contribution of family, individual, school, and social structural factors as determinants of a young person's educational attainment and occupational status. They have also collected a wide range of data on the subjective well-being, attitudes, and values of American adolescents (Bachman, 1970; NCES, 1981).

Since 1975, the "Monitoring the Future" project at the Institute for Social Research at the University of Michigan has been surveying high school seniors across the United States on an annual basis (Bachman & Johnston, 1978; Johnston et al., 1980). The project is explicitly designed to generate social indicators on youthful behaviors, attitudes, and values. The primary focus is on student drug use and related attitudes, but data are also collected on students' educational aspirations, occupational aims, and marital and family plans; on their attitudes toward government, social institutions, race relations, and changing roles for women; as well as on a variety of family background and demographic factors. For the study of child development, the project has several limitations: It covers only late adolescence and early adulthood; it provides no data on high school dropouts; and it relies exclusively on information furnished by the students themselves. Nevertheless, the project has already produced some challenging trend data, such as the finding that student drug use is leveling off and perhaps even declining.

The National Survey of Children, sponsored by the Foundation for Child Development and conducted by the Institute for Survey Research at Temple University during 1976–1977, included the first national sample of children ages 7 to 11 to be personally interviewed and given a chance to speak for themselves about their lives and upbringing (Zill, 1983). Information about this probability sample of 2,301 American children was also obtained from parents and teachers. In order to measure changes in child health and behavior over the preceding decade, some questions for parents and teachers were replicated from the 1963–1965 Health Examination Survey of Children and other earlier studies. National surveys of children comparable to the Foundation for Child Development study were conducted subsequently in Japan (Sengoku & Iinaga, 1979) and France (Fédération Nationale des Ecoles des Parents et des Educateurs, 1980). National samples of children in the United States have also been interviewed for *The General Mills American Family Report* (Yankelovich, Skelly, & White, Inc., 1977) and the Newspaper Readership Project (1980).

Limitations of surveys. Although surveys of children can provide a wealth of indicator data, these surveys do have their drawbacks and limitations. For example:

They are expensive to conduct. This is especially true of nationwide studies using in-home interviews.

The large sample sizes that are needed to generate reliable statistics impose limitations on the amount of information one can collect on any given child in the sample and on the level of expertise that can be expected of those gathering the data, whether by interview, observation, or testing.

Some groups of great interest, such as children with specific handicaps, children who live with their fathers only, or children of migrant workers or illegal aliens, are likely to be sparsely represented in general population surveys. This is due to such factors as a low incidence in the population, an unwillingness to cooperate with surveys, and language barriers. In general, sample surveys do a good job of describing the midrange of a population and a less adequate job of describing the extremes of the population. Yet it may be that conditions at the extremes reveal more about the state and progress of a society than conditions in the middle.

As far as national surveys are concerned, it has been argued that no one lives in "the nation" and that national averages do not describe any particular neighborhood or setting very well. Most national samples do not have sufficient cases in any one area to provide reliable statistics about that area.

The validity of survey data depends on the respondent's accuracy of recall and willingness to report the information in question. Problems with retrospective recall of childrearing behavior are well documented in the child development literature.

The limited vocabularies of elementary-school-aged children and their imperfect understanding of the frequency, recency, and duration of events impose restrictions on the kinds of survey questions that these children can be expected to answer meaningfully. The responses of young children (especially those under the age of nine) are generally less reliable than those of older children and adults (Vaillancourt, 1973; Zill, 1983). This does not necessarily mean that their responses are worthless. But it does mean that correlations involving child-based measures will generally be weaker than those based on adult responses.

Some of the problems described above may be overcome through the use of alternative survey designs and innovative data collection procedures. It is possible, for example, to oversample hard-to-reach groups and to compensate for the oversampling through statistical weighting. It is also possible to modify the usual national sample design so as to provide a larger number of cases in each of a smaller number of sampling points, although this would result in some loss of sampling efficiency. Supplementary ecological data may be gathered about each community in the sample.

As far as data collection procedures are concerned, it would seem desirable to make greater use of in-home observations and other "objective" measurement methods in large sample surveys. However, these methods are likely to be expensive and may pose problems as far as respondent cooperation is concerned. Child Trends, Inc., an organization devoted to improving the scope and quality of statistics on children, is currently exploring these and other methods for strengthening child and family surveys.

The uses of childhood indicators

Childhood social indicators can perform a number of useful functions that assist the expert in child development, the policy analyst, and the concerned citizen. Having identical measures repeatedly applied over time to comparable populations of children is essential if one is to monitor progress or deterioration in child welfare and achievement. These measures also make it possible to evaluate the validity of common beliefs about the state of the younger generation. Indicators on children put the results of child development research into a broader social perspective. They can help to guide the efforts of child advocates and program planners who are attempting to improve children's lives. And they furnish the raw materials for developing and testing theories that relate social change to children's development.

Monitoring progress or deterioration in child welfare and achievement. By tracking changes over time in the functioning of the child population as a whole and in the development of different groups of children, a system of childhood indicators makes it possible to identify problem areas as they emerge. Childhood indicators can also reveal areas where progress is being made and corrective programs seem to be working.

The decline in average scores on the Scholastic Aptitude Test (SAT) and on other standardized tests used in various school systems around the country during the late 1960s and 1970s is a prime example of the "warning light" function that childhood indicators can serve. Although the reasons for the decline in test scores are still open to debate, there can be little doubt that continued evidence of deterioration in student achievement led to extensive criticism of educational practices in this country and helped to trigger reform efforts such as the "back to basics" and competency-testing movements.

Since 1970, the National Assessment of Educational Progress (NAEP) has been providing a more comprehensive and detailed picture of how student achievement in the United States is changing over time. The trends in student achievement that have been charted by NAEP are more varied and less bleak than the simple downhill path that SAT scores have followed. NAEP has found, for example, that reading scores at the elementary level actually improved between 1970 and 1980, particularly among traditionally low-achieving groups such as black children, pupils from the South, and students from low-income urban and rural areas (NAEP, 1981). These findings have been interpreted as evidence that federal programs to support compensatory education for disadvantaged children have begun to pay off. The NAEP results were specifically cited in congressional debate during 1981 and 1982 as part of the effort to preserve the funding and integrity of the compensatory programs.

Correcting misconceptions about the nation's children and youth. Childhood indicators can document areas of real deterioration (and real improvement) in the condition of our children and youth. Accurate trend data can also help to dispel common misconceptions about the younger generation. There are, for example, so many reports in the popular media about the health hazards in our environment and the deficiencies in our health care arrangements that it would be easy to conclude that the current state of child health in the United States is not good. Indeed, the impression created by some of these accounts is that American children are in dire peril from breathing dirty air, drinking chemical-laden water, eating junk food, failing to get inoculations, or being exposed to nuclear radiation (Norwood, 1980). The facts are, however, that infant and child mortality rates have never been lower, life expectancies have never been longer, and, based on virtually all of the traditional indicators, the physical health status of children in the United States has never been better (Kovar, 1978; Rice & Danchik, 1979).

This is not to say that the environmental and health care problems reported in the media are not worthy of attention and concern. But the concern should be tempered by a realization that the overall trend is one of continued improvement in child health, thanks to advances in medical care, better sanitation and safety procedures, increases in parent education levels, and government programs that have made adequate nutrition and health care available to indigent families. Child advocates naturally want to arouse public anxiety and outrage over the problems that remain in the hope that these sentiments will stimulate corrective actions. However, the constant emphasis on what is wrong with our children, rather than on the genuine progress that has been made in some areas, has probably helped to bring about the current public willingness to see many social programs reduced or dismantled. Yet federal programs such as food stamps, Medicaid, and consumer product safety regulations have clearly contributed to the improvement in child health in the United States.

Another exaggerated notion concerning young people is that they subscribe to attitudes and values that are vastly different from those of their elders. Surveys of adolescents and young adults have found that the "gap" between the generations is far less profound than is commonly believed (Adelson, 1979; Johnston et al., 1980). For example, most young people do *not* condone the use of a variety of illegal drugs (Johnston, 1973; Johnston et al., 1981). However, the attitudes and actions of a deviant minority of youngsters often overshadow the positive development and prosocial behavior of the majority. The distorted picture of youthful attitudes that many older Americans have leads to hostility toward adolescents as a group and makes it difficult to build support for programs aimed at benefiting children and youth. By developing an accurate statistical profile of youthful attitudes and behavior, and by getting the facts out to the voting-age public, it may be possible to counteract some of the negativism about young people that is now so prevalent.

Providing an ecological context for child development research. By describing how children live and function in the real world, childhood indicators provide an ecological context for interpreting research results and assessing policy prescriptions. For example, much university-based research in child development has been conducted with the children of college-educated parents. Yet national statistics on educational attainment show that, even though educational levels have risen, the majority of American children are not being raised by college graduates. Indeed, as of the mid-1970s, less than 20% of all children in the United States were growing up in families where one of the parents was a college graduate. More than a third of all children under 18 years of age were being raised by parents who had not even completed high school (Kovar, 1981). Since the parents' educational level is significantly correlated with measures of children's intellectual development, health, and behavior, we should be cautious about drawing broad conclusions from studies which are based only on children from a narrow range of educational backgrounds. Studies in which the treatment or program in question is confounded with the parents' educational level are even more likely to be misleading. Yet comparatively few studies seek to determine how a given program or treatment might work for children from different educational levels. Knowledge of the composition and distribution of the child population in terms of parent education, family structure, parent occupation, family income, family size, ethnic group, and area of residence can help to make child development research more valid ecologically and hence more useful.

Guiding social policies on behalf of children. The existence of accurate descriptive information can strengthen the hand of policy makers, program planners, or child advocates in their attempts to improve children's lives. At a minimum, indicator data furnish guidance as to the size, nature, and distribution of a particular problem. This can improve decisions about resource allocations. Indicator data can also show whether and how rapidly conditions are changing in the child population as a whole and in specific subgroups of children. Child indicators may even provide insights into what kinds of intervention would be most effective. The availability of "before and after" data means that the effect of a new program or of a major historical event can be assessed more convincingly than if baseline information were not available.

Of course, better information about high-risk groups, such as runaways, children involved in custody disputes, abused children, and children of migrant farm worker families does not inevitably result in actions on behalf of those groups. Nor does better analysis of the costs and benefits involved in various approaches to specific child-related problems necessarily lead to more sensible policies. It is not always possible to show immediately how a new fact or finding from indicator research can be translated into policy reform or direct action. Nevertheless, childhood social indicator data do work their way into actions for the good of children. As Brim wrote a few years ago:

The Children's Defense Fund must rely on such data as the basis of its legal actions, as in the recent successful suit on behalf of children excluded from school. And, two decades ago, the 1954 Supreme Court desegregation decision was based on just such statistical description of group differences between black and white children. [Brim, 1975, p. 524]

Today, child advocacy organizations are relying to an even greater extent on social indicator data bases to document areas in which progress has been made and to emphasize continued inequality in health care, education, day care, youth employment, and other areas (Edelman, 1980; National Black Child Development Institute, 1980). Indicator data are being used to bolster the case for continuation of certain existing government programs and for changes in others. As already mentioned, data on declines in pupil achievement spurred reform efforts in public schools across the nation, and more recent data on gains in achievement among disadvantaged pupils have helped to preserve federal funding for compensatory education programs. Underscoring the important role of social indicator data for effective advocacy efforts, the Children's Defense Fund has published a guide to assist advocates in obtaining such information (Shur & Smith, 1980).

Improving the quality and usefulness of data on children

Despite the wide range of research and reporting on childhood indicators sponsored by public and private agencies, much remains to be done. The statistical portrait of children that can be assembled from existing data is still fragmented and incomplete. The potential of an integrated childhood social indicator system – called for by Bronfenbrenner (1965, p. 364) and Brim (1975) and endorsed in the National Academy of Sciences' report, *Toward a National Policy for Children and Families* (National Research Council, 1976) – has yet to be achieved. Statistics bearing on children that are generated by all levels of government are in need of integration, secondary analysis, and more effective dissemination. Steps for improving childhood indicators are the subject of a recent report published by the Social Science Research Council (Watts & Hernandez, 1982).

Coordination among agencies. The number of federal agencies with some involvement in data collection on the health, education, behavior, nutrition, welfare, or development of American children is large. It includes such organizations as the Bureau of the Census (in the Department of Commerce), the Bureau of Labor Statistics (in the Department of Labor), the National Center for Education Statistics, the National Center for Health Statistics, and the Department of Justice. The successful development of social indicators on children depends upon cooperative relationships, or at least some communication, among these agencies as well as on coordination between federal statistical agencies and those at the state and local levels.

At a minimum, work should be carried out to bring about the standard definitions of variables and comparable measurement and tabulation procedures. Currently, there are unnecessary variations in the way terms are defined, questions asked, and data tabulated, not only across agencies, but even within the same agency.

Beyond this, strategies could be developed for linking data collected by the same organization at different time periods and across geopolitical jurisdictions. Much of the information now collected about children cannot be related to the general populations of which they are a part or compared across different time periods. Cohort analyses are even more difficult. The linking procedures are simple and well known, cost little, and would yield great benefit in our understanding.

Secondary analysis of existing data sets. The potential value of existing data on children from national surveys and large-scale longitudinal studies conducted at considerable expense is not fully realized because data are not sufficiently analyzed by the original investigators or made available for secondary analysis by other investigators in a timely fashion. Furthermore, many graduate students in child development receive virtually no training in secondary analysis of large data sets, so that the demand for public-use tapes of government surveys has been limited. An inventory of existing data sets offering a broad array of opportunities for secondary analysis has been prepared by Watts and Santos (1978) of Columbia University.

Dissemination. Systematic data about children can only be of use if they become known to those – from individual parents to political leaders – who make decisions affecting children's lives, or at least to the experts whose analyses and teachings eventually shape public opinion and policy. Yet, in the past at least, many important statistics concerning U.S. children were known only to regular readers of *Current Population Reports* (Bureau of the Census), the *Vital and Health Statistics* series (National Center for Health Statistics), and other relatively obscure government publications. Federal statistics have become more visible in recent years. As noted above, several agencies are now publishing regular indicator chartbooks, and national, state, and local "state of the child" reports are being issued by a growing number of organizations. This is all to the good. Our knowledge about social change in America depends on the way in which federal and other statistical agencies present their data as well as on the content of those data.

Recommendations of the Social Science Research Council. A series of recommendations for improving national statistics on children has been put forth by the Child and Family Indicators Advisory Group, a panel convened by the Social Science Research Council at the request of the Foundation for Child Development (Watts & Hernandez, 1982). The group was composed of scholars from both the academic community and the federal statistical establishment. Their report emphasizes the need to maintain the quality, comprehensiveness, and timeliness of the major federal surveys and data collection programs on which our basic child and family indicators depend. With respect to the analysis and reporting of federal data, the report calls for the use of the child as the unit of observation and analysis; for the adoption of consistent definitions and tabulation procedures with respect to age and other background variables; and for the timely dissemination of reports and public-use tapes. The panel strongly recommends the publication of a federally sponsored biennial report on children that would bring together the major child and family indicators in a single volume and the establishment of a data archive to make existing data on children available in a readily accessible form to scholars, students, and policy analysts.

In order to strengthen the child indicators data base, the report calls for the replication of earlier national surveys of children and for the institution of a new National Youth Panel Study. The report stresses the need for greater breadth in measuring the contexts and environments in which children develop, for indicators that reflect a child's cumulative experience rather than just his or her current situation, and for data on family support networks that extend outside the boundaries of the residential household.

As the availability and quality of the child indicator data base improve, these indicators will be increasingly relied on in policy debates. To one extent or another, childhood social indicators were drawn upon in each of the policy developments described in other chapters in this volume. The transformation of knowledge into action, of descriptive information into intelligence and then into policy, is not easy. But it is increasingly clear that the availability of good national, state, and local data on the health and well-being of children *can* fundamentally affect the ability of public and private programs to assist children and their families.

References

Achenbach, T. M., & Edelbrock, C. S. Behavioral problems and competencies reported by parents of normal and disturbed children aged four through sixteen. *Monographs of the Society for Research in Child Development,* 1981, Serial No. 188, *46*(1), entire issue.

Adelson, J. Adolescence and the generation gap. *Psychology Today,* September 1979, pp. 33–37.

Andrews, F. M., & Withey, S. B. *Social indicators of well-being: Americans' perceptions of life quality.* New York: Plenum Press, 1976.

Arkansas Advocates for Children and Families. *Arkansas children have problems.* Little Rock, 1980.

Austin, G. R., & Garber, H. (Eds.). *The rise and fall of national test scores.* New York: Academic Press, 1982.

Bachman, J. G. *Youth in transition.* Vol. 2: *The impact of family background and intelligence on tenth-grade boys.* Ann Arbor: Institute for Social Research, University of Michigan, 1970.

Bachman, J. G., & Johnston, L. D. *The monitoring the future project design and procedures.* Ann Arbor: Institute for Social Research, University of Michigan, 1978.

Bachman, J. G., Johnston, L. D., & O'Malley, P. M. Smoking, drinking, and drug use among American high school students: Correlates and trends, 1975–1979. *American Journal of Public Health,* 1981, *71,* 59–69.

Bachman, J. G., Kahn, R. L., Mednick, M. T., Davidson, T. M., & Johnston, L. D. *Youth in transition.* Vol. 1: *Blueprint for a longitudinal study of adolescent boys.* Ann Arbor: Institute for Social Research, University of Michigan, 1969.

Bachman, J. G., O'Malley, P. M., & Johnston, J. *Youth in transition.* Vol. 6: *Adolescence to adulthood: A study of change and stability in the lives of young men.* Ann Arbor: Institute for Social Research, University of Michigan, 1978.

Bane, M. J. *Here to stay: American families in the twentieth century.* New York: Basic Books, 1976.

Bauer, R. A. (Ed.). *Social indicators.* Cambridge: MIT Press, 1966.

Biderman, A. Aversions to social concepts. *Proceedings of the Social Statistics Section, American Statistical Association,* Washington, D.C., 1979, pp. 328–333.

Breen, P. *Raising a new generation in the South.* A report for the Task Force on Southern Children. Research Triangle Park, N. Car.: Southern Growth Policies Board, 1981.

Brim, O. G., Jr. Macro-structural influences on child development and the need for childhood social indicators. *American Journal of Orthopsychiatry,* 1975, *45,* 516–524.

Bronfenbrenner, U. Socialization and social class through time and space. In H. Proshansky & B. Seidenberg (Eds.), *Basic studies in social psychology.* New York: Holt, Rinehart and Winston, 1965.

Bureau of the Census, U.S. Department of Commerce. *Current population reports.* Series P-20: *Population characteristics.* Series P-23: *Special studies.* Series P-25: *Population estimates and projections.* Series P-60: *Consumer income.* Washington, D.C.: U.S. Government Printing Office.

Bureau of the Census, U.S. Department of Commerce. *Child well-being study: Stage II* (Interim Report). Washington, D.C.: U.S. Government Printing Office, 1977. (a)

Bureau of the Census, U.S. Department of Commerce. *Social indicators, 1976.* Washington, D.C.: U.S. Government Printing Office, 1977. (b)

Bureau of the Census, U.S. Department of Commerce. *Characteristics of American children and youth, 1976 (Current population reports,* Series P-23, No. 66). Washington, D.C.: U.S. Government Printing Office, 1978.

Bureau of the Census, U.S. Department of Commerce. *Social indicators III.* Washington, D.C.: U.S. Government Printing Office, 1980. (a)

Bureau of the Census. U.S. Department of Commerce. *American families and living arrangements (Current population reports,* Series P-23, No. 104). Washington, D.C.: U.S. Government Printing Office, 1980. (b)

Bureau of the Census, U.S. Department of Commerce. *Child support and alimony, 1978 (Current population reports,* Series P-23, No. 112). Washington, D.C.: U.S. Government Printing Office, 1981.

Bureau of the Census, U.S. Department of Commerce. *Characteristics of American children and youth, 1980. (Current population reports,* Series P-23, No. 114). Washington, D.C.: U.S. Government Printing Office, 1982. (a)

Bureau of the Census, U.S. Department of Commerce. *Characteristics of households and persons receiving selected noncash benefits, 1980 (Current population reports,* Series P-60, No. 131). Washington, D.C.: U.S. Government Printing Office, 1982. (b)

Bureau of the Census, U.S. Department of Commerce. *Marital status and living arrange-*

ments, March 1981 (*Current population reports*, Series P-20, No. 372). Washington, D.C.: U.S. Government Printing Office, 1982. (c)

Bureau of Labor Statistics, U.S. Department of Labor. *Half of nation's children have working mothers* (News Release USDL 81-522). Washington, D.C., November 15, 1981.

Campbell, A. *The sense of well-being in America: Recent patterns and trends.* New York: McGraw-Hill, 1981.

Campbell, A., & Converse, P. E. (Eds.). *The human meaning of social change.* New York: Russell Sage Foundation, 1972.

Campbell, A., Converse, P. E., & Rodgers, W. L. *The quality of American life.* New York: Russell Sage Foundation, 1976.

Cherlin, A. J. *Marriage, divorce, remarriage: Social trends in the United States.* Cambridge: Harvard University Press, 1981.

Coleman, J. S., Campbell, E. Q., Hobson, C. J., McPartland, J., Mood, A. M., Weinfeld, F. D., & York, R. L. *Equality of educational opportunity.* Washington, D.C.: U.S. Government Printing Office, 1966.

College Entrance Examination Board. *National college-bound seniors.* Princeton, N.J.: Educational Testing Service, 1982.

Condran, J. G. Changes in white attitudes toward blacks, 1963–1977. *Public Opinion Quarterly,* 1979, *43*(4), 463–476.

Davie, R., Butler, N. R., & Goldstein, H. *From birth to seven.* London: Longmans/National Children's Bureau, 1972.

Davis, J. A. Communism, conformity, cohorts, and categories: American tolerance in 1954 and 1972/73. *American Journal of Sociology,* 1975, *81*, 491–513. (a)

Davis, J. A. The log linear analysis of survey replications. In K. C. Land & S. Spilerman (Eds.), *Social indicator models.* New York: Russell Sage Foundation, 1975. (b)

Davis, J. A. The parental families of Americans in birth cohorts, 1890–1955: A categorical, linear equation model estimated from the NORC General Social Survey. *Social Indicators Research,* 1981, *9*, 395–453.

Davis, J. A., Smith, T. W., & Stephenson, C. B. *General social surveys, 1972–1978: Cumulative data.* Chicago: National Opinion Research Center (producer); New Haven: Roper Public Opinion Research Center, Yale University (distributor), 1978.

Douglas, J. W. B. *The home and the school.* London: MacGibbon and Kee, 1964.

Douglas, J. W. B., & Blomfield, J. M. *Children under five.* London: Allen and Unwin, 1958.

Douglas, J. W. B., Ross, J. W., & Simpson, H. R. *All our future.* London: Davies, 1968.

Duncan, O. D. *Toward social reporting: Next steps.* New York: Russell Sage Foundation, 1969.

Duncan, O. D. *Social indicators, 1973: Report on a conference.* In R. A. Van Dusen (Ed.), *Social indicators, 1973: A review symposium.* Washington, D.C.: Social Science Research Council, Center for Coordination of Research on Social Indicators, 1974.

Duncan, O. D. Measuring social change via replication of surveys. In K. C. Land & S. Spilerman (Eds.), *Social indicator models.* New York: Russell Sage Foundation, 1975.

Duncan, O. D., Schuman, H., & Duncan, B. *Social change in a metropolitan community.* New York: Russell Sage Foundation, 1973.

Edelman, M. W. *Portrait of inequality: Black and white children in America.* Washington, D.C.: Children's Defense Fund, 1980.

Education Commission of the States. *The children's needs assessment handbook.* Denver, 1976.

Edwards, L. M., & Grossman, M. The relationship between children's health and intellectual development. In S. Mushkin & D. Dunlop (Eds.), *Health: What is it worth?* New York: Pergamon Press, 1979.

Fédération Nationale des Ecoles des Parents et des Educateurs. *Enfants et parents en questions: L'Enfant de 7 à 11 ans, sa famille, son environnement.* Paris, 1980.

Ferri, E. *Growing up in a one-parent family.* London: NFER, 1976.

Fishburne, P. M., Abelson, H. E., & Cisin, I. *National survey on drug abuse: Main findings, 1979* (Contract No. 27-78-3508). Rockville, Md.: National Institute on Drug Abuse, 1980.

Flanagan, J. C., & Cooley, W. W. *Project TALENT: One-year follow-up studies* (Technical Report, Cooperative Research Project No. 2333, U.S. Office of Education). Pittsburgh: University of Pittsburgh, Project TALENT Office, 1966.

Flanagan, J. C., Dailey, J. T., Shaycroft, M. F., Gorham, W. A., Orr, D. B., & Goldberg, I. *Design for a study of American youth.* Boston: Houghton Mifflin, 1962.

Flanagan, J. C., Davis, F. B., Dailey, J. T., Shaycroft, M. F., Orr, D. B., & Goldberg, I., & Neyman, C. A. *Project TALENT: The American high school student* (Final Report, Cooperative Research Project No. 635, U.S. Office of Education). Pittsburgh: University of Pittsburgh, Project TALENT Office, 1964.

Fogelman, K. (Ed.). *Britain's sixteen-year-olds.* London: National Children's Bureau, 1976.

Glick, P. C. Children of divorced parents in demographic perspective, *Journal of Social Issues,* 1979, *35,* 170–182.

Glick, P. C. *Children from one-parent families: Recent data and projections.* Paper presented at Charles F. Kettering Foundation, Special Institute on Critical Issues in Education, American University, Washington, D.C., June 22, 1981. (Distributed by U.S. Bureau of the Census.)

Gold, M., & Reimer, D. J. Changing patterns of delinquent behavior among Americans 13 through 16 years old, 1967–1972. *Crime and Delinquency Literature,* 1975, *7,* 483–517.

Gross, B. M., (Ed.). *Social intelligence for America's future.* Boston: Allyn & Bacon, 1969.

Grossman, A. S. Working mothers and their children. *Monthly Labor Review,* 1981, *104*(5), 49–54.

Grossman, M., Coate, D., Edwards, L. M., Shakoto, R. A., & Chernichovsky, D. *Determinants of children's health* (Final Report, Grant No. 1 R01 HS 02917, National Center for Health Services Research). New York: National Bureau of Economic Research, 1980.

Hindelang, M. J., & McDermott, M. J. *Juvenile criminal behavior: An analysis of rates and victim characteristics* (National Institute for Juvenile Justice and Delinquency Prevention, Law Enforcement Assistance Administration, U.S. Department of Justice). Washington, D.C.: U.S. Government Printing Office, 1981.

Johnston, L. D. *Drugs and American youth.* Ann Arbor: Institute for Social Research, University of Michigan, 1973.

Johnston, L. D., Bachman, J. G., & O'Malley, P. M. *Monitoring the future: Questionnaire responses from the nation's high school seniors, 1979.* Ann Arbor: Institute for Social Research, University of Michigan, 1980.

Johnston, L. D., Bachman, J. G., & O'Malley, P. M. *Highlights from student drug use in America, 1975–1980* (National Institute on Drug Abuse). Washington, D.C.: U.S. Government Printing Office, 1981.

Kellam, S. G., Branch, J. D., Agrawal, K. C., & Ensminger, M. E. *Mental health and going to school: The Woodlawn Program of assessment, early intervention, and evaluation.* Chicago: University of Chicago Press, 1975.

Keniston, K., & Carnegie Council on Children. *All our children: The American family under pressure.* New York: Harcourt Brace Jovanovich, 1977.

Kleinman, J. C., & Kessel, S. S. The recent decline in infant mortality. In *Health: United States, 1980* (DHHS Publication No. [PHS] 81-1232, Public Health Service). Washington, D.C.: U.S. Government Printing Office, 1980.

Kogan, L. S., & Jenkins, S. *Indicators of child health and welfare.* New York: City University of New York, Center for Social Research, 1974.

Kovar, M. G. Children and youth: Health status and use of health services. In *Health: United States, 1978* (DHEW Publication No. [PHS] 78-1232, Public Health Service). Washington, D.C.: U.S. Government Printing Office, 1978.

Kovar, M. G. Some indicators of health-related behavior among adolescents in the United States. *Public Health Reports,* 1979, *94*(2), 109–118.

Kovar, M. G. *Better health for our children.* Vol. 3: *A statistical profile: The Report of the Select Panel for the Promotion of Child Health.* Washington, D.C.: U.S. Government Printing Office, 1981.

Langner, T. S., Gersten, J. C., McCarthy, E. D., Eisenberg, J. G., Greene, E. L., & Jameson, J. D. A screening inventory for assessing psychiatric impairment in children 6 to 18. *Journal of Consulting and Clinical Psychology,* 1976, *44,* 286–296.

Lash, T. W., & Sigal, H. *State of the child: New York City.* New York: Foundation for Child Development, 1976.

Lash, T. W., Sigal, H., & Dudzinski, D. *State of the Child: New York City II.* New York: Foundation for Child Development, 1980.

Lueck, M., Orr, A. C., & O'Connell, M. *Trends in child care arrangements of working mothers (Current population reports,* Series P-23, No. 117). Washington, D.C.: U.S. Government Printing Office, 1982.

Masnick, G., & Bane, M. J. *The nation's families, 1960–1990.* Boston: Auburn House, 1980.

Mayeske, G. W., Okada, T., & Beaton, A. E., Jr. *A study of the attitude toward life of our nation's students* (U.S. Office of Education, DHEW Publication No. [OE] 73-01700). Washington, D.C.: U.S. Government Printing Office, 1973.

Mayeske, G. W., Weinfeld, F. D., Beaton, A. E., Jr., Davis, W., Fetters, W. B., & Hixson, E. E. *Item response analysis of the Educational Opportunities Survey student questionnaire* (Technical Note No. 64). Washington, D.C.: U.S. Office of Education, 1968.

Mayeske, G. W., Wisler, C. E., Beaton, A. E., Jr., Weinfeld, F. D., Cohen, W. M., Okada, T., Proshek, J. M., & Tabler, K. A. *A study of our nation's schools* (U.S. Office of Education, DHEW Publication No. [OE] 72-142). Washington, D.C.: U.S. Government Printing Office, 1972.

McDermott, M. J., & Hindelang, M. J. *Juvenile criminal behavior in the United States: Its trends and patterns* (National Institute for Juvenile Justice and Delinquency Prevention, Law Enforcement Assistance Administration, U.S. Department of Justice). Washington, D.C.: U.S. Government Printing Office, 1981.

McHale, M. C., & McHale, J., with Streatfeild, G. F. *Children in the world.* Washington, D.C.: Population Reference Bureau, 1979. (a)

McHale, M. C., & McHale, J., with Streatfeild, G. F. World of children. *Population Bulletin,* 1979, *33*(6), entire issue. (b)

Medrich, E. A., Roizen, J. A., Rubin, V., & Buckley, S. *The serious business of growing up: A study of children's lives outside school.* Berkeley: University of California Press, 1982.

National Assessment of Educational Progress. *General information yearbook* (Education Commission of the States, Report No. 03/04-GIY). Washington, D.C.: U.S. Government Printing Office, 1974.

National Assessment of Educational Progress. *Three national assessments of reading: Changes in performance, 1970–80* (Report No. 11-R-01). Denver: Education Commission of the States, 1981.

National Black Child Development Institute. *The status of black children in 1980.* Washington, D.C., 1980.

National Center for Education Statistics. *The condition of education.* Washington, D.C.: U.S. Government Printing Office, annual.

National Center for Education Statistics. *The national longitudinal study of the high school class of 1972: A capsule description of second follow-up survey data.* Washington, D.C.: U.S. Government Printing Office, 1977.

National Center for Education Statistics. *High school and beyond: A capsule description of high school students* (NCES Publication No. 81-244). Washington, D.C.: U.S. Government Printing Office, 1981.

National Center for Health Statistics. *Vital and Health Statistics.* Series 1: *Programs and collection procedures.* Series 10: *Data from the Health Interview Survey.* Series 11: *Data from the Health Examination Survey and the Health and Nutrition Examination Survey.* Series 20: *Data on mortality.* Series 21: *Data on natality, marriage, and divorce.* (Public Health Service.) Washington, D.C.: U.S. Government Printing Office.

National Center for Health Statistics. *Plan, operation, and response results of a program of children's examinations* (*Vital and Health Statistics,* Series 1, No. 5, Public Health Service). Washington, D.C.: U.S. Government Printing Office, 1967.

National Center for Health Statistics. *Plan and operation of a health examination survey of U.S. youths 12–17 years of age* (*Vital and Health Statistics,* Series 1, No. 8, Public Health Service). Washington, D.C.: U.S. Government Printing Office, 1969.

National Center for Health Statistics. *Parent ratings of behavioral patterns of children, United States* (*Vital and Health Statistics,* Series 11, No. 108, Public Health Service). Washington, D.C.: U.S. Government Printing Office, 1971.

National Center for Health Statistics. *Behavior patterns of children in school, United States* (*Vital and Health Statistics,* Series 11, No. 113, Public Health Service). Washington, D.C.: U.S. Government Printing Office, 1972.

National Center for Health Statistics. *Plan and operation of the Health and Nutrition Examination Survey* (*Vital and Health Statistics,* Series 1, No. 10a & b, Public Health Service). Washington, D.C.: U.S. Government Printing Office, 1973. (a)

National Center for Health Statistics. *Examination and health history findings among children and youths, 6–17 years, United States* (*Vital and Health Statistics,* Series 11, No. 129, Public Health Service). Washington, D.C.: U.S. Government Printing Office, 1973. (b)

National Center for Health Statistics. *Behavior patterns in school of youths 12–17 years, United States* (*Vital and Health Statistics,* Series 11, No. 139, Public Health Service). Washington, D.C.: U.S. Government Printing Office, 1974.

National Center for Health Statistics. *Health interview survey procedure, 1957–1974.* (*Vital and Health Statistics,* Series 1, No. 11, Public Health Service). Washington, D.C.: U.S. Government Printing Office, 1975. (a)

National Center for Health Statistics. *Self-reported health behavior and attitudes of youths 12–17 years, United States* (*Vital and Health Statistics,* Series 11, No. 147, Public Health Service). Washington, D.C.: U.S. Government Printing Office, 1975. (b)

National Institute on Drug Abuse. Nature and extent of marijuana use in the United States. In *Marijuana Research Findings, 1980* (NIDA Research Monograph 31). Washington, D.C.: U.S. Government Printing Office, 1980.

National Research Council, Assembly of Behavioral and Social Sciences, Advisory Committee on Child Development. *Toward a national policy for children and families.* Washington, D.C.: National Academy of Sciences, 1976.

Nesenholtz, D. Early childhood needs assessment in Texas. In *The children's needs assessment handbook.* Denver: Education Commission of the States, 1976, pp. 50–70.

Newspaper Readership Project. *America's children and the mass media.* New York: Newspaper Advertising Bureau, 1980.

North Carolina Division of Policy Development. *Indicators of children's needs in North Carolina.* Raleigh, N. Car.: Department of Administration, 1979.

Norwood, C. *At highest risk: Environmental hazards to young and unborn children.* New York: McGraw-Hill, 1980.

Office of Management and Budget, Executive Office of the President. *Social indicators, 1973.* Washington, D.C.: U.S. Government Printing Office, 1973.

Olson, M., Jr. The plan and purpose of a social report. *Public Interest,* 1969, *15,* 85–97.

Organisation for Economic Co-operation and Development. *List of social concerns common to most OECD countries.* Paris, 1973.

Organisation for Economic Co-operation and Development. *Measuring social well-being.* Paris, 1976.

Organisation for Economic Co-operation and Development. *Child and family: Demographic developments in the OECD countries.* Paris, 1979.

Parke, R., & Peterson, J. L. Indicators of social change: Developments in the United States of America. *Accounting, Organizations, and Society,* 1981, *6*(3).

Parnes, H. S., Miljus, R. C., Spitz, R. S., & Associates. *Career thresholds: A longitudinal study of the educational and labor market experience of male youth 14–24 years of age.* Columbus: Ohio State University Center for Human Resources, 1969.

Population Reference Bureau. *World children's data sheet.* Washington, D.C., 1979.

President's Research Committee on Social Trends. *Recent social trends in the United States.* New York: McGraw-Hill, 1933.

Pringle, J. L. K., Butler, N. F., & Davie, R. *Eleven thousand seven year olds.* London: Longmans/National Children's Bureau, 1966.

Reinhold, R. Data on cuts imperiled by cuts in data. *New York Times,* October 18, 1981, Sec. E, p. 4.

Rice, D. P., & Danchik, K. M. *Changing needs of children: Disease, disability, and access to care.* Paper presented at Institute of Medicine Annual Meeting, Washington, D.C., October 25, 1979. (Distributed by National Center for Health Statistics.)

Robinson, J. P. *How Americans use time.* New York: Praeger, 1977.

Rutter, M., Tizard, J., & Whitmore, K. (Eds.). *Education, Health, and Behaviour.* London: Longmans, 1970.

Sengoku, T., & Iinaga, K. *Elementary school children of Japan: An international comparison.* Tokyo: NHK, 1979.

Sheldon, E. B. Social reporting for the 1970s. In *Report of the President's Commission on Federal Statistics.* Vol. 2: *Federal Statistics.* Washington, D.C.: U.S. Government Printing Office, 1971.

Sheldon, E. B., & Moore, W. E. *Indicators of social change.* New York: Russell Sage Foundation, 1968.

Sheldon, E. B., & Parke, R. Social indicators: Social science researchers are developing concepts and measures of change in society. *Science,* 1975, *188,* 693–699.

Shur, J. L., & Smith, P. *Where do you look? Whom do you ask? How do you know? Information resources for child advocates.* Washington, D.C.: Children's Defense Fund, 1980.

Simons, J. M. *America's children and their families: Key facts.* Washington, D.C.: Children's Defense Fund, 1982.

Smith, T. W., Taylor, D. G., & Mathiowetz, N. Public opinion and public regard for the federal government. In A. Barton & C. Weiss (Eds.), *Making bureaucracies work.* Beverly Hills, Calif.: Sage, 1979.

Snapper, K. J., Barriga, H. H., Baumgartner, F. H., & Wagner, C. S. *The status of children, 1975.* Washington, D.C.: Social Research Group, George Washington University, 1975.

Snapper, K. J., & Ohms, J. S. *The status of children, 1977* (DHEW Publication No. [OHDS] 78-30133). Washington, D.C.: U.S. Government Printing Office, 1977.

Social Indicators Newsletter. Washington, D.C.: Social Science Research Council, Center for Coordination of Research on Social Indicators, irregular.

Social Indicators Research. Hingham, Md.: Reidel Publishing Company, quarterly.

South Carolina Department of Social Services. *Children and their families: A statistical profile.* Columbia, S. Car.: Office of Child Development, 1977.

Szalai, A. (Ed.). *The use of time: Daily activities of urban and suburban populations in twelve countries.* The Hague: Mouton, 1972.

Testa, M., & Wulczyn, F. *The state of the child: Volume one of a series of research reports on children in Illinois.* Chicago: Children's Policy Research Project, School of Social Service Administration, University of Chicago, 1980.

Texas Department of Community Affairs, Human Resources Branch, Early Childhood Development Division. *Seventy-eight things you need to know about Texas children: Still the darker side of childhood.* Austin, 1978.

Tracy, D. F., & Pizzo, P. D. *State of the child in Appalachia: Report of a conference.* Atlanta: Appalachia Child Care Conference Planning Committee, 1977.

U.S. Department of Health, Education, and Welfare. *Toward a social report.* Washington, D.C.: U.S. Government Printing Office, 1969.

U.S. Department of Health and Human Services, Office of Human Development Services, Administration for Children, Youth, and Families. *The status of children, youth, and families, 1979.* Washington, D.C.: U.S. Government Printing Office, 1980.

U.S. Department of Health and Human Services, Public Health Service. *Health: United States.* Washington, D.C.: U.S. Government Printing Office, annual.

Vaillancourt, P. M. Stability of children's survey responses. *Public Opinion Quarterly,* 1973, *37*(3), 373–387.

Veroff, J., Douvan, E., & Kulka, R. A. *The inner American: A self-portrait from 1957 to 1976.* New York: Basic Books, 1981.

Virginia Division for Children. *Children, youth, and families in Virginia: Assessing their needs.* Richmond: Virginia Division for Children, 1978.

Watts. H. W., & Hernandez, D. J. (Eds.). *Child and family indicators: A report with recommendations.* Washington, D.C.: Social Science Research Council, Center for Coordination of Research on Social Indicators, 1982.

Watts, H. W., & Santos, F. P. *The allocation of human and material resources to childrearing in the United States: A theoretical framework and analysis of major data sources.* New York: Center for the Social Sciences, Columbia University, 1978.

Wedge, P., & Prosser, H. *Born to fail?* London: Arrow, 1973.

White House Conference on Children, 1970. *Profiles of children.* Washington, D.C.: U.S. Government Printing Office, 1970.

Wirtz, W., & Howe, H. *On further examination: Report of the advisory panel on the Scholastic Aptitude Test score decline.* New York: College Entrance Examination Board, 1977.

World Bank. *World atlas of the child.* Washington, D.C.: World Bank, 1979.

Yankelovich, Skelly, & White, Inc. *The General Mills American family report, 1976–77: Raising children in a changing society.* Minneapolis: General Mills, 1977.

Zelnick, M., & Kantner, J. F. Sexual and contraceptive experience of young unmarried women in the United States, 1976 and 1971. *Family Planning Perspectives,* 1977, *9,* 55–71.

Zelnick, M., & Kantner, J. F. Sexual activity, contraceptive use, and pregnancy among metropolitan-area teenagers, 1971–1979. *Family Planning Perspectives,* 1980, *12*(5), 230–237.

Zill, N. *Happy, healthy, and insecure: A portrait of middle childhood in the United States.* New York: Anchor, 1983.

13   Social policy and the media

Susan Muenchow and Susan Shays Gilfillan

"Nothing will be done about the social problems besetting America's children and families," argues Edward Zigler, director of Yale's Bush Center in Child Development and Social Policy, "until the public has a shared sense that these problems exist" (Zigler & Finn, 1981). Zigler consequently calls on policy analysts and advocates to work with the media in educating the public about these problems and a range of policy options. Undoubtedly, the media have an important role to play in raising public consciousness. However, once having accepted this notion in principle, further questions arise: What precise role do the media play in alerting the public to certain problems or educating them to a range of policy options? How does a social problem such as child abuse or teenage pregnancy emerge as a media issue, and who determines how the problem will be presented or framed? Finally, what strategies can the child advocate use to improve media coverage of family-related issues?

Changes in the media and in the function of journalism

Although this discussion tends to emphasize the role of television and major newspapers in influencing social policy, the authors by no means intend to limit their definition of media to the print and broadcast press alone. In the age of the instant paperback, sophisticated direct-mail techniques, and public relations or "news subsidizers," media must be understood in the broadest sense. Moreover, at a time when cable television is revolutionizing the concept of broadcasting, technological changes are even forcing us to redefine the concept of audience. An entire network may soon be designed for persons over 50, another for Southern Baptists, and still another for fans of video computer games.

223

Thus, it is becoming increasingly easy to reach a narrow, clearly defined audience and difficult to reach a "mass" audience with any controversial message. Because research (Whiting, 1976) indicates that media impact is related not so much to reaching the largest audience as to reaching the most appropriate audience, policy advocates who ignore these outlets to specialized audiences would severely limit the effectiveness of their messages.

Not only is the concept of audience undergoing dramatic changes, but also the concept of mass media journalism has been changing during the last decade. Controversy emerges around the question of where education stops and advocacy and propaganda begin. The rise of advocacy journalism, wherein the reporter tries to advance a point of view or to become a part of the news, may indeed have compromised the journalist's role as objective observer (Kampelman, 1978). But it can be argued that limiting the role of journalists to "passive transmitters of descriptions or specific events" (Weaver & McCombs, 1980, p. 491) does not serve the public interest. The journalist must also be an active truth seeker. Many trends in journalism – interpretive, investigative, and public affairs reporting – are simply forms of recognition of this responsibility. Perhaps the newest trend, "precision journalism" – the direct application of social science methodology to reporting – demands the most active role yet for journalists as educators. It calls on journalists not only to "pay attention to what social scientists are doing, but also that they use the research methods of social scientists" (Weaver & McCombs, 1980, p. 489). In some cases the tendency for journalists to conduct "social science in a hurry" is disturbing, for it has led to the proliferation of public opinion polls, many of which are improperly conceived and poorly conducted. But the application of social science methodology to journalism also holds much promise, for it allows journalists to become better investigative reporters "with better tools for probing social reality" (Weaver & McCombs, 1980, p. 490).

At the least, the blurring of the line between the journalist's and the social scientist's functions has the potential to improve both of their contributions to public decision making. As Charles Silberman (1964) states in his book *Crisis in Black and White,* journalists and social scientists need each other: "The journalist is sometimes too impatient with the scholar's concern for substantiation; the scholar sometimes fails to remember what the journalist can never forget – namely that life can never wait until all the evidence is in, that important decisions must always be made on the basis of incomplete information" (p. IX).

Agenda setting: a theory of how the media influence social policy

To what extent, then, do the media influence social policy in the current setting just described? As will become apparent, the media's influence is crucial but not primary, powerful but indirect.

History of theories of media influence

Whether or not the media play any significant role in influencing public decision making has been a subject of controversy. Among communications scholars, theories asserting the powerful role of the media have tended to wax and wane. Throughout World War II, social scientists tended to share an assumption with the general public "in the ability of mass communications to achieve significant, perhaps staggering, social effects" (Mc Combs & Masel-Walters, 1976, p. 3). Based on the effects of wartime propaganda and the demonstrated ability of the media to sell products, both the public and scholars were convinced that the media could mold public opinion at will. But more precise quantitative research "soon brought the academic world to a jaundiced view of the power of mass communication" (McCombs & Masel-Walters, 1976, p. 3). Evidence of selective exposure, selective perception, and selective retention seemed to reduce the role of the media to one of minimal consequences. For example, a study by Lazarsfeld, Berelson, and Goudet (1948) concluded that the media had little influence on the outcome of the 1940 election. Most voters, the study indicated, had made up their minds before the campaign and tended to expose themselves selectively to media coverage that reinforced their choice while avoiding information opposed to their choice (McLeod, Becker, & Byrnes, 1974). The dominant postwar view became that the mass media might be "all pervasive, but not particularly persuasive" (Shaw, 1979, p. 96).

More recently, however, a theory called "agenda setting" has tended to restore a view of the media as a powerful influence on public decision making. Cohen (1963), apparently the first to use the term *agenda setting,* stated that the press "may not be successful much of the time in telling people what to think, but it is stunningly successful in telling its readers what to think *about*" (quoted in McLeod et al., 1974, p. 134). Media coverage may not directly alter public attitudes, but it does much to focus public attention on certain events, issues, and persons and to determine how much importance people attach to these matters (Shaw, 1979). For example, in one of the first studies to verify agenda-setting theory, Maxwell McCombs and Donald Shaw (1972) found substantial correlations

between the issues emphasized in the news media and those the undecided voters regarded as the key issues in the election. Thus, media
coverage may not have changed voter decisions, but, at least among the
undecided voters, media coverage was effective in shaping the criteria
upon which they made their decisions.

Agenda setting: powerful influence, but indirect

Assuming that the agenda-setting model has some validity, what are the
mechanisms by which the media's agenda becomes the audience's agenda?
In the simplest sense, media coverage confers status to certain events,
people, or problems. Simply by virtue of its presence in the media, a
phenomenon may be "afforded a level of status or 'worth' in the eyes of the
audience members that was previously absent" (Baran, 1977, p. 140). For
example, in 1972, Geraldo Rivera's television documentary "Willowbrook: The Last Great Disgrace" (WABC-TV, New York) brought national attention to the problems of the institutionalized mentally retarded
(O'Brien, Schneider, & Traviesas, 1980). The documentary's contribution
was not so much the advocacy of any particular policy, but rather the
focusing of public attention on a social problem that is easy to ignore.

Similarly, "Roots," the eight-segment television series that attracted
one of the largest audiences in television history (Hur & Robinson, 1978),
may not have altered the prejudices of any white supremacists, but it was
tremendously successful in making black American history a topic of
discussion. Approximately one-half of all black viewers and one-quarter
of white viewers sampled in one study reported discussing the program
with persons of another race (Goldberg, 1979). Moreover, "Roots"
conferred status not only on the history of black Americans, but also on
the study of history and genealogy in general. The program also
prompted an explosion of American interest in travel to Africa (Johnson,
1977). An official of a Cleveland institute that sponsors travel–study tours
to Africa summed up the impact of "Roots" by saying, "Africa has become a real place in the minds of many Americans" (Johnson, 1977).

Media coverage, especially television coverage, not only confers status
on a subject, but it also burns images into our minds, images to which we
react in countless ways for years afterward (Rubin, 1977). Simply by
virtue of bringing the image of body bags into our living rooms on a
nightly basis during the Vietnam War, points out columnist George Will,
television complicated the government's task of holding public support
for the war. It was not that media coverage was deliberately antiwar.
Rather, as Will says, television coverage of any war might lead to an

antiwar movement: Had there been television cameras at Gettysburg during the Civil War, had the public seen the carnage of that war and "the bloodiest day in American history at Antietam," Will reasons, the United States would be at least two nations now (in Daly, 1979, p. 15). "This does not mean that the press corps in the 1860s would have been pro-Confederacy. It means that the media's exposure of the war would have had certain consequences" (in Daly, 1979, p. 15). Thus, without any deliberate attempt to promote or discourage any public policy, the media can arouse strong public response through their vivid presentation of visual images.

Far from being limited to news transmission, the agenda-setting function, particularly in the case of television, extends to fictional programs as well. As a result of the disproportionate amount of violence on television, heavy viewers tend to "overestimate the amount of violence in the world, overestimate the chances that they will be the victims of violence," and be less trusting of their neighbors (Gandy, 1980, p. 108). By the age of 14, the average child in the United States has "witnessed the assault on or destruction of more than 18,000 people" on television (J. Stein, 1979, p. 80). Undoubtedly, television has helped to create a disproportionate fear of violence in our society.

Of particular interest to those in the field of child and family policy, agenda setting can operate as much by omission as by commission. The most powerful media influence on child and family policy may therefore be the omission of certain news stories that should be of popular concern and the absence of certain characters in television drama. Despite the overemphasis on violence in general, the media have tended to ignore violence experienced by whole classes of citizens, especially the poor and minorities (Rubin, 1977). Similarly, Gerbner (1980) points out that both television news and drama tend to devalue children by grossly underestimating even the sheer presence of children in American society. Indeed, children may the largest of the invisible minorities.

Newspapers also tend to relegate coverage of children to the "family" pages at the back of the paper. When the Carnegie Council on Children began plotting its media strategy in the mid-1970s, "council staffers became aware of the media's general attitude that 'children aren't news,' and are not so-called 'hard' news in particular" (Keniston et al., 1980, p. 28). Even when a story affecting children has a clear-cut economic angle, such as a budget cutback affecting prenatal care for low-income women, it may wind up in the "family and leisure" section (Conrad, 1981). Too often, any story about child and family issues is automatically assigned to the family or education reporter, not to the correspondents who cover unemployment, inflation, and economic issues that are more apt to receive front-page coverage.

How a social issue gets on the media agenda

So far this discussion has tended to stress the role of television and newspapers in the placement – or omission – of social issues on the nation's agenda. But among the various "stages in the natural history" of the emergence of social concerns (Henderson, 1978), television and even the mass-circulation print media frequently come into play later, rather than earlier, in the process. Henderson lists six stages in the buildup of social energy in response to an emerging public issue, from exposés in low-circulation books and periodicals to the passage of legislation. Although in some cases, such as the emergence of Watergate as a public issue, the mass media may initiate the buildup of social energy, more often television and major newspaper coverage appear midway in the process, serving only to amplify messages that originated in lower-circulation media. Thus, it would be a mistake to conclude that television and the major newspapers are the advocate's most important tools. Social change may be said to result as much from just the right message to the right audience (Whiting, 1976), even in a much smaller medium.

To appreciate the importance of the right message to the right audience, one need look no further than the emergence of poverty as a national issue in the 1960s. One might even be able to trace the beginnings of the War on Poverty back to a couple of influential books: Oscar Lewis's study of Puerto Ricans living in the culture of poverty (*La Vida,* 1966) and Michael Harrington's *The Other America* (1962). When *The Other America* first appeared, it received favorable but not rave reviews (Harrington, 1975). By January 1963, Harrington assumed the book had run its course. But in that same month the *New Yorker* printed Dwight MacDonald's review of *The Other America,* and it was this single review, in a magazine with a circulation of under 500,000, that really made *The Other America* a matter for discussion in the Northeast corridor (Harrington, 1975). In fact, Harrington says that it was in response to the *New Yorker* review that "John F. Kennedy borrowed a copy of *The Other America* from Walter Heller, read some other analyses, and decided to launch his attack on poverty" (Harrington, 1975, p. 7).

In some cases a social issue can go all the way from exposé in relatively limited-circulation media to major legislation without much television or major newspaper coverage. In tracing the rise of the environmental movement, Schoenfeld, Meier, and Griffin (1979) credit specialized periodicals, agency reports, and books like Rachel Carson's *Silent Spring* (1962), not newspaper or television coverage. In fact, the *New York Times* and the national press did not acknowledge the passage of the National Environmental Policy Act in 1969 as a landmark piece of federal legislation. It was not until a year after the legislation's passage that newspapers began to establish environmental reporting as a "beat" (Schoenfeld et al., 1979).

This analysis of the emergence of poverty and the environment as social issues seems to make two key points. First, although neither the problems of poverty nor those of the environment were new, they became "news" because some persons succeeded in framing old problems in a new light. Harrington and Lewis succeeded in changing the focus on poverty from a moral or biological problem to a cultural problem. Carson and others converted the problems of "conservation" into the problems of the "environment," a conceptualization bound to have broader appeal.

At the same time, neither the War on Poverty nor the environmental movement would have escalated to the level of widespread public support had not certain "media events" intervened on their side. In the case of poverty, the civil rights demonstrations and urban riots of the 1960s provided dramatic action that prompted mass media coverage, which in turn impressed the vicissitudes of poverty on the public mind. As for the environmental movement, the Santa Barbara oil spill and the 1969 "view from the moon of a fragile, finite spaceship earth" (Schoenfeld et al., 1979, p. 43) provided the images necessary to dramatize environmental problems.

Direct mail: circumventing the agenda-setting process

More recently, the efficacy of conveying the proper message to the proper audience may have been carried to its ultimate extreme. With the rise of direct-mail advertising and its electronic equivalent, cable television, advocates can mobilize a powerful lobby without ever having to deal with the conventional media at all. "You can think of direct-mail advertising as *our* TV, radio, daily newspaper and weekly news magazine," states Richard Viguerie, one of the masterminds behind direct-mail advertising for the New Right (Viguerie, 1980, p. 7).

Although the role of direct-mail advertising in political fundraising is well known, direct mail has also been influential in decisions on key pieces of child and family legislation. When passage of comprehensive child development legislation seemed assured in 1971, Congress was deluged with sacks of opposing mail, with most letters containing the same charges, even the same phrases. In part, the letters echoed a syndicated column by James J. Kilpatrick, who charged that the bill would lead to the "Sovietization of American youth" and a communal approach to child rearing (Kilpatrick, 1971). But according to a *Conservative Digest* profile of "profamily" forces, the orchestration of the letter campaign can be attributed to one Washington State "citizen activist." June Larson, head of Citizens for Constructive Education, is said to have alerted profamily forces promptly on the pending legislation and thereby orchestrated the movement that forced President Nixon to veto Senator Walter Mondale's child development bill in 1971 ("The pro-family movement," 1980). Without ever engaging extensive mass media coverage at all, right-wing groups were thus able to make their views prevail through the presidential veto.

The agenda setters

With some understanding of the process of agenda setting, the next question that must be asked is "Who sets the agenda?" As has been suggested above, mass media professionals are not the primary initiators of most news stories. Rather it is persons outside the conventional media, sometimes called "issue energizers," who succeed in communicating their concern about a particular issue and the expectation of a solution to others (Schoenfeld et al., 1979). These claimsmakers or advocates in effect "subsidize" the news with their own information and interpretation (Gandy, 1980).

It would be difficult to overestimate the role of news subsidizers in determining the media's agenda. Of the major sources of news – routine channels, informal sources, and reporter interviews and investigations – routine channels are by far the easiest and the least expensive for the reporter and publisher (Gandy, 1980). Thus, even in major newspapers such as the *New York Times* and the *Washington Post*, nearly 60% of the stories come from such routine sources as press releases or hearing reports. Of nearly 3,000 stories published in the *Times* and the *Post*, 58.2% came from routine sources, 15.7% came from informal sources, and only 25.8% came from enterprise sources (L. V. Sigal, as cited in Gandy, 1980).

These routine channels are in turn heavily subsidized by news sources who want to influence public and private decision making. Some of these news subsidizers are private, others are tax-supported. According to Gandy (1980), the Civil Service Commission estimates that there are over 20,000 civilian government information and public affairs officials, and the former Department of Health, Education, and Welfare (DHEW) reportedly spent $23 million annually disseminating public information.

One can argue that subsidized news performs an important educational function and that, in any case, in a free society news subsidizers with conflicting views will eventually cancel out one another. The problem with this rationale is that news can only be as good as its sources, and news subsidizers that offer sensationalism or a story with guaranteed public appeal have a much better chance of getting past the media "gate-keepers" than others.

Frequently, news subsidizers succeed in giving a problem – and their particular approach to a problem – an air of "expert" or scientific author-ity on the basis of very limited data. Media critic Peter Schrag (1976) relates the strange story of how the "CBS Evening News" began calling child abuse a "social problem of epidemic proportions." As CBS reporter Steve Young related on December 1, 1975, "Authorities say as many as 3,000 children were killed by their own parents last year in America, and that 15,000 were brain damaged for life." The report had the aura of hard, scientific data based on what CBS called the "first national study" on child abuse. But when Douglas Besharov, the official source of the figures and then head of the National Center for Child Abuse and Ne-glect, was later questioned, he could not substantiate the figures, for no such national study had yet taken place. Schrag charges that Besharov "pulled the figures out of a hat" in an effort to build public support for the Child Protective Services Act, which Schrag in turn calls "the most extensive invasion of personal and family privacy ever proposed in this country" (Schrag, 1976, p. 22).

Another example of a news-subsidized story on child abuse occurred on "60 Minutes," with the story "Mommy, Why Me?" As Mike Wallace acknowledged, the report was "triggered by a letter from Parents Anony-mous, at a time when the organization was having financial difficulties. The raft of mail and telegrams that followed the program helped the organization to secure funds and continue its work" (O'Brien et al., 1980, p. 233). Although Parents Anonymous offers one valid, important ap-proach to child abuse, its primary selling point to "60 Minutes" seems to have been that it could package and deliver a group of parents willing to confess and describe their abuse of their children in vivid detail.

Unfortunately, as Schrag (1976) observes, child and family news cover-age often may be particularly vulnerable to domination by individuals and organizations who push untested approaches to problems. The media may have "learned enough about government propaganda to find someone to question White House or Pentagon pronouncements about Russian missile strengths," he notes, "but somehow assertions from DHEW or from any of scores of private organizations about child abuse . . . are legitimized as fact by nothing more than their pious veneer of good intentions" (Schrag, 1976, p. 22). The fact that a news subsidizer claims to represent children seems to automatically make him a reliable source. To turn around W. C. Fields's adage, the assumption is that anybody who loves children can't be all bad.

Thus, a press release related to children may be more likely to escape the critical eye of media "gatekeepers," such as editors and producers. These gatekeepers ordinarily perform a crucial link in the agenda-setting process. They not only have the power to publish or broadcast, but also to edit or doublecheck a story, or to qualify or balance it with an opposing perspective. But when it comes to stories about children and families, media gatekeepers may feel that they are "soft news," and therefore not worth doublechecking. Editors may accept stories about children and families uncritically because they do not perceive these stories as serious or potentially controversial.

At the same time that a press release related to children is less likely to be questioned by media gatekeepers, it is also less likely to get past them at all. Gatekeepers are influenced by many factors, such as the availability of broadcast time or newspaper space, the time of day when a news event occurred or a story was filed, and their implicit trust in the reporter – or wire service – that supplied the story (Einsiedel & Fielder, 1980). But the most crucial factor to gatekeepers is the perceived importance of an issue, not only for media personnel, but also for the audience the media are trying to reach. It is this last factor that poses the major stumbling block for stories about child and family policy – or for any social policy, for that matter. Editors and producers, who are in turn influenced by advertisers and audience or subscriber ratings, perceive that coverage of child and family policy does not rank high with adult viewers or subscribers. As an associate editor for a major family magazine explains, advertising departments frequently remind editorial departments that mothers are more than mothers, that they are interested in makeup and beauty, too. However, advertisers do not encourage magazines to offer more coverage of social policy because they do not think articles on social policy sell magazines.

The power of advertisers and the purchasing public in limiting the news agenda offers one explanation for the decline in news coverage generally of social issues such as poverty, poor housing, and inadequate health care. Joyce Lynn (1980) points out that 10 or 15 years ago nearly every daily newspaper had a civil rights or antipoverty beat, and stories about Great Society programs rated front-page coverage. But by the end of the Carter administration, she noted: "No top national newspaper or television network covers social services as a beat, and stories about social services are relegated to the local sections of the nation's newspapers, if they are covered at all" (Lynn, 1980, p. 33). In part, social service news probably declined simply because, for a time at least, there were "no events in the streets or new programs, or because the country is bored with the issue" (Lynn, 1980, p. 33). But there are other factors that lead publishers to ignore the problems of lower-income citizens. "Advertisers are not much interested in the part of a newspaper's circulation that is lower income," Lynn asserts, and she reports that Otis Chandler, publisher of the *Los Angeles Times,* believes "it would not make sense 'financially' for the *Times* to direct the newspaper to low-income readers because [according to Chandler] 'that audience does not have the purchasing power and is not responsive to the kind of advertising we carry' " (Lynn, 1980, p. 34). Thus, news subsidizers, advertisers, and media gatekeepers all play a role in determining the media's agenda.

Obstacles to media coverage of social problems

The chief obstacle to fair, thorough, and persistent coverage of social issues by the media is the conflict between the goals of education and entertainment. This conflict can in turn be traced partly to the commercial ownership of the mass media, particularly television, in the United States. Unlike other Western nations (e.g., Britain, West Germany, and Canada), the United States from the outset allowed television to develop as a commercial venture. In a medium designed primarily to attract the largest audience in order to maintain ratings and thus advertiser revenues, education was bound to take second place to entertainment.

Yet the commercial nature of television and the major print media in the United States is not the only barrier to fair, thorough coverage of social issues. There are other obstacles that are endemic to the basic dilemmas of public education in any society. It is no simple matter to educate a broad spectrum of people, even on crucial issues. The Public Broadcasting System, despite its impressive efforts at public affairs reporting, has trouble reaching more than a small percentage of the television audience in prime time (Shorenstein, 1981). Even in societies where there is no competing commercial network, such as the Soviet Union, there is the problem of losing the audience to boredom or weariness with public affairs pronouncements. Thus, in every society the mass media must frequently sacrifice some educational goals for the sake of entertainment.

News as entertainment

In order to maximize dramatic impact, the mass media in the United States cover action and events. Yet, as columnist George Will points out, much that should be factored into public policy decisions does not fall under the category of "event," and as a result does not get media coverage (Daly, 1979).

For example, the daily struggles of the poor simply don't attract an audience of a profitable size. In Bernard Rubin's study *Media, Politics, and Democracy* (1977), Boston reporter Alan Lupo recounts a story of a woman in a South Boston housing project who called some reporters and said, "We've had it, we want to explain to you people what it is we're objecting to down here, why this project is so awful, and we'd like to get something done about it" (Rubin, 1977, p. 13). According to Lupo's account, two television crews arrived and unpacked their equipment. But suddenly over their portable radios they heard a "fire–fire" announcement, and they packed up and raced off to cover the fire. Even though the woman tried to tell the reporters that the fire was in an abandoned building, they apparently thought the fire merited more coverage than what she had to say about the injustices of life in an overcrowded housing project. As Harrington explains, "The media want dramatic events, not wearying and wearing social conditions which are going to look pretty much the same tomorrow as they did yesterday" (1975, p. 8).

Even when the media do cover the dramatic consequences of social problems, the coverage is most often superficial and does not elucidate the complexities of the problems. As Rubin states (1977, p. 12), "Terrorists strike, but the moral and political arguments raised against their rampages are ignored or played down; . . . a school busing crisis in a large city goes on and on . . . and little cogent information is provided as to why the situation is out of control." Similarly, a fire in an Atlanta day-care center prompts national television coverage and front-page placement in major newspapers. Meanwhile, the Senate's defeat of federal standards to help protect children enrolled in federally supported centers gets relegated to a few inches in the back of the *New York Times*.

Although it is tempting to attribute the superficiality of media coverage to corporate journalism's indifference to children and families, the honest critic must acknowledge the difficulty in dramatizing the underlying social policy issues. A fire in a day-care center simply makes more exciting television than a Senate vote on day-care standards. Similarly, readers of popular magazines may be acutely interested in how to prevent an unwanted pregnancy or what to tell their own teenagers about sex. But the same readers are apt to turn the page on an abstract discussion of the nation's teenage pregnancy problem and the policy options for reducing it.

The trick to attracting media coverage for social policy, therefore, is to find ways to dramatize it. One media technique is to seduce the reader or viewer into a policy discussion by offering a portrait of one victim of the social problem to be discussed. Newspaper and magazine writers often begin a social policy article with personal anecdotes or weave them in and out of statistics and comments by policy analysts. Television programs like the "Donahue" show also attempt to personalize social problems. For example, in a recent program on suicide among gifted teenagers, the "Donahue" show found parents willing to tell their own stories of what led to their children's deaths (Singer, 1981). Clearly, the audience is much more likely to identify with a father expressing his anguish than with a social scientist citing statistics on teenage suicide. Nevertheless, media attempts to personalize social problems also run the risk of misleading the audience. As James Gallagher, director of the Bush Institute for Child and Family Policy at the University of North Carolina pointed out at a Bush-sponsored media workshop on April 10, 1981, how *typical* of the social problem is the person the media chooses to represent the problem?

Another media approach to dramatizing social policy, framing policy issues in confrontational style, is best illustrated by CBS's "60 Minutes." This weekly program successfully bridges the gap between education and entertainment. The program not only conducts courageous public affairs reporting, but also ranks consistently in the top 10 in the ratings and generates more viewer mail than any other program on the air. Nevertheless, "60 Minutes" also illustrates the potential conflicts posed by its "dual aspirations . . . to produce reports that both meet the highest journalistic standards and work as drama" (H. Stein, 1979, p. 76). "Sixty Minutes" is frequently accused of staging confrontations just for the sake of entertainment and of sacrificing ambiguity and fairness to the demands of "docudrama."

The media tendency to sell solutions almost like products

Even when the media do present a social problem in some depth, the demands of news as entertainment often lead both the broadcast and print media to focus on simplistic, even spurious, solutions to those problems. The popular press may not deliberately intend, for example, to push kidney machines as the solution to kidney disease or "patterning" as a solution to mental retardation. But these sorts of solutions have the merit of being easy to depict and to dramatize.

The media seem particularly vulnerable to selling policy proposals that are the easiest to package or that most closely resemble products. Thus, in coverage of health problems, the press, eager for dramatic medical discoveries, often inadvertently push public expenditures for expensive medical technologies such as artificial kidney machines and neonatal intensive-care nurseries. Although each of these technological advances has merits, the media, in their fascination with "high tech," too often fail to stimulate real public understanding of the policy tradeoffs involved. That is, which policy is likely to prevent more infant deaths and birth defects and at less public expense – the expansion of neonatal intensive-care nurseries or the expansion of routine prenatal care to low-income pregnant women? Health policy analysts credit maternal and child health programs, not medical technology, for most of the dramatic (40%) reduction in infant mortality in the United States since 1965 (Select Panel for the Promotion of Child Health, 1980). But the media rarely balance their dramatic pictures of premature babies in neonatal-care nurseries with evidence that many premature births could be prevented by routine prenatal care.[1]

In some cases, the popular press help to promote "solutions" that would otherwise never survive the process of scientific peer review. In a particularly disturbing example of media promotion of an unproven treatment, the press has continued to push a rigorous program called "patterning" for helping brain-damaged children. Publications as diverse as *Midnight* ("Seventy people needed," 1976) and the *New York Times* (Campbell, 1976) and television programs such as "That's Incredible" (November 29, 1982) relate the same scenario: A child declared "hopeless" by physicians is helped through a demanding treatment that requires great efforts of the family and 60 to 70 volunteers per week to work with the child in small groups for hours every day, 365 days a year. Yet "few of these articles even allude to the fact that a controversy over the value of patterning has raged in scientific journals for twenty years," report Zigler and Weintraub (1979). In truth, not only is there no scientific evidence that patterning works, but there is some indication that patterning leads to "wasted effort and money, shattered marriages, and guilt-ridden parents strained to the breaking point" (Zigler & Weintraub, 1979, p. 7).

Why, in the absence of scientific support for patterning, does the press continue to promote this treatment? The answer lies in the dramatic appeal and the visual impact of patterning. In the first issue of the new *Life* magazine, a photo story appeared entitled "Hands of Hope for a New Life" (Lanker & Frook, 1978). The first photograph shows the agonized expression on a brain-damaged child's face; the next shows the hands of six adult volunteers placed on the boy's small body, trying to stimulate the crawling motions he can't make himself. In the face of this child desperately in need of help, it would seem callous to shatter parents' hopes by countering with cool, scientific data that no miracle cure exists. In the face of the volunteers' courageous efforts, it would seem anticlimactic to suggest that more traditional methods – such as a regular visit from a foster grandparent or homemaker – would be as helpful.

Perhaps worst of all, the media coverage of "patterning" illustrates the failure of the press to take any responsibility for monitoring the validity of the "solutions" it promotes. It is curious that press accounts nearly always focus on families just beginning the "patterning" treatment. "We know of no accounts relating the experiences several years after completing the treatment," note Zigler and Weintraub (1979, p. 7). Thus, whereas other proposed supportive policies such as expanded access to homemaker services or respite care can offer immediate and enduring support to the family of the brain-damaged child, it is the drama of a miracle treatment, which places an extraordinary burden on the family, that attracts media coverage.

Ultimate irony: "action" news promoting boredom

Perhaps the ultimate irony is that, despite efforts to dramatize the news, public apathy toward all public affairs reporting may be increasing. *New Yorker* television critic Michael Arlen states the problem succinctly: "If Hitler's troops were reoccupying the Rhineland now," he imagines, "we would be hearing a good deal more about it than people did in 1936, and worrying about it less" (Arlen, 1977, p. 119). Unless news is perceived as having a direct personal or immediate significance, reasons Bernard Rubin, "most people accept information in the same manner as they accept the sounds of the music they like" (Rubin, 1977, p. 11). Or, in the words of George Will, news is becoming like advertising – "the background noise of American life" (Daly, 1979, p. 19).

Although such observations may seem to contradict the agenda-setting theory, they do not: They merely illustrate how complicated agenda setting has become. Mere exposure through the media to human suffering no longer necessarily raises public consciousness of that suffering, because overexposure to the violent and the desperate dulls the senses, building its own wall of indifference. Even though the public may view the world in general as more violent than it is, a distancing phenomenon may also take place, in which readers or viewers tend to protect themselves by thinking, "But that person is not like me, so that calamity cannot befall me." Thus, the challenge for those who want to increase public support for action to address social problems is to portray the similarities between the audience and the people whose problems are receiving media attention. For it is only through identification between viewer and victim that a social problem is likely to be added to an individual's personal agenda.

Strategy for improving media coverage of social issues

Discussions of how to improve media coverage often focus on the need for structural reforms. Recommendations range from measures to avert the trend toward the increasing consolidation of newspaper and other media ownership, to requirements that commercial television exempt public affairs reporting from the tyranny of ratings, to suggestions for how to protect public broadcasting in the United States from government interference and corporate dependence. Although each of these structural reforms and the problems they address deserves serious consideration, they are beyond the scope of this chapter. Moreover, as we have tried to emphasize, one of the primary obstacles to fair, thorough coverage of social issues is the conflict between education and entertainment, a conflict that seems to afflict the mass media regardless of the ownership or economic structure.

This discussion will therefore focus on less ambitious measures that do not depend on immediate changes in the commercial structure of the media. Our major proposals will be aimed at policy analysts or advocates who want greater access to media coverage and at journalists trying to overcome the current obstacles to sound reporting of social issues affecting children and families.

Strategy for improved access to media coverage

Choose the right audience and medium. As suggested earlier in the section on how a social issue gets on the media agenda, policy analysts and advocates need not always aim first for coverage in the largest-circulation media aimed at the largest audience. As Brian Lamb, former director of Congressional and Media Relations of the White House Office of Telecommunications Policy, says, "Television is all-powerful when it comes to influencing the masses. The printed word is all-powerful when it comes to influencing the people who are influencing the masses" (Benson, 1977, p. 12).

Before constructing a media campaign, advocates should first determine the nature of the audience they are trying to reach. Advocates should consider whether the message to be conveyed is best directed at a mass audience or at various specialized subaudiences who have the power to effect desired change. The genius of direct-mail advertising is simply an appreciation for the power of the right message aimed at the right subaudience. As Whiting (1976, p. 207) states, "the most creative and ingenious message sent to the wrong audience – the audience whose behavior and actions will not effect the crucial change – will be futile." Too often, Whiting adds, in an effort to save time and money, advocates omit the necessary inquiry into the nature of the audience and simply assume "the audience to be just like the individuals who are constructing the message" (Whiting, 1976, p. 205).

Aim for consonance with audience. Closely related to the importance of choosing the right medium to reach the right audience is the need to aim for consonance with the audience. Advocates must choose their issues carefully and present them in a manner that is consonant, or in harmony, with the basic values of the audience they want to reach. Direct assault on audience values rarely works. As Whiting states, even "a flood of cigarette advertising fails to dent the resistance of a devout Mormon or Seventh Day Adventist" (1976, p. 209).

In part, aiming for consonance entails a good sense of timing. If Harrington's *The Other America* had been released during the recession of the 1980s rather than during the relatively affluent 1960s, the book may not have had the effect that it did. Perhaps no amount of publicity about the fate of the nation's poor could have overcome the popular sentiment that the middle classes could no longer afford to support the alarming numbers of poor and unemployed and that compensatory programs would be mere "Band-Aids" applied to an increasingly debilitated economy. Similarly, it is unlikely that any media campaign could succeed in making the central message of the Carnegie Council on Children – that income redistribution is the only real solution to the problems facing America's families – attractive to Middle America. Aware that this message was apt to hit a discordant note, particularly in a period of inflation and general economic retrenchment, the council's media strategists tried to downplay the call for income redistribution and to emphasize other council recommendations instead (Keniston et al., 1980).

This is not to suggest that advocates should abandon all attempts to convey an unpopular message. But the principle of consonance does indicate that an untimely or disconsonant message must be framed in a non–

self-righteous manner that does not immediately repel the intended audience or put them on the defensive. Whiting argues that the best strategy may be to find a way to couch an unpopular message in values the audience currently holds: "Information about a previously rejected course of action which is couched in terms of the criteria for approval held by the individual," he writes, "may lead to re-evaluation of the course of action" (Whiting, 1976, p. 210). For example, media strategists often try to present recommendations for income redistribution as a way of avoiding "interventionist" federally supported social services, and proposals to help the poor are sometimes offered as a way to combat crime in the streets.

Not only must advocates frame their issues carefully, but they must learn to find spokespersons who can communicate with mass-media professionals. Reflecting on why conservationists long had a problem garnering widespread public support, Schoenfeld et al. (1979, p. 52) point out that the early advocates were too elitist; they simply did not speak the same language as the editor-reporters they were trying to influence. Child advocates frequently confront a similar barrier. How often we hear well-intentioned child and family policy analysts call for "early intervention." This term may be clear and acceptable to developmental psychologists, but it is likely to offend the ear of many Americans who are apt to equate "intervention" with federal interference in family life (Muenchow, 1981).

Perhaps no contemporary group has demonstrated more sophisticated awareness of the importance of consonance than the New Right. In advice to conservatives prior to the 1978 election, media strategist Brien Benson recommended the use of words and phrases currently popular with the media. "If you want to attack IRS intrusion into a local business," he counsels, "talk about threats to 'privacy,' not to free enterprise" (1977, p. 10). Benson also advises conservatives to "be sure your press releases emphasize what is newsworthy, not the conservative message you want to sell" (p. 10). Finally, he suggests how conservatives can dress up an old policy to appear innovative: "If you want the school board to replace 'social adjustment' courses with reading, writing and arithmetic, release a *recent* study showing that our *modern* economy requires a *new* emphasis on verbal and mathematical skills. Don't say, 'We ought to return to the three R's' " (p. 10).

Cultivate reporters outside the regular family and education "beat." As noted earlier in the section on agenda setting, too often news coverage of child and family issues is relegated to the "soft news" category. The success of the Carnegie Council on Children in attracting major news coverage, as opposed to "kiddy" or "family" page treatment, stems largely from its efforts to reach beyond the correspondents who normally cover children to those responsible for unemployment, welfare reform, and other front-page economic issues (Keniston et al., 1980, p. 29). The council not only compiled a nationwide press list, but also made personal contact with key reporters in a small number of major daily and national outlets, such as the wire services, the *New York Times,* and the *Washington Post.*

Similar advice applies to advocates working at the local level. Personal contact with reporters and knowledge of the way the media operates are indispensable. "Learn and exploit the peculiarities of your local paper or broadcast station: its deadlines, its slow news days, who are its decision makers, which of its reporters can be cultivated with background tips," advises Benson (1977, p. 10).

Focus on specific issues of immediate significance to audience. The most effective media campaigns seem to be those that focus upon changing specific rather than diffuse attitudes. More than other child advocacy organizations, the Children's Defense Fund (CDF) seems to understand this principle. In an attempt to set up a Children's Policy Network in each state, CDF has found that addressing child and family policy as a broad area does not succeed; instead, CDF focuses on a single issue such as child health or foster care. Similarly, whereas many advocacy groups saw the International Year of the Child as an opportunity to release a laundry list of every reform ever considered to benefit children, CDF focused major attention on one issue – foster care. CDF's report *Children without Homes* (1978) received extensive press coverage. This coverage can in turn be at least partially attributed to CDF's press release: Rather than dwelling on the statistics of the nation's foster-care problem, it focused on the lives of several particular children who through no fault of their own or of their parents had no place to call home. According to Pamela Decker (1981), publications coordinator for CDF, the impact of the report was dramatic, generating tens of thousands of requests for CDF literature – more than CDF ever before received.

Frame issues in media events. Media strategists also advise advocates to learn to frame their issues in media events. New Right strategist Bill Rhatican cites a prime example of this "framing theory" that he helped orchestrate in 1977. Before the National Organization of Women's conference in Houston that year, Rhatican advised conservative profamily leader Phyllis Schlafly to arrive early to hold a press brunch the day before the conference opened. "As it turned out, in the press and on the networks, Phyllis fought the Bella Abzug crowd to a draw in national coverage" (Fowler, 1980, p. 18). Had Schlafly not arrived early, Rhatican reasons, she would have enjoyed only scant media coverage.

Strategy for journalists to improve coverage of social issues

Throughout the preceding section on strategy, it should be apparent that the line between the legitimate techniques of mass communication and the devices of propaganda is thin indeed. As the Institute for Propaganda Analysis observed during World War II, media campaigns thrive on "the glittering generality, or the association of an idea with a virtue word"; on testimonies from respected persons, and on card stacking, "or the arranging of facts or falsehoods . . . in order to present the best (or the worst) possible case for an idea, program, person or product" (J. Stein, 1979, p. 77). As Stein observes, mass media campaigns are as likely to serve the Devil as the Lord.

Thus, whereas media campaigns have their place, the best hope for transcending propaganda does not lie in media campaigns of any kind. The proper role of the media in social policy is not to serve as propagandist, whether intentional or inadvertent, for special interest groups. Rather the media, at their best, serve as active truthseekers, helping to hold policy and politicians accountable.

Eric Sevareid argues that the nation needs more serious reporting of "accountability." That is, did the War on Poverty change things, he asks, and "did the Peace Corps have anything to do with the rise of the per capita income or the growth of democracy in a country?" (in Daly, 1979, p. 8). This is the type of question the press has insufficiently investigated, and the answers could be controversial and dramatic. Similarly, one of the most important tasks of the media during the Reagan administration may be to keep track of whether the cutbacks in the social programs achieve the administration's expressed aim, namely a reduction in tax dollars. For example, will reductions in maternal and child health programs save the taxpayers' money, or will they lead to increased birth defects and tax expenditures for special education and institutionalized care? Will cutbacks in welfare aid save tax dollars, or will they eventually lead to the disintegration of vulnerable families, thereby increasing public expenditures for foster care? By holding public policy accountable, the media not only rise above propaganda, but also help penetrate it.

How can the media better serve the function of active truthseeking and of holding public policy accountable? In part, the answer lies in better training for journalists in the tools of systematic research. Already schools of journalism are placing more emphasis on social science methods in news reporting. But employed journalists could also benefit from time out in the form of internships, or even workshops, such as those sponsored by the Bureau of the Census and the News Research Center of the American Newspaper Publishers' Association (Weaver & McCombs, 1980). In addition to training in how to read and report social science findings, journalists could benefit from a social scientist's perspective on what constitutes a good example of a media-sponsored poll as contrasted with what constitutes a bad one. Since "social science in a hurry" serves a useful purpose, perhaps it is time to stop denigrating it and to start a dialog among journalists and social scientists about its possibilities as well as its limitations.

Training for journalists in social science research methods, however, does not fully address the issue of how to dramatize social policy without compromising accuracy or content. Sheri Singer (1981), producer for the "Donahue" show, explains her dilemma in trying to put complex social policy issues on television. Although she tries to balance policy issues with dramatic appeal, she tends to seize the stories that are easiest to tell and to highlight the people with whom the audience is most apt to identify. Singer acknowledges that social scientists might prefer that the show only air "experts," or that it present issues more thoroughly, with supporting research and qualifications. But, argues Singer succinctly, if no one is going to listen, there is not much point in putting a program on the air.

As stated near the outset of this chapter, the chief obstacle to fair, thorough coverage of social policy issues is the conflict between the media goals of education and entertainment. The authors suggested some strategies for reducing or circumventing this conflict, but the conflict remains. On the one hand, it is clear that those who disdain audience preference for entertainment are apt to lose the audience and, with it, the opportunity to inform. On the other hand, always allowing entertainment to take precedence over education in media coverage reflects the ultimate disdain for the audience.

Note

1 In an excellent exception to this critique, see Conrad (1981).

References

Arlen, M. J. The air: "The news." *New Yorker,* October 31, 1977, pp. 119–127.

Baran, S. J. TV programming and attitudes toward mental retardation. *Journalism Quarterly,* 1977, *54,* 140–142.

Benson, B. How to fight bias in the news. *Conservative Digest,* 1977, *3*(9), 10–13.

Campbell, B. Sixty volunteers a week aid retarded boy. *New York Times,* April 26, 1976, p. 1.

Carson, R. L. *Silent spring.* Boston: Houghton Mifflin, 1962.

Children's Defense Fund. *Children without homes: An examination of public responsibility to children in out-of-home care.* Washington, D.C., 1978.

Cohen, B. C. *The press, the public, and foreign policy.* Princeton, N.J.: Princeton University Press, 1963.

Conrad, D. Some premature births are preventable. *New Haven Register,* April 10, 1981, pp. 37–39.

Daly, J. C. (Moderator). *The press and public policy.* Washington, D.C.: American Enterprise Institute for Public Policy Research, 1979.

Decker, P. Personal communication, April 9, 1981.

Einsiedel, E. F., & Fielder, V. D. Newspaper treatment of a controversial series: A case study of "Johnny Still Can't Read." *Newspaper Research Journal,* 1980, *1*(4), 30–37.

Fowler, G. Bill Rhatican: Super salesman for the New Right. *Conservative Digest,* 1980, *6*(1), 18–19.

Gandy, O. H. Information in health: Subsidized news. *Media, Culture, and Society,* 1980, *2,* 103–115.

Gerbner, G. Children and power on television: The other side of the picture. In G. Gerbner, C. J. Ross, & E. Zigler (Eds.), *Child abuse: An agenda for action.* New York: Oxford University Press, 1980.

Goldberg, M. A. "Roots: The next generation": A study of attitude and behavior. *Television Quarterly,* 1979, *16*(3), 71–74.

Harrington, M. *The other America: Poverty in the United States.* New York: Macmillan, 1962.

Harrington, M. Meanwhile in the other America. *MORE,* 1975, *5*(11), 6–8.

Henderson, H. *Creating alternative futures: The end of economics.* New York: Berkley, 1978.

Hur, K. K., & Robinson, J. P. The social impact of "Roots." *Journalism Quarterly,* 1978, *55,* 19–24, 83.

Johnson, T. A. "Roots" has widespread and inspiring influence. *New York Times,* March 19, 1977, p. 46.

Kampelman, M. M. The media: Out of control? *Conservative Digest,* 1978, *4*(12), 14.

Keniston, K., Towers, C. R., Almond, P., Cory, C. T., Diamond, A., & Kneerim, J. *Final report of the dissemination unit, Carnegie Council on Children, to the Carnegie Corporation of New York.* Unpublished manuscript, September 22, 1980.

Kilpatrick, J. J. *Congressional record* (daily ed.). Washington, D.C.: U.S. Government Printing Office, December 2, 1971, p. E12897.

Lanker, B., & Frook, J. Hands of hope for a new life. *Life,* October 1978, pp. 42–50.

Lazarsfeld, P., Berelson, B., & Gaudet, H. *The people's choice.* New York: Columbia University Press, 1948.

Lewis, O. *La vida: A Puerto Rican family in the culture of poverty.* New York: Vintage, 1966.

Lynn, J. Filed and forgotten: Why the press has taken up new issues. *Washington Journalism Review*, 1980, *2*, 32–37.

McCombs, M., & Masel-Walters, L. Agenda setting: A new perspective on mass communication. *Mass Communication Review*, 1976, *3*(2), 3–7.

McCombs, M., & Shaw, D. The agenda-setting function of mass media. *Public Opinion Quarterly*, 1972, *36*, 176–187.

McLeod, J. M., Becker, L. B., & Byrnes, J. E. Another look at the agenda-setting function of the press. *Communication Research*, 1974, *1*(2), 131–166.

Muenchow, S. How the pro-family movement and child advocates use the media: Ethics, strategy, and effectiveness. In S. Muenchow & M. L. McFarland (Eds.), *What is profamily policy? Proceedings of the Bush interest group/symposium, May 18, 1981,* New Haven, Conn. Yale Bush Center in Child Development and Social Policy, 1981.

O'Brien, D. H., Schneider, A. R., & Traviesas, H. Portraying abuse: Network censors' round table. In G. Gerbner, C. J. Ross, & E. Zigler (Eds.), *Child abuse: An agenda for action.* New York: Oxford University Press, 1980.

The pro-family movement. *Conservative Digest*, 1980, *6*(5/6), 14–30.

Rubin, B. *Media, politics, and democracy.* New York: Oxford University Press, 1977.

Schoenfeld, A. C., Meier, R. F., & Griffin, R. J. Constructing a social problem: The press and the environment. *Social Problems*, 1979, *27*(1), 38–61.

Schrag, P. The epidemic that never was. *MORE*, 1976, *6*(2), 22, 24.

Select Panel for the Promotion of Child Health. *Better health for our children: A national strategy.* Washington, D.C., 1980.

Seventy people needed to help 3-year-old become normal. *Midnight*, September 13, 1976, p. 6.

Shaw, E. F. Agenda-setting and mass communication theory. *Gazette*, 1979, *25*, 96–105.

Shorenstein, S. A. Does public television have a future? *Wilson Quarterly*, 1981, *5*(1), 66–75.

Silberman, C. E. *Crisis in black and white.* New York: Random House, 1964.

Singer, S. Decision-making in topic selection and treatment on the "Donahue" show. Presentation at the Bush Media Workshop on Children and Families, Quail Roost Conference Center, N. Car., April 10, 1981.

Stein, H. How "60 Minutes" makes news. *New York Times Magazine*, May 6, 1979, pp. 28–30, 75–90.

Stein, J. W. *Mass media, education, and a better society.* Chicago: Nelson-Hall, 1979.

Viguerie, R. The new right: We're ready to lead. *Conservative Digest*, 1980, *6*(10), 3–17.

Weaver, D. H., & McCombs, M. F. Journalism and social science: A new relationship? *Public Opinion Quarterly*, 1980, *44*, 477–494.

Whiting, G. C. How does communication interface with change? *Communication Research*, 1976, *3*(2), 191–212.

Zigler, E., & Finn, M. From problem to solution: Changing public policy as it affects children and families. *Young Children*, 1981, *36*(4), 31.

Zigler, E., & Weintraub, E. "Patterning" is unproven hope for brain-damaged children. *New Haven Register*, January 5, 1979, p. 7.

Part V

From problem to policy

14   Child daycare policy in chaos

Gwen Morgan

The American system of child daycare is largely composed of separate and competing programs, each vying for scarce resources. In addition, there is disagreement among funding sources on child daycare's central mission, reflected by a lack of universally accepted overarching goals and even by a lack of agreement on whether or not there is an unmet need for day childcare. This chapter looks at the various domains that are concerned with different child daycare programs, analyzes supply and demand in the child daycare market to determine just where child daycare policy should focus, and then proposes several ways in which child daycare policy can be designed to support the family, given today's economy. The author argues that through the addition of a few new elements to the present purchase-of-service delivery system, the chaos now overwhelming child daycare policy can be overcome.

Child daycare and its competing constituencies: problems with the "program approach" of the 1960s

The reasons for policy chaos in the field of child daycare are related to the struggle to understand "daycare" from overlapping perspectives, representing various domains of interest. These domains of interest belong to members of the child growth and development field, advocates for the poor, advocates for equality for ethnic minorities, family specialists, child welfare specialists, labor policy experts, feminists, and welfare reform proponents. Because of professional and academic specialization, and because each domain relates to different agencies and offices in the government bureaucracy, the child daycare industry has been constrained, first, by an inability to communicate across conceptual frameworks, and second, by competition and turf guarding.

Instead of conceptualizing overall policy for child daycare, the emphasis on developing individual programs during the 1960s and 1970s led to a fragmented and inconsistent system. This "program approach" involved the establishment of several new projects aimed at helping children and families. Each individual program was conceived as "the solution" to "the problem," instead of being designed as one link in a diverse – yet comprehensive and coordinated – master plan, building on the strengths of what already existed. The programs included Head Start, preschools under Title I of the Elementary and Secondary Education Act, and Title XX daycare funded by the Social Security Act, among others. Each program was housed in a different government agency, oriented to a different profession, and funded independently; each program defined its own goals and approaches; and each program developed its own bureaucracy and constituency at the federal, state, and service delivery levels. There was no master policy for children and families that could coordinate theory and practice among these funding sources. Table 14.1 gives a very simplified representation of the different domains of interest and displays differences in the basic missions associated with each group.

The existing system of scattered programs has created a number of actors on the local scene committed to their valid missions, protecting their ever-threatened turf, and competing for scarce resources. Mechanisms for unifying the child daycare pieces of this system into a cost-effective and accessible community service have been given little emphasis. This fragmented service system includes staff, parents, the bureaucracies that administer it at the federal, state, and local levels, and the experts who see child daycare from very different perspectives. These comprise the cast of characters among whom consensus must be reached before child daycare policy action can be taken. It is small wonder that so little successful policy has been made in this complex cross-disciplinary field.

The economics of child daycare: supply and demand

Child daycare defined

Child daycare can serve many purposes. The term is variously used to mean the following: all the ways that children are cared for, including care by their parents; all the ways that children are cared for except for parent and sibling care and the hours in school; or the ways children are cared for only by centers, family day care, and babysitters, to the exclusion of schools and part-day Head Start and nursery–preschool programs.[1] In this discussion, the term *child daycare* is used to cover all the ways children are cared for when they are not being cared for by a nonemployed

Table 14.1. Child daycare programs and their missions

Social service	Employment	Child development
Subgoals: To help families care for their own children whenever possible, and to assure children the right to a permanent family in reasonable time	*Subgoals:* To assure the availability of an adequate supply of quality child daycare to enable the self-sufficiency and productivity of families, at a price parents can afford	*Subgoals:* To assure children a positive group experience for learning and social development when needed, for any reason
Programs: Treatment programs for child abuse and neglect Emergency shelter care Subsidized adoption; income maintenance of various types Preventive programs; family life education	*Programs:* Child daycare programs for working families, public and private Sliding-fee policy for subsidy Tax credit Employer initiatives: flextime; shared jobs; help with subsidy and/or information CETA; WIN; Welfare reform	*Programs:* Nursery–kindergarten programs Head Start for the poor Special education; respite care Title I ESEA programs Parent–child centers; family support centers in Head Start and in schools
Domains of Interest: Family specialists Child welfare specialists	*Domains of Interest:* Advocates for the poor Advocates for equality for minority groups Labor policy experts Feminists Welfare reformers	*Domains of Interest:* Child developmentalists Advocates for the poor Health and mental health specialists

parent or during regular school classes. Care for a child may not be the primary purpose of a particular program, but if the child is in that program, he or she is not available to fill a space in a full-day center or family daycare home. In order to define supply and demand for child daycare, it is important to know all the places where the children are.

Child daycare can be provided within the resources of the family or the family can search for and choose an arrangement outside the family. Types of nonmarket child daycare within the resources of the family include a "latchkey" child who is given keys to his or her home and allowed to remain there for unsupervised periods of time; a parent caring for a child while working; parents staggering work hours to provide tandem care; an older sibling caring for a child; a relative caring for a child, in the child or relative's home; and a close friend caring for a child. Types of child daycare outside the family (the child daycare market) include care in the child's home by a babysitter, housekeeper, au pair person, and so on; family daycare (usually up to 6 children in the caregiver's home); group homes (usually 6 to 12 children); mixed care, combining nursery school or Head Start with either in-home or family daycare; full-day center; and school-age programs, combined with public or private school.

Table 14.2 charts the results of four noncomparable surveys that examined the types of care that children of working mothers were actually in. It is interesting to note the trends over time to more care in relatives' and caregivers' homes and decreasing percentages of children being cared for in their own homes.

Arrangements that can be made within the family are outside the market of child daycare as it is conceived in this chapter. They are beyond policy in some ways, since the government does not regulate families and cannot provide relatives to families that do not have them. However, families often choose care within their own family when they can get it, in part because the care is generally free, but also in part because families prefer it (Rodes & Moore, 1976). Relatives may have the same irrational commitment and love for the child that parents have; they may have the same culture and values the parents want transmitted to the child. Interestingly, parents who prefer relative care often report making this choice for "child development" reasons (Moore, 1980).

Since the mid-1960s, the rate of care by relatives in their own homes and the children's homes has held fairly steady; some see this as reassuring evidence that the extended family is still alive. Hofferth (1979) predicts that with the pressures of today's economy, relatives will become less and less available, since they too will be working. This, however, has not happened and still may not.

There is evidence that relative care is becoming monetized, partly because with inflation relatives may need to be paid, at least for their expenses, and partly because government policy has begun to subsidize the reimbursement of relatives. Almost half of the children whose mothers work are cared for by relatives. Close friends also exchange child care, but these arrangements may lack stability for full-time working parents.

Of children in the child daycare market (in arrangements outside the family), only a small percentage are in child daycare centers. This percentage is misleading because the total number used in figuring this per-

Table 14.2. Types of care used according to four different surveys

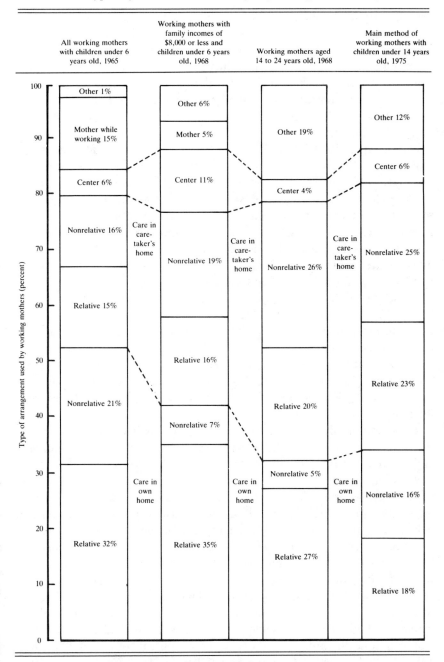

Type of arrangement used by working mothers (percent)

All working mothers with children under 6 years old, 1965
- Other 1%
- Mother while working 15%
- Center 6%
- Nonrelative 16%
- Relative 15%
- Nonrelative 21%
- Relative 32%
- (Care in own home)

Working mothers with family incomes of $8,000 or less and children under 6 years old, 1968
- Other 6%
- Mother 5%
- Center 11%
- Care in caretaker's home
- Nonrelative 19%
- Relative 16%
- Nonrelative 7%
- Care in own home
- Relative 35%

Working mothers aged 14 to 24 years old, 1968
- Other 19%
- Center 4%
- Care in caretaker's home
- Nonrelative 26%
- Relative 20%
- Nonrelative 5%
- Relative 27%
- Care in own home

Main method of working mothers with children under 14 years old, 1975
- Other 12%
- Center 6%
- Care in caretaker's home
- Nonrelative 25%
- Relative 23%
- Care in own home
- Nonrelative 16%
- Relative 18%

Note: The percentages do not add up to 100 because of rounding.
Sources: Levitan and Alderman (1975, p. 24) (cols. 1, 2, and 3); Low and Spindler (1968, p. 71) (col. 1); Westinghouse Learning Corporation and Westat Research (1971, pp. 177–178) (col. 2); Shea et al. (1971, p. 136) (col. 3); Rodes and Moore (1976, vol. 1, pp. 4–29) (col. 4).

centage usually includes children of all ages, even though there are few centers available for children under two-and-a-half and over age five. Most child daycare centers, nursery schools, Head Start programs, and preschools are designed for three- to five-year-olds. Of all parents with children this age, working and nonworking, 64% enroll their children in part- or full-day nursery-type programs (Kamerman & Kahn, 1979). In-school programs for four-year-olds are also increasing (Hymes, 1981). In 1965, the overall total of three-, four-, and five-year-olds in school was under 30%; in 1978 it was 50.3%. The National Center for Education Statistics predicts a 43% increase from 1979 to 1989, with a 71% rise in three-year-olds, and a 51% rise in four-year-olds in preschool programs.

More children are in family daycare than in child daycare centers. It is sometimes difficult to get accurate data on the numbers of children in family daycare, since the numbers tend to get mixed in with relatives' care. Table 14.2 suggests that as many as 25% of the children of working mothers are in family daycare or in similar programs (Levitan & Alderman, 1979, p. 24; Rodes & Moore, 1976, pp. 4–29).

These statistics on child daycare utilization reflect important changes in family life. Every day in the United States 3.5 million children under 13 go off to meet their friends in child daycare centers, nursery schools, and family daycare homes, where they will stay for more than 30 hours a week. Another 4 million children spend part of their days out of their own homes (Rodes & Moore, 1976). Finding and selecting an environment where their children will learn and grow is an important new task for families.

To determine demand for child daycare, it has been customary since the early 1960s to compile the most recent figures on working mothers and to compare the number of their children with known available child daycare arrangements. Each year the numbers of working mothers have become more dramatic. As our country entered the 1980s, it became impossible to ignore the fact that there was a massive movement of women into the workforce. The fastest rise has been among mothers of children under age three. In 1978 over 39% of mothers with children under age three were in the labor force. Of all children between ages three and five, 46% now have mothers in the workforce. The proportion of women who have school-age children and are participating in the labor force has grown at an even faster rate than the proportion of working women without school-age children. The school-age child whose mother works is now the rule, not the exception (Bureau of Labor Statistics, 1979, 1980; Hofferth, 1979; Johnson, 1980; Smith, 1979; Women's Bureau, 1977).

Most women, like most men, work because they need the money. They may also enjoy their jobs, and often strive for equity of opportunity and reward on a par with men. From a policy perspective, it does not make sense to argue whether women "should" or "should not" prefer to work outside the home when their children are small if the economy does not permit them both options. In 1977, 23% of working women were single parents, and another 25% were married women whose husbands earned less than $10,500 per year (Kamerman & Kahn, 1979). The country is dependent on their labor and the family is dependent on their earnings.

The economy in this country does not often support a two-parent, one–wage-earner family. Most families need a second source of income. The median full-time job paid $10,140 in 1977. Out of a total of 69,428,000 full-time wage and salary workers that year, 38,200,000 earned less than $15,600 (Hedges & Mellor, 1979). Most jobs will not support a family of four, and families with one wage earner holding such a job will have to work other full-time or part-time jobs in order to put food on their tables and a roof over their heads. The probability of a wife working in a two-parent family is greatest when the husband's earnings are near the top of the poverty range, but not enough to support the family (Thurow, 1975). The bulk of families in America's middle-income population has achieved their basic standard of living by dual job earnings.

Nor is this trend likely to reverse. Between 1950 and 1976, the country added 9 million new jobs. Only 3 out of 10 of these new jobs in the private sector, and two-thirds of the new government jobs, can be classified as "good" jobs in terms of wages, working conditions, fringe benefits, job security, and opportunities for advancement. Overall, 6 out of 10 of the new jobs must be classified as poor (Ginzberg, 1977). Under these economic conditions, the continued influx of mothers into the workforce is ensured. By 1990, analysts are projecting, 3 out of every 4 mothers will be working and 66.7% of all two-parent families will have both parents in the workforce (Hofferth, 1979).

Single-parent families, primarily headed by women, suffer the dual problems of shortage of time and low income because of job discrimination. Children in single-parent families are six times more likely to live below the poverty line than children of two-parent families (Masnick & Bane, 1980). Single parents are more likely for that reason to be eligible for government subsidy for child daycare. If they are among the few fortunate enough to enter a field where the jobs are higher-paying, they will probably not be eligible for any subsidy, and may not be able to get their children into publicly supported child daycare even if they pay. Thirty-eight states limited Title XX daycare subsidies to those making below 80% of the median income (Kilgore & Salmon, 1980), even before drastic cutbacks in 1981. This limitation works as a ceiling on wages that can be earned by parents in subsidized child daycare.

Families where both parents work tend to be ineligible for subsidy for child daycare because the combined incomes usually take the family beyond the state-established income eligibility limits. A handful of states have sliding fee scales that permit families to increase their child daycare payments gradually as they increase their earnings. In most states, however, subsidized programs are forced by low-family-income eligibility limits to drop or exclude families who move to higher income brackets. For this reason, government-funded programs include a heavy proportion of single-parent families, whereas two-parent working families are found in higher proportion in private, unfunded programs (Jenkins, 1974).

Problems with the child daycare market

Roughly $10 billion is spent annually by parents and the government on child daycare (Congressional Budget Office, 1978), and the amount is increasing. If the child daycare market works and parents can find and buy the child daycare they need, then there is little need for additional policy except for regulating the quality of child daycare alternatives. If there is a market failure, more policy decisions are needed.

Parent preferences for market care vary. The present system offers diversity to meet the choices parents might want to make. If parents are finding a range of options, are choosing them, and are accepting employment, some argue that there is no market failure. It seems fairly clear, however, that the child daycare market is complex and cannot be viewed as if supply and demand were separable. One important factor is the parents' ability to pay. If parents, by virtue of income, tax credit, or subsidy, can afford the service, supply will probably develop to meet the demand. Perceived problems can then be interpreted as poor distribution of supply or as a lag in time as the service takes time to start up. If parents cannot afford the cost of the service and there is no subsidy, then supply will not develop (Glantz, 1980). In that case, parents may be using a form of child daycare, such as care by siblings, that is not their preferred choice. They have dropped down to what is affordable.

Parents' ability to pay is therefore a major factor, perhaps the central factor, in child daycare supply and demand, if the purchase of services in the market system remains the major supply mechanism. There is no evidence that in the next decade free, publicly subsidized child daycare will be available except for the very poor, handicapped, or abused children. Congress passed an improved personal income tax credit in 1981 that helps a little, but is not enough to bring child daycare into the affordable range for most families. Even with the credit, few families could afford to pay as much as 20% of their total family income for the care of all their children, given the other major expenses of food, shelter, and taxes. Ten percent is a more likely share. The cost of child daycare is still beyond the means of families at the income median and far beyond the means of families at half the median, even with the credit.

The ability to pay influences whether families are in the market for child daycare, and it determines the type of care that is within their financial reach. The relationship between ability to pay and supply can be most clearly seen in the case of infant care. All sections of the country report a high demand for infant care, especially in areas of economic growth and low unemployment. Yet this type of care calls for a fairly low ratio of infants to staff, meaning that the per-child cost will be very high. With only a small segment of the population earning enough to pay these high costs, infant care is in short supply in homes as well as in centers. If rates of payment are inadequate, responsible providers will not serve subsidized children. There is a danger in urban areas of the growth of cheap underground infant-care centers that merely "warehouse" large numbers of infants without adequate staff.

There is some evidence that the existence of subsidies will not attract parents to high-quality center care if they prefer relative care (Weiner, 1978). At the same time, when parents are offered subsidy for previously unmonetized relative care, they will shift rapidly toward monetizing this preferred arrangement, which will also bring more money into the family (Weiner, 1978). The public cost of monetizing all the presently unmonetized relative care would be very great indeed. The demand for partial subsidy to help those parents that need to pay for market child daycare would be less.

Another point relevant to supply and demand of child daycare is the fact that demand will fluctuate with the economy. In growing communities with low unemployment there will likely be high child daycare demand. In times of recession and unemployment, child daycare demand will decrease, forcing centers to operate substantially below capacity. This may cause a loss of stability to the services themselves as they lose money rapidly. A stable policy would encourage a core of center care and would add to it a number of family daycare homes, since the latter are better able to start and stop without heavy cost and to shift as patterns of demand shift. Rather than the more static view of needs assessment used in the past, some ongoing source of data is needed for the assessment of fluctuating needs and resources, given the economic and geographic shifts in patterns of need and preference.

A final important characteristic of the child daycare market is its hidden subsidy by the caregivers themselves. At present, the fees and reimbursement rates are set low because of parents' limited ability to pay or because of lack of resources available to the government. The caregiving staff accepts wages that are clearly far below the value of their work. Of the 149,000 child daycare teachers in full-day centers, 60% have incomes below the poverty level. Only 8% earn above the Bureau of Labor Statistic's Lower Living Budget for a family of four (Roupp et al., 1979). Caregivers in family daycare settings also earn very little (Fosburg, 1981).

All these data indicate a partial market failure. Although many parents' preferences for relative care appear to be based on genuine satisfaction, this is not always an available option. Parents may be forced by a lack of in-family resources to use care outside the family. They may find that the care they need is not available, as is often the case with infant care; or they may find that it exists but costs more than they can afford, forcing them to choose a less stable arrangement. Finally, care may exist, but parents may not know about it. There appears to be a need for compiling data on what services exist across different systems, not only to help parents find care, but also to help decision makers plan incrementally or decrementally in response to demand. Sensitive mechanisms for stimulating new supply where demand fluctuations are being expressed are also needed.

Child daycare in the 1970s: confusion and division

The evolution of a diverse child daycare system

In 1970, facing a new decade, the White House Conference on Children included the small Task Force on Delivery of Services as part of the Day Care Forum. Chaired by Dr. Alfred Kahn, the group included representatives of the different kinds of child daycare then in existence and experts from different disciplines. The group began their work asking this basic question: Are we talking about creating a new child daycare "program" in this country, or are we talking about making policy that would build on, improve, and link up the existing network of public and private services that now provide care for children at the community level? The group resolved that there was a need to build on the existing child daycare system. From that agreement flowed decisions about other elements of the child daycare system. The results were not published, however, and advocate groups subsequently continued to pursue federal development of a new "program" for meeting the need for child daycare.

Child daycare in 1970 was in the midst of an expansion. Most states had licensing systems in place and were somewhat interested in a public child daycare subsidy for child welfare and work-related reasons. Federal Interagency Day Care Requirements (FIDCR) adopted in 1968, and the model of Head Start, had inspired new concepts of quality that emphasized parental involvement. An open-ended federal reimbursement policy for child daycare for welfare recipients or "former or potential" welfare recipients and new fund-matching potentials had made possible many creative expansions. At the local level, United Way agencies and the agencies they had funded in the past began to expand, improve, and form child daycare associations. New services were also stimulated by the anti-poverty and Model Cities programs. Technical information on innovative funding and matching arrangements spread through the federally stimulated Community Coordinated Child Care (4-C) system, as well as through other important systems in the child daycare arena: United Way, Community Action programs, Model Cities, social service agencies, and the early childhood professional groups. Child daycare did not wait for comprehensive federal legislation. Between 1970 and 1976 the number of child daycare centers serving three- to five-year-olds jumped from 14,000 to 18,300, a 30% increase (Westinghouse Learning Corporation & Westat Research, 1971; Coelen, Glantz, & Calore, 1979). This number was also a substantial increase in not-for-profit child daycare, probably stimulated by the availability of public money and United Way–public money partnerships. Before 1965, 60% of child daycare needs were largely met by small profit-making "mom and pop" centers. Much of the growth during the 1970s took place in the not-for-profit sector, so that the percentage of profit-making centers is now only 40.7%, while the not-for-profit centers make up 59.3%.

There was another change in type of ownership as well. Large corporate chains and franchise operations began, in the 1970s, to serve significant numbers of families, particularly in the above-median-income groups. Although some franchise operations did not work out very well, chains continue to grow. They now constitute about 10% of all profit-making centers and are considered the fastest-growing type of organization in day care.

By 1980 this diverse spectrum of service delivery systems was in place, and expanded child daycare was a reality. Child daycare advocates, meanwhile, continued to discuss daycare policy as if the creation of a new

Table 14.3. Percentage distribution of benefits from direct spending programs and tax expenditures for child care by annual income, 1977

Annual income	Direct-spending programs	Tax expenditures
$0–5,000	60%	1%
5,000–10,000	25	13
10,000–15,000	12	19
15,000–20,000	3	24
20,000–30,000	—	33
30,000–50,000	—	8
Over 50,000	—	2
Total	100%	100%

Note: Percentages are estimates.
Source: Congressional Budget Office (1978).

"program" was the objective, as indeed it was to those who did not like the diverse service system that had grown up.

Child daycare in the 1980s: a need for overarching goals

The needs of working parents

Child daycare stands at a crossroads as the decade of the 1980s has brought a different climate of opinion. Given the unlikely prospect in the foreseeable future of a new child daycare "program" or free child daycare for all, a vision of the delivery system needs to take into account the system that was built piecemeal in the 1970s and that is still evolving.

This purchase-of-service system has been regulated by state licensing systems, with fairly high coverage for centers, but less coverage for family daycare (Morgan, 1980). Child daycare today is largely paid for by parents, with direct public subsidy going to the poorest and a tax credit reaching the upper middle class, as shown in Table 14.3. The group that receives the least amount of direct or indirect government subsidies consists of two-parent families where out of financial necessity both parents are working. Yet this is a group with a clear need for child daycare.

Failure to address the needs of this group has another unwanted consequence. The more wealthy middle-class parents can buy services in child daycare programs and the government can buy into the same system for poor, abused, or handicapped children. However, if child daycare is unable to serve the group in the middle – those two-parent working families who are the mainstream of America – the system will develop in the future as two segregated streams: one – stigmatized even if standards are high – for the poor, another for those who can afford to pay.

The American mindset and financial pressures for program accountability may tend to push the future in the direction of such segregation. Indeed, the 1970s went far in this direction. In the practice of child daycare, possibly because of the healthy experience of serving working families as a support system under the Lanham Act in the years of World War II, there is resistance to these trends and a struggle to create a community-based system of support for all families with children. Unless the pressure to segregate segments of the population into different child daycare markets is consciously addressed, it is possible that the segregating trend cannot be reversed, despite aspirations of those in the field.

A purchase-of-service delivery system: What should it look like?

In order for a delivery system to accomplish what Dr. Kahn's task force suggested in 1970 – unifying but preserving a diverse market – the delivery system would have to be conceptually clear and politically and pragmatically feasible. Such a delivery system must include present providers and the major administrative bureaucracies; one could not "win out" over another. Added to that system would be new elements as needed to provide what is missing in the present system, including:

> *Broadened goals,* so that the system is seen as accomplishing the diverse goals of different interest domains and constituencies.
>
> *Major reform of the regulatory system* to remove systematic obstacles to the growth of a needed service and to build the reality, as well as the image, of a vigorous consumer protection system, with a strong parent role. The federal government should have model standards, and use them to inspire state funding requirements and the training for the field of practice.
>
> *Emphasis on parent choice of program type.* States that have emphasized center care exclusively need to encourage a mix of center and family child daycare as the direction for future growth of the system. Some operating agencies may begin to offer both.
>
> *Centralized, nonstigmatized access to child daycare,* such as was available during the Lanham Act days. A child daycare information and resource center (perhaps modeled on the old 4-C program or the re-

source and referral system in California) or another central point of access is needed, although parents should always be able to obtain access to the system at the provider level as well.

Data about where children are, across agencies, so that decision makers have current information about the supply of Title XX daycare, Head Start, school-based services, licensed private programs, and health-related and other programs.

Broadened income eligibility criteria for subsidy at least to the median income. When child daycare is related to work, priority for eligibility should be based on the need for work, and fees should be based on income. Child daycare eligibility should never be based on earnings that the care makes possible.

This eligibility policy might not be consistent with Head Start's commitment to low-income families. In that case, Head Start should continue to serve low-income families without full-time employment, but should not enter the field of work-related child daycare, even though issues of quality should be identical in both types of programs. Welfare caseworkers should target family referrals more appropriately to work-related child daycare when improved income is the family need, or to Head Start when improved income is not the objective.

New attention to the needs of the two-parent working family. Two-parent families are usually excluded from direct subsidy. Working-class families benefit less from the tax credit than do the middle class. An approach to tax credits and direct subsidy must be worked out so that child-care benefits are distributed more equitably. Data on families should be compiled and presented in such a way that two-parent working families are not lumped in the same income category as families that receive their income from one job. These two types of families at the same income do not have the same resources of time available; they have different problems, and therefore different policy needs. Most important, policy should not defer help to a two-parent family until after family breakdown has occurred.

More access to partial direct subsidies for parents who need them in order to make a real choice. Work-related child daycare subsidies should always slide, to avoid limiting the potential of any family for increased earnings. Voucher systems can be used by employers, United Way, and many different bureaucracies so that different constituencies can buy into the same community-based services. Child daycare must be recognized as a support that is needed by families with young children if they are to participate in work, training, educational opportunities, or rehabilitation.

More accurate information on child daycare costs, and reimbursement that is related to cost, when significant public dollars are spent. This is not to say that the funding agency has to pay the whole cost; it may well be unable to do so. At present, however, the funding agency may not know what the real cost is, and may believe it is paying a greater proportion than it really is. For contracts or grants, the reimbursement negotiations should be true cost negotiations, regardless of what portion of the costs the public agency will pay. For Aid to Families with Dependent Children subsidy, allowable cost maximums should be the same as those for the tax credit. Vouchers can be based on the "going rate" or on costs.

Continuation of Head Start programs and school-based preschool services, as well as Title XX daycare. Head Start is a valuable federally controlled demonstration program that can be used to forge new directions for low-income American children and families. Schools, too, should be encouraged to continue in the direction of more family-supportive educational services for young children. There is no need to choose one domain of program administration over another. Title XX child daycare funding at some future date might be broken out as an identified program.

Child daycare that supports families

These improvements in the child daycare system are needed, and are flexible enough so that child daycare could develop differently to respond to the situations in different localities. Because they do not inject a new "program" into an already diverse system, these suggestions are not threatening and could lead to greater sharing and coordination. In the long run, however, more structure and cohesion are needed. The different domains of interest in child daycare need to relate to one another's objectives and to respect some overarching goals for child daycare. At the very least, there should be agreement among all the constituencies that child daycare should be supportive of, and never undermine, the family. Families have a number of important functions, including child rearing, emotional support of members, and economic self-support. Any policy that supports one of these functions, but undermines another, is undermining the family.

Ultimately, the policy question facing us in the 1980s is not whether we will have child daycare; it is what kind of child daycare we will have, how it will be delivered in terms of what we know of the needs of children and families, and what can be done to assure parents' ability to find and pay for their choice of service.

It is necessary to broaden the perspectives of the various constituencies represented in child daycare to include the interests of children, their parents, and a healthy society. Most importantly, child daycare policy must be designed never to be substitutive, but always supportive, of all the functions of families.

Note

1 In its most general sense, the term *daycare* (or *day care*) connotes care for the elderly, retarded, severely handicapped, and so forth, as well as care for children. The term *child*

care connotes residential child welfare services as well as daytime care for children living with their families. For the sake of clarity, and following the lead of the National Campaign for Child Daycare for Working Parents, in which the issue of terminology was discussed at great length, this chapter uses the term *child daycare* in referring to its subject.

References

Bureau of Labor Statistics. *Marital and family characteristics of workers, 1970 to 1978* (Special Labor Force Report No. 219). Washington, D.C., 1979.
Bureau of Labor Statistics. *Current population survey.* Washington, D.C., March 1980.
Coelen, C., Glantz, F., & Calore, D. *Daycare centers in the U.S.: A national profile, 1976–1977.* Cambridge, Mass.: Abt Associates, 1979.
Congressional Budget Office. *Childcare and preschool: Options for federal support.* Washington, D.C., September 1978.
Fosburg, S. *Family day care in the United States: Summary of findings* (DHHS Publication No. [OHDS] 80-30282). Cambridge, Mass.: Abt Associates, September 1981.
Ginzberg, E. The job problem. *Scientific American.* 1977, *237*(5), 43–51.
Glantz, F. Unpublished lecture for Day Care Council of America, Washington, D.C., June 1979, and Wheelock College, July 1980.
Hedges, J. N., & Mellor, E. F. Weekly and hourly earnings of U.S. workers, 1967–1978. *Monthly Labor Review,* 1979, *102*(8), 31–41.
Hofferth, S. L. Day care in the next decade: 1980–1990. *Journal of Marriage and the Family,* 1979, *41*(3), 649–658.
Hymes, J. L. *A look at 1980. Early childhood education: The year in review.* Berkeley, Calif.: Hacienda Press, 1981.
Jenkins, S. Child welfare as a class system. In A. L. Schorr (Ed.), *Children and decent people.* New York: Basic Books, 1974, pp. 14–15.
Johnson, B. L. Marital and family characteristics of the labor force. *Monthly Labor Review,* 1980, *103*(4), 48–52.
Kamerman, S., & Kahn, A. The day care debate: A wider view. *Public Interest,* 1979, *54*, 76–93.
Kilgore, G., & Salmon, G. *Technical notes: Summaries and characteristics of states' Title XX social services plans for fiscal year 1979.* Washington, D.C.: U.S. Department of Health, Education, and Welfare, Office of the Assistant Secretary for Planning and Evaluation, 1980.
Levitan, A., & Alderman, K. C. *Child care and ABC's too.* Baltimore: Johns Hopkins University Press, 1979.
Low, S., & Spindler, P. G. *Child care arrangements of working mothers in the United States.* Washington, D.C.: U.S. Government Printing Office, 1968.
Masnick, G., & Bane, M. J. *The nation's families, 1960–1990.* Cambridge: Joint Center for Urban Studies of MIT and Harvard University, 1980.
Moore, J. C., Jr. *Parent decisions on the use of day care and early education services: An analysis of amount used and type chosen.* Ann Arbor, Mich.: University Microfilms, 1980.
Morgan, G. G. Can quality family day care be achieved through regulation? In S. Kilmer (Ed.), *Advances in early education and daycare.* Greenwich, Conn.: JAI Press, 1980.
Rodes, T. W., & Moore, J. C. *National Child Care Consumer Study, 1975* (ERIC Document Number Ed 151 931). Washington, D.C.: U.S. Department of Health, Education, and Welfare, Office of Child Development, 1976, 3 vols.

Roupp, R., Travers, J., Glantz, F., & Coelen, C. *Children at the center.* Cambridge, Mass.: Abt Associates, 1979.

Shea, J. R., Roderick, R. D., Zeller, F. A., Kophen, A. I., and Associates. *Years for decision: A longitudinal study of the educational and labor market experience of young women* (Vol. 1). Columbus: Ohio State University, Center for Human Resource Research, 1971.

Smith, R. (Ed.). *The subtle revolution: The movement of women into the labor force.* Washington, D.C.: Urban Institute, 1979.

Thurow, L. *Generating inequality.* New York: Basic Books, 1975.

Weiner, S. The child care market in Seattle and Denver. In P. Robins & S. Weiner (Eds.), *Child care and public policy.* Lexington, Mass.: Lexington Books, 1978.

Westinghouse Learning Corporation & Westat Research. *Day care survey 1970: Summary report and basic analysis.* Washington, D.C., Office of Economic Opportunity, 1971.

Women's Bureau, U.S. Department of Labor, Employment Standards Administration. *Working mothers and their children.* Washington, D.C., 1977.

15   Head Start: a case study in the development of social policy for children and families

Jeanette Valentine and Edward F. Zigler

Students of social policy and child development are concerned with a variety of issues at the interface of the social sciences and public policy formation. In the era of the War on Poverty, social science theories ranging from preschool education to juvenile delinquency enjoyed extensive popularity. These theories provided information for numerous public policy decisions during the 1960s, decisions that by the end of that decade were held in widespread disrepute as "failed reforms." Many of the social programs built during those years were either radically transformed or eliminated altogether as the nation approached the 1970s. Our experience with the programs of the War on Poverty raises generic questions about the role that social science plays, or can potentially play, in social policy development. What is the relationship between social science theories and the construction of social policy? Is this relationship the same in all areas of social policy, or just some? How do theoretical formulations change in response to the translation of theories into policies and programs? Pondering those questions leads to a series of related, perhaps more important issues. How can we explain the emergence of a given social policy at any particular point in time? Once a policy has been implemented, how can we explain its continued existence? What role does the evaluation of program effectiveness play in decision making?

These questions are guided by a fundamental interest in impacting the policy-making process to achieve social change. Social scientists have historically played significant roles in policy making, but social science theories alone can never entirely explain the acceptance or continuation of a policy. Proven effectiveness and the development of a large and vocal constituency are important factors in the survival of social programs. Understanding the relationship between research findings from social science, advocacy, and constituency building among consumer and special interest groups is necessary to successfully change social policy.

266

Within the field of child development and social policy, scholars are beginning to ask these questions, with a focus on policy initiatives that affect children and families. Project Head Start, which was a program of the War on Poverty and has been in existence now since 1965, provides an excellent case study to explore many of the questions posed above. Head Start represents a successful collaboration between social science and public policy. Expertise from the fields of education, child development, mental health, and medicine contributed to the design of the Head Start program, and representatives from these fields have worked with consumer groups to maintain the program over time.

Head Start provides a good example of the relationship between social science theory and social policy construction in a number of ways. Information for the design of the Head Start program was informed, first, by theories of child development (e.g., the role of the environment and the importance of critical periods), and secondly, by implicit and explicit theories of social reform (the culture of poverty, opportunity theory). Head Start has often been described as an "idea whose time had come." The time that the program emerged and the form that it took reflect a convergence of social, political, and economic factors with social science theories. To explain why a particular policy emerges at a given point in time requires an appreciation of how the social and political climate "set the stage" for the acceptance of the theories and problem definitions that lead to policy formation. The controversies over the outcomes of evaluation studies of Head Start exemplify some general problems in the relationship between evaluative research and decision making. The limitations of program evaluation methodologies, the political uses and abuses of evaluation research, and goal definitions for social programs are all issues that arose in the attempts to understand the impact of Head Start and decide its future. What is especially interesting about Head Start is the stability of the program through changes in political climates over the years. Advocacy and constituency building have played key roles in maintaining the integrity of Head Start through political and economic crises.

These issues will be examined in detail in this chapter, with the intent of identifying some general principles about the relationship between social science and the construction of social policy that can be applied to other social policy initiatives on behalf of children and families in America today. We will discuss the current state of the Head Start program and analyze its origins as illustrative of dilemmas in social science and public policy. The relationship between the social climate, domestic policy, and child development theories will be examined to explain the emergence of family policies at particular points in time. Studies of Head Start effectiveness will be reviewed as examples of the political uses of evaluations of social programs. These analyses can enlighten our contemporary work in social policy for children and families. As a result, we can hopefully make use of more appropriate and effective strategies to support America's families.

What is Project Head Start?

On the 15th anniversary of the Head Start program, President Carter praised Head Start for its contribution to hundreds of thousands of children and their families served over the years: "The flexibility of Head Start to accommodate changing times . . . has been one of its innate strengths" (Carter, 1980). Head Start is a social program born in an era of social reform (1965 was the first year of operation) that has survived into the 1980s. The current era reflects not only a different political climate, one in which social programs are unpopular, but also different issues in family-life development. When originally conceived, Head Start represented a particular approach to addressing the developmental needs of children, one that emphasized early educational experiences for poor children to maximize their learning potential. Over the years Head Start has developed a focus on family support to enhance child development. The history of the Head Start program itself, then, is a history of the evolution of social policy development for children and families.

In describing the Head Start program, Marian Wright Edelman noted that "Head Start is not one program, it is a family of programs" (Edelman, 1978). The basic program is a center-based preschool educational program serving predominantly poor children between the ages of three and five. Every program is mandated to provide the following services: education, health screening and referral, mental health services, social services, nutrition (hot lunches and nutrition education), and parent involvement. In 1980, the basic program served 376,000 children in full-year and summer programs. Because of federal guidelines, at least 90% of these children come from families with income below the poverty line, and nearly 12% are handicapped (*Statistical fact sheet*, 1980).

Through demonstration efforts, Head Start expanded the types of services offered beyond those mandated by legislation. Parent–Child Centers provide health, social, and educational services to 3,500 children and their families beginning in the prenatal period and carried through age three. Under Project Developmental Continuity, approximately 7,000 children receive educational services beyond Head Start into the early primary grades. This demonstration effort reinforces parental involvement in the primary grades and provides continuity in educational and developmental experiences for children as they make the transition from preschool into primary school.

The Child and Family Resource Program is a comparatively small demonstration effort that assists families in obtaining necessary services and benefits to which they are entitled. This is a family-oriented program, offering a wide range of direct services (prenatal care, pediatric screening, social services, and education), as well as advocacy for services not available through the Head Start program.

The Home Start demonstration (1972 to 1975) brought special services into the homes of economically disadvantaged families. Parenting education, developmental assessments, and social services were provided either in combination with a center-based program of early intervention or as a separate program, in and of itself, to families with young children. As a result of its proven success, "home-based options" are now available to supplement or replace center-based Head Start programs. The availability of this option not only facilitates local autonomy and flexibility in meeting the needs of particular communities, but reflects the evolutionary nature of the Head Start program.

Special services to handicapped and bilingual children, career development for staff, and programs in parenting education for high schoolers are among the other services that comprise the Head Start family of programs. These efforts incorporate a commitment to families, as well as to children, with a view of child development as a continuous process. Children have multiple needs at each and every stage of development, and social programs should be comprehensive enough to address these needs.

Dilemmas in child development theory and the construction of social policy

Although Head Start is not one program but many, the program did not have its beginnings as one that was comprehensive and family-oriented in nature. In the first summer of operation, Project Head Start was primarily a program of preschool intervention for economically disadvantaged children. The focus was educational in nature, with the goal of reducing intellectual deficits among the young participants. Although the planners listed a range of services that should be available at each site and stressed the importance of parental involvement, the reality of starting and implementing a six-week summer program that served 500,000 preschool children nationally made it impossible to offer multiple services at every site.

The early Head Start program derived from a particular theoretical strain in the field of child development at that time, one that had as its starting point the prime importance of intellectual development and its malleability. The classic works of Benjamin Bloom and J. McVicker Hunt posited that environmental enrichment has the potential to improve one's intellectual abilities (Bloom, 1964; Hunt, 1961). This theoretical framework echoed a rejection of strict hereditarian views of development that held sway in the 1950s.

The early planners of Head Start were influenced by studies that assessed the impact of environmental enrichment on intellectual development. One of the early "intervention" studies that influenced the Head Start planning committee was done by Susan Gray and her collaborator Richard Klaus (Gray & Klaus, 1965). Their work evaluated the benefits of educational enrichment to mentally retarded children in the Nashville, Tennessee area. Similar studies in other parts of the country were initiated: New Haven, Connecticut; New York City; and Ypsilanti, Michigan, among others (Palmer, 1978). Intervention in the preschool years improved the intellectual performance (as measured by intelligence tests) of mentally retarded children, and the concept was extended to apply to socially disadvantaged children (the term *cultural familial retardation* was coined to describe this latter group). A "culture of poverty" was ascribed to the poor by Oscar Lewis, an anthropologist who studied poor families of Hispanic background in border towns of the Southwest United States (Lewis, 1966). An adaptation of that concept to America's poor provided a framework to explain the transmission of economic and social disadvantages from one generation to the next. At the risk of oversimplification, the theory maintains that, through patterns of socialization and a lack of appropriate environmental stimulation, the poor develop a world view and intellectual capabilities that do not equip them for "success" in mainstream American culture. These cultural deficits are transmitted across generations, creating an endless cycle of poverty. Intervention, based on environmental enrichment, could possibly break this cycle of poverty.

When is the optimum time to intervene in the life of the disadvantaged child? Bloom (1964) defined the first five years of life as the "critical period" during which the benefits of enrichment could be maximized. Later, other theories would insist on narrower age ranges (e.g., the first three years of life), but the first early intervention studies reached children in the preschool age period (three to five years). The concept of critical periods came to be accepted as an important component of early-intervention programs for the disadvantaged. The earlier the better was the rule of thumb, but the age of five was certainly too late.

These ideas constituted the conceptual basis for Head Start. The theories informed the policy-making process, primarily through the Head Start Planning Committee, which consisted of educators, child development experts, and pediatricians. The small-scale studies of early intervention became a model for the Head Start program. The major public policy issue for the Planning Committee was how to implement this "model" on a national scale. This problem was not insurmountable, as history has demonstrated.

The theories that laid the foundation for Head Start did not remain static. The many years of the program's existence witnessed a backlash of sorts to the "naïve environmentalism" that characterized this era. Geneticists resurfaced in the late 1960s to explain the apparent "failure" of efforts at educational reform. Developmental psychologists countered with explanations of the innate developmental stages unique to every individual, which reflected underlying competencies that may or may not be expressed in performance. This latter view, sometimes referred to as "neomaturationist," rejects the idea of critical periods per se and considers intelligence the result of the interaction of genetic potential and unique learning experiences. Every child passes through fixed stages of development, acquiring skills and competencies that permit him or her to pass to the next stage of development. The speed of developmental progress through these stages is individually determined (Ginsburg, 1972; Keddie, 1973).

This same period witnessed a reaction to the culture of poverty as the explanatory framework for the perpetuation of poverty (Ryan, 1971; Valentine, 1968). The roots of poverty do not lie in individual and family socialization, the new argument went, but rather in social institutions that limit education and job opportunities. Efforts at social reform should then be geared to changing schools, increasing job opportunities, and increasing access to services. Administrators and evaluators of the Head Start program accepted many of these criticisms over the years and recognized that the concept of the culture of poverty disparaged the poor. A more meaningful approach to social programs for the poor should build upon the inherent strengths and competencies of poor children and their families (Stipek, Valentine, & Zigler, 1979).

One of the major strengths of the Head Start program is its flexibility and adaptability to changing goals and problem definitions. As Head Start developed, the program incorporated theoretical criticisms as well as theoretical advances into new foci. Thus, social policy construction has been responsive to theoretical advances in the field of child development. Because of the application of theoretical developments to policy construction, Head Start has evolved into a program that emphasizes the importance of the family, considers all periods of a child's life as important, recognizes that children and families have needs for multiple kinds of services, and has developed social–emotional measures of program success beyond intellectual ones (Zigler & Trickett, 1978). These perspectives are apparent in the components of the basic program, as well as in its demonstration efforts. Furthermore, program administrators and evaluators no longer expect Head Start to be a solution to the problems of poverty.

An explanatory framework for the emergence of social policy: the political and economic climate

Project Head Start was conceived during a time of economic prosperity for the majority of Americans. Social concern focused on the "other America," the one in which a minority of people were economically and socially deprived. At the same time, the civil rights movement was burgeoning, having achieved some success with the Civil Rights Act of 1964. These forces, along with the passage of the Economic Opportunity Act (EOA) in 1964, sparked social unrest. This act provided programs and funds directly to local communities to redress some of the social, political, and economic inequities that were becoming increasingly apparent during this time. Reformist sentiment was great, legitimated to a large extent by social science theories about the need for political change to impact social injustice (Cloward & Ohlin, 1960).

Sargent Shriver became the director of the Office of Economic Opportunity (OEO), and the legislation (EOA) as designed had no spending ceiling nor real matching requirements and could transfer monies to local community groups without going through entrenched local political interests that typically excluded the poor (Katznelson, 1976). Head Start was not part of the original package of OEO programs, but was developed shortly thereafter. Sargent Shriver supported the concept of doing something for children, and the Planning Committee for Head Start was convened in January 1965 (Shriver, 1979). The time was ripe for a program like Head Start in 1965. Social programs were expanding, seemingly unlimited funds were available, and social science theories held out the promise of social change through social reform. When conceptualizing a program for children, the members of the original planning committee drew upon then-current strains of thought in child development, as discussed above, which fit well with other social science theories of reform, federal responsibility for the disadvantaged, and an expanding economy that could support such responsibility. The concepts behind Head Start had been "on the drawing boards" for some time before the program started, but only in 1965 were the political and economic bases there to actualize the program.

Preschool educational programs to aid economically disadvantaged children had been implemented in small-scale demonstration efforts, but the translation of theories about child development into a nationwide program for children was made possible because these theories meshed well with the reformist sentiment so prevalent in social policy at that time. Concerned social scientists could take full advantage of the opportunity, insofar as the programmatic models had been tested and had been proven effective. Timing is of utmost importance in making use of research findings to impact public policy, but, as Head Start demonstrates, the availability of theories and models alone does not explain their implementation into social programs.

Once Head Start was under way as a program, the political and economic bases that made the program possible quickly began to change. Neither the theories themselves nor the scientists who espoused them could sustain the continuation of the program. As the political climate changed, other factors came into play that determined the program's successful continuation, not the least of which was the proven effectiveness of the program and the development of a supportive political constituency.

The politics of evaluating program effectiveness

From a rational social policy perspective, assessing the impact of social programs is of prime importance. Especially difficult is the evaluation of a social program that has multiple goals, or one in which the "process" of implementation is as important as any measure of "outcome." In contemporary social policy, virtually every social program is scrutinized and confronted with the questions: How effective is this program? Is it worth the money we are spending on it? Of course, in the most immediate sense, budget balancing has forced program cuts regardless of effectiveness. However, in general, program evaluation is a useful tool in developing rational approaches to decision making regarding the allocation of social resources (Dye, 1978).

"Linear" evaluation models (in which program inputs lead to certain outcomes), first used in Defense Department accounting, were applied to social programs for the first time in the mid-1960s (Cohen, 1970; Williams & Evans, 1969). Head Start had an evaluation scheme when the program first started (Gordon, 1979). However, the evaluation component was hastily conceived, was mostly descriptive in nature, and proved not useful to program planning (i.e., when could/should changes be made based on what was found in the evaluation?). The first major evaluation of Head Start, conducted by the Westinghouse Learning Corporation, was based on the linear model of program inputs that lead to defined program outputs (Westinghouse Learning Corporation, 1969). A sample of Head Start programs was studied to determine the impact of the Head Start experience on disadvantaged children. Outcomes were defined primarily in terms of school performance measures and of intellectual development using IQ measures.

It is well-known history now that the Westinghouse study found preschool children who went through Head Start had significantly improved performance on intelligence tests. In addition, children with the Head Start experience performed better on tests of school readiness when compared with non–Head Start children. The study found, however, that these observed benefits were "immediate" and that the gains these children made were not lasting gains. By the time the children reached the primary grades, the gains on the intellectual performance measures faded (Datta, 1979). This research was used as the basis for policy recommendations of program cutbacks in 1969. Within the research community, this study touched off an important controversy regarding the value of early intervention as well as methodological problems with evaluating effectiveness. This controversy emerged at a time when the programs of the War on Poverty were being attacked as demonstrated failures of social reform (Moynihan, 1969). At the same time, federal policy initiatives dismantled the Office of Economic Opportunity (the administering agency of the poverty programs) and gradually phased out a number of programs of the War on Poverty.

From a scientific standpoint, one of the problems with the Westinghouse study was that the research design did not take into account different levels of program implementation. Some programs were very good in terms of staff quality, staff/child ratios, program content, and service availability, whereas others offered fewer services and had higher staff/child ratios. Program quality is uneven in Head Start, as in other nationwide programs, and this factor played an important role in outcomes (Campbell, 1969). The focus on intellectual development was very narrow, especially since Head Start has multiple program goals. Some researchers also suggested that a longitudinal study might be more appropriate to evaluate the impact of Head Start. Longitudinal studies of Head Start impact were conducted by the Educational Testing Service (ETS)

(Emmerich, 1973). These studies attempted to measure program quality as a significant factor in observed outcomes and broadened the scope of what could be considered legitimate outcomes (qualitative and quantitative data on socioemotional development, parental involvement, and consumer satisfaction). Findings from the ETS study of Head Start children showed important gains in the children's school readiness and IQ performance in the short run, as well as improved social behavior. School performance in later years among Head Start children was significantly better than among children who had not had a Head Start preschool experience.

The Westinghouse study probably received more attention from government than some of the other research findings about the impact of early intervention because the data added to the antireformist sentiment prevalent in the late 1960s. Although the impact of this on the program's existence was not devastating, expansion of Head Start (as indexed by budget appropriations and increasing the numbers of children served) leveled off. From 1970 onward, appropriations for Head Start have remained about the same until recently. In 1979, the Head Start program experienced a budgetary increase of almost $2 million, primarily as a result of new findings concerning the long-term impact of early-intervention programs for disadvantaged children (Brown, 1978; Kleinman, 1980; Palmer & Anderson, 1979). The Developmental Continuity Consortium that conducted this research brought together several small-scale studies of model early-intervention programs among disadvantaged preschool children. Each of the studies involves a population of children very similar to a Head Start population. (The New Haven program is actually a Head Start population.) These programs followed a group of disadvantaged children who had enrichment experiences in the middle to late 1960s. Combining the findings from each of these studies, the Consortium found that by the eighth grade, children who participated in an early-intervention program were less likely than matched controls to be held back in school or to need special educational services. In addition, these children performed better in reading and math than their counterparts who did not have the special preschool experience. Parental involvement was found to be an important factor that mediated these effects (*Lasting effects,* 1978).

Some general themes emerge from the review of the program evaluation literature on Head Start. The availability of good data on program effectiveness is crucial to make informed public policy decisions. It seems evident that evaluation research can be manipulated to serve a variety of political ends. Open debate within the scientific community best serves social policy development in the long run. Also important is an appreciation of the limitations of the methodologies used to evaluate social programs. The case of Head Start demonstrates the difficulties of assessing the effectiveness of a program that has multiple goals (Zigler, 1979). Evaluation should not focus on narrowly conceived goals, such as cognitive development, while other, equally important goals go unrecognized. A third point to consider in evaluating social programs is that program evaluation should be used to enhance the quality of the program, not merely to justify its existence. Head Start has achieved this goal by becoming a "national laboratory" to test out different approaches to the delivery of services to young children and their families.

How to impact the policy-making process: the role of advocacy

Whereas scientific evidence has played a key role in the construction of social policy in the case of Head Start, the existence of a broad-based political constituency has been a major reason for its survival through major political upheavals. Among the supporters of Head Start have been legislators (Walter Mondale, John Brademas, Robert Brooke), child advocates, and a cadre of social scientists, educators, and medical practitioners. Most important of all is the national organization of Head Start parents and advocates (National Head Start Association).

Since the inception of the program, attempts have been made to radically alter the character of Head Start. The integrity of the program was threatened in the late 1960s because of claims that early intervention was not effective. Research countering these claims and effective lobbying on the part of parents and other groups led to a strong commitment to continuing the program. There have been numerous attempts to shape Head Start into a strictly education-based program. A key strategy has been to try to shift the administration of Head Start from the Administration for Children, Youth, and Families (ACYF) into the Department of Education (formerly the Office of Education within the Department of Health, Education, and Welfare). The most recent battle – to transfer Head Start into the newly created Department of Education – took place in 1978. At that time, congressmen, child advocates, and Head Start parents lobbied effectively to maintain Head Start within ACYF. Although Head Start programs are in fact administered at the local level, many under the aegis of school boards, national-level administration must remain within an agency whose primary mission is the enhancement of the lives of children and families. Under such circumstances, such an agency can advocate change from "outside" the school system, representing the interests of children and families.

Discussion

Project Head Start has withstood past attempts to dismantle the program as well as attempts to shift its focus away from a program of comprehensive family services to one of strictly educational services. There seem to be two reasons for this. At the grass roots level, Head Start became a popular program. This popularity was evidenced by the formation of the National Head Start Association, which is composed to a large extent of parents of former Head Start children. The second reason for Head Start's continued survival is that various groups who have an interest in Head Start have been able to successfully work together forming coalitions and lobbying to maintain the program. This is not to say that the popularity of a social program can maintain its existence independent of proven effectiveness. The experience with the Head Start program suggests that there are many indicators of program effectiveness. An effective program with a broad base of national and grass roots support need not be eliminated either because of changing political climates or because of narrow definitions of program impact.

In terms of social science and public policy development, the Head Start experience has contributed to the advancement of the field of child development and the role of government. Head Start has provided a national laboratory to test the best approaches to enhance child development and support family life. Almost two decades of program operation have addressed such diverse yet related problem areas as the importance of social competence in the development of children, the effectiveness of different teaching models on children's learning, the role of parents as primary educators and socializers of children, and continuity of human development in the learning process. Children are greatly affected by their environments, some in ways that we do not yet fully understand, at the same time that they bring to their environments their own unique characteristics. Disadvantaged children and their families have strengths that should be supported. We have also learned that intellectual development is not, and should not be, the single goal of special programs for children. Developing socially competent human beings who can participate fully in society is a worthwhile goal of any social program for children.

Head Start has demonstrated that development is a continuous process, and as such every period in a child's life is important. Children can benefit from special services at many points in their lives, and some children will reap more benefits than others. A key factor in the extent to which children benefit from special programs is the involvement of a parent or parents. Programs should be family-oriented, which means that through the education and participation of parents in program planning, parents can reinforce program goals with their children in their own homes.

In the social policy arena, Head Start has demonstrated that it is indeed possible to mount a national program on behalf of children and families and that it can be maintained. It is especially encouraging that our society has been able to offer a comprehensive social program, as opposed to the more narrowly focused categorical programs in health, education, and social services that characterize most federal child welfare programs. Head Start is a comprehensive service program with multiple social goals including learning, physical and mental health, and family support. Program evaluation must utilize multiple indices of program impact, giving weight to each. Finally, Head Start has shown that a preschool intervention program for economically disadvantaged children, as Head Start primarily was in its early days, is no panacea for poverty. Head Start, with its focus on family support and comprehensive services, can achieve some important social goals, but the elimination of poverty is not one of them. Head Start can increase young children's readiness for school. It can provide some useful social and intellectual skills to support children throughout the school years, leading to better performance in the later grades. Head Start can deliver to parents important social and educational services that they can use to reinforce their children's learning experiences.

Head Start provides a model of successful collaboration between the field of child development and the construction of social policy. It has provided experience that has important implications for other policy initiatives on behalf of children and families. Timing of policy recommendations is of utmost importance. A broad-based constituency is a second essential factor in successful lobbying for a program. At some point, special interest groups must put aside their differences to work together on a set of shared goals. Once a program is mounted, studies of program impact should be designed to reflect multiple possible outcomes, and should even permit finding serendipitous effects. In developing a rationale for particular programs, we should be careful not to overstate the changes the program might produce. The goals that are set should be realistic. And finally, a social program should be flexible enough to make changes as the theories upon which they were based advance.

The development of standards for federally funded day care provides a good contemporary example of the application of these principles. Child development research has provided the basis upon which standards for federally funded day care have been developed (Cohen & Zigler, 1977).

Various proposals to upgrade these existing standards have been on the drawing boards for years and have not been implemented. The reason is that the ingredients for a successful launching of these initiatives have not been there. First, the timing has not been "right" to implement these changes; second, special interest groups have not been able to put aside their differences to coalesce around a common interest; and third, implementation of the new standards would be more costly than the current standards at a time when social service expenditures are contracting, not expanding. Although policy analysts must be conscious of the costs of policy proposals, we would hazard a guess that broad-based political action can tip the balance of the cost/benefit equation in social policy. The development of advocacy strategies then become key.

The heyday of the social scientist's role in policy making with respect to social problems is past, yet social problems persist and social scientists still can play a key part in certain aspects of the policy-making process. Although the current political and economic climate is vastly different from the one in which Head Start was conceived, we have nonetheless learned lessons from that era that can and should be carried into the present. Equity is still an attainable goal of social policy in the United States. To achieve this goal, we may have to use some of the strategies that proved successful in the past and discard others that were not useful. In the realm of child and family policy, this could mean new roles for scientists and experts as advocates. All of this can point the way to social change.

References

Bloom, B. S. *Stability and change in human characteristics.* New York: Wiley, 1964.

Brown, B. (Ed.). *Found: Long-term gains from early intervention.* Boulder, Colo.: Westview Press, 1978.

Campbell, D. Reforms as experiments. *American Psychologist,* 1969, *24,* 411–415.

Carter, J. *Remarks on the fifteenth anniversary of Head Start.* Washington, D.C., 1980.

Cloward, R. A., & Ohlin, L. E. *Delinquency and opportunity: A theory of delinquent gangs.* Glencoe, Ill.: Free Press, 1960.

Cohen, D. Politics and research: The evaluation of social action programs in education. *Review of Educational Research,* 1970, *40,* 213–218.

Cohen, D. J., & Zigler, E. Federal day care standards: Rationale and recommendations. *American Journal of Orthopsychiatry,* 1977, *47*(3), 456–465.

Datta, L. Another spring and other hopes: Some findings from national evaluations of Project Head Start. In E. Zigler & J. Valentine (Eds.), *Project Head Start: A legacy of the War on Poverty.* New York: Free Press, 1979.

Dye, T. R. *Understanding public policy.* Englewood Cliffs, N.J.: Prentice-Hall, 1978.

Edelman, M. W. *Head Start's future: If there is no way we'll find a way anyway.* Paper presented at the Fifth Annual Conference on the National Head Start Association, May 26, 1978.

Emmerich, W. *Disadvantaged children and their first school experiences: ETS–Head Start longitudinal study*. Princeton, N.J.: Educational Testing Service, 1973.

Ginsburg, H. *The myth of the deprived child: Poor children's intellect and education*. Englewood Cliffs, N.J.: Prentice-Hall, 1972.

Gordon, W. Evaluation during the early years of Head Start. In E. Zigler & J. Valentine (Eds.), *Project Head Start: A legacy of the War on Poverty*. New York: Free Press, 1979.

Gray, S. W., & Klaus, R. A. An experimental preschool program for culturally deprived children. *Child Development*, 1965, *36*, 887–898.

Hunt, J. McV. *Intelligence and experience*. New York: Ronald Press, 1961.

Katznelson, I. The crisis of the capitalist city: Urban politics and social control. In W. D. Hawley & M. Lipski (Eds.), *Theoretical perspectives in urban politics*. Englewood Cliffs, N.J.: Prentice-Hall, 1976.

Keddie, N. (Ed.). *The myth of cultural deprivation*. Baltimore: Penguin, 1973.

Kleinman, D. Preschool program is called beneficial. *New York Times*, December 14, 1980, p. 35.

Lasting effects after preschool (A report of the Consortium for Longitudinal Studies [DHEW Pub. No. OHDS-79-30178]). Washington, D.C., October 1978.

Lewis, O. The culture of poverty. *Scientific American*, 1966, *215*, 19–25.

Moynihan, D. P. *Maximum feasible misunderstanding*. New York: Free Press, 1969.

Palmer, F. H., & Anderson, L. W. Long-term gains from early intervention. In E. Zigler & J. Valentine (Eds.), *Project Head Start: A legacy of the War on Poverty*. New York: Free Press, 1979.

Palmer, H. The effects of early childhood intervention. In B. Brown (Ed.), *Found: Gains from early intervention*. Boulder, Colo.: Westview Press, 1978.

Ryan, W. *Blaming the victim*. New York: Pantheon Books, 1971.

Shriver, S. Head Start: A retrospective view. In E. Zigler & J. Valentine (Eds.), *Project Head Start: A legacy of the War on Poverty*. New York: Free Press, 1979.

Smith, M., & Bissell, J. S. Report analysis: The impact of Head Start. *Harvard Educational Review*, 1970, *40*, 51–104.

Statistical fact sheet: Project Head Start. Washington, D.C.: U.S. Department of Health, Education, and Welfare, Office of Human Development Services, February 1980.

Stipek, D., Valentine, J., & Zigler, E. Project Head Start: A critique of theory and practice. In E. Zigler & J. Valentine (Eds.), *Project Head Start: A legacy of the War on Poverty*. New York: Free Press, 1979.

Valentine, C. A. *Culture and poverty: Critique and counterproposals*. Chicago: University of Chicago Press, 1968.

Westinghouse Learning Corporation. *The impact of Head Start: An evaluation of the effects of Head Start on children's cognitive and affective development–executive summary* (Report to OEO, ED 036321). Washington, D.C., June 1969.

Williams, W., & Evans, J. W. The politics of evaluation: The case of Head Start. *Annals of the American Academy of Political and Social Science*, 1969, *385*, 118–132.

Zigler, E. Project Head Start: Success or failure? Reprinted in E. Zigler & J. Valentine (Eds.), *Project Head Start: A legacy of the War on Poverty*. New York: Free Press, 1979.

Zigler, E., & Trickett, P. IQ, social competence, and evaluation of early childhood intervention programs. *American Psychologist*, 1978, *33*(9), 789–798.

16 Social policy and the schools: the case for educational equity

Edmund W. Gordon and Carol Camp Yeakey

This chapter discusses the problem of achieving educational equity and social justice in a population of diverse people with pluralistic standings. Contemporary efforts to democratize schooling, to make it more egalitarian, are not new in American society, but in fact have historical precedent that is centuries old. What accounts for today's resurgent efforts to achieve educational equity and parity is attributable in part to a change in the school's clientele as well as to the failure of past reforms to adequately address causality rather than the symptoms of educational malcontent. The ineffectiveness in achieving educational equity may be related to the manner in which we conceptualize our notions of justice and equity as well.

By way of distinction, status characteristics refer to such traits as ethnicity and sex, and functional characteristics refer to cognitive style and temperament. This chapter examines some of these underlying functional and status characteristics of youngsters as a way of crystallizing some of the fundamental issues related to equalizing educational opportunity. After providing the conceptual framework, the chapter focuses upon the heightened synergistic relationship among status, achievement, and opportunity, providing a historical as well as contemporary perspective of the school's relationship to the various client groups it has served. Further, this chapter analyzes the manner in which the schools have attended, almost exclusively, to status rather than functional differences in learners and the results of that myopia for both the individual learners and society at large. The phenomenon known as blaming the victim, as well as a discussion of the school's capacity to function, are among the relevant issues presented in the summary commentary.

The terms *social justice* and *equality of educational opportunity* have been used with such frequency and ambiguity that they have become rather hackneyed and vague, serving almost as an injustice to the very

281

profound concepts that they were designed to signify. To make our language more precise, the authors first assert that a society begins to approach social justice when the rewards and positions of that society are freely accessible to all its members; and, second, that the available treatments to offset inequities bear a positive relationship to the functional characteristics of the people for whom they are prescribed.

Equality of educational opportunity is not simply measured by equal access to schooling. Equal access is an accepted standard, albeit not a totally accomplished one. Rather, the other dimension of the concept of equality of educational opportunity requires that treatments be appropriate and sufficient. In the pursuit of a just society, the United States has tended to hold equal treatment as its criterion measure. Yet for educational equity to be served, treatment must be specific to one's functional characteristics and yet sufficient to one's condition. To address the problems of appropriateness and sufficiency, we seek to go beyond the status labels that apply to individuals and groups and examine their functional characteristics, which in concert with their status may handicap them in their school experience.

Conceptual framework

This chapter utilizes the conceptual framework posited by Rawls (1971) in *A Theory of Justice*. Rawls cogently developed a conceptual framework for the examination and implementation of a system of justice in which a concern for fairness as an expression of equal treatment is a central feature. His effort at explicating such a theory rests upon two principles of justice. The first is:

Each person is to have an equal right to the most extensive total system of equal basic liberties compatible with a similar system of liberty for all. [Rawls, 1971, p. 302]

His second principle holds:

Social and economic inequalities are to be arranged so that they are both: (a) to the greatest benefit of the least advantaged, consistent with the just savings principle, and (b) attached to offices and positions open to all under conditions of fair equality of opportunity. [Rawls, 1971, p. 302]

Rawls's principles rest on the dual notions that justice requires not only equality in the treatment of all members of the society but also the protection of the least advantaged members of the society. It is the concern for equal treatment that has dominated much of the United States' efforts toward the achievement of democracy. Through constitutional provisions, court decisions, legislative actions, and administrative mandates United States citizens have affirmed their nation's official commitment to equal access and equal justice. Although they recognize that these goals have not been achieved, and debate continues as to how best to achieve them, there is almost no open debate as to the validity of the commitment to equality as a national value. Rawls's concern for the least favored has not gained wide acceptance as a guiding principle in the United States, yet it may be that with respect to equalizing educational opportunity, it is the sensitive protection of the least advantaged that may be at the heart of this problem.

One of the traditional roles of American schooling has been the broadening of opportunities for productive, influential, and rewarding participation in society through the development of knowledge, skills, and credentials necessary for economic, political, and social participation. As the requirements for participation have increased and become more technical and as perceptions of the role of schooling have become more acute, the pressure on the schools to better serve the least advantaged members of the society has increased. If we keep this view in mind, Rawls's guiding principles enable us to examine closely the issues of equity and justice as they relate to the public schooling of those least advantaged in the United States.

Status, achievement, and opportunity

Among the many functions of American schools, none are more important than the following three: socialization or the process by which the young learn the ways and mores of the dominant society; the transmission of the dominant culture; and the selection and sorting of students into various educational and vocational streams. In this third function, the school helps to determine the particular way of life and the set of values a student acquires by discriminating among students on the basis of academic achievement. Academic achievement aids in determining the student's curricular program, scholastic standing, motivational directions, and opportunities for further schooling. Ascriptive factors such as race, ethnicity, social status, sex, age, and family background also figure prominently and have a circuitous and mutually reinforcing effect on opportunities for achievement and advancement in the larger society.

Research efforts have long established and reestablished the fact that actual school achievement is related to the socioeconomic status of one's family. Perhaps the three classic studies that best demonstrate the catalytic relationship between social status, achievement, and opportunity in the United States are Lynd and Lynd's *Middletown* (1929), Warner, Havighurst, and Loeb's *Who Shall Be Educated?* (1944), and Hollings-head's *Elmtown's Youth* (1949). These three studies, as well as corroborating research by Conant (1961), Wylie (1963), and others, suggest that a strong positive correlation exists between a student's social status and his or her educational opportunity. The converse is also true in that the lower one's social status, the lower will be one's educational opportunity. From the research evidence by Bowles and Gintis (1976), Carnoy (1974, 1975), and Bell (1976), it would appear that the school reinforces this handicapping relationship.

The immigrant experience

A view of history is appropriate in understanding the school's relationship to the larger society and to the various client groups it has sought to serve. Perhaps nowhere have the school's functions been more manifest than in the socialization and acculturation of lower-status immigrant groups to the mores and values of American society. Almost from the beginning of the settlement by Europeans in the New World, malevolent distinctions were drawn between new (those from Southern and Eastern Europe) and old (those from Northern and Western Europe) immigrants. Generally speaking, incoming immigrants to the United States, for much of the nineteenth century, were drawn from Northern and Western European countries (Britain, Germany, France, Scandinavia, Belgium, the Netherlands). Toward the latter part of the century, a growing number of immigrants were from Southern and Eastern Europe (Italy, Yugoslavia, Hungary, Czechoslovakia, Poland). The prevailing sentiment was that the "old immigrants" constituted a superior race of tall, blond, blue-eyed Nordics or Aryans whereas the "new immigrants" included the inferior Eastern and Southern Europeans (Gordon, 1961).

Elwood P. Cubberley, an educational historian, bespoke the prejudices of the time:

These southern and eastern Europeans are of a very different type from the north Europeans who preceded them. Illiterate, docile, lacking in self-reliance and initiative, and not possessing the Anglo-Teutonic conceptions of law, order and government, their coming has served to dilute tremendously our national stock, and to corrupt our civic life. . . . Everywhere these people tend to settle in groups or settlements, and to set up their national manners, customs and observances. Our task is to break up these groups or settlements, to assimilate and amalgamate these people as a part of our American race, and to implant in their children, so far as can be done, the Anglo-Saxon conception of righteousness, law and order, and popular government, and to awaken in them a reverence for our democratic institutions and for those things in our national life which we as a people hold to be of abiding worth. [Cubberley, 1909, pp. 15–16]

With the great migrations at the end of the nineteenth century and the beginning of the twentieth century, each new wave brought an addition of at least temporary second-class citizens whose status was determined on the basis of the part of Europe from which they had come. The acculturation and socialization of this diverse stock was a dominant theme during most of the first half of the twentieth century. The degree to which members of these groups experienced upward mobility in the existing economic order was positively correlated with the degree of socialization and acculturation of those members to the dominant cultural mores of American society.

Add to this scenario the introduction of blacks as slaves in the mid-1600s and their subsequent emancipation in the mid-1800s, and a caste-like differential was enmeshed into an already stratified societal order. Those individuals and groups who refused to adapt to and adopt the dominant culture, or failed to become upwardly mobile in the existing economic structure – because of their undeveloped abilities, because of limited opportunities available in the system, or as a result of their caste-like status – began to constitute a permanent underclass of ethnic and racial minorities (blacks, Hispanics, native Americans, and low-income whites) (Glascow, 1980).

Conventional wisdom has long postulated the fact that the school is the place to break the cycle of poverty and scale the social class ladder. This belief is underlain by an almost impervious faith in the value of schooling. Following this line of reasoning, it had been assumed that schooling provided the means by which European immigrants moved into the social, cultural, and political mainstream, whereas blacks, Hispanics, native Americans, and lower-status whites have evinced far less prosperity (Weinberg, 1969). Research by Greer (1972) and Cohen (1970) belie such conventional wisdom and sustain the fact that, only with certain notable exceptions, city schools were not the ladders of social class mobility for European immigrants, for, in many fundamental respects, city schools related to European working-class immigrants in much the same way as they related to blacks. Moreover, the emergence of parochial schooling in America was testament, in part, to the severities that the Irish and Italian immigrants, in particular, suffered at the hands of the public schools. And today's educational problems – cultural and linguistic curricular content, the ethnic and racial mix of schools and their staffs, and the overall ineffectiveness of the schools in educating lower-status youngsters – are but contemporary versions of old problems: the inability of the schools to overcome the educational consequences of poverty and lower social class status and to recognize the legitimacy of working-class and diversified ethnic cultures.

The notion that schools should act as social levers is attributable, in large measure, to progressive educational ideology. In the latter half of the nineteenth century, progressive education began as part of a larger program of social and political reform called the progressive movement (Cremin, 1961). The effort was designed to recast the school as a ladder for social class mobility and political regeneration, viewing the school as an "adjunct to politics" (Cremin, 1961, p. 88) while simultaneously adding to its functions and gradually transforming it into a multipurpose social service center. It was at this juncture that school curricula were expanded to include vocational subject matter and to attract a more diversified clientele, as part of a larger movement toward egalitarianism. It should be noted that while the foregoing was occurring, the former decentralized school decision-making structure was dismantled and removed from the hands of the local clientele and given to more centralized authorities. Just as the liberal and progressive philosophy and spirit created a climate that made concern for greater access and service to all children more acceptable, it really enabled the society to retard progress and equalization in the interest of social control. The result was that the progressive education movement was not as benevolent and beneficient as initially perceived (Hays, 1963; Tyack, 1970).

Equalizing educational opportunity

To the initial efforts at egalitarianism and attempts to maximize educational opportunities for the European immigrant populace must be added more contemporary attempts to equalize educational opportunities for the public schools' present populace of blacks, Hispanics, low-status whites, native Americans, females, and the physically and mentally handicapped. There is a long and uneven history of attention given to the educational problems of these groups. At no point in that history, however, has there been more national attention and direction focused on these groups than during recent years. Despite various attempts to effectuate a greater equalization of opportunity, there appears to be only modest progress in both the achievement of equality of opportunity or outcomes. The implicit social commitment, the relatively large and varied efforts, and the rather modest results have contributed to a decline of interest in such efforts in some circles and to a reexamination of such efforts in other circles.

Efforts at equalizing opportunity and freeing achievement from its ubiquitous association with status have been made difficult by a complicity of factors including the diversity of characteristics in the population as well as the fact that such diversity is accompanied by pluralism. Not only are the members of society different, but they aspire to different goals and adhere to different values even as they embrace and pursue common goals. Thus the very process of equalization of educational opportunity is challenged to accommodate different characteristics, values, and goals, even as it serves those features that all groups share in common.

What, then, is equity in educational opportunity and educational outcomes in a society of diverse populations and pluralistic goals, standards, and values? By what criteria can we judge the achievement of either? Our concern for equity has most often been debated in legislative and judicial arenas. We have seen the establishment of constitutional provisions as reflected in the Bill of Rights. There are legislative provisions for equity in federal and state laws. There is a long history of court decisions in support of equal justice and equal rights. Most of this concern has had as its focus the assurance of equity in regard to populations defined by ethnicity, sex, language, handicapping conditions, and to a lesser extent economic status. These legal expressions, however, have asserted the right to equality, not the insurance of it. The courts have specified the conditions of equality relevant to a specific problem like school desegregation. Yet the meaning of equality and the implications of that meaning for the functioning of the society and its institutions have not been adequately addressed in the judicial and legislative arenas.

Efforts at defining equality of educational opportunity in a diverse and pluralistic society demand that, because what children bring to the school is diverse and unequal, what the school puts in may have to be distributed unequally and customized in order to ensure equity at the basic levels of the achievement of competence. Equalization of educational opportunity in a society that espouses democracy requires parity in achievement at a baseline corresponding to the level required for social satisfaction and productive democratic participation. It also demands opportunity and freedom to vary with respect to achievement ceilings. Borrowing from our conceptual frame of reference as posited by Rawls, the concept of equal educational opportunity must therefore refer to both necessary and sufficient learning conditions for all youngsters as well as the possibility for equal enjoyment of the benefits and rewards of schooling according to their accomplishments. It is in these sometimes conflicting requirements that equality of opportunity is tested. At some points in the development of a society, it may be necessary to favor universality at the expense of uniqueness. At other times, universality may need to be sacrificed in the interest of unique achievements. If preferential attention is continuously given to one while neglecting the other, equality of opportunity is precluded. That the schools may not yet know how to provide this individualized, specialized, and diversified treatment and to creatively respond to the dialectical needs of pupils and society is a central part of the problem. That such issues are posed and solutions actively pursued that inform policy and practice may be the purpose that best defines the work of those who actively pursue educational equity and social justice.

Rawls's principles of justice and the varied definitional emphases discussed above suggest that there are two overriding issues with which we must be concerned. These issues relate to the relevance of human differences in status and differences in function for pedagogical practice and public policy.

Status and functional characteristics

Our concern for equalizing educational opportunity has brought us to examine some of the underlying status and functional characteristics of youngsters as a way of better understanding the issues related to equity and social justice. Reference has been made to differences in ethnicity, family background, sex, and income as characteristics by which status is determined in our society. Such characteristics in and of themselves fail to tell us much about how people function, but more about their position in the society. In the United States, knowledge of a person's ethnic group or social class membership can tell us a great deal about that person's relative position in the society and the manner in which the person is likely to be treated. Thus, status characteristics refer to those human attributes that generally determine one's individual or group position in the social hierarchy, the nature of one's access to the opportunities and resources of the social order, the manner in which one is perceived and treated by the institutions and members of the social order, and, to some extent, the nature of the roles to which one is socialized by the institutions of the society.

Recent U.S. court decisions and civil rights legislation have gone far to at least make illegal any government-supported or government-condoned discrimination based on several of these status characteristics. However, such judicial and legislative action has not and probably cannot eliminate the more subtle differentials in the way the society responds to and treats people of different statuses. What thus becomes important in education is that status be recognized as a category of characteristics that influence not so much the way in which the group member functions, but more significantly the way in which the status group member is likely to be treated.

To better understand the learning behavior of pupils, concern with functional rather than status characteristics is likely to be more informative and illuminating. Functional characteristics refer to those attributes that are descriptive of the adaptational behavior of the pupil. They tell us how the person operates, behaves, or functions, in what manner the behavior is expressed, from what interests and motivation the behavior is derived, and in response to what ecological conditions behavior is likely to be expressed. These functional characteristics include affective and cognitive response tendencies usually called style, interests, identification, motivation, culture, and environmental press. Although almost any teacher will describe the many variations of these characteristics in the behaviors of pupils and, in many instances, cite examples of teachers' adaptations of instruction to fit some of these variants, schooling has not been officially responsive to such functional dimensions of diversity (Hunt, 1976). Rather, schools have attended, almost exclusively, to status differences in pupils.

If we begin to look at differences in the ways in which children function in learning environments, then we have a case for adapting treatments and interventions to meet those functional characteristics. To further crystallize this point of view, the issue of bilingual education in the United States is illustrative. In their decision in *Lau* v. *Nichols* (1974) the Supreme Court ruled that a youngster whose dominant language was not English was not being granted an equal educational opportunity when provided an education solely in one of the standard English dialects. Why? Because his functional characteristics, his language behavior, made him unable to benefit from whatever standard treatment the school provided. Although one's language, in part, defines one's status, with respect to schooling it may have a more significant relationship to the manner in which he or she interacts with the learning experience. Because languages differ not only in their symbols but in the way in which particular symbols are used, if the learning experience is provided in a language with which the learner does not have facility, the learning experience may be rendered dysfunctional. The youngster may not only have difficulty understanding the material to be learned, but in addition may be prevented from ever relating to the learning experience.

Status was not the crucial variable in the above exmaple. Status is important, but its salience is related to its contribution to the way in which this society responds to lower-status youngsters rather than to its contribution to the way in which such youngsters function cognitively. A relevant question is: How can one differentiate between treatment and function? The fact is that there is not much about one's learning behavior that is attributable to the mere fact of one's socioeconomic, ethnic, or racial status, despite what Jensen (1969) and others would suggest. There is, however, a great deal about the way in which the school and the society treat such individuals and the way in which such individuals are perceived that is related to status. If one wants to know how individuals function and behave, one needs to look at functional characteristics as well. Is this child a happy person? A spontaneous person? Is this young-ster highly motivated, and if so, by what? Is this child a gestaltist, one who looks at the world as a whole, or one who looks at the world in detail? These are some of the variables that inform us as to how such a child would solve intellectual tasks. We may continue to speculate about such important variables, as most of our compensatory efforts in the past have done, but if we want to know certain dimensions about the learning behavior of children, especially lower-status children, then we cannot continue to rely solely upon status, class, race, and ethnicity as predictive variables. We must begin to assess functional characteristics. Most of the efforts directed at equalizing educational opportunities have focused too narrowly on status to the exclusion of key functional variables.

In terms of the actual teaching and learning situation, focusing on functional differences in youngsters leads us to more customized, indi-vidually designed learning experiences. Bloom's (1976) concept of mas-tery learning and the utilization of frequent assessment probes comes close to our ideas of what customized learning experiences could entail. But in reality, customized instruction is what good teachers have been doing all along.

Blaming the victim

One of the primary reasons that our efforts have been guided more by status than by functional characteristics grows out of a mythology that has guided the United States. The national creed begins with "all men are created equal," and the assumption, as evidenced by the school's institu-tional processes, is that all persons start from roughly the same position. The fact is that such mythology has not only permitted U.S. nationals to maintain a high degree of inequality, but concurrently has prevented them from questioning and challenging the underlying assumptions that are perceptibly false.

It has therefore been possible to project, on a societal scale, a notion of equality and then to "blame the victims," as William Ryan has so aptly put it (Ryan, 1975). Many of us in the United States presently blame blacks, Hispanics, native Americans, and others for being unable to use the school as it is thought, however erroneously, European immigrant groups have done. As Colin Greer suggests:

The legend supports a . . . policy which is secure in its faith that the agency for the amelioration of most social problems already exists – and that those problems whose solutions elude us now will be resolved, or are beyond solution, through no fault of that great nation, but because of deficiencies in particular people who cannot seem to solve their problems as countless other Americans have before them. [Greer, 1972, p. 3]

The school's limited capacity

The reality is that public schools in the United States are limited in their capacity to respond to the diverse characteristics of people and that they serve best those youngsters who place the fewest demands upon them. Proponents of this view hold that the roots of inequality in the United States are based in the class structure and in the system of racial and ethnic (and sexual) power relationships. The school system is but one of a series of institutions serving to perpetuate existing privilege. Given this, the school system is relatively powerless to correct economic inequality because the racial, ethnic, and status biases in schooling do not produce, but rather reflect, the pyramidal structure of property, privilege, and power in American society at large (Bowles & Gintis, 1976; Carnoy, 1974, 1975; Reich, 1978). It is believed, therefore, that it is primarily the economic system that reinforces racial, ethnic, and other ascriptive distinctions of birth.

To be sure, the schools as well as other societal institutions have served both discriminative and assimilative functions. But it is the school's discriminating function, in particular, that has made it increasingly and *predictably* difficult for racial and ethnic minority youngsters to acquire both quantity and quality of schooling necessary for successful competition in our highly industrialized society.

The school is also limited, in part, because educators have not made pedagogy very scientific. One could argue that although there are elements of art in pedagogy, there are also elements of science, a knowledge base that can be utilized and with which most educators are largely unfamiliar. Educators know far more about teaching and learning than is practiced. For example, if one examines the impact of group experience on learning in psychotherapeutic exchanges, one can identify a number of conditions that facilitate or impede learning, and a skillful group therapist will manipulate those variables in a therapy situation to enhance learning. Valuable insights from such experiences might easily be adapted to the classroom situation.

Similarly, educators have learned, from research on desegregation, the concept of social contagion – that is, behavior demonstrated by high-status persons in the group, or by models that are identified within the group, will be emulated by the lower-status persons within that group. In essence, then, certain learning modes, behaviors, and styles are contagious. Unfortunately, a concept with such profound ramifications has yet to be sufficiently utilized by educators in the school environ.

Further, let us take the concept of discovery in learning. From experiment after experiment it is known that youngsters learn better in situations that are structured in ways that enable them to discover relationships. Yet most teaching is didactic – youngsters are told what the underlying relationships are. It is known that, with the exception of rote memorization, repetition does little to enhance learning, yet teachers go far beyond the rote memorization of the multiplication tables in using repetition as an accepted teaching modality. What most often occurs with repetition is a reinforcement of errors rather than the creation of an understanding of interlacing and interlocking associations.

Finally, youngsters are expected to learn in environments that are so distracting that they cannot concentrate on the task at hand. Research on environmental pressure shows that if there is too much disruption and "static" in the environment, the "time on task" is greatly reduced, leading to impaired learning. Experimental research further shows that if children are allowed to spend enough time on the task, most will eventually master the task.

Part of what prevents school professionals from using such scientific knowledge in the classroom is their lack of awareness of timely developments in the field. In addition, however, professionals tend not to use ideas, especially experimental notions, that they do not fully understand. Coupled with this fact is teachers' reliance on habit and tradition, a tendency to fall back on past practices. In the final analysis, much depends on how the scientific research findings are formulated into ideologies, how such ideas get translated into practice, and by whom.

Conclusion

Concern for equalizing educational opportunity has led the authors to examine the underlying functional characteristics of youngsters as a way of better understanding the problems surrounding the issues of equity and social justice in schooling. One of the difficulties with the conceptions of justice and educational equity, as popularly conceived, is that attempts to implement these concepts have focused too sharply on efforts at equalizing treatments. In devising strategies to provide equal educational opportunity, policy makers, researchers, and practitioners alike have too often assumed a homogeneity among a vast populace that is, in reality, heterogeneous and diverse. If youngsters do not begin from an equal position, then providing equal treatment at some point in their school experience will not serve to achieve equity but will more likely retard its achievement. Moreover, what is created is an illusion of equity and justice when in fact none exists. For equal educational opportunity to be served, prescribed treatment must be specific to one's functional characteristics, yet sufficient to one's condition. Since the justification for society's interventions is to enable one to function adequately, then treatment must be measured in relation to what one needs rather than in relation to what one is given.

What this means with regard to the public schools is that educational planning and policy will have to be much more individualized and customized. Portions of this ideology are reflected in the long history of special programs in education, and even though past efforts in this area have been far from exemplary, the guiding principle of these efforts held that the nation or state could supplement the resources available to schools that had large numbers of youngsters with learning dysfunctions. But the fact is that the supplementary resources provided were insufficient to the needs of those schools. What occurred was a reduction in the gap between what the best schools offered to high-status youngsters and what the poorer schools offered to low-status youngsters. If the nation were really going to follow the spirit of equalizing educational opportunities, it would have provided, for low-status youngsters, educational opportunities that were richer and more varied than the opportunities provided for high-status children. In addition, it would have made treatments specific to the functional characteristics of these youngsters.

It is this interaction of status and functional characteristics that brings us back to Rawls. He argues for "the most extensive total system of equal basic liberties," and for "social and economic inequalities . . . arranged so that they are . . . to the greatest benefit to the least advantaged" (1971, p. 302). Equality of access meets both of these criteria. Making available special resources to persons with special needs is movement in the direction of creating a total system of equal basic liberties. But what of the requirement that such inequalities provide the greatest benefit to the least advantaged? To meet this standard, it is not enough to ensure participation to the poorest or even to make available a compensatory or rehabilitative mechanism. Since the real problems posed by diverse characteristics can be exacerbated by factors of status, a just system must ensure that special treatments do not require privileged status as a condition of availability. It may well be that neither low status nor atypical function as separate conditions constitute significant handicaps. The culpable circumstance may be the atypical function in the presence of a status characteristic that deprives one of supporting and compensating experiences or resources.

Lower-status persons are generally the least likely to command access to the supporting and compensating resources necessary when the school is unable or unwilling to respond to the diversity of its pupils. Under this circumstance low status and functional differences combine to make these the "least advantaged" persons served by the school. In order to provide the greatest benefit to the least advantaged, the system must be so designed that both access and reward are not limited by status and that prescription and amelioration are responsive to the functional characteristics of the learner. Such a condition may result in unequal access and treatment, but this is consistent with Rawls's argument that "all social goods – liberty and opportunity, income and wealth, and the bases of self respect – are to be distributed equally unless an unequal distribution of any or all of these goods is to the advantage of the least favored" (Rawls, 1971, p. 302).

A final word is in order. The salience of this discussion on equalizing educational opportunity and educational equity should not be narrowly confined to schooling issues per se, for the relevance of these ideas far surpasses the school's immediate environment. If the United States continues its present course of uneducating and undereducating its clientele, the slow but overwhelming process of allowing humans to go to waste will continue unabated, with unparalleled social, economic, and political ramifications. What is being created presently, in a climate of reactionary conservatism, is a seedbed of discontent that will serve to erode the very basis of society, which professes equality and homogeneity at the expense of the least advantaged.

References

Bell, D. *The cultural contradictions of capitalism.* New York: Basic Books, 1976.
Bloom, B. *Human characteristics and school learning.* New York: McGraw-Hill, 1976.
Bowles, S., & Gintis, H. *Schooling in capitalist America.* New York: Basic Books, 1976.
Carnoy, M. *Education as cultural imperialism.* New York: McKay, 1974.

Carnoy, M. *Schooling in a corporate society.* New York: McKay, 1975.

Cohen, D. K. Immigrants and the schools. *Review of Educational Research,* February 1970, *40,* 13–27.

Conant, J. B. *Slums and suburbs.* New York: McGraw-Hill, 1961.

Cremin, L. A. *The transformation of the school.* New York: Vintage, 1961.

Cubberley, E. P. *Changing conceptions of education.* New York: Riverside Educational Mimeographs, 1909.

Glascow, D. G. *The black underclass.* San Francisco: Jossey-Bass, 1980.

Gordon, M. M. Assimilation in America: Theory and reality. *Daedalus,* 1961, *90,* 263–285.

Greer, C. *The great school legend.* New York: Basic Books, 1972.

Hays, S. P. The politics of reform in municipal government in the progressive era. *Pacific Northwest Quarterly,* 1963, *55,* 157–169.

Hollingshead, A. *Elmtown's youth.* New York: Wiley, 1949.

Hunt, L. Teacher's adaptation. *Journal of Teacher Education,* 1976, *27,* 268–275.

Jensen, A. A. How much can we boost IQ and scholastic achievement? *Harvard Educational Review,* 1969, *39,* 1–123.

Lynd, R. S., & Lynd, H. M. *Middletown: A study in American culture.* New York: Harcourt, Brace, 1929.

Rawls, J. *A theory of justice.* Cambridge: Harvard University Press, 1971.

Reich, M. The economics of racism. In R. Edwards, M. Reich, & T. Weisskopf (Eds.), *The capitalist system.* Englewood Cliffs, N.J.: Prentice-Hall, 1978.

Ryan, W. *Blaming the victim.* New York: Penguin, 1975.

Tyack, D. City schools at the turn of the century: Centralization and social control. Unpublished paper, Stanford University, 1970.

Warner, W. L., Havighurst, R. J., & Loeb, M. B. *Who shall be educated?* New York: Harper, 1944.

Weinberg, M. A yearning for learning: Blacks and Jews through history. *Integrated Education,* 1969, *7,* 20–29.

Wylie, R. C. Children's estimate of their schoolwork ability as a function of sex, race and socioeconomic level. *Journal of Personality,* 1963, *31,* 203–225.

17 Forging educational policy: the quest for a balanced curriculum

John I. Goodlad

The formal curriculum, the body of courses offered ideally as a cohesive whole to the students of an educational institution, should reflect the educational standards and values the institution considers necessary to well-balanced schooling. This chapter traces how curricular policy is made: first in higher education, then in secondary education. It then examines the underlying assumptions behind past curricular decisions and how data can be used or misused to support such decisions. Then, there is an examination of how current state policies, particularly with regard to teacher education, affect curriculum development. This chapter concludes with recommendations for a new agenda for curriculum development and schooling.

The politics of curriculum in higher education: a closed book

The late Beardsley Ruml, one-time dean of the Social Science Division and professor of education at the University of Chicago, once said that it is impossible for faculty members to reform the college curriculum. Ruml was referring primarily to the politics of formulating institutional policy with respect to the scope and depth of the curriculum to be made available and the restraints to be placed on students' choices. The policies established determine the fate of departments: the amount of curricular turf each occupies, professors hired, professors ultimately given tenure, and the like. Decisions reached often involve power struggles and trade-offs having little or nothing to do with educational benefits to students, rhetoric to the contrary notwithstanding.

But even if the political aspects were minimal, the task of formulating comprehensive curricular policies for an entire institution remains formidable. Old, tough questions arise to challenge the most able of us. What knowledge is of most worth? How much of it should students study in common? How much integration of knowledge should be attempted in the organization of the institutional curriculum? What should be the total smorgasbord of offerings, and how much freedom of choice should be allowed? Should students be tested on abilities transcending the specifics of each course?

Although these questions are directly addressed only infrequently by the total faculty, they are answered over time by both commission and omission so that the curricula of higher education do change. Departments sometimes become suspect and are eliminated. Some evolve from one emphasis to another. Scholarly investigation of complex phenomena produces new fields, such as biochemistry. Waves of humanism, such as those following major wars, crowd some fields with students and starve others, creating new courses in the process. Shifts in vocational demands affect programs of study more than some educators would like to believe. How legislators respond to these and economic trends sends out ripples and sometimes shock waves that affect curricular decisions in public and sometimes private institutions. Many colleges respond to both the form and substance of periodic curricular revisions undertaken at prestigious universities such as Harvard and the University of Chicago. The form of institutional curricula[1] and the course offerings of departments in colleges and universities all across the United States are shaped by faculty members who, in turn, were shaped by the major universities where they took their doctorates.

In sum, the curricula of higher education are formed through an amorphous process of expansion and contraction, with accretions significantly outweighing deletions. (It is very difficult to retire a department once it has an established constituency of faculty and students.) It is not a highly rational, deliberate process of setting goals, determining knowledge relevant to these goals, organizing this knowledge to facilitate students' learning, and using evaluation to determine the need for curricular revision. Pervading the whole is the basic assumption that the faculty knows best. Although faculty members may not be able to agree on a cohesive, symmetrical, institutional curriculum, they close ranks when their autonomy is seriously threatened. Through good times and bad times, they manage to retain this autonomy largely because of a sometimes fragile image that they are professionals and are therefore qualified to decide.

Curriculum development in secondary education: shared decision making

All of the political and substantive complexities of curriculum development in American higher education, and more, pertain to the lower schools as well. The secondary school has been referred to as the Bermuda Triangle of curriculum reform (Goodlad, 1978, p. 144). Here, too, departmental fiefdoms prevail. Because the faculty is not generating new knowledge, however, there is little generation of new fields from within. The curricular questions requiring attention are essentially the same as in higher education, but they must be answered for an even more heterogeneous student population.

Virtually all of the differences between higher and secondary education conspire to further complicate curriculum development for the latter. First, there is the *system* of public schooling. However loosely coupled (Weick, 1976) it may be, it is clearly more regulated and hierarchical than the system of higher education. (Recall Clark Kerr's description of the modern university: "a series of individual entrepreneurs held together by a common grievance over parking" [1963, p. 20].) When principals and teachers in my inquiry into schooling, "A Study of Schooling,"[2] were asked to rate the influence of various individuals and groups on *their* school, the superintendent and the board came out as being most influential. Authority is dispersed throughout the system, with responsibilities not clearly defined. Even though both the principals and the teachers in this sample, overall, would put their respective groups in the top position in answer to who should have the most influence, it is difficult to find research suggesting that the principal and teachers assume that they have clear authority and responsibility for developing the school's curriculum. Lacking such authority, teachers associations frequently bargain for a major decision-making role in curriculum planning.

Second, not only is the system of public secondary education somewhat hierarchical, with authority distributed but not clearly distinguished among board, superintendent, principal, and teachers, but it also is relatively open at the top and on the sides (Goodlad, 1978, pp. 141–142). Despite charges that the system is "closed," belief, rhetoric, and some aspects of practice attest to a public school system belonging to the people. Individual parents confer with individual teachers over classroom practices. Groups of parents intervene to remove books from libraries. Legislators hesitate not one moment in passing laws designed to affect everything from courses offered to how classroom time is spent. They rarely ask, "Whose decision is this?" By contrast, higher-education communities enjoy enormous autonomy regarding curriculum and instruction.

Third, the public has lost most of whatever innocence it once had regarding the professional status and accompanying perquisites of teachers. Educators have not fallen as rapidly and as far on the public faith index as have politicians, for example, but they can no longer count on being trusted to know what is best for Dick and Jane. Although the majority of parents surveyed in "A Study of Schooling" would put the principal and teachers in their school ahead of themselves, the superintendent, and the board when asked who *should* have the most influence, they want to participate in school affairs – not just in social events but in more fundamental matters pertaining to school programs.

It should not surprise us that systematic, rational, institutional curriculum planning is not characteristic of secondary schools, just as it is not characteristic of higher education. Even if there were clarity with respect to faculty responsibility and authority for curriculum decision making, there is no time allocated for it. There is an irony in the fact that teachers frequently bargain for more authority in determining the curriculum and simultaneously for restrictions on using their time beyond lesson preparation, teaching classes, and counseling students. If a reasonably cohesive, symmetrical curriculum is desirable for a secondary school, then presumably some group should be busily designing and implementing it. If not the principal and teachers, then who?

There is not much, if any, serious work being done now to design comprehensive secondary curricula for the American systems of public and private education. Some of the discipline-centered approaches initiated in the 1950s and 1960s continue, and a few new projects have emerged. The faculties of individual departments in many secondary schools find some time to discuss curricular matters on a fairly regular basis. Publishing houses work hard in a very competitive market to place their curricular wares in the hands of teachers. But all of this falls far short of deliberate, sustained efforts to provide every student with a balanced curriculum for his or her academic, social, vocational, and personal development. There are few signs of existing or emerging policies designed to assure this right to learn according to a sensibly coordinated plan.

From standards to policy: two models

The autonomy of teachers: Can they be trusted?

So what? Behind the classroom door, teachers have always exercised considerable autonomy in determining what and how Dick and Jane learn. Data from "A Study of Schooling" suggest that they still exercise this autonomy, regardless of the many bills bearing on instruction passed in state capitols. Indeed, teachers appear frequently to be quite unaware of the content of these enactments (Hill, 1979, pp. 101–127). Teachers surveyed in "A Study of Schooling" claimed to be influenced most in their teaching by their own experience and by students' interests and needs, and much less by state and district guides, supervisors, or even textbooks. Should we not be encouraged by this? In spite of extensive public interest in the schools and the endless intervention of legislators, teachers appear to have retained the autonomy they need to make relatively independent decisions in the classroom. Is this not the best way to assure the education our children need?

Values and standards: the conventional model

Policy presumably grows out of some recognition and clarification of a problem. A problem emerges when something appears to be malfunctioning, departing from a norm, or inadequate in the light of new or increased expectations. But words such as *malfunctioning, norm,* and *expectations* imply standards, interests, or values. Somebody's standards or interests determine the presence and nature of the problem. The initial diagnosis shapes the formulation of policy.

The conventional standard for determining the presence of a problem in schooling is achievement test scores. When Scholastic Aptitude Test (SAT) scores hold steady for a period of years or when they are on the rise, there is no problem worthy of concerted effort; society's response mechanisms are at rest. When test scores drop over a period of years, there is a problem; responses range from criticism in the press, to an increase in remedial courses, to governmental intervention.

The decade of the 1970s was just such a "problem" period. The diagnosis focused on the need for improvement in student achievement in easily testable areas. The "obvious" solution was to give greater attention to teacher accountability for students' learning. State policies for the accreditation of teacher education programs favored precise definitions of teaching skills, implying that everyone knows what these are. Teachers possessing these skills would be able to improve student achievement. Change strategies drew their rationale from the familiar ends–means model, with the means being a reduction of goals to behavioral objectives and the attainment of these then measured as though they were ends in themselves. The application of this process of reductionism to teaching and learning is not new. Bobbitt spelled it out in 1924 but shifted his position dramatically in later writings (1941). The shift in state policies later in the decade, from emphasizing teachers' accountability to stressing students' responsibility, was predictable. Accountability not asked for and not sitting well with teachers was shifted to students. Today, more and more states are developing proficiency tests to be passed for high school graduation and, sometimes, for passage from grade to grade. Only the details of this response are new. Some Americans still recall sitting for examinations in the 1920s and 1930s in order to graduate from elementary school and then, later, from high school. This was done in large part to assure that graduation would "mean something" and to prevent laggards from entering the next level (and presenting that level with the problem of teaching a more heterogeneous student population).

This, too, shall pass. The surest sign of the ending of one era and the transition to another in schooling is the shifting of major, virtually sole, responsibility to students. The ultimate rhetoric is "shape up or ship out" (Ebel, 1980). It assuages the conscience of everyone. Americans now need only better tests, not more creative state and local policies and delivery systems. Nonlearning is due to students' deficiencies, not defective curricula and teaching strategies. There is less need to sacrifice financially for the public education of the young.

We must never forget that policies reflect interests and values, their substance resulting from one set of interests winning out over another. Those seeking to influence policy seek out research that supports their views, eschewing research that does not. The astute political maneuver is to make it appear that solid evidence dictated the policy, rather than admitting that the proposed policy limited the search for truth. This is particularly desirable when political debate is in a domain where alternative theories and sketchy evidence prevail, as is often the case in matters of education and schooling. Then, legislated policy can appear to be akin to truth, pushing aside alternative positions. Fortunately, truth needs no legislated validation.

An alternative: the Dewey tradition

It is difficult for new policies reflecting alternative interests and theories to emerge if the state has created a great deal of baggage accompanying existing legislation. The greater the baggage, the less the flexibility to seek new diagnoses of problems as prevailing analyses and solutions appear increasingly dubious. The greater the state's investment in rules, regulations, mandated programs, and tests, the more difficult it is to effect change. Consequently, the trappings of the state surrounding existing educational policies should always be spare and lean.

The existence of an alternative theory vying with the dominant theory for attention and expression in educational policy and practice is not new either. The guiding rhetoric of this alternative usually speaks to individual discovery and growth, the creation of one's own world, setting one's own goals, self-actualization, and personal autonomy. The teaching process is what parents and teachers do to help the individual acquire the knowledge and skills needed for daily living and continued growth. The curriculum provides for the sustained cultivation of individual traits in a nurturing environment. Power in learning is derived from understanding basic principles; the learning of facts and mechanics is instrumental and important, but not in itself basic.

Bobbitt, having moved from one philosophical position to another, ended up sounding very much like John Dewey in aligning himself with the alternative position sketched above:

> Education then is to help children and youths day by day and year by year to see things truly, to think about them clearly, to feel toward them rightly, to plan wisely their daily dealings with them, and then forcefully to achieve their purposes. Their education is to help them to the experiences each day and year that gradually make them proficient in worthy living.
> . . . The good life is the thing that is to be learned, and the pupils learn it by living it. [Bobbitt, 1941, p. vii]

The concepts are slippery. They do not easily lend themselves to operationalization for Monday morning's lessons. Further, they are easily converted into romantic belief in the virtue of spontaneous, unpremeditated, nonreflective action. Such belief, in turn, "translates itself into an educational methodology that is anti-intellectual and anti-developmental where purposes, plans, goals and directions are eschewed in favor of feelings and emotions" (Doll, 1979, p. 340). Dewey perceived such a methodology to be off base because of its misconception of the conditions required for independent thinking (1974, pp. 153–154).

Because the methods of applying this alternative theory are not readily translated into a technology, they are not easily translated into state policy either. Legislators neither want nor have the luxury to wait, listening to the importance of nurturing pedagogical behavior on the part of teachers, while they are reading about declining test scores. They want to author a bill that will directly address their perception of the problem as well as appease their constituents. But now that we are down to the core of indifferent students as the heart of the malaise, there's not much left to legislate. Perhaps we're ready to consider alternative diagnoses of what needs to be set right in education and schooling.

The need for a new agenda for schooling

The wedding of data and theory

Persons who sense that the SAT and other standardized test scores do not tell them much about the quality of education in schools employ alternative standards of quality and look for alternative kinds of clues. They look for evidence to substantiate (or even reject) their initial ideas. They bring norms and values to an inquiry that becomes more and more intriguing as the pieces begin to suggest different hypotheses. Ultimately, it is these norms and values, illuminated by *selected* data, that guide the formulation of policy – norms and values that prevail over others' norms, values, and selected data. One policy then replaces another, or a policy appears where there was none before. Unfortunately, those who argued and won in the political arena too often come to believe that what has now been legislated is truth, not just a hypothesis reflecting current beliefs and selected data. New trappings replace the old. One hopes that the best theory, with the best supporting evidence, is embedded in the new policy.

It is in anticipation of imbuing policy with sound theory and evidence that most scholars become involved in the making of policy. Yet despite their protestations, they usually believe "that a working hypothesis is far more than a hypothesis – that it is a principle, that it is correct" (Conant, 1964, p. 30). Otherwise, they would not become involved, as they so often do, in advocacy.

A new agenda: the data

The major problems of American schooling are not those that have attracted prime attention in recent years. We have been addressing symptoms, not problems. The perspective with which this chapter views the educational scene differs markedly from the one currently guiding policy and action. Consequently, the body of data referred to here differs from the data most commonly cited. Needless to say, this proposed agenda differs from or at least goes beyond what others have proposed, and its implementation calls for alternative policies. Further, this analysis suggests that continued stress on the most visibly dominant state policies of recent years will contribute to worse, not better, quality of education in schools (Goodlad, 1979b).

Two sets of data from "A Study of Schooling" suggest a new agenda. First, senior high school students in the sample who are judged to be the most able study curricular offerings that are quite different from those curricular offerings studied by students judged to be the least able. Second, the range of instructional procedures encountered in progressing upward from elementary through middle and senior levels of schooling is extraordinarily narrow. Several different kinds of findings add up to these generalizations.

The comprehensive high school ideal. Today's secondary school curriculum is a far cry from Conant's concept of the comprehensive high school in the 1960s. He recommended that more than half of each student's program be required – a condition that most high school principals and teachers would claim pertains today. But he went on to insist that this common core would be made up of several *courses* required of all students, irrespective of ability (1959, p. 47). Differences in ability to learn would be met by placing students in sections, each at a different level *of the same subject.* Whether or not one agrees with Conant's advocacy of achievement grouping, it is clear that he had in mind students studying common subject matter, albeit at differing rates of speed. Less than half of their time would be spent in electives, which he hoped would include art and music. His concept of the comprehensive high school included the development of marketable skills through vocational education programs, but not at the expense of the required core. He urged that every effort be made to prevent the separation and isolation of students in and into vocational courses.

The reality: data from "A Study of Schooling." Against the backdrop of students' curricula in the high schools observed in "A Study of Schooling," Conant's recommendations appear austere and dated. Large numbers of students are in predominantly academic *or* vocational programs. According to principals and counselors, few of those completing their sophomore year in the predominantly vocational track would find it possible to complete Conant's recommended program by the time of graduation. In effect, using Conant's criteria, their curricula are already woefully out of balance. Further, to varying degrees depending on the high school, many of the vocationally oriented students take their academic subjects together rather than with the more academically oriented students.

In 8 of the 13 high schools in this sample, students were found to be "tracked" in the 4 basic subjects required for college admission: English, social studies (Conant specified history and American government), mathematics, and science. Students in the other 5 schools were tracked in 3 of these. Little evidence was found to suggest that this tracking was in different sections of essentially the same sequential subject matter. Indeed, in spite of the labels, it often was difficult to conclude that all of the options available under, say, the social studies label were even in that field. Many of the so-called tracks were not, then, tracks, in the sense of providing guiding rails for trains spaced at different intervals and traveling at different rates of speed.

"A Study of Schooling" data suggest that a major response to student individuality in these schools is separation of students into different *kinds,* rather than *levels,* of subject matter. The explanations that come to mind are not charitable. One is that there has been little thought about what knowledge is of most worth. Consequently, all courses are of equal value. Another explanation pertains to dominant beliefs about human ability. If one assumes that ability is innate and immutable and that some subject matter is harder than other subject matter, then one separates the high and low achievers accordingly. But if, with Carroll (1963), we assume ability to mean ability to understand instruction, then we open up the possibility of meeting individual differences by differentiating instructional procedures for students enrolled in the same, not different, courses. Indeed, we would expect such pedagogical adaptations even if high and low achievers were separated into different courses. But this would not be likely to occur if the culture of schooling both included and reinforced a tacit pedagogy of limited variability.

Implications of the data

Let us turn now to inferences from the data on teaching practices. The impression that results from observations in over 1,000 classrooms is that instruction through the grades, whatever the subject, is characterized by an extraordinary sameness: teachers lecturing and questioning, students responding, classes covering textbook pages in concert, individuals reading and completing workbook exercises, quizzes, and tests. By the fourth grade, there are few surprises. In general, the atmosphere of teaching and learning appears "flat" more than punitive or abrasive. Increasingly, as students in the sample move upward from elementary to secondary schools, they perceive time to be spent more on instruction than on routines or controlling student behavior. They become socialized into school and to a considerable degree become rather accepting of it. Meanwhile the social and athletic ambience and activities of school become increasingly important.

Teachers' praise and encouragement of students engaged in learning, sparse at all levels, is half as frequent in secondary as compared with primary classes. There is no evidence to suggest that teachers instructing the lower tracks engage in more creative efforts to reach children and youths who are placed there, presumably because of learning difficulties. Indeed, such evidence as exists points precisely to the opposite (Oakes, 1981). Curricular rather than pedagogical adaptations appear to be a common response to individual differences. Of course, there are deviations. Some teachers rise above the norm, unique because of their starlike qualities, regardless of the setting in which they work. There is more "hands-on" activity, movement, and even involvement in decision making, for example, in the arts, physical education, and vocational education (which consistently are the most liked subjects) than in the more academic subjects. The common experience of students in the schools studied appears to be much less the subject matter studied by all and much more the teaching experiences commonly encountered.

If we give ourselves the latitude to leap from these contextual data, as others leap from achievement test scores, we see alternative diagnoses of school problems and an alternative agenda for policy and practice emerge. This agenda suggests no "quick fix."

The effect of current state policies on curricula

Curriculum development to date

Earlier, questions were raised about prevailing diagnoses of school problems and state policies addressed to them. The first part of this new diagnosis points to the institutional curriculum and particularly to the curriculum experienced by secondary school students. Let us review briefly what has been happening in curriculum development.

The curriculum work begun in the 1950s emphasizing structure and method in the subject disciplines (Goodlad, 1964) has virtually dried up. In part because of congressional concern over *Man: A Course of Study* (Bruner, DeVore, & Balikci, 1970) financed by the National Science Foundation, federal agencies have been markedly skittish over becoming involved in curriculum development. When the National Institute of Education tentatively explored a potential involvement in curriculum development, the response from groups supposedly interested in the school curriculum was for a piece of any pending action, not an identification of basic need (National Institute of Education, 1976). Few fundamental curriculum issues were put forward.

Curriculum activity at the state level has been in support of special interests: bilingual education, vocational education, education of the handicapped, drug and alcohol education, and so on. There are few curriculum generalists in state departments of education and little conceptual or developmental work designed to provide a guiding framework for schools seeking to address the question of what constitutes a balanced, general education for all children and youth. State guidelines and interventions have stressed the development of minimum competencies and proficiencies in teachers and students. The task of overall curriculum development is left to local districts and schools, if only by default.

Local energy, too, is taken up largely by meeting these minimum requirements and demonstrating accountability as conventionally defined. Teachers teach. The summer workshops of principals, teachers, and consultants that attempt to address the curriculum are of another era, even in relatively prosperous school districts. The times are not hospitable to budgetary allocations for curriculum planning and development. But is the absence of funds an indication of their unavailability or a sign of inadequate diagnoses and misplaced priorities?

Gaps in teacher education

Colleges and universities have both fueled and reflected trends and priorities. Since the early 1970s teacher education programs have been guided and accredited primarily on the basis of precise definitions of competencies desired in teachers, even though verification of these is at best heuristic. Relatively little attention is given to the classic questions of curriculum development, the social context of schooling, or the epistemology by means of which teachers might acquire some understanding of the phenomena with which they deal. Lacking sufficient understanding, many teachers become particularly vulnerable to limited pedagogical procedures that adequately address only a small part of their daily work. Such procedures may cheer teachers on Monday morning but leave them looking for something else on Tuesday.

With little emphasis on curriculum development in the system of teacher education, one should not be surprised to find disarray in the secondary school curriculum. The data from high schools in "A Study of Schooling" alert one to the possible nature of the problem. But others might conclude that the picture revealed is precisely as it should be. One brings to data a set of norms. The fit or lack of fit between data and norms conveys discomfort or a sense that all is well. The author's reaction is one of discomfort. Are young people gaining access in schools to the knowledge and skills they need for personal development and responsible citizenship? Is there equity with respect to access to knowledge? Are self-fulfilling prophecies being created for segments of the student population because of early, possibly faulty judgments about their ability to learn?

These worries compound when a diagnosis of instructional methods is added. Data from the 38 elementary, junior high, and senior high schools in "A Study of Schooling" suggest a narrow, unimaginative range of pedagogical procedures. There is also evidence of a falling off in praise, encouragement, and other indices of demonstrated concern for students' learning problems as students progress through the grades. The consistency of these findings suggests the possibility of a serious problem extending beyond this sample.

A misdiagnosis of need: the mechanistic approach to teaching

State and local policies focused on instructional improvement are apparently addressed to an existing need. But one is forced to wonder whether the need has been correctly diagnosed and whether the response is likely to be helpful. Competencies defined for teachers and proficiencies required for students may be of some help, but they suggest both a mechanical model of education and a rather punitive approach to improvement. Further, there is a simplistic rationality (Wise, 1979) to this approach that simply does not recognize the complexity of the context within which teaching and learning occur (Sarason, 1971). Analyses of such approaches in recent years question the appropriateness of implied assumptions about change and improvement (House, 1974).

A mechanistic model of teaching and learning probably reinforces some of the kinds of teaching found in schools as described earlier. It always has been difficult for teachers to transcend the circumstances of 25 or more students in a confined space. Teachers become preoccupied with control and look for classroom activities appearing to help maintain that control. And since *some* of what learning involves *is* mechanistic, it is useful for teachers to be able to be efficiently mechanistic.

Efficient control of the classroom and even mechanical skill are not sufficient, however. There are many other kinds of learning, some of them suggested by such terms as *problem solving, inquiry, discovery, interpolation, extrapolation*. There are interests to be met, new interests to be aroused, talents to be cultivated, creativity to be encouraged. And there is nurturing to be done. Teachers' lack of concern for students as persons, and especially students' awareness of this, frequently will negate teachers' technical skill. Many of the parents surveyed in "A Study of Schooling" expressed concern over teachers' attention to their children as individuals and about whether average students were getting a good education.

Policies developed in good faith do not necessarily have their intended effects. It may be that recent state policies with respect to expectations for teachers and students have reinforced those very characteristics of classrooms that most need to be remedied. A careful study of the impact of existing policies and strategies is very much needed.

Policy recommendations: the new agenda

The tacit agenda: our goals for schooling

Implicit in the foregoing sections is the belief that it is the tacit underpinnings of policies and not their literal wording that influences – especially in domains such as schooling where much of what goes on already is infused with tacit understandings. Because so much of what commonly goes on in schools arises and proceeds without expressed or written agreements, specifications from the outside are often ignored unless they happen to reinforce the existing tacit understanding. Even many regulations in state education codes are ignored because they do not fit teachers' perceptions of their role. Regulations that cannot be ignored are frequently given lip service, sometimes with accompanying symbolic exchanges of paper designed to give the impression that requirements are being met. Such tactics infuriate legislators and others concerned about the schools. Not surprisingly, the policies they then propose reflect this frustration and carry punitive messages. Holding students accountable and defining the specifics of that accountability become last resorts.

Perhaps it is time to convey a different message, tacitly and overtly. It should begin with the nature of state and local expectations for schools. Over more than 300 years we have evolved for our schools four sets of goals: academic, social and civic, vocational, and personal. Each of these is endorsed by parents surveyed in "A Study of Schooling." State task forces that get serious about what our schools are for come up rather consistently with a dozen or so educational goals reflecting these four broad areas (Goodlad, 1979b, pp. 46–52). Might not the articulation of these be sufficient statement of policy guidelines regarding purposes for schools and those in them?

But these goals are invariably very general, it is said, and subject to interpretation. Of course, that is precisely their beauty. Broad, comprehensive goals convey something of the scope and complexity of the educational process. The tacit message to teachers is that the scope of their work is broad and cannot be reduced to mechanics. They are there to develop the wholeness of the individual's learning.

Tyler often is cited as "the father of behavioral objectives." But this is not the Ralph Tyler known today, nor is it the Tyler who wrote the commonly cited monograph entitled *Basic Principles of Curriculum and Instruction* (1949). He recommended, over three decades ago, that about a dozen broad goals are sufficient. Further, he urged that these goals include the domains of knowledge within which the needed understandings, skills, and values are to be developed. Tyler went on to recommend that a secondary school English department consider not just the learnings most naturally derived from literature, for example, but that the teachers examine their potential contribution to all of the goals. Presumably, the faculty of a high school would address the matter of developing a program to encompass the full set of goals.

These are not the kinds of activities being assiduously pursued today. Their importance is not conveyed in the message of state policy. Time for them is not built into yearly schedules. To repeat that there is curricular neglect should come as no surprise. Without a cohesive set of goals and educational priorities, there is no foundation for a coordinated curriculum.

The first plank in an alternative state policy for schools, then, is a carefully conceived and articulated set of goals in each of the four broad areas: academic, social and civic, vocational, and personal development. These goals should not be further reduced to precise behaviors. Let there be continued search for better tests. Let there be continued diagnostic national and state assessments. But let there not be legislated pedagogical skills for teachers nor proficiencies for students' grade progression and graduation. Let us help teachers define and use behavioral objectives as just *part* of their teaching repertoire.

The development of a coordinated curriculum

Next, independent of legislation and licensing, we need centers to address the whole of the curriculum. If not university-based, they must be university-related. Much of their work would be conceptual, directed to the scope and sequence of K–12 programs designed to be balanced in all four goal areas. These centers might well be regional rather than state or local.

Closer to schools, there needs to be resuscitation of and improvement upon the fine curriculum services once provided local school districts by such intermediate agencies as county offices. These, in turn, need to be linked to curriculum centers and to district and individual school planners.

None of this badly needed activity will be successful, however, unless the authority and responsibility of school faculties, in collaboration with their communities, is clarified and supported. Time for faculty planning during the year (lengthened to provide for it), rotation of teachers from teaching to curriculum development, and intensive "hands-on" summer workshops are essential elements. Planning a school's curriculum is extraordinarily difficult – for both substantive and political reasons (McClure, 1979). Before we throw up our hands over assumed costs involved, we should examine present spending priorities.

Basic to the necessary curriculum work are appraisal systems to determine the programs actually engaged in by students. A balanced institutional curriculum is not necessarily a balanced curriculum experienced by the individual student. We need for each student an inventory of studies engaged in from kindergarten on up and sensitive monitoring designed to guide him or her in course selection. However useful certain kinds of tests may be, they do not give us the needed picture of what is being studied year after year or at any given time.

School improvement through reforms in teacher education: a view of the future

Just as we need policies and logistics to assure access to knowledge for our young, we also need instructional procedures designed to engage them meaningfully in this knowledge. Present approaches to the improvement of instruction are woefully inadequate: a brief orientation for educators at the beginning of the school year, a few days of in-service education during the year, and summer attendance at how-to workshops – usually hyped up with "name" speakers and recreational activities designed to create a vacation atmosphere for teachers who must foot the fees and living costs themselves. Is this the way a successful corporation would seek improved performance by its employees? The more one thinks about what we do and don't do to improve the effectiveness of teachers, the more pitiful it appears and the angrier one becomes. We complain about inadequate schools, yet do nothing seriously designed to assure their improvement and continue to vote against school bonds (often with the excuse that the schools are not good enough to warrant more money!).

More than the improvement of pedagogical skills is required if education in schools is to improve. Some of the initiatives must come from outside the system of schooling, with its implicit agreements and resistance to fundamental reforms. The teaching profession has nurtured the myth that instructional technology is merely an extension of the teacher. Technology is only one more tool, of course, but with the advent of computers and computer-dependent learning systems, it has become apparent that only modest utilization of teacher energy is required to create productive learning situations where students interact directly with electronic energy. Teachers generally fail to understand the economics of their vocation, that it is a labor-intensive enterprise unlikely to eventuate into greater financial benefits for them until they embrace the potential benefits of technology. The school of the future, whether or not a building on 10 acres of ground, will feature human and machine teachers working productively and appropriately side by side.

Substituting one course for another, or redefining competencies for teachers more clearly, is merely playing at the edges of needed reform in the education of educators. Teacher education is one of the few domains of "professional" education where the tacit assumption is that most of what is required for practice of the profession will be learned later, on the job, after a degree representing minimal preparation has been awarded. This is not assumed in medicine or law, although it is assumed that doctors and lawyers will continue to do whatever is required later for continuing competence. For the physician, the M.D. is the first and last professional degree, unless related professional activity is contemplated, as in psychiatry or certain kinds of research where the Ph.D. frequently is added.

Teachers graduating with bachelors degrees and preliminary certification struggle toward masters degrees while teaching and raising families. The individual effort is commendable, but the implied societal indifference to teachers and teaching is a disgrace. Cremin (1978) has recommended the doctor of education degree as the professional degree in teaching (paralleling the doctor of medicine degree as the professional degree in medicine). This will be perceived as far too radical by most people, but surely a master of teaching degree should be regarded as minimal. Further professional growth would be expected, but another degree would not – unless for related professional activity, as with psychiatry.

Once more, hands rise in protest over costs. But must we continue to think only of self-contained classrooms of 25 students each and a teacher? We have had experience with other models of educational delivery systems, and there are also models worth adapting from parallel areas of human endeavor. Schooling and education in the future will be characterized by greater differentiation of the roles to be played in educating the young. There will be apprentices, there will be master teachers, and there will be electronic learning systems, and surely there will be much more use of adult role models and specialized instructors drawn from all sectors of the community. Can we not afford this? Or, better, can we afford not to have this?

What policies and logistics do we need now as the medium to carry us surely to where we next need to be? Whatever the policies, they will convey implicit messages to people as well as serving as guides to practice. Let these be messages of hope, of high expectations for human accomplishments, and of extraordinary faith in the ability of individuals, when trusted and supported, to fulfill these expectations.

We have come through a decade of contrary messages, and our schools still survive, albeit badly shaken. Perhaps this is because, as Parkinson (1957) so aptly warned, to deprive people of hope takes time.

Notes

1 For definition and further clarification of the institutional level, as contrasted with other levels of curriculum decisions, see Goodlad (1979a, pp. 17–41).
2 For further information regarding the research project "A Study of Schooling," see Goodlad, Sirotnik, and Overman (1979, pp. 174–178).

References

Bobbitt, F. *How to make a curriculum.* Cambridge, Mass.: Riverside Press, 1924.
Bobbitt, F. *The curriculum of modern education.* New York: McGraw-Hill, 1941.
Bruner, J., DeVore, I., & Balikci, A. *Man: A course of study.* Washington, D.C.: Curriculum Development Associates, 1970.
Carroll, J. B. A model of school learning. *Teachers College Record,* May 1963, *64,* 723–733.
Conant, J. B. *The American high school today.* New York: McGraw-Hill, 1959.
Conant, J. B. *Two modes of thought.* New York: Trident Press, 1964.
Cremin, L. A. *The education of the educating professions.* Nineteenth annual Charles W. Hunt lecture. Presented at the meeting of the American Association of Colleges for Teacher Education, Washington, D.C., February 21, 1978.
Dewey, J. Individuality and experience. In R. D. Archambault (Ed.), *John Dewey on education: Selected writings.* Chicago: University of Chicago Press, 1974.
Doll, W. E., Jr. A structural view of curriculum. *Theory into Practice,* December 1979, *18,* 336–348.
Ebel, R. L. The failure of schools without failure. *Phi Delta Kappan,* February 1980, *61*(6), 386–388.
Goodlad, J. I. *School curriculum reform in the United States.* New York: Fund for the Advancement of Education, 1964.
Goodlad, J. I. Political issues in curriculum reform. In W. I. Israel (Ed.), *Political issues in education.* Washington, D.C.: Council of Chief State School Officers, 1978.
Goodlad, J. I. The scope of the curriculum field. In J. I. Goodlad and Associates, *Curriculum inquiry: The study of curriculum practice.* New York: McGraw-Hill, 1979. (a).
Goodlad, J. I. *What schools are for.* Bloomington, Ind.: Phi Delta Kappa Educational Foundation, 1979. (b)
Goodlad, J. I., Sirotnik, K. S., & Overman, B. C. An overview of "A study of schooling." *Phi Delta Kappan,* November 1979, *61,* 174–178.
Hill, H. W. Societal decisions in curriculum. In J. I. Goodlad and Associates, *Curriculum inquiry: The study of curriculum practice.* New York: McGraw-Hill, 1979.

House, E. R. *The politics of educational innovation*. Berkeley, Calif.: McCutchan, 1974.

Kerr, C. *The uses of the university*. Cambridge: Harvard University Press, 1963.

Man: A Course of Study. Educational Development Center, Inc. Cambridge, Mass., 1970.

McClure, R. M. Institutional decisions in curriculum. In J. I. Goodlad and Associates, *Curriculum inquiry: The study of curriculum practice*. New York: McGraw-Hill, 1979.

National Institute of Education. *Current issues, problems, and concerns in curriculum development*. Washington, D.C.: Department of Health, Education, and Welfare, 1976.

Oakes, J. *A question of access: Tracking and curriculum differentiation in a national sample of English and mathematics classes* (Tech. Rep. 24). Los Angeles: Laboratory in School and Community Education, Graduate School of Education, University of California, 1981.

Parkinson, C. N. *Parkinson's law*. Boston: Houghton Mifflin, 1957.

Sarason, S. B. *The culture of the school and the problem of change*. Boston: Allyn and Bacon, 2d ed., 1982.

Tyler, R. W. *Basic principles of curriculum and instruction*. Chicago: University of Chicago Press, 1949.

Weick, K. E. Educational organization as loosely coupled systems. *Administrative Science Quarterly*. March 1976, *21*, 3–9.

Wise, A. E. *Legislated learning*. Berkeley: University of California Press, 1979.

18   Public Law 94–142 and the formation of educational policy

Seymour B. Sarason

Before World War II, American society was in the most minimal way confronted with the formulation of public policies that required special knowledge of human behavior, especially in regard to those considered to have distinctive problems or needs, including children, the elderly, and the handicapped. For all practical purposes, public policy for such groups referred to the intervention by state and local governments in aiding the needy. It was not until after World War II that the federal government, in large part because of pressure from state and local government, came onto the scene and initiated a cascade of legislation that has only recently abated. Before the war, for example, the Office of Education was small and impotent; after the war it began to expand exponentially as a result of legislation addressing the needs of special groups in the schools. New national institutes were formed to support and improve research and practice in regard to certain "special-need" groups in the population. The growth in size of the federal government is in no small measure due to the acceptance of the proposition, itself a policy, that it is in the self-interest of the society to promote better understanding of and help for specified groups whose core problems raise questions about their "psychology." It should be emphasized that this proposition contains two parts: (1) these groups need (deserve) special understanding and help, and (2) at the present time neither our understanding nor helping practices are based on firm knowledge.

The direction or the means through which knowledge could be increased were relatively clear to the policy makers because there were institutions in the society whose main reason for existence was to contribute to knowledge. These institutions were the universities. The task, then, was to make funds available to individual researchers. That task had four major parts: to support researchers already working on the problem, to attract the interest of other researchers, to train new genera-

315

tions of researchers, and to support a variety of approaches to the particular problem areas. The obvious assumption was that just as university researchers in the physical sciences had demonstrated their worth to society, so would the behavioral sciences. That assumption seemed so obvious, so unchallengeable, so "natural" that no thought was given to its possible limitations. This chapter argues that the assumption had limitations, not that it was wrong.

At this point it is important to note that policies about research in human behavior derived from conventional wisdom within the institution we call the university. Policy makers had been – and their advisors were – university people. Had not the university demonstrated its practical worth to the society? In fact, policy makers frequently argued that the society had been derelict in supporting behavioral science research in the university. There seemed no grounds for questioning where, and by whom, research should be conducted.

When we turn to the other part of the proposition – increasing and supporting helping services – policy makers were confronted with dramatically different, more complicated, and more murky issues. It has almost always been the case that public policy has at the same time two directions: to further research *and* improve practice. But how do policy makers decide the direction and means for improving practice and service? In the matter of furthering research, the direction and means were relatively simple: Announce and promote the policy and guidelines and await applications for grant support from *individual* researchers in the university. To improve practice and service, however, one did not seek individuals but rather agencies and institutions that provided services to the targeted populations.

Assessing the merits of an individual research proposal is less complicated than assessing a proposal from a complex social institution (e.g., a school or school system, a social agency, or a residential institution). In the case of the individual researcher, the reviewers can read what he or she has previously done and published, check to see if the researcher is knowledgeable about the relevant research literature, and conduct a site visit to get a better feel for whether the researcher can accomplish what he or she has proposed to do. In the case of a complex social setting, the assessment task is more difficult and problematic because the culture of the setting – its traditions, formal and informal organization and sources of power, relationship to clients and the community, everyday ambiance and morale – is, under the best circumstances, difficult to fathom. The difficulty is increased when, as is frequently the case with federal legislation, the number of eligible organizations is too large to make site visits a possibility, with the result that decisions have to be made on the basis of the written application alone.

A case study: the Experimental Schools Program

A case in point is the Experimental Schools Program (ESP). This program represented a federal initiative to make it possible for selected school systems to overcome their internal fragmentation and unrelatedness to their communities. Until this program, different parts of a school system could be receiving support from different parts of the Office of Education, thus reinforcing rather than overcoming fragmentation and markedly constricting the spread of hoped-for benefits. After two decades of piecemeal support to schools, it was apparent that the capacity of school systems to integrate their programs and services had not been strengthened and that community participation in the affairs of school systems was still a slogan and not a reality. So with great fanfare, including a special message to Congress by President Nixon, the Experimental Schools Program was announced. The program became operational in 1971 when 8 urban sites were awarded planning grants. By 1973, some 18 sites, 8 urban and 10 rural, were being funded.

The author was a consultant to those who had to choose the schools that would be funded. Not atypically, decisions had to be made before the end of the fiscal year. The decision makers were confronted with scores of applications, the average weight of each being around four pounds. By criteria unknown to me, the pile of applications had been reduced to about twice the number for which funds would be available. There had been many telephone conversations between the decision makers and officials from the school systems of the final running. The consultants had been asked to read these applications and to make recommendations. Obviously, the applications could not be read with any care unless the consultants had been given sabbaticals. This author, therefore, made no recommendations. But what if there had been more time to read and even to make visits to each site? With what confidence could one decide if a particular school system had really put it all together and therefore deserved to get a large sum of money? Before addressing these questions, let us backtrack and ask what the new policy to improve educational practice and service was reacting to. What had policy makers learned from past policies that had failed? Cowden and Cohen (1979), who evaluated the ESP, put it this way:

The Experimental Schools Program was based on the policy notion of comprehensive change. This notion remains a familiar one to the federal practice of social policy but at the time of ESP, it offered a novel approach to federal reform efforts in education. Throughout the sixties, a number of efforts in education, including Title I, Head Start, and Teacher Training, had attempted to change local schooling by focusing on a particular population or aspect of a school system. As an alternative "hypothesis" to reform, federal ESP reformers advanced the notion that significant improvements in the outcomes of formal education were not likely to result unless there was "holistic" or "comprehensive" change; that is, unless the different "pieces" were both compatible and mutually reinforcing in a "synergistic" way.

Put in another way, past policies to improve educational practices and service were based on faulty understanding of the culture of schools (Sarason, 1982). Policy makers thought they understood a single school and a single school system to a sufficiently comprehensive and valid degree to base efforts to change educational practices and services. On the basis of what is known about the ESP, it seems that whatever lessons were learned from previous failures were also faulty.

A problem of institutional change: conceptualizing the whole system

We cannot begin to understand the basis for the failures in policies unless we recognize that policy makers were dealing with the problem of institutional change. The policies were directed to improving educational services for children by changing the attitudes and behavior of school personnel, by changing relationships among personnel and between them and the community, and by altering in significant ways the organizational pattern of individual schools and school systems. That is and was a tall order! One can dream up myriad ways about how to change a school and school system, but each of these ways derives from an explicit and implicit picture of what a school system is and how it works. That picture determines the means one employs. If the picture is faulty, then the means one employs will be unproductive and perhaps even faulty.

What pictures were policy makers using that led them to adopt means that have so frequently led to disillusionment? To answer that question is beyond the scope of this chapter, but it is fair to say that policy makers never pursued that question in a systematic way. For one thing, policy makers are people of action who operate under all kinds of pressures to act, to do something, to get things done, to meet deadlines, to ponder and deal with the political arena, to be sensitive to different constituencies and pressure groups, to protect themselves against criticism. Policy makers do not operate in a process or arena that permits reflection, candor, and study. Some educational policy makers have never worked in schools, and although that restriction does not necessarily invalidate whatever picture they have, it does not automatically validate it either. Similarly, the fact that a policy maker may have once worked in schools does not give face validity to whatever picture he or she may have.

As is pointed out elsewhere (Sarason, 1982), it is surprising how many people who work in schools have a very parochial view of the school culture. Inevitably, the picture one has is a function of where one is in the system. Indeed, the failure of policy makers to recognize that a school system is comprised of different groups (e.g., classroom teachers, special class teachers, principals, a variety of administrators, the superintendent, a board of education, psychologists, social workers) who see and define "the system" differently, and who react differently to any effort at system change, in part explains why policies have misfired.

It should be obvious from the preceding that the author is sympathetic to the frustration arising from built-in obstacles that policy makers experience. If there is any criticism to make of policy makers, it is their tendency to present a policy as if it were based on a firmer conceptual foundation than they know it has and to raise public hopes too high by presenting a picture of the process of policy formulation that is incomplete, misleading, and unrealistic. Policy makers generally do not disagree with these criticisms, but some of them have retorted that however valid the criticisms may be, one must see them as inherent in the relationship between politics and the substance of policy. To paraphrase one policy maker: We are not paid to be theoreticians, scholars, or researchers. We are expected to be knowledgeable and to seek advice from those who devote their time to thinking about and researching the issues. And we do seek their advice and we are influenced by them. So when you criticize us you are at the same time criticizing the theorists and researchers who advise us. When we participate in the formulation of a policy we, of course, draw on our own experience and values, but we also draw on a lot of "idea people." Most of us have been away from schools a long time, and we no longer have a first-hand feel for what is going on.

One can be sympathetic to the plight of the policy makers, but that does not excuse them from recognizing more clearly that the central problem is how one conceptualizes a school and a school system. It makes no difference whether the policy is about reading, math, community participation, drug prevention programs, or handicapped children – the effort at change and improvement is directed at a complicated system that has a long tradition and a variety of interconnections with the surrounding community. It may be unfair to ask the policy maker to have a differentiated conceptualization of the school system, but it is not unfair to ask that he or she recognize what the central problem is.

We have seen that policy makers seek the advice of theorists and researchers, and we saw earlier that supporting research is almost always part of a policy. Let us then turn to educational research and theory, if only to determine to what extent they have contributed to a sorry situation.

Educational research and theory

For the most part, educational researchers and theorists are in universities. It is extremely difficult to survive in the university by attacking large, global, fuzzy problems that do not easily lend themselves to traditional conceptions of "good research" and cannot be written up in the length and form that "good journals" require. The socialization of the graduate student and young faculty member into his or her field inculcates, explicitly or implicitly, criteria for what is good and bad research and what is good and bad theory. However people may differ about what is good and bad educational research and theory (and how theory and research should relate to each other), in practice they have one thing in common: The educational problems they work on are *narrow* ones. "Narrow" is not being used in the pejorative sense. Look at any journal of educational research and theory and you will see what is meant by "narrow." The problems are narrow in contrast to what was earlier described as the central or overarching problem: how one conceptualizes a school or a school system. They are legitimate problems, and nothing in this chapter is meant to suggest that they should not be supported. But the ultimate goal is not narrow, and it is the ultimate goal that justifies research expenditures from the federal government.

This does not mean that it is the individual researcher's responsibility to demonstrate how the knowledge he or she gains can be successfully introduced into the school system. That may not be possible or desirable for a variety of reasons. All educational researchers hope that their findings will be a basis for improving something in the school system. All researchers have a picture of where, how, and with what consequences their research will impact in schools. That picture may never be alluded to directly in their research reports, but there is no question that they have it in mind. The picture is also unquestioned by the researcher, who in this respect differs not at all from the policy maker. Because in an ultimate sense research findings have to be seen in relation to the school system, researchers, however narrow their research, cannot long avoid two questions: What is my conception of a school or a school system? and

What are the characteristics contained in that conception that work for or against efforts at change based on the research? The fact is that educational researchers have avoided these questions, which is why the new math, the new biology, and the new physics (among other things) were such debacles (Sarason, 1982).

In the 1960s and early 1970s there were many educational researchers and theorists who asserted that what they were really lacking in their efforts to change and improve school systems were the "right" means, technology, or methodology. The phrases *change agentry* and *change agent* were very fashionable. These terms were used in just the same way that *marketing techniques and strategies* are used in the business world, with the enormous difference that in the business world marketing is based on a lot of homework about the characteristics of the market. This kind of homework is what educational researchers and theorists have not done, and it is this kind of homework that policy makers have neither encouraged nor supported.

The following examples of experiences the author has had with several small groups of educational policy makers and researchers elaborates on this point. In discussions the author posed the following problem:

Assume that you will be able to make one and only one change in schools. There is only one restriction to what that change might be: It would require little or no additional expenditure of money. Obviously you would choose and justify the change in terms of its "ripple effect," that is, it is a change that over time will percolate and have more desirable effects than other changes you could come up with. What would that change be?

(A word about the money restriction: The problem was almost always posed after discussion had produced agreement that even with money, and sometimes a good deal of it, the consequences of efforts at school change provide no basis for satisfaction.)

The reaction to the problem was usually one of silence and obvious puzzlement. The puzzlement did not stem from incomprehension but rather from unfamiliarity with how to think about what one person called the "whole shebang." Each person was knowledgeable about a substantive educational issue that had meaning for a part of the educational system, but none had ever tried to conceptualize systematically the system as a whole. Once people were able to let their minds roam, a variety of proposals arose, of which the following are samples:

1. Eliminate the role of the school principal and place responsibility for the school in the hands of teachers and parents.
2. Drastically deemphasize the teaching of reading and arithmetic in the early grades.

3. Eliminate boards of education as they are currently constituted. Have a board for each school that will then send a representative to a district or central board.
4. Change the curriculum and organization of the high school so that students spend at least half of the day in a community activity that is educationally and intellectually justifiable. These participants came up with this proposal recognizing that it derives from *Youth: Transition to Adulthood* by Coleman (1974).
5. Change the substance of teacher preparation programs in the direction of much more emphasis on child and adolescent development.
6. Make it illegal for schools to mount any "human service" program that diverts attention and time away from the teaching of fundamentals.
7. Require teacher preparation programs to provide their students with a better understanding of cultural and racial diversity as it relates to the school setting.

The proposals did not come easily, and at least half of the group participants felt too uncomfortable or simply were unable to come up with a response. Almost everyone participated in vigorous critiques of each proposal. Each proposal was found wanting in many respects: Either it would have no effect, or it would not benefit students, or the cure was worse than the disease. Given the nature of these meetings, discussion could not go on very long, but it lasted long enough for most of the participants to agree that they really rarely thought about the system as a whole or that they lacked anything like a clear idea or set of criteria by which to judge proposals for change. Yet almost every participant was working on an educational problem or issue that would lead to conclusions that they hoped would have beneficial effects if they were incorporated throughout the educational system. They did not view their work as having applicability to a single school only but to all schools in a system.

What characteristics of the system should researchers examine in order to determine how they would assimilate and accommodate their conclusions and proposed changes? How should the answer to that question guide researchers to the action strategies they or others should adopt? These two questions can never be kept separate from each other (regardless of how narrow the research and the proposals for change derived from it). Consider what it means to think about the system as whole – its different parts, their interrelationships, sources of informal and formal power, the selection and socialization of its personnel, sources of conflict and vehicles for conflict resolution, decision makers and the processes of decision making, the inevitable discrepancies between the rhetoric of policy and the realities of practice, the quantity and quality of interconnectedness with other community agencies, the interconnectedness with the political system, the criteria by which students and personnel are judged deviant, and so on. As soon as one begins to think this way and tries to build a differentiated conception of a school system, one becomes aware that he or she is drawing on experiences (one's own or someone else's) about how each part or process or group tends to respond to a proposal for change. These experiences may never be formally represented in the picture, but that omission says more about the inadequacies of our conception of the system than it does about the importance of the experience. Omitting what these experiences signify results in a description of what the system is supposed to be and not what, in practice, it is. In almost every instance of failure to introduce a change into the educational system, a major causative factor was the failure to distinguish between what is supposed to be and what is, between appearance and reality, between the part and the whole, and between a static and a dynamic system.

Past attempts to change the system

The educational scene has had a surfeit of conceptions about how to introduce a change into a system. They have included the wholesale use of group techniques to change attitudes; changes at the top that were then supposed to trickle down to "the troops"; changes at the bottom that would somehow trickle upward; altering, by administrative fiat or legislation, power relationships within the system and between the system and outside groups; the use of financial and other incentives that would either increase or change motivation and cooperation; the introduction of a voucher system that would force the system to become competitive and therefore presumably better; and demonstrating in one school that a particular change is both desirable and possible and expecting that the rest of the system would then want to get on the bandwagon. The results have not been, to say the least, reassuring. Indeed, the decision to resort to legislation is in large part a recognition that these approaches have had little success, and that unless schools are forced to change they will not change.

Policy makers and policy influencers outside the school system often view schools as one would view a recalcitrant, unmotivated, stonewalling child intent on defeating efforts to change him or her. That analogy is a serious one because the picture many people have of a school system derives from an individual psychology: Individuals (e.g., principals, teachers) are in the foreground, and their embeddedness in a "local" social structure and the interconnectedness of the local to other structures are vaguely, if at all, in the background. We can *see* individuals; we cannot see social structures. Social structures have to be conceptualized in a way that acts as a control against the tendency to forget that what we term *figure* has the characteristics it has because of its ground. That is no less true for perceiving any individual in any part of a school system than it is for perceiving an object in our environment. Unfortunately, too many policy makers, researchers, and "change agents" learned that truism after they failed to achieve their goals.

Shortly after World War II, for example, a national highway policy was formulated and implemented. The aim of the policy was no less than to beribbon the continental United States over time with interstate highways. It was a policy that had a great deal of public support, conjuring up the fantasy that one could get on a highway in New York and never see a traffic light until the West Coast. For all practical purposes no serious consideration was given to the question: Given the nature of the complex and differentiated American society and the traditions, ideologies, and socio-economic, structural, and geographic–demographic features that characterize it, what might be the *adverse* consequences of the highway policy? What groups would be massively dislocated and with what consequences? What could happen to our cities? With the advantage of hindsight, one could add more questions. This is not to suggest that if these questions had been raised, the answers were at hand or the policy would have been altered. The point of the example is that just as efforts to change schools have not been based on an adequate conception of what a school system is, the highway policy did not confront the nature of American society and its social order. It was only after the highway program began and its adverse consequences were recognized that opposition to the policy was articulated. There are more than a few people today who would argue that on balance the highway program, at best, has had mixed consequences and, at worst, has been a social disaster. Even those who view such conclusions as extreme and unwarranted are aware that many consequences of the highway program have been mixed blessings.

Public Law 94–142: a lack of vision

The intent of the law

Let us now turn to a federal educational policy that, like the highway policy, was intended to have beneficial widespread effects. Public Law 94–142, enacted in 1975, is popularly known as the "mainstreaming law." The policy from which that law and the accompanying regulations derive was that all handicapped children should be integrated into a regular classroom and routine school activities according to the criterion of the least restrictive environment. That is to say, it would no longer be desirable and/or possible to segregate handicapped children simply because they were handicapped, and it became the schools' obligation to study and plan for each handicapped child so that his or her program would meet the criterion of the least restrictive alternatives. Policies are not dreamed up; they have a social, political, moral, historical, judicial background. In the case of P.L. 94–142 that background is quite complex and beyond the scope of this chapter. Suffice it to say that the new policy reflected several factors: court decisions invalidating segregation in the schools; court decisions that required schools to assume responsibility for the education of all children; the organized pressures of different parent groups to get schools to be more responsive to the needs of handicapped children; and the belief, held by many people, that the formulation of educational policy in local districts did not sufficiently or meaningfully involve parents or other interested community individuals and groups.

Although it was recognized that schools would need additional resources to implement the new policy – funds to obtain only some of those resources were included in the legislation – the origins of the policy are not comprehensible if one leaves out the belief that the structure and traditions of our schools, and the attitudes of school personnel, have not only been inimical to the objectives of the new policy but would continue to remain so unless schools were forced to change. A close study of the legislation and the somewhat voluminous administrative guidelines that were developed make it hard to avoid the conclusion that schools were seen not as part of the solution but as part of the problem. Whatever doubts the author may have had about this conclusion evaporated when an individual who was influential in formulating the policy and in writing the guidelines told him that the "guts" of the legislation was due process: a set of detailed procedures that would give parents more of a role in decision making about their children. He went on to say: "Even though 94–142 is known as the mainstreaming law, the fact is that the word mainstreaming never appears in the legislation. What we were after was institutionalizing due process."

The implicit conception of schools, embodied in the law

Two things are incontrovertible. First, and most obvious, P.L. 94–142 was intended to change school systems in discernible ways. Second, these changes were not sought by schools but by forces outside of schools. These two factors bring us to an old question: What conception of schools and school systems informed the strategies contained in the legislation?

On the basis of talking to many people who pushed for the new policy and legislation and with a few people influential in writing the legislation, the author concludes that they had nothing resembling a clear conception of what a school system is and how it works. These talks were reminiscent of experiences with the Experimental Schools Program and of discussions with those who were pushing the new math programs.

There was no conception of the system qua system. There was concern about the means and direction for change, but relatively little attention to the basis on which one justified the means. Especially when one is dealing with something as complicated as a school system, any conception of that system does not direct one to one, and only one, means of changing that system. In changing that system, one is always faced with a universe of alternatives for action even when the goal of change is clear. The more differentiated the conception of the system, the more alternatives for action are apparent. The task is to examine each alternative in terms of intended and unintended consequences. A differentiated conception of a system alerts one to possible unintended consequences. If anything has characterized efforts to change schools, it has been the recognition of unintended consequences *after* failure in action. Some of these consequences could have been known ahead of time if one had a differentiated conception of the system that is the object of change. Awareness of and passionate commitment to intended consequences are in practice effective obstacles to thinking systematically about unintended consequences. A partial control against such an error is the attempt to gain clarity about the complexity of the system that is the object of change.

The importance of external forces

In the case of 94–142, decisions about the means for change were (or should have been seen as) more complicated because the pressures for change were coming from without the system rather than from within. What are the different ways the system might react to such outside pressures? More specifically, where in the system would conflict be engendered? What impact might these conflicts have on decisions about the use of resources and on preexisting, within-system conflicts? One could raise many more questions to emphasize that the new conflicts 94–142 would engender would, willy-nilly, begin to interconnect with preexisting conflicts.

In 1978, several months before the funding of 94–142 was to begin, the author attended a small meeting to discuss problems the legislation was already creating. On the morning of the meeting, the author noticed that the first-page story of the local newspaper concerned a board of education meeting the night before where the decision had been made to lay off scores of classroom teachers. The superintendent of the city's school system was to be at the day's meeting. Just before the meeting began, some of the participants jocularly commiserated with the plight of the superintendent. To paraphrase the superintendent's reply: What the headline did not say was that last night the board voted to hire several special education teachers. Can you imagine how the teachers who will be laid off will react? Some of the teachers I have to lay off are superb teachers, but I can't use them for the new positions. The union is going to yell and so will parents and a lot of other groups. The net result is that all the flak that has been directed to the schools for all kinds of reasons is going to increase, on top of which I am going to have a horrible problem among my staff. And guess how the new special class teachers and their students are going to be looked at? I'm glad I'm at this meeting because I can just imagine the telephone calls that are coming into my office right now from teachers, parents, the union, and my administrative staff. Don't expect me at this moment to think kindly about 94–142.

Officials of local teachers unions have made it perfectly clear that they would vigorously oppose any provisions of 94–142 that conflicted with the substance of existing contracts or the substance of issues being negotiated. It was not that these officials were in principle against the spirit of the new policy and legislation (they were not, for the most part), but rather that they had enough points of conflict with officialdom of the system to look with jaundice on anything that would further complicate matters. P.L. 94–142 was being "put" into a school that was very far from being conflict-free.

The impact of the law

It is too early to speak with security about the impact, intended or unintended, of 94–142. As might have been expected, the impact seems to vary depending on many factors (e.g., urban–suburban–rural regions, level of economic activity in the region, the scope and commitment to past programming for children with special needs, the strength of parent groups). But if the data on which to base secure conclusions are not yet available, it does not mean that people are not arriving at conclusions stemming from their local experiences. From the time the law began to be implemented in school systems, the author has talked with scores of people from around the country with a vested interest in, or bearing some kind of responsibility for, the implementation of P.L. 94–142. Some people were "outside" the system (e.g., parents, university trainers of educational personnel, federal and state educational officials), whereas others were from within (e.g., teachers, principals, pupil personnel staff, district administrators, superintendents, members of boards of education). The following conclusions were shared by most people (and they varied widely pro and con on the legislation):

1. The paperwork required in formulating an Individual Education Program (IEP) for each handicapped child was unconscionably high.
2. Between the paperwork and the hours of meetings required of those who have to participate in formulating IEPs, there has been a drastic reduction in the amount of time personnel can spend in rendering direct service to children and teachers.
3. The larger the city system, the more glaring were points 1 and 2, and the mere implementation of 94–142 had all the hallmarks of empty ritual.
4. The spirit of 94–142 obligated school systems to create new least-restrictive alternatives and not to restrict themselves to two traditional alternatives: regular or special class. Generally speaking, that obligation is not being met.
5. Pupil personnel staff frequently make a recommendation because of pressure from administrative staff and not because they consider the recommendation to be either in the best interest of or in keeping with the spirit of 94–142. The pressure stems largely from budgetary considerations (i.e., recommendations that will require additional funds are frowned upon or simply forbidden.)[1]
6. School officials were amazingly naïve about the fiscal implications of 94–142, and it did not take them long to realize that local funds would be needed to supplement federal funds. As a consequence, backlash sentiment toward the new program is appearing, especially as local school districts are being forced to cut staff.

From the perspective advanced in this chapter, what requires explanation would be a situation in which the major intended consequences of 94–142 were successfully institutionalized and the unintended consequences were minimally adverse. This is not said because the author is a pessimist or because, on a sheer actuarial basis (i.e., based on past efforts to change educational systems) one should bet, and even give odds, that on balance 94–142 will fall short of its mark. The prediction stands because neither the many factors that shaped the legislation nor the details of its implementation were based on some kind of serious attempt to understand or conceptualize the system qua system.

Conceptualizing the educational system

It may seem odd, if not obtuse, to have said little or nothing about children in schools. After all, is not the major justification for efforts to change schools the increased benefits that pupils will derive?[2] Is not educational policy for and about children? The answer returns us to where this chapter began: Policy gives rise to legislation that essentially says how the educational system should educate children. It is the dynamics of the educational system that determine whether or not children will derive benefits from the attempt to alter that system. You can possess the most valid knowledge of child development, but that in no way guarantees that efforts to incorporate such knowledge into the school system will be successful.

Conceptualizing the educational system is a staggering task, but one that can no longer be avoided. Thomas Green (1980) in his recent book *Predicting the Behavior of the Educational System* has begun that task. It is a stimulating, engrossing, beginning attempt that compellingly demonstrates why the task is so absolutely crucial if Americans are not to continue down the road to cynicism and disillusionment. Here is one of Green's more challenging conclusions as stated in his prefatory remarks:

The supreme irony, however, is that in the attempt to study the future, I discovered most of all the obligation to revisit the past. If this disposition to find the countertrends in every vision of the future is to be more than sheer perversity, then it must rest in a carefully documented study of those stabilities that being discoverable in the past are, therefore, likely to persist. In the midst of a concern for change and endless happy visions of the future, I began to search for what, in the world of education, does not change, and what is unlikely to change because of its rootedness in realities more fundamental than can be touched by so crude an instrument for change and control as public policy. The system began to announce itself! For if the system exists at all, then it will consist of those relationships, those structural necessities, and arguments of behavior that endure and remain unaltered no matter what results from the hard-fought but short-term battles that are waged over the formation of educational policy. *The system, whatever it is, is precisely what doesn't change* in the established arrangement of educational institutions and in the reiterated arguments that guide their behavior. [Green, 1980, p. xv; emphasis mine]

The author hopes that Green's book is a harbinger of the direction that theory and research about the educational system will take.

This chapter has criticized the federal effort to alter and improve our schools. In presenting a more balanced perspective, the following should be noted: The individuals, bureaus, and agencies (on the federal, state, and local levels) who were part of this well-intentioned effort had very little experience in the arenas of politics, policy, and institutional change. What is distinctive about the past 25 years is the unprecedented seriousness and degree to which so many segments of the U.S. population have been involved with educational change. If these people were babes-in-the-woods, this would say as much about the ways American society was changing as it would about the inadequacies of the disciplines. So when criticisms are directed at the policy makers and implementers, it should be remembered that, with very little preparation, they were asked (and they agreed) to attack problems the complexity of which staggers the mind. Although these efforts don't receive high marks in terms of ultimate accomplishment, it is unwarranted to suggest that nothing was learned or that future efforts should be eliminated.

What would be monumentally ironic is if, in the present move to admit the federal role – be it in policy, research, or implementation – it were simply assumed that "things will get better." The important substantive issues in American education are not of a kind that get clarified by shifting sites of power and policy. Indeed, it is likely in the current debate about what powers, policies, and resources should be shifted from the nation's capital to our states' capitals that the substantive issues will be all but forgotten.

Notes

1 At the urging of some of its members who were school psychologists, the American Psychological Association (its Board of Ethical and Social Responsibility) held a meeting to explore ethical problems psychologists were experiencing in relation to 94–142. Two things became clear: School placement teams were frequently under pressure not to make recommendations that would require increased funding, and the intent of the legislation to involve parents meaningfully in decision making about their children was, more often than not, circumvented in diverse ways.
2 The author holds the belief that no less important than what children experience in schools is what school personnel experience.

References

Coleman, J. S. (Chairman). *Youth: Transition to adulthood*. Report of the Panel on Youth of the President's Science Advisory Committee. Chicago: University of Chicago, 1974.
Cowden, P., & Cohen, D. *Divergent worlds of practice: The federal reform of local schools in the experimental schools program*. Cambridge, Mass.: Huron Institute, 1979.
Green, T. *Predicting the behavior of the educational system*. Syracuse, N.Y.: Syracuse University Press, 1980.
Sarason, S. B. *The culture of the school and the problem of change* (2d ed.). Boston: Allyn & Bacon, 1982.

19 Understanding child abuse: a dilemma for policy development

Edward F. Zigler

The area of child abuse is replete with contradictions on all fronts – scientific, social, and public policy. Scientists, to begin with, disagree on the very fundamental issue of what they are studying. Some see only overt acts of physical harm such as beatings and torture as the proper definition of child abuse. Others include more common practices like spanking or hollering at a child, and a few even consider subtle behaviors such as emotional rejection or failure to understand a child's needs as quiet but genuine abuse. Since there is such a difference between murdering a child and criticizing one, it is not surprising that scientific research offers a wide diversity of conclusions. The literature reveals that the incidence of child abuse in the United States is increasing (Newberger & Hyde, 1975) or unchanged (Kempe & Kempe, 1978), that the most likely abuser is the mother (Gelles, 1980) or the father (Gil, 1970), and that child abuse is more common in poor (Pelton, 1978) or more affluent (Parke & Collmer, 1975) families.

Contradictions also abound in the social dimensions of the child abuse problem. Perhaps the greatest contradiction is seen in the act itself. The physical battering of children seems monstrously perverse to parents who cherish and nurture loving relationships with their offspring, and the thought of a small, helpless child at the hands of a big, violent adult elicits revulsion and moral outrage. In fact, some professionals and laymen have resurrected an outmoded approach to human behavior and asserted that child abuse runs contrary to the basic instincts of the human species, particularly the "maternal instinct." Yet whereas American society is unanimously opposed to child abuse, one does not have to look far to see that it sanctions and even encourages abuse in many ways. For example, although Americans no longer horsewhip adult criminals, there is widespread acceptance of physical punishment as an appropriate means of disciplining children. Permissiveness in child rearing was a short-lived

331

trend that is now disdained; more common now is the "spare the rod and spoil the child" approach to parenting. More generally, there is a growing acceptance of physical hostility in national attitudes and pastimes. Today aggressiveness is commonly seen as a positive personality trait, and the movies, sports, and TV shows with the most violence typically occupy the top of the box office and ratings charts. "G" seems to have gone the way of the peace movement in the United States' modern brute society, the same society that claims to be "child-oriented" and anxious to wage public war against child abuse. Perhaps "war" is a most fitting word.

The inconsistencies in the American social climate cannot help but be reflected in the governmental bodies that concretize the public will. Although there are child abuse reporting laws, there is also a Supreme Court ruling that upholds the use of corporal punishment in the nation's schools. The Child Abuse Prevention and Treatment Act (1974) symbolizes the federal government's commitment to solving the child abuse problem, but the bill is little more than symbolic since legislators failed to back it with meaningful funding. The most serious lack of money is for research, despite the fact that there is a logical relation between the knowledge base in any area of social policy and the nation's ability to mount effective prevention and intervention programs. To date there is relatively little *reliable* information about child abuse, and many incongruous findings await clarification – a state of affairs that would seem to preclude any successful solutions to the problem. Yet today's trend to concentrate funds on the provision of services, as well as the negative attitude toward behavioral science research currently in vogue in the Congress, means that this area of expanding public concern will face dwindling funds for vital information gathering. Given the fiscal austerity of the times and the historical reluctance of the U.S. government to assign high priority to children's issues, we seem to have set out to solve a dilemma we have neither the knowledge, means, nor dedication to solve.

Through all this confusion, one fact stands consistently clear: Child abuse is a pressing social problem that every scientist, citizen, and policy maker desires to eradicate. In spite of these good intentions, child abuse cannot be eliminated overnight, nor can it be legislated away with a single bill. Social change occurs not by the stroke of a pen but by intensive and persistent efforts to restructure the human ecology within which the problem exists. Researchers must pinpoint the underlying roots of the problem. Scholars, professionals, and laymen across the United States can contribute their knowledge, experience, and expertise to mount programs that research shows can be effective. Finally, the federal government must commit itself both politically and financially to supporting these efforts and to implementing policies that will address the conditions that perpetuate abuse. The path from research to policy to practice may be as complex as the problem itself, but the joint efforts of these diverse interest groups are our only hope for reducing the incidence of child abuse in America.

Child abuse as a major or minor problem

The lack of a standardized definition of *child abuse* has a dramatic impact on incidence data because statistics reflect phenomena ranging from the number of children killed to the number spanked each year. This problem is exacerbated since researchers, who themselves have diverse views about what constitutes abuse, are relying more and more on public interviews to calculate incidence rates. Despite the most careful wording of survey questions, respondents may have differences in beliefs so basic as to make their answers incomparable. Attitudes toward child abuse depend on whether individuals believe that all forms of physical aggression against children are abusive; whether they give primary consideration to the adult's motivations (if the harm was purposeful or unintentional) or focus only on the actual consequence to the child; and even whether they view social services (and pollsters) as benign or intrusive. Survey results therefore often yield estimates that range as widely as do personal opinions. A national survey by Gil (1970), for example, revealed that between 2.5 and 4 million adults each knew of a separate case of child abuse (defined as deliberate injury of a child by a caretaker) in the preceding year. In a reanalysis of these statistics, Light (1973) suggested that between 200,000 and 500,000 children are abused annually. In a household survey, Gelles (1980) found that between 1.4 and 1.9 million children were intentionally injured by their parents in the preceding year. Although such surveys are certainly of some value, it is hardly informative to state that the incidence of child abuse ranges from 200,000 to 4 million cases annually.

Another way of calculating incidence data is based on the number of cases of child abuse actually reported to public authorities. The most commonly cited estimate of this type, released by the National Center on Child Abuse and Neglect in 1975, is that approximately 1 million cases of abuse are reported each year. Douglas Besharov, director of the center at the time the figure was released, maintained that the American Humane Association furnished the statistic, yet that organization reportedly claimed that it was "groundless" and "excessive" (Divoky, 1976). This type of debate may lead some workers to question the accuracy of the 1 million estimate. Yet any number based on reported child abuse cases is at best a very rough index of the actual incidence rate. There is no doubt that many, many instances of abuse are never reported. Social class differences compound statistical accuracy, as studies have shown that reporting rates differ dramatically between classes (e.g., Garbarino, 1976; Gil, 1969; Newberger et al., 1975). Undetected cases of child abuse are especially numerous in the more affluent segments of the population. There are reasons to believe that some private pediatricians are reluctant to report an injured child from a "good" home as a victim of abuse (Newberger et al., 1975). And since poor families have more contact with social service agencies, they are more likely to be reported for abuse than are wealthier families. On the other hand, poor persons may hide their knowledge of abuse in order to protect their neighbors from the authorities. None of these hypotheses has been unequivocally proven, but they all contribute to the unreliability of estimates of child abuse.

The absence of reliable data has made it difficult to determine whether the incidence of child abuse has increased or decreased over recent decades. The abuse of children is not unique to contemporary society. Throughout history children have suffered from harsh physical punishment, the hardships of child labor, and strenuous living conditions. Comparisons over time are made difficult because the ambiguous definitions used today to determine incidence rates do not necessarily coincide with situations that were considered abusive in the past (Ross, 1980). Furthermore, although incidence rates are sketchy and unreliable today, they were virtually nonexistent in the United States before state legislatures passed mandatory reporting laws in the mid-1960s. The number of child abuse cases reported to public authorities has increased ever since, which suggests that the problem is worsening. Many researchers, however, maintain that the actual rate of abuse is the same and that heightened public awareness has swelled reporting statistics (Bourne & Newberger, 1979; Kempe & Kempe, 1978).

The answers to questions about the pervasiveness of child abuse and whether the problem is growing or diminishing have grave implications. As can be said for most social problems, if this one is widespread and increasing at a rapid rate, policy makers must quickly mobilize all available forces to put it in check. On the other hand, if the problem affects relatively few individuals and remains limited, it will hardly deserve so much effort. Proponents of both options can be heard where child abuse is concerned, since the lack of credible incidence data leaves the question wide open. Certainly child abuse is not nearly as common as childhood accidents, diseases, and other traumas that often befall children. Even leading researchers in the field have questioned whether child abuse is statistically a major social problem. For instance, Gil wrote that the "battered child syndrome" occurs relatively infrequently. "Even if allowance is made for the gross under-reporting of fatalities, physical abuse cannot be considered a major killer and maimer of children" (1969, p. 862). Using the comparative approach to determine which social problems are major, however, can be counterproductive. Taken to its extreme, that approach could lead child advocates to delay their efforts to improve the status of children until they all agreed on which problems were extensive enough to merit intervention. This possibility gives good reason to support the absolute approach to the problem of child abuse – that is, regardless of how many children are abused each year, that number is too many. This line of thought, coupled with the fact that public concern about interfamily violence has intensified in recent years, can help policy makers justify the amount of attention, money, and effort they commit to eradicating abuse.

Scholars too should heed the suggestion to stop quibbling over numerical niceties. Determining the overall magnitude of the child abuse problem may be impossible, and little corrective action can be taken if workers focus all of their time on comparing incidence trends and debating an undefined issue. Moving away from inaction based on doubts regarding the pervasiveness of abuse, however, does not mean that we should abandon efforts to collect reliable incidence data. The National Center on Child Abuse and Neglect, for example, should work at compiling statistics on the number of cases reported each year. Researchers should join the effort by attempting to determine the relation between the number of reported and actual cases of abuse in different communities. Determining the magnitude and demography of the problem will help guide decisions about funding and service implementation priorities. Finally, policy makers must make a firm resolution to devote a considerable amount of financial and human resources to the problem of child abuse. Without this kind of commitment, the problem will never be solved.

Mandate for a definition

Perhaps nothing reveals the difficulties facing those working to alleviate child abuse better than the fact that no standardized definition of the phenomenon has yet been accepted by all the involved professions (Bourne & Newberger, 1979; Lauderdale, Anderson, & Cramer, 1978; National Center on Child Abuse and Neglect, 1978; Parke & Collmer,

1975). Without common agreement on what constitutes maltreatment, research findings are misleading because identical labels are used to describe different things. Laws are applied unevenly because prosecutors have different perceptions of which behaviors justify court intervention. Social services are extended or withheld depending on the caseworker's feelings about what is harmful to children. Finally, policy makers find themselves faced with the impossible task of solving a problem whose magnitude, causes, and very nature remain undefined. The intricacies of the child abuse problem demand a highly differentiated, conceptually based classification system, and the need is urgent.

Conceptual compromises

The development of a commonly acceptable definition of child abuse is a prerequisite for the development of any tenable solutions. That is, the scope of the solutions proposed to eliminate abuse will be linked to how broadly the limits of abusive behavior are defined. Employing a narrow and precise definition, for instance, will reduce the size of the problem, qualify a limited number of families for social assistance, and foster policies that address only the severest cases of physical abuse. A broad definition, on the other hand, might encompass all ways in which the environment fails to meet a child's developmental needs. Child abuse would thus be seen as rampant, most families would be considered in need of aid to improve their child-rearing practices, and policies would be drawn to improve the lives of all children in the society. The two extremes differ in that one places an emphasis on individual solutions to abuse, whereas the other focuses on structural social solutions. In terms of actually reducing the incidence of abuse, however, both perspectives will prove to be of limited value. The emphasis on cases of extreme physical abuse cannot make a dent in the problem because it excludes less dramatic but far more common instances of assault and neglect. The broader definition implies that the labels "abusive" and "neglectful" are applicable to (1) all parents who use any form of physical discipline and perhaps verbal reproaches, and (2) socially sanctioned practices such as behavior modification techniques that could conceivably have detrimental effects on a child's physical or emotional development. For the purposes of devising studies on the characteristics of abusive persons or abused children and developing guidelines for state intervention, this definition is too comprehensive to be of any practical use.

In developing a viable definition of child abuse, workers need to consider blending ideas from both the narrow and the broad perspectives. The definitions must be broad enough to take into account forms of abuse less obvious than cigarette burns and torture but not so broad as to make it impossible to distinguish abusive behavior from "normal" parental practices. These guidelines indicate that we must abandon the currently used two-category system that discriminates only between parents who abuse their children and those who do not. This system simply does not describe realistically the complex nature of family interactions. As has been suggested before (Burgess, 1978; Zigler, 1979), child abuse might best be reconceptualized as a continuum of behaviors that includes all the ways adults relate to children. The continuum might range from affection on the one end to horrendous abuse or murder on the other, with all the forms of occasional violence between parents and children positioned somewhere in between. Types of child neglect would also be spread across the continuum so that it would be possible to discriminate between a parent who habitually starves a child, for example, and one who occasionally leaves the child home alone. Finally, the simple two-class typology that draws a sharp line between abuse and nonabuse could rarely account for less tangible harm that children might suffer. For example, repeated emotional rejection may lead to more serious long-term damage than would isolated instances of physical abuse. The diversified classificatory system proposed here would finally allow workers to consider the less obvious ways that parental behavior can hinder a child's development.

The continuum model illustrates that abusive acts differ in degree rather than kind and suggests that similar distinctions apply to child abusers. Whereas the narrow definition would reserve the label "abuser" solely for parents who maim or kill their children, the continuum approach implies that child abusers are not necessarily strange or psychopathic human beings. On the contrary, they are usually indistinguishable from parents who are never reported for abuse. And where the broad definition intimates that all parents are knowingly guilty of abuse at one time or another, the continuum makes allowance for the adult's intentions. In many cases of child abuse, the parent did not ever mean to inflict such pain. Very often parents start out rather innocently using some mild form of punishment and end up, to their own horror, seriously injuring their child. The continuum approach thus implies that, depending on static familial and environmental circumstances, all parents are capable of abusing their children. This view is obviously threatening to the majority of people who are more comfortable with the belief that the child abuser is some sort of "sick" individual quite unlike themselves. Yet by breaking down the distance between abusers and nonabusers, this perspective has wide-ranging theoretical and practical benefits.

First, with such a differentiated classificatory system, workers – particularly those involved with legal impositions – could avoid the problems inherent in labeling every act of child abuse as the equivalent of every other. Research results would be more easily comparable since investigators could work within standard, circumscribed areas of abuse rather than each going by his or her perception of what constitutes child abuse phenomena. Most importantly, recognizing the nature of abuse and abusers has ramifications for the nature of appropriate interventions. By conceptualizing abusive behavior as part of a continuum of possible parental behaviors, people will have to face the potential for abuse in everyone and thus support *preventive* programs. To date American society has sought mostly after-the-fact treatment, demanding "justice" or some sort of secondary intervention to keep the abuser from committing the same sin again. Primary prevention efforts to curb abuse before it occurs can receive much broader support if the notion of "abuser" is taken out of its psychopathic limits (and perhaps given a less value-laden name that connotes parents at *risk* of abuse rather than guilty of it). To advocate primary programs, however, policy makers must be willing to reformulate their cost/benefit equations (by which they justify the cost of a policy in terms of its successes) to allow for benefits that are sight-unseen. For instance, it is much more difficult to predict the number of parents who will not become abusive because they completed a parenting education course than it is to count the number of families served by a crisis day-care center. Yet if primary prevention measures are to receive adequate funding, policy makers must accept the fact that there is no reliable way to gauge their immediate effectiveness.

Working definitions

Definitions are not so much right or wrong as they are useful or not useful (Farber, 1975; Zigler, 1963). The definitional dilemma stems in part from the fact that some groups, including lawyers and government officials, use the definition to determine standards for intervention into families, whereas other groups, including scholars and social service workers, use it to focus attention and funding on at-risk families and those in need of assistance. Although these aims are not entirely mutually exclusive, each group needs a definition tailored to its major social goals and practical objectives. The standardization of the differentiated *concept* of abuse discussed above would facilitate accurate communication within professions as well as among members of different disciplines. A narrower definition will be required for the purposes of legal action (Solnit, 1980; Uviller, 1980) in order to protect family rights. For the purposes of research or the provision of services on a voluntary basis, the definition must be broad enough to encompass all forms of child neglect and maltreatment. Clinical case management and social policy development may well merit their own definitions of child abuse. In other words, because it is difficult to develop a single definition of abuse that can fulfill all the statistical and social functions required by various professions, what appears to be needed are separate working definitions for legal, clinical, social service, and research requirements. Each definition must be standard within its field, have an appropriate range, and be clear as to the exact objectives and uses for which it is intended. Each must also be harmonious with aspects of the broader-based conception of child abuse in order that professionals may recognize that they share a common goal

Medical. The most limited definitions of abuse will necessarily be employed in the medical and legal fields, since this is where intervention and invasion into family privacy are typically enjoined. The first formal recognition and definition of child abuse occurred in medicine, when radiologists noticed a number of fractures appearing on children's X rays that parents could not adequately explain. The term *battered child syndrome* was coined to describe this constellation of conditions and events (Kempe et al., 1962). The purposes and processes of classifying a case as "battered child syndrome" now constitute a medical diagnostic definition of child maltreatment (see Giovannoni & Beccera, 1979). The general aim of a diagnostic definition is to identify a pathological condition in a way that enables therapeutic intervention. Thus adult abusers are thought to be the source of the pathology and in need of cure on the individual case level. This somewhat limited approach is natural and appropriate in the health sciences because physicians require a diagnostic assessment tool and because each case is so different in terms of its symptoms, severity, and chronic or acute nature. Yet the label "abused child" is so accusatory that it may discourage doctors from applying it or parents from accepting help. On the other hand, the term, when it is used, gives families immediate access to crowded programs that otherwise might not admit them. This is where the broad concept of abuse, coupled with a narrow definition, might aid in the development of some discretionary guidelines that physicians can apply on a case-by-case basis.

Legal. The legal definition of child abuse must be more explicit and particularly stringent in order to guard family autonomy. The Judicial Administration–American Bar Association has proposed a set of criteria to limit the judgment of child abuse to cases where a child has suffered or is in imminent danger of suffering serious physical harm or emotional damage (Juvenile Justice Standards Project [JJSP], 1977). Such harm must be supported by documented evidence; for example, emotional damage must be "evidenced by severe anxiety, depression, withdrawal, or untoward aggressive behavior toward self or others" (JJSP, 1977, pp. 55–58). There is also recognition that different legal objectives or intrusions require different definitions to guide decision making. Hence, removing a child from the home might be restricted to cases of physical injury only, whereas other types of coercive court intervention such as referral to state social service agencies might include "endangered" (at-risk) children, those suffering emotional damage, and the like. In all cases, however, the standards are based on such general principles as the presumption of family autonomy in child rearing, protecting cultural differences, and designing an intervention system that promotes a child's need for a continuous and stable living environment and that reflects developmental differences among children of various ages. Such value preferences are necessary but must be clearly spelled out, or the technical merit of the definition is likely to suffer. Still, the proposed legal definition appears to remain on solid ground because it limits the state's right to intervene in family life unless an identifiable threshold of risk is passed.

Sociological. The sociological approach to child abuse allows room for a much broader definition that includes more minor forms of child neglect and "probable" hindrances to a child's development. The process of defining maltreatment is not done with clinical–scientific precision but rather becomes a social judgmental task. That is, parental acts are considered abusive when they deviate from our culture's values of acceptable child-rearing and adult role expectations. The judgment is made by social agents in order to protect social standards as well as individual members of society. Because child abuse is socially defined, social solutions are implied. Whereas the medical and legal definitions focus on the problem as caused by individuals and therefore requiring case-level solutions, the sociological definition sees its roots in political, economic, and human conditions over which individuals have little control. Factors that can correct a family's ecology are sought for the long run, with short-term aid provided within the social support system. At the practical level, the sociological definition serves to establish eligibility criteria for voluntary services and to evaluate the environment as a factor in identifying and treating child abuse.

Research. The principal functions of the medical, legal, and sociological definitions of child abuse are to guide diagnosis and decision making. Research efforts aim to explain child maltreatment – especially its nature, causes, and effects – and to evaluate programs to control or prevent the problem. The definition of child abuse for research purposes thus involves all the primary foci of the other three fields – the parental characteristics, the abusive behavior, and the social and cultural environmental conditions – as well as the child's characteristics and developmental status. Empirical explanations are sought for the interrelations among all these factors. The number of dimensions involved make it clear that the need for a distinct definition of abuse is no less pressing for researchers than it is for those who make decisions concerning families. The definitional task may seem formidable, but the complexity is not insurmountable if investigators are clear as to the explicit aim of each branch of study. For example, if the goal is to increase the scientific reliability of the child abuse classification, the definition must use very narrow and distinct behavioral terms. On the other hand, if the purpose is to discover what will reduce the incidence of abuse in a certain community, aspects of what is potentially harmful to children, unavailable to them, or anything else that strays from ideal developmental conditions might come under consideration.

The research definitions of abuse must not only be consistent across related studies, but they must also be commonly accepted by members of the various behavioral sciences. A welcome sign as to the improved quality of child abuse research is that workers have begun to draw from theoretical and empirical offerings of several established disciplines. For instance, scholars in psychology and related disciplines have augmented their child abuse work with knowledge from the socialization literature concerning child rearing, attachment, and human aggression. Comparative psychology offers a rich source of information on parental violence in infrahuman species (Harlow & Harlow, 1971). A research tradition based upon the theoretical work of Bronfenbrenner (1979) focuses on the ecology of human development and has produced illuminating studies of family–environment transactions. Such cross-fertilization enhances the sophistication of thinking in the child abuse field, broadening the knowledge and understanding of the roots of interfamily violence and subjecting it to the methodological rigor of procedures, approaches, and measures used in related areas. To pursue this course, it behooves workers to arrive at mutual working definitions.

The research mandate

The definitional dilemma is one reason why the current state of knowledge about child abuse is so limited. There is very little consistent evidence concerning which children are prone to being abused, which adults are prone to being abusers, and why. Further research about all aspects of child abuse would provide the knowledge necessary to design effective social policies. A detailed examination of research priorities – including studies on the etiology, treatment, prevention, and effects of abuse on children and families – is beyond the scope of this chapter.[1] What will be discussed here are ways in which basic research can aid in the definition of child abuse and, on the negative side, problems the lack of research has caused for both policy and program formation. The purpose is to expound through a very few specific examples the crying need for sound information about child abuse if we are ever to do something about it.

Developmental considerations

Research can help refine the definitional schemes of child abuse required by the various professions. As discussed above, each scheme has strengths and weaknesses when viewed from the perspective of establishing a *common* definition of child abuse. Yet the definitions do not have to be logically inconsistent if they are all based on a common understanding of the basic nature of child maltreatment. Recognizing the continuumlike scope of parental behaviors, with each discipline acknowledging its interest in a wide or narrow range of that continuum, is one step toward achieving that consistency. Another is for all definitions to take into account the developmental nature of child abuse phenomena (Aber & Zigler, 1981), an area where further empirical and theoretical efforts are required.

The importance of emphasizing the developmental nature of child abuse has been most clearly articulated by legal scholars in their efforts to construct legal definitions. This interest is consistent with debates in other areas of juvenile law over such issues as at what age a child should be held responsible for criminal acts or how the child's age should enter into custody decisions. It also follows the powerful suggestion of Goldstein, Freud, and Solnit (1973) that knowledge of child development should form the basis for more enlightened legal policies. Although it is now accepted that developmental issues should influence the creation and application of definitions of child abuse, this is easier said than done.

Consider the Juvenile Justice Standards Project (JJSP) proposal to premise all forms of state intervention in child abuse cases on documented harms to the child. With respect to physical harm, documentation is relatively straightforward through medical technology, although specific impairments such as internal organ damage or malnourishment may be more or less serious depending on the victim's age. Less tangible harms like emotional damage can have more drastic developmental consequences than physical injuries and are more frequent as grounds for intervention. Yet reliable documentation of emotional harm is an extremely difficult and complex task, so much so that some commentators have suggested abandoning the use of the phenomenon as grounds for coercive state intervention (Solnit, 1980). The difficulties occur in part because the expression of a psychological construct such as depression or withdrawal varies enormously with the child's developmental stage and because age-appropriate methods of assessing the construct are not always available. Still, developmental data on specific forms of emotional damage could help operationalize these constructs for use in definitional schemata.

According to the proposed JJSP standard, emotional damage must be evidenced by "severe anxiety, depression or withdrawal" or "untoward aggression." A depressed toddler presents a very different symptom picture than does a depressed third-grader. While research on childhood depression is still rare, there are some theoretical statements as to its stagelike nature. For example, Philips (1979) suggested that failure to thrive might be one indicator in infants, whereas refusal to attend school, learning problems, and hyperactivity may be symptoms of depression in older children. The age-specific nature of withdrawal also merits closer attention. The child's relation to his or her primary caretaker assumes special importance in the first years of life. Obviously if an adult is an attachment figure of crucial importance, the consequences of withdrawal can be severe. For an older child physical withdrawal from an adult does not necessarily entail psychological withdrawal, although the two types of reaction have drastically different ramifications. Developmental trends in the structure and dynamics of aggression are better documented. In the preschool years the child's aggression is usually in the action mode and is directed at inanimate objects. Hostile aggression is more common in the school years and is directed at a person who is a source of threat. Language and "psychological weapons" eventually become alternatives to physical hostility. Thus to determine whether a child's aggression is severe enough to indicate emotional damage, one cannot simply ask if the target is a person or object, or if the mode was physical or verbal, since all these dimensions are in a state of flux over the course of development.

Such developmental trends in the expression of psychological phenomena suggest the need for further research to describe more accurately their stagelike nature. Developmental norms would not only assist in the reliability and validity of the "emotional damage" classification, but they would greatly aid legal and clinical decision makers in identifying children who suffer emotional harm. Obviously, too much systematic variation exists in the expression of psychological constructs to attempt to determine emotional damage without a research-based calculus of behavioral traits.

The developmental perspective has at least two additional implications for case management and research definitions of maltreatment. First, the stimulus value of the child for provoking abusive behaviors from the parent is likely to vary with developmental level. For instance, much has been made of the rage some parents feel under some conditions toward helpless, inconsolable infants. Other parents find toddlers' uncontrollable temper tantrums or emerging abilities to locomote and cause a mess more provocative. As children approach the "age of reason" (the shift from preoperational to concrete operational thought), they are more likely to be viewed by parents as capable of intentional actions for which they can and should be held responsible. As S. Feshbach (1980) pointed out, a provocative action is more likely to result in an aggressive response if it is seen as the intentional act of a responsible person. Within the JJSP's definition, the provocativeness of the child should have no influence on the declaration of child abuse since the focus is exclusively on harms to the child. But to the extent that a clinical or research definition of maltreatment also considers parental characteristics and the nature of the act, an unprovoked action might be more easily defined as abusive than a provoked action.

Finally, there are also systematic changes in children's vulnerabilities to types of maltreatment. For instance, severe emotional damage due to separation and loss may be particularly easy to inflict during the child's earliest years, whereas vulnerability to sexual abuse seems to increase with age. Parental fostering of delinquency holds its greatest risk during the early school-age years when social standards are being internalized. Such shifts in children's vulnerabilities must be more clearly delineated if they are to be useful factors in defining maltreatment or a child in "imminent danger" of abuse.

Research vacuum

Studies of abused children and abusing adults have yielded some tentative evidence and several promising directions for policy makers to pursue in their efforts to curb the incidence of child abuse. In other instances, inconsistent or insufficient findings place information more in the realm of suggested risk factors. Certainly more facts about child abuse are needed, but this does not mean we should delay action until every last piece of data is verified. For example, in the case of the finding that premature infants are more often the victims of abuse than are full-term infants, we need await no lengthy program of research to assert that a national effort to reduce the incidence of premature births could impact the incidence of child abuse (and have many other beneficial effects). In other cases the lack of bedrock evidence has created such havoc that all we can do is step up research efforts to confirm or disconfirm the course of inquiry.

To illustrate, consider one factor that research has associated with parent–child violence but where the evidence is simply too boggling to indicate a clear course of action. Assuming that human stress is a crucial factor leading to abuse, and given the difficult conditions in which poor families live, it would not be surprising to find more cases of abuse among low-income groups. Whereas this is certainly suggested by many studies, Parke and Collmer (1975) dispute the claim that child abuse is more common in impoverished families and maintain that it is simply better concealed in wealthier ones. Pelton (1978), on the other hand, disclaims the notion that child abuse is equally prevalent in all social classes and contends that the "myth of classlessness" diverts money from poverty programs. True, scholars and politicians are often reluctant to make a connection between class and abuse because similar links have been made in the past as a means of disparaging the poor. Although more studies are needed to show whether or not poor children do suffer more abuse, this present tendency to disassociate class from abuse can dilute the effectiveness of current preventive and/or treatment efforts. Researchers often conclude that child abuse is more common among poor families, but scarcity of analysis has made that information difficult to translate into nonpunitive policy.

Further directions

Many questions for basic research remain unanswered. In the areas of prevention and service delivery, for example, it would be important to determine what correlation, if any, exists between the availability of support services in a community and the incidence of abuse. Does the very knowledge that services exist ease family tension and reduce the incidence of violence? How much child abuse really exists, and is it concentrated in particular areas or subpopulations? How well are different models of social service programs succeeding in reducing abuse? Do parents from ethnic groups that maintain strong extended-family ties and who live near their relatives engage in less abusive behavior than more isolated parents?

Obviously, much work remains to be done before workers can arrive at some definitive answers to explain and prevent abuse. Yet the child abuse problem continues, and so must our efforts. First, those in the field must diligently continue their search for hard facts about abuse and about how to make programs more effective. Because child abuse policy is in a relatively formative stage and is expanding rapidly, research is crucial and policy makers should give it a high priority in funding. Secondly, poor though the knowledge base may be, there exist some data about the extent and causes of child abuse and about effective intervention and prevention tactics. Policy makers must put to use what information is available about the best ways to meet the needs of abusive or potentially abusive families. We do not yet know enough to provide solutions, but what we do know should be translated into social programs and used to inform policies. This very complex task will require the efforts of all those involved with children and families.

Mobilization of forces

A wide range of organizations and individuals have roles and responsibilities in solving the problem of child abuse. Research has offered many suggestions for corrective action that need further consideration and refinement by those most concerned with children. The legal profession, the helping services, scholars, legislators, and the communities whose child-rearing values should be supported and enhanced by social policies all have invaluable contributions to make. Representatives from such groups must begin to coordinate their special skills and plan a unified course of action. Widespread discussion, reassessment, and the development of working plans will certainly take time, but Americans must at least put their best foot forward *now*. Somewhere a child is being abused.

The government must begin in its own backyard. The state and its agents must set the highest possible standards for the care of children in their charge because of the state's symbolic importance in molding the behavior of private citizens toward children. Forms of socially sanctioned abuse – including corporal punishment in schools; mistreatment of children in protective, therapeutic, or corrective institutions; and abuse in the foster care and juvenile justice systems – suggest that widespread reforms in how the states care for children are overdue (Aber, 1980; Blatt, 1980; N. D. Feshbach, 1980; Uviller, 1980). Deepseated social approval of corporal punishment seems to legitimize institutional abuse of children. Several immediate steps can be taken that would attack both the underlying attitudes that perpetuate mistreatment of public wards and the abuses themselves. Personnel who staff public institutions should receive training on children's needs and acceptable disciplinary techniques. States should establish mechanisms to assist parents and concerned citizens in monitoring the quality of care, reporting malfeasances, and lobbying for necessary statutory changes. The use of such structures to encourage and support the help of citizens is a very practical step that has precedents in other areas of institutional care. Finally, government agencies should be empowered to withhold funds from facilities where mistreatment continues. Although this extreme measure should be reserved for repeated or flagrant violations, the threat of that ultimate action would help to effect reforms.

Change is also mandated in another social institution that, after the family, is the most important socializing agent in American society – namely the school. The philosophies and practices of the school not only reflect the values of society but also influence familial attitudes and behavior. Only four states presently ban corporal punishment in schools, despite evidence that such punishment fails to deter misbehavior, discriminates against boys and members of minority groups, and teaches the use of physical aggression while militating against a positive environment for learning (N. D. Feshbach, 1980). Of course, the frequent occurrences of school fights, assaults, and melees stimulate the fears of teachers and school officials such that there is a general unwillingness to relinquish corporal punishment as a means of self-protection against student violence. Yet if the use of physical harm is to be discouraged in public settings, teachers must receive training in alternative methods of discipline and classroom management. Although such alternatives require a greater commitment of time and energy from teachers, the benefits of that extra effort must be made to seem compelling. State and federal legislation should prohibit corporal punishment, and parents, government agencies, and advocacy groups should lend force to the law by monitoring schools. The United States is unlikely to adopt the Swedish position that bans parents from using corporal punishment on their children, but prohibitive legislation affecting schools can communicate changing attitudes to parents – and to the students who will be the parents of tomorrow.

Besides teaching by example, schools can take a more active and positive role by supporting education for parenthood. Much research on abusing parents suggests that parenting education may be a promising means of stemming child abuse. For instance, parents' lack of knowledge about children's physical vulnerabilities contributes to the likelihood of their losing their tempers or using methods of discipline with unanticipated results (e.g., many adults do not realize that giving an infant a "good shaking" or that an open-handed slap to a child's head can cause brain damage). Knowledge about child development and skills for handling children would undoubtedly lessen the incidence of unintentional abuse. Unrealistic expectations of a child's capabilities also lead to age-inappropriate demands, parental frustration, and abuse. Even a middle-class parent's efforts to raise a child's IQ by 20 points or to teach a two-year-old to read can be considered forms of abuse because they put such a strain on both the developing child and the struggling parent. Thus, because parents of all backgrounds can have unrealistic expectations of their children, all young people should receive training for parenthood.

Policy makers must of course determine the efficacy of implementing any social program by measuring its demonstrated effectiveness, cost, and social acceptability. It would be difficult to demonstrate that parenting education courses are an effective means of reducing child abuse. Yet the cost of implementing these courses in schools is relatively small. In terms of acceptability, scholars, professionals, parents, and young people themselves have championed parent education for many years, and available courses are typically popular and well attended. Of course, some people will undoubtedly resist publicly subsidized education for parenthood, interpreting such programs as yet another encroachment by government into family affairs. Courses should thus avoid the inculcation of values and emphasize instead basic information about children, including units on physical development and behavioral capabilities of children at different developmental stages and ages. An added plus is that parenting courses would be offered to persons from all racial and economic backgrounds and, when carefully designed to protect cultural diversity, need not discriminate against any socioeconomic or ethnic group. In this they would differ from other child abuse prevention programs that are directed at a targeted segment of the population. Parenting education classes address some of the common problems faced by all parents, and their effectiveness does not depend on any arbitrary distinctions between abusive, nonabusive, and potentially abusive parents.

Education and support for the difficult task of parenting should also be available to new and expectant parents. Hospitals and doctors should educate adolescent parents as well as parents of premature, handicapped, and other children at high risk of abuse about the kinds of problems they may encounter and the services available to them. This suggestion implies that Americans must reeducate the "gatekeepers" in each community – that is, in addition to doctors, the clergy, teachers, child care workers, and social service personnel – so that they will offer guidance and support instead of negative judgment alone to troubled parents. Such counselors should aim to encourage self-help (instead of merely to report suspects) in a way that will enhance, not undermine, the confidence of parents in their own skills and family roles. This type of expert advice, as well as the implicated social services, should be available before, not just after, a family finds itself in serious trouble. If Americans are to prevent rather than simply treat child abuse, they must develop policies that secure supportive family and child programs that are there as the need arises.

Many supportive services and institutions already exist in virtually every community (Richmond & Janis, 1980), but oftentimes those who are in need do not know the help is there. Every locality needs an inventory and evaluation of general services for families experiencing difficulties. (Examples of this kind of inventory are catalogs of local day-care facilities, often compiled by volunteers.) Such a listing would simplify the call for help, since families may be confused by the number of different service agencies they come in contact with. There should also be an integration of child abuse prevention programs not only within the social welfare system but with the network of agencies with which most families interact, including schools, churches, and places of employment. An immediate and essential step involves communication, cooperation, and coordination among the groups that serve parents in each community. In this way workers would know which services are available, which are duplicative, and which are apparently lacking. Such a broad-based approach would cost relatively little over the separate services system and would enhance the efforts of all concerned with reducing an area's incidence of child abuse.

Although programs to prevent child abuse cannot await broader social reform, we cannot ignore the relation between social reform and the quality of life for children and families. Despite the current mood of fiscal austerity regarding social welfare, the United States cannot turn its back on the need to improve its social environment, confront structural problems, and support policies that enhance family life. A credible and fiscally responsible child abuse act must be constructed by Congress and implemented without delay. A national commitment to the well-being of children would be further reflected in policies designed to guarantee every child decent medical care and nutrition, reduce the unemployment often associated with violence toward children, and guarantee baseline standards of living, adequate housing, day care, and social services (Keniston & the Carnegie Council on Children, 1977; National Academy of Sciences, 1976; Silver, 1978). Interested professionals should monitor all proposed legislation to see how it will affect children. Further, large companies should be encouraged to expand their efforts to devise employment policies and services that foster family life. Child-care professionals and advocates should offer their services in setting up such programs. Ongoing coalitions among government and the private sector would facilitate social changes beneficial to all American families.

Thus, legislators, localities, and concerned citizens have already made a start. But popular reconceptualization of the definition and scope of child abuse and an integration of existing programs and ideas are overdue. Finally, even though specific actions may help to prevent and contain child abuse, the problem is so closely related to the general difficulties facing American children and families that in the long run massive social reform and advocacy seem necessary.

Note

1 See Gerbner, Ross, and Zigler (1980) for many suggested questions for future exploration.

References

Aber, J. L., III. The involuntary child placement decision: Solomon's dilemma revisited. In G. Gerbner, C. J. Ross, & E. Zigler (Eds.), *Child abuse: An agenda for action.* New York: Oxford University Press, 1980.

Aber, J. L., III, & Zigler, E. Developmental considerations in the definition of child maltreatment. In D. Cicchetti & R. Rizley (Eds.), *New directions for child development.* San Francisco: Jossey-Bass, 1981.

Blatt, B. The pariah industry: A diary from purgatory and other places. In G. Gerbner, C. J. Ross, & E. Zigler (Eds.), *Child abuse: An agenda for action.* New York: Oxford University Press, 1980.

Bourne, R., & Newberger, E. H. (Eds.). *Critical perspectives on child abuse.* Lexington, Mass.: Lexington Books, 1979.

Bronfenbrenner, U. *The ecology of human development: Experiments by nature and design.* Cambridge: Harvard University Press, 1979.

Burgess, R. L. Child abuse: A behavioral analysis. In B. B. Lahey & A. E. Kazdin (Eds.), *Advances in clinical psychology.* New York: Plenum, 1978.

Divoky, D. Child abuse: Mandate for teacher intervention? *Learning,* April 1976, pp. 4–22.

Farber, I. E. Sane and insane: Constructions and misconstructions. *Journal of Abnormal Psychology,* 1975, *84,* 589–620.

Feshbach, N. D. Corporate punishment in the schools: Some paradoxes, some facts, some possible directions. In G. Gerbner, C. J. Ross, & E. Zigler (Eds.), *Child abuse: An agenda for action.* New York: Oxford University Press, 1980.

Feshbach, S. Child abuse and the dynamics of human aggression and violence. In G. Gerbner, C. J. Ross, & E. Zigler (Eds.), *Child abuse: An agenda for action*. New York: Oxford University Press, 1980.

Garbarino, J. A preliminary study of some ecological correlates of child abuse: The impact of socioeconomic stress on mothers. *Child Development*, 1976, *47*, 1780–1785.

Gelles, R. A profile of violence toward children in the United States. In G. Gerbner, C. J. Ross, & E. Zigler (Eds.). *Child abuse: An agenda for action*. New York: Oxford University Press, 1980.

Gerbner, G., Ross, C. J., & Zigler, E. (Eds.). *Child abuse: An agenda for action*. New York: Oxford University Press, 1980.

Gil, D. G. Physical abuse of children: Findings and implications of a nationwide survey. *Pediatrics,* 1969, *44*(5), Part 2 (Supplement), 857–864.

Gil, D. G. *Violence against children: Physical child abuse in the United States*. Cambridge: Harvard University Press, 1970.

Giovannoni, J. M., & Becerra, R. M. *Defining child abuse*. New York: Free Press, 1979.

Goldstein, J., Freud, A., & Solnit, A. *Beyond the best interests of the child*. New York: Free Press, 1973.

Harlow, H. F., & Harlow, M. K. Psychopathology in monkeys. In H. D. Kimmel (Ed.), *Experimental psychopathology: Recent research and theory*. New York: Academic Press, 1971.

Juvenile Justice Standards Project. *Standards relating to abuse and neglect*. Cambridge, Mass.: Ballinger, 1977.

Kempe, C. H., Silverman, F., Steele, B., Droegemueller, W., & Silver, H. The battered child syndrome. *Journal of the American Medical Association,* 1962, *181*, 17–24.

Kempe, R. S., & Kempe, C. H. *Child abuse*. Cambridge: Harvard University Press, 1978.

Keniston, K., & the Carnegie Council on Children. *All our children: The American family under pressure*. New York: Harcourt Brace Jovanovich, 1977.

Lauderdale, M., Anderson, R., & Cramer, S. (Eds.). *Proceedings of the second annual conference on child abuse and neglect* (Pub. No. OHDS 78-30147). Washington, D.C.: U.S. Department of Health, Education, and Welfare, 1978.

Light, R. J. Abused and neglected children in America: A study of alternative policies. *Harvard Educational Review,* 1973, *43*, 556–598.

National Academy of Sciences. *Toward a national policy for children and families: Report of the Advisory Committee on Child Development*. Washington, D.C., 1976.

National Center on Child Abuse and Neglect. *Annual review of child abuse and neglect research, 1978* (Pub. No. OHDS 79-30168). Washington, D.C.: U.S. Department of Health, Education, and Welfare, 1978.

Newberger, E. H., & Hyde, J. N. Child abuse: Principles and implications of current pediatric practice. *Pediatric Clinics of North America,* 1975, *22*, 695–715.

Newberger, E. H., Reed, R., Daniel, J., Hyde, J., & Kotelchuck, M. *Toward an etiologic classification of pediatric social illness: A descriptive epidemiology of child abuse and neglect, failure to thrive, accidents, and poisonings in children under four years of age*. Paper presented at the biennial meeting of the Society for Research in Child Development, Denver, April 11, 1975.

Parke, R. D., & Collmer, C. W. Child abuse: An interdisciplinary analysis. In M. E. Hetherington (Ed.), *Child development research* (Vol. 5). Chicago: University of Chicago Press, 1975.

Pelton, L. H. Child abuse and neglect: The myth of classlessness. *American Journal of Orthopsychiatry,* 1978, *48*, 608–617.

Philips, I. Childhood depression: Interpersonal interactions and depressive phenomena. *American Journal of Psychiatry,* 1979, *136*, 511–515.

Richmond, J. B., & Janis, J. Child health policy and child abuse. In G. Gerbner, C. J. Ross, & E. Zigler (Eds.), *Child abuse: An agenda for action*. New York: Oxford University Press, 1980.

Ross, C. J. The lessons of the past: Defining and controlling child abuse in the United States. In G. Gerbner, C. J. Ross, & E. Zigler (Eds.), *Child abuse: An agenda for action*. New York: Oxford University Press, 1980.

Silver, G. A. *Child health: America's future*. Germantown, Md.: Aspen, 1978.

Solnit, A. J. Too much reporting, too little service: Roots and prevention of child abuse. In G. Gerbner, C. J. Ross, & E. Zigler (Eds.), *Child abuse: An agenda for action*. New York: Oxford University Press, 1980.

Uviller, R. K. Save them from their saviors: The constitutional rights of the family. In G. Gerbner, C. J. Ross, & E. Zigler (Eds.), *Child abuse: An agenda for action*. New York: Oxford University Press, 1980.

Zigler, E. Metatheoretical issues in developmental psychology. In M. Marx (Ed.), *Psychological theory* (2nd ed.). New York: Macmillan, 1963.

Zigler, E. Controlling child abuse in America: An effort doomed to failure? In R. Bourne & E. Newberger (Eds.), *Critical perspectives on child abuse*. Lexington, Mass.: Lexington, 1979.

Juel Janis

Nineteen-eighty was a watershed year for child health advocates. In that year members of a federally appointed panel, consisting of child health professionals and consumer advocates, submitted to Congress and the secretary of health and human services a report entitled *Better Health for Our Children: A National Strategy.* The report not only presented the most comprehensive and detailed analysis of child health programs and policies ever done in the United States, but it also provided, for the first time, a framework for the development of a national policy on child health. The circumstances that led to the report reveal a good deal about the way social policy regarding child health has developed in the United States.

Before looking at this issue, however, it is important to note that the health of the American children has never been better (Office of the Assistant Secretary . . . , 1979). This has been achieved as a result of a combination of fortuitous factors ranging from the efforts of health professionals and volunteers in the private sector; to improvements in housing, sanitation, and nutrition; to advances in scientific medicine; to the leadership and financial resources provided by the public sector. This chapter focuses on the last factor – on the ways federal agencies, programs, and policies have affected children's health in the United States. In particular, it attempts to trace the evolution of federal involvement in helping to assure high-quality health services for the nation's children.

Child health: a historical perspective

Beginnings: the Children's Bureau

Children's health did not become a matter of public concern until the second half of the nineteenth century. By 1858 reports had been prepared

353

in New York City noting the relationship between contaminated milk and diarrhea, dysentery, and other diseases affecting children. These reports quickly led to efforts by private groups and municipalities to require pasteurization. In the 1890s, public schools assumed an increasingly active role in the promotion of child health, and by 1908 New York City had created a separate agency within its Health Department to deal with all problems related to child health (Bremner, 1971, pp. 811–814).

The first highly visible effort to address children's services on a national level was initiated in 1909 when President Theodore Roosevelt convened over 200 child welfare workers in what was to become the first of a series of decennial White House Conferences on Children. The 1909 conference has been credited with acceleration of efforts to aid mothers with dependent children, establishment of a national voluntary child welfare organization, growth of adoption agencies, and development of higher standards on the part of child-care agencies (Steiner, 1976, p. 121). From the standpoint of a federally defined focus on child health, the most significant outcome of the conference was the creation, in 1912, of the Children's Bureau in the Department of Labor. Although it is unclear whether this bureau was established as a result of direct political follow-up to the conference or, as some have alleged, was simply the result of "osmosis" (Steiner, 1976, p. 122), its existence provided a major focus for federal activity in child health for over four decades.

The Sheppard–Towner Act. The initial mandate of the Children's Bureau limited its activities to investigating and reporting on "matters pertaining to the welfare of children." Accordingly, in the area of health, its early efforts focused on ensuring birth registration, studying infant mortality, and publishing health education pamphlets that stressed the importance of breast-feeding, clean milk, and "civic cleanliness" (Bremner, 1971, p. 967). Although these activities seemed uncontroversial, it was the first time that a federal agency had produced data linking infant mortality to factors that clearly could be controlled. This information was subsequently used to support the adoption of the Sheppard–Towner Act in 1921. This act established the framework for federal–state cooperation in the provision of maternal and child health services. The legislation "established the national policy that the people of the United States through their federal government, share with the states and localities the responsibility for helping to provide community services that children need for a good start in life" (Bremner, 1971, p. 1003). Administrative responsibility for the act, which represented the first federal commitment to children's health services, was assigned to the Children's Bureau.

This act was a source of considerable controversy from its inception. Critics charged it with propagating "European Socialist and Bolshevist" doctrines promulgated by "endocrine perverts" and "derailed menopausics" that wouldultimately result in the "right to State visitation and espionage" (quotations from Bremner, 1971, pp. 1016–1020). In 1929, eight years after the enactment of Sheppard–Towner, the combined opposition of organized medicine and the Catholic church resulted in the law's termination.

It is difficult to assess whether or not the opposition to this legislation was representative of public opinion at that time. The critics who suggested that legislation such as this would ultimately result in the "assumption by the State of the authority to interfere in family relations" (Bremner, 1971, p. 1016) were expressing a point of view that has continued to appear in opposition to proposals for public support of children's services up to the present time.

Rejection of a governmental role in providing care for children has typically been accompanied by calls for voluntary efforts. The roots of this thinking are deeply entrenched in American political philosophy. For example, in an address made over 50 years ago, President Herbert Hoover attributed the advances that had been made in child health in the preceding 3 years to a "great campaign of voluntary work." He concluded this address with the admonition that "these efforts on behalf of children should be built upon the solid rock of inspiration in the local community . . . and not . . . upon the shifting sands of over centralization" (quoted in Bremner, 1971, pp. 1063–1064). It is not difficult to find such prose in political speeches today.

The Maternal and Child Health Act: Title V. Although Congress failed to renew the Sheppard–Towner Act in 1929, a bill proposing its reenactment was introduced in every session until 1935. Then, as a result of the Depression and new reports from the Children's Bureau on the declining health status of children, Congress included, as Title V of the Social Security Act of that year, the most significant piece of legislation charting federal responsibility for services for maternal and child health enacted until then.

The Maternal and Child Health Act, or Title V as it is more frequently called, is the only federal program concerned exclusively with health care for mothers and children. It provides support to the states to enhance their ability "to promote, improve and deliver" maternal and child health (MCH) care and crippled children's (CC) services, particularly in rural areas in severe economic distress.[1] Until the passage of the Medicaid program in 1965 and the Early and Periodic Screening, Diagnosis, and Treatment program in 1967, the Title V program provided the most significant federal financial support for children's health services.

The initial intent of the Title V program was to improve the health status of the mothers and children who were in greatest need by means of a federal–state grant program. Until World War II, the MCH component of the program focused primarily on preventive health care services with almost no direct delivery of medical care. Then, as a result of pressure to provide pregnancy care for wives of servicemen as a morale booster, funds for direct medical care were appropriated (Davis & Schoen, 1978, p. 123). Shortly after the war ended, however, most of these services were discontinued, and the Title V program returned to its earlier concern with preventive health and educational services (immunization programs, vision and hearing screenings, well-child conferences, etc.).

From the standpoint of federal involvement in the direct delivery of child health services, it is worth noting that the services provided to servicemen's wives during World War II, as well as the services provided by the CC program, represented examples of successful large-scale federally financed efforts in the delivery of high-quality services.

The 1950s: a period of stagnation

The decade of the 1950s has sometimes been referred to as the time of a "long drugged sleep." In child health this was a period when the nationwide infant mortality rates, long recognized as perhaps the most sensitive index of a nation's health, ceased to decline, maternal mortality remained a problem for certain groups within the population, and a large percentage of children in low-income families were receiving no medical or dental care. In addition, following World War II many of the rural poor had moved into urban areas, straining existing resources beyond their capacity.

The infant mortality rates in some cities in those years reflected these strains. For example, Baltimore's infant mortality rate increased by 19% in the 1950s. Even during the first half of the 1960s "only three of the 21 largest cities had significant annual reductions in their infant mortality rates." For the nation as a whole between 1956 and 1965, infant mortality rates decreased by only 5% (Lesser, 1969, p. 894).

In the spring of 1963, Dr. Arthur J. Lesser, who was then director of health services in the Children's Bureau, noted the special burden that was being placed on large urban hospitals by the influx of poor people into the cities. "Time is working against us," he observed: There were not enough physicians, "clinics won't admit a patient who applies in the third trimester," mothers had to wait long hours with their children for care at overcrowded hospitals, and some hospitals were about to lose their accreditation because of overcrowded conditions (Grotberg, 1977, pp. 109–110).

The response to public declaration of these problems was almost immediate. This was not the first time that a highly placed government official had expressed concern about the health of the nation's children, and it certainly was not the first such warning issued from the Children's Bureau. However, this time the warning was made in a political climate in which there was a young and vigorous new president. The nation was ready to address the social problems ignored in the previous decade and to correct inequities caused by years of discrimination and neglect.

The 1960s: a time of growth

Amendments to Title V. Although the nation ended the 1960s with a sense of frustration over the war in Vietnam, it is important to recall the excitement and optimism that characterized the early part of that decade. Reservations about federal involvement in social programs were overshadowed by a belief that the War on Poverty could ultimately be won. Success was thought to be merely a matter of dedicated work and will. Programs to improve children's health were in the forefront of political activity in that period.

In 1963, as a result of recommendations made by President Kennedy's Panel on Mental Retardation, Congress legislated the first of several amendments to the Title V program. (Until this time the Title V program had remained relatively unchanged since its enactment in 1935.) The 1963 amendments provided grants to local health departments for maternity and infant care (M&I) projects that were aimed at reducing retardation and infant mortality through the provision of prenatal care and family planning. Two years later, in 1965, another amendment to Title V created the Children and Youth (C&Y) projects. These projects picked up where the M&I projects left off by providing comprehensive health care services to children and youth up to age 20 in poverty areas. In 1967, Title V was amended again to provide special grants for dental services to children from low-income families.

Significantly, all of these amendments essentially bypassed the states and allowed the Title V dollars to go directly to local health departments and teaching hospitals, primarily in urban areas, to establish special project grants to support maternal and child health activities in low-income areas. The political decision to bypass the states in the allocation of Title V dollars reflected a belief by liberal congressmen and administration officials that the only way to assure the effectiveness of these programs was to assume direct federal control. In particular, the failure of many state health programs to deal effectively with the health problems of the poor up to that time was thought to be due to bureaucratic ineptitude, discriminatory practices, or both.

By 1973, federal Maternal and Child Health project grants supported 56 M&I projects and 59 C&Y projects. The importance of these grants can be seen in terms of the large increase in program dollars that took place in funding for the Title V program from 1950 to 1973. Specifically, this program "grew from a total of $29 million in federal, state, and local expenditures in 1950 to a total of $443 million in 1973. Most of the growth occurred after the expansion of the program in 1963" (Davis & Schoen, 1978, p. 127).

The success of these programs was evident almost immediately. Reversing the trend of the early 1960s, some of the nation's largest cities soon began reporting greater reductions in infant mortality than the nation as a whole. At the national level, the difference in the rate of decline in the infant mortality rate for blacks provides the most dramatic example of the impact of these programs: From 1965 to 1977 there was a 43% decline in black infant mortality rates, compared to a decline of only 5% in the previous 15-year period.[2]

Equally dramatic findings were reported for the C&Y programs, which had been created to provide comprehensive services for children and youth. Here, too, the record of the program's success is impressive: There was a 50% decrease in the number of children needing hospitalization since the beginning of the program. Even for those children needing hospitalization, the average number of hospital days per 1,000 registrants declined from 101 at the end of 1968 to 42 at the end of 1972 (Davis & Schoen, 1978, p. 133).

Title XIX and EPSDT: new dollars for child health. In addition to the M&I and the C&Y projects, the 1960s and early 1970s saw the creation of numerous other social programs that affected the health of children (Community Health Centers, School Lunch Program, Head Start, the Women, Infants, and Children Supplemental Food Program, etc.). The Medicaid program, legislated by Title XIX of the Social Security Act and its 1967 amendment, required states to provide Early and Periodic Screening, Diagnosis, and Treatment (EPSDT) for children under 21 as a mandatory Medicaid service. It was Title XIX and the EPSDT program that had the most significant effect on the financing of health services for children.

Specifically, by 1970, only three years after the enactment of Title XIX, the total federal expenditure under Title XIX for children under 21 was more than double the amount spent on such children in Title V programs. Whereas the Title V program grew from over $22 million in federal funds in 1955 to over $223 million in 1970, in 1970 the Title XIX program expenditures were $481 million (Foltz, 1978, p. 24).

From the standpoint of dollars expended, the period of the 1960s and early 1970s would appear to represent a significant level of responsiveness at both the state and federal level to the health and welfare needs of this nation's children. In 1940 total federal expenditures for the Title V program were approximately $8 million. However, by 1970 the combined federal expenditures for the Title V and Title XIX program were over $700 million (Foltz, 1978, p. 24).

This increase in expenditures for children's health and welfare was paralleled by an increase in the number of federal programs in these areas – by 1976 an estimated 106 such programs. Although the majority of these programs were concentrated within the Department of Health, Education, and Welfare, altogether they were administered by 5 distinct departments, by 15 different agencies within these departments, and by 45 offices and bureaus within the agencies. Further, these programs were subject to review by 6 full congressional committees and 23 congressional subcommittees whose members represented different constituencies with different priorities (Office of Child Health Affairs, 1977).

The 1970s: concern for consolidation

The argument and evidence for coordination. By the mid-1970s, despite the new infusion of federal dollars, it was apparent that maternal and child health programs needed to be better coordinated in order to reduce the fragmentation and duplication that was seen as hindering their effectiveness (Davis & Schoen, 1978; Foltz, 1978; Richmond, 1977; Steiner, 1976). From a policy standpoint, critics alleged that problems with child health programs were due to haphazard policy decisions as well as to the fact that the legislation establishing these programs was so vague and ambiguous that it was difficult to execute them effectively.

Added to concerns about the need for a coordinated approach to child health problems was the issue that despite the impressive statistics documenting the effectiveness of many of the programs started in the 1960s, by the mid-1970s other child health data were documenting the fact that significant numbers of children still were not receiving needed health care services (Davis & Schoen, 1978; Richmond, 1977). Several significant descriptive studies on the status of child health in the United States were published. They noted that the multiplicity of new programs had paradoxically created a situation in which there was no single voice for children's health problems and that certain groups of children in the United States were still inadequately served (Davis & Schoen, 1978; Harvard Child Health Project, 1977; Keniston, 1977; Newberger, Newberger, & Richmond, 1976).

With respect to the lack of a single strong voice for children, it should be noted that over the years the Children's Bureau had become relegated to an increasingly less significant position in the bureaucracy. In 1969, with the transfer to the Public Health Service of all maternal and child health programs, crippled children's services, and research and training programs related to mothers and children, the Children's Bureau lost its most powerful programs.

The maternal and child health programs of the 1960s and 1970s were developed in response to identified problems. Yet with each new study of children's health the need for a more centralized focus for children's health problems became clearer and the demand for some type of coordinating group more insistent. Essentially it was felt that only through some "integrating force" would it be possible "to remedy the fragmentation of federal programs and to provide a focal point for them, within the federal government, for serving the best interests of children and their families" (Richmond, 1977, p. 258).

Although a study group convened by the secretary of health, education, and welfare in 1971 recommended "that the Secretary initiate necessary planning of a comprehensive national health care system for mothers and young children," there was no follow-up to this proposal (Lesser, 1973). Then, in 1977, staff from the Public Health Service's Office of Child Health Affairs prepared a report entitled *A Proposal for New Federal Leadership in Maternal and Child Health in the United States* (Office of Child Health Affairs, 1977). This report outlined the existing barriers to comprehensive child and maternal health care in the country and noted that the "multiple and fragmented array of programs makes it nearly impossible for the federal government to impose any real accountability for the use of public funds, or for the collection of the kind of data necessary for effective planning." It pointed to the fact that "no single agency or bureau has been given the major federal responsibility for children" (p. 47). For a variety of reasons, little response was made to this report.

One year later, the final report of the President's Commission on Mental Health (PCMH) appointed by Jimmy Carter reiterated some of the same concerns and again emphasized the need for a coordinated child health policy. The PCMH report, issued in the spring of 1978, recommended that "the Secretary of Health, Education, and Welfare review federal programs that pertain to health and mental health services for infants and children and design a coordinated national plan to make available comprehensive services for all children" (PCMH, 1978, p. 52). One year later, as a result of several fortuitous circumstances – primarily supportive leadership in the Office of the Assistant Secretary of Health and enterprising work on the part of a young Congressional Fellow on the staff of the House Health Subcommittee – a legislative proposal was passed to create a Select Panel for the Promotion of Child Health, charged with developing "a comprehensive plan to promote the health of children and pregnant women in the United States" (H.R. 12370, 95th Cong., 2d sess., May 15, 1978).

Social policy and political expediency. The congressional mandate to the Select Panel was a milestone insofar as it represented, for the first time, an acknowledgement at the federal level of the need for a coherent national child health policy. From the inception of the Children's Bureau in 1912 and its limited charge as a data-gathering agency, to the originally narrowly conceived prevention-oriented services of the Maternal and Child Health program, to the proliferation of categorical programs in the 1960s, there had been steady growth in federal efforts to improve children's health. Yet policy decisions in each instance always represented an attempt to deal with specific, carefully delineated problems. Even the several studies in the 1960s that encouraged closer collaboration between programs affecting children's physical and mental health had a limited focus (Joint Commission on Mental Health, 1973).

In the 1970s, it became something of a cliché to describe child health policy in the United States as a "nonpolicy." Child health programs were typically characterized as being "uncoordinated," "ambiguous," and "contradictory" (Davis & Schoen, 1978; Foltz, 1978; Office of Child Health Affairs, 1977; Richmond, 1977; Steiner, 1976). Not surprisingly, these charges were similar in many respects to those being made about the health care system in general.

Individuals responsible for decision making in health were described as "afraid of imposing overall or systematic solutions" and trying "to do a little bit of everything at once" (Langer, 1967, p. 5). Yet such criticisms ignore the historic aversion of Americans to "systematic solutions" and their long-standing antipathy to national planning. Criticisms of a perceived lack of a child health policy in the United States also ignore the prevalent fear of Americans of government infringement on the rights of the family. Given these attitudes, it is not difficult to understand why the development of a coherent national child health policy has been such a slow process.

Steiner (1976, p. vii) described public action on children's policy issues as being a "federal-agency-by-federal-agency, congressional-committee-by-congressional-committee, state-by-state or city-by-city assortment of unrelated decisions that are as likely to be contradictory as complementary." Foltz (1980, p. 141) amplified this theme in her assertion that federal child health policy has been a mixture of "care and carelessness," "care" being the passage of legislation such as the Sheppard–Towner Act and the Title V and Title XIX programs, "carelessness" referring to the fact that the Sheppard–Towner Act was allowed to lapse, that the congressional appropriation of federal dollars for Title V has been "miserly," and that the EPSDT legislation was written and the program implemented in an ambiguous and confusing way.

According to Steiner, "political accidents and back-door approaches rather than rational responses to rational proposals explain most federal actions in child health questions" (1976, p. 206). Given a purely factual review of the history of the development of child health programs, such a criticism might appear appropriate. However, for anyone familiar with the history of the development of almost all social programs and policies in the United States, it is apparent that "political accidents and back-door approaches" also "explain" most federal actions in these areas as well.

Basically, such criticism assumes that individuals within the federal executive and legislative branches have both the power and the responsibility to develop national policy on domestic issues. Yet if one looks at either the power or the responsibility held by such individuals, it is apparent that this is not the case. This is so partly because of the "laissez-faire" attitude embedded in the political philosophy of the United States that advocates noninterference by the federal government, and partly because of the structure of the U.S. government with its system of checks and balances that requires a level of cooperation between the executive and legislative branches that rarely exists.

Examination of the development of social policy in almost any social program in the United States from welfare to housing to health yields little evidence to suggest that national policy in these areas ever developed as a result of "rational responses to rational proposals." Almost without exception, the major domestic programs in the United States developed in response to events that made their creation politically expedient.

What has occurred reflects ad hoc responses to social problems. From the Social Security Act of the 1930s, to the housing programs both before and after World War II, to the Great Society programs of the 1960s, federal action in social programs occurred in response to recognition of crises that could not be ignored. Further, in each instance, although the creation of separate, discrete programs was sanctioned by Congress, they were never *conceptualized* as a part of some larger plan or national policy. Suggestions that there was a need for a comprehensive national plan to deal with a particular problem have typically been denounced as being both socialistic and anti-American. Nowhere has this been truer than with efforts to formulate a national health policy.

For example, over 40 years ago a group of physicians known as the Committee of 430 (referring to the number of its members) banded together to enunciate the principle that "the health of the people is a direct concern of the government" and that "a national public health policy directed toward all groups of the population should be formulated" (Richmond, 1969, p. 17). The response by organized medicine (in the form of the AMA) was immediate. Warning of the "dangers of Federal subsidies," an editorial in the *Journal of the American Medical Association* raised the specter of eventual federal "determination of the curriculum and administration of service" and suggested that the "unthinking" physicians who endorsed these principles and proposals submit some prompt disclaimers (Richmond, 1969, p. 19).

Years later Medicaid and Medicare met with similar, though in this case unsuccessful, efforts to prevent federal involvement in the provision of health services. The absence today of a national health insurance plan for the United States speaks to the strength of this political philosophy. What is surprising today is not that the United States has not had a national child health policy in the past, but rather that in 1980 it was so close to having one. It was not coincidental that the major components of the proposed child health policy closely paralleled those of the national health policy enunciated by the health leadership in the Carter administration.

Child health: present and future

The status of child health – 1980

The rationale for the national health policy that had been developed by the end of the 1970s in the Department of Health and Human Services and for the policies outlined in the report from the Select Panel for the Promotion of Child Health reflects an effort to respond to the major changes that have occurred in the health status of the American people and more particularly of American children: "Between 1965 and 1979, infant mortality declined by 47 percent to 13 deaths per 1,000 live births" (Office of Health Research . . . , 1980, p. 39). Mortality rates for children 1 to 4 years of age dropped even more dramatically, from 641 per 100,000 population in 1925 to a low of 69 in 1978 (Office of the Assistant Secretary . . . , 1981, Vol. 3, p. 133). A child born in 1900 had a life expectancy at birth of 47 years, whereas in 1977 life expectancy at birth was 73 years (Office of Health Research . . . , 1980, p. 201). At the turn of the century, infectious diseases were the principal causes of death. In 1920, the death rate from influenza for children 1 to 19 years of age was 39 per 100,000 population (Bureau of the Census, 1920). By 1977, this rate had dropped to 1.4 (National Center for Health Statistics, 1979). Today accidents are the leading causes of childhood death and account for 45% of total childhood mortality (Office of the Assistant Secretary . . . , 1979, p. 33).

These changes in child health have been paralleled by equally dramatic changes in the health status of American people of all ages. However, current data show that there is a persistent gap in health status and use of services between rich and poor, white and nonwhite. Specifically, in 1977 the black infant mortality rate was nearly double that of whites; approximately one-third of all black children had some kind of nutritional deficit, while less than 15% of all white children had such a deficit; children under 6 years of age in the poorest families had almost twice as many bed disability days and a third more restricted-activity days as those in the highest-income category; among children under 18 years old in the highest-income families, 70% were reported to be in excellent health, as compared to 41% in the lowest-income families; and the number of hospital days per child under 17 was almost four times as great for the lowest-income group as for the highest, with average length of stay more than twice as long (Office of the Assistant Secretary . . . , 1981, Vol. 1, p. 38). The preceding statistics on the health of American children lead to several conclusions: (1) The overall status of children's health has never been better; (2) certain groups of children are still not receiving adequate health care; and (3) accidents are the most significant threat to a child's health and thus present a problem that must be addressed not only by health professionals but by other disciplines as well.

Further, although not immediately detectable in the data, the decline in infectious diseases has allowed for the recognition of health problems that Dr. Robert Haggerty (1975) has called the "new morbidity." Basically, the term *new morbidity* is now used to encompass a wide range of behavioral and psychosocial problems, including developmental disabilities, the social and emotional aspects of handicapping conditions, excessive risk taking, alcohol and drug abuse, and suicide. Although in fact none of these is a new problem, they can now claim added attention since the threat of infectious diseases has been almost eliminated. Most importantly, this changed profile in children's health needs has significant implications for future developments in the training of health professionals as well as the organization, financing, and delivery of child health services.

The Select Panel for the Promotion of Child Health

The Select Panel for the Promotion of Child Health began its work in 1979 with a charge to "review all the significant medical, scientific, behavioral, and epidemiological studies concerning the promotion of child health, and the prevention of childhood diseases" (H.R. 12370, 95th Cong., 2d sess., May 15, 1978). Based on this review it was to "develop a comprehensive national plan" to achieve the desired goals. The legislative mandate specified the types of recommendations to be covered in such a comprehensive plan, noting that they should include an analysis of preventive services; plans for financing and service delivery, as well as for coordinating and consolidating programs; research needs; health education; and the training of health personnel.

The panel consisted of 17 members from throughout the United States, 5 of whom were Department of Health, Education, and Welfare officials. The other members included representatives, as was specified in the act, from the scientific, medical, allied health, mental health, preventive health, public health, and education professions, as well as consumers and representatives from state and local health agencies. The panel was to complete its work in 18 months and was authorized for a $1 million budget.

A substantial part of the panel's report deals with the broad issues of financing, service delivery, manpower, research, and federal administrative arrangements in maternal and child health. However, one of its most significant contributions, reflective of an increased awareness of the change in the nature of children's health problems, is its acknowledgment that many "of the strongest influences in child health lie beyond the reach of personal health services" (Office of the Assistant Secretary . . . , 1981, p. 3). Specifically, almost one-third of the report concerns issues related to "environmental risks," "health and behavior," and "nutrition."

The most powerful conclusion of the report is its unequivocal endorsement of universal access to three essential sets of services: (1) prenatal, delivery, and postnatal care; (2) comprehensive care for children through age five; and (3) family planning services. Other recommendations in the report call for changes in the organization and financing of health services; note the need to modify the training and utilization of health professionals to address the psychosocial and behavioral components of child health problems; propose specific mechanisms for restructuring programs to ensure better coordination at the local, state, and federal levels; cite the need to strengthen the knowledge base in maternal and child health; and urge the involvement of a variety of both public and private institutions to help reduce accidents and risks in the physical environment, improve nutrition, and promote healthier ways of living. In the summary section of the report, the panel members characterized the report as representing "a long-term prospectus for a sound investment in America's future" (Office of the Assistant Secretary . . . , 1981, p. 2).

This four-volume report is the most comprehensive study done to date on child health in the United States. The responsibility for assessing its full impact will fall to future historians, since it is now too early to speculate on its fate. To seasoned and cynical observers of the Washington scene, commission and panel reports are most frequently associated with shelves and dust gathering. Given the severe budgetary problems in the United States when this report was submitted, as well as the Reagan administration's vigorous efforts to reduce or eliminate the federal role in health and other social service programs, the administration's response to the report's recommendations in the first two years after it was published was certainly one of apathy. The only significant congressional action taken in relation to child health was the establishment in 1982 of the Select Committee on Children, Youth, and Families in the House of Representatives.

Regardless of action taken in response to the panel's recommendations, the report itself provides a blueprint for a child health policy in the United States for the rest of this century.

Toward a national child health policy

The three strong themes that emerged from the Select Panel's report (Office of the Assistant Secretary . . . , 1981) were:

1. The importance of prevention – a recognition especially of the need to develop health promotion strategies aimed at reducing accidents, improving nutrition, and encouraging individuals to "adopt and sustain behaviors that can enhance health and well-being" (p. 20);
2. The assurance that "all needed health and health-related services are available and accessible to *all* infants, children, adolescents, and pregnant women" (p. 20);

3. The need to support research in order to continue to build "the knowledge base necessary to further enhance maternal and child health" (p. 21).

The three major themes outlined in the Select Panel's report mirror those enunciated previously by the chief health officer of the United States, Dr. Julius B. Richmond, surgeon general of the Public Health Service and a member of the panel. Throughout his tenure (1977–1981) in the Department of Health, Education, and Welfare (later Health and Human Services), Dr. Richmond presented a conceptual framework for national health policy priorities that emphasized three key areas: disease prevention and health promotion; access to health services for all Americans; and health research. Federal health activities during the Carter administration were directed toward the promotion of these priorities. The congruence between the national health priorities identified by the administration and those identified by the Select Panel reflected the close working relationship between the panel members and the key health officials in the administration.

Still another level of activity in the arena of national health policy that has implications for future actions affecting children's health was the publication in 1979 of *Healthy People: The Surgeon General's Report on Health Promotion and Disease Prevention* (Office of the Assistant Secretary . . . , 1979). This was followed in 1980 by *Promoting Health/Preventing Disease* (Public Health Service, 1980), a document that outlined specific and quantifiable objectives for attaining the national "prevention" goals identified in the surgeon general's report.

The 1980s began, therefore, with a clearly formulated national health policy and with a policy outline for improving child health. Specific measurable goals had been set at the federal level to assess progress toward the attainment of these goals. The question is: Where will we go from here?

If program developments in child health over the past two decades were to be classified according to an Eriksonian typology (Erikson, 1950), the 1960s would probably be classified as a decade of "industry" – an assertion of new strength and competence – and the 1970s as a decade of "identity" – a struggle to establish a set of definitively recognizable characteristics. To carry the analogy further, the question now is whether the 1980s will be, in Erikson's terms, a period of "generativity" or of "stagnation."

Certainly developments in U.S. child health policy have been influenced by the larger political picture:

> The days of significant federal expenditures for categorical programs are over. (The block grant approach to maternal and child health pro-

grams approved by Congress in the summer of 1981 has resulted in a 25% reduction in federal funding for the programs included in this block.)

Reduction in support for categorical programs has been accompanied by efforts to limit growth in "entitlement" programs (i.e., programs, such as Medicaid, that provide aid to all people who fit certain eligibility standards).

Control and administration of many health and welfare programs is being decentralized, thereby minimizing the role of the federal government and providing increased responsibilities to state and local governments. The establishment of a separate Maternal and Child Health block grant program that gave federal funds for maternal and child health directly to the states with little or no restrictions illustrates this decentralization effort.

Regulations, reporting requirements, and other restrictions affecting the use of federal dollars for social programs have been greatly reduced or in some cases eliminated. In the early part of the Reagan administration a statement was placed in the *Federal Register* noting that, with respect to the Title V program, "we will not burden the States' administration of the programs with definitions of permissible and prohibited activities, procedural rules, paperwork and recordkeeping requirements, or other regulatory provisions" (46 *Fed. Reg.* 48583, October 1, 1981).

Special interest groups will continue to battle for the limited available dollars and will also compete with each other for support from private foundations.

These are some of the major constraints that will affect future activity in child health. Any speculation about future developments in child health must keep them in mind. If the 1980s can, in fact, be a period of "generativity," the following should occur:

Prevention should be acknowledged as one of the most effective and least costly ways to improve the health status of children. New efforts should be made in areas such as accidents, teenage pregnancy, substance abuse, and child abuse.

There should be a special effort to target the reduced existing dollars for child health on programs for those special populations at greatest risk, including women who do not seek early prenatal care, women who are at risk for bearing a low-birth-weight infant, pregnant teenagers, and unserved segments of the population in rural and low-income urban areas.

There should be more local, state, and private sector involvement in social programs once seen as the federal government's responsibility. Individuals with expertise in areas affecting children's health, who in earlier years had gravitated to Washington, should turn their talents toward work at the local and state level.

There should be greater acceptance of interdisciplinary activities and continued moves toward a team approach to service delivery.

Efforts to ensure that services are coordinated among health, mental health, employment, housing, and other relevant social programs must be made. Limited service would make it imperative that services not be duplicative.

New ways should be found to finance child health services, ways that are not based exclusively on a fee-for-service model.

Prevention, targeting of resources, greater state and private sector involvement, more interdisciplinary emphasis, improved coordination between health and other social programs, and more creative ways of financing services are the likely future trends for child health programs and policies.

It is essential that those who wish to promote these trends – be they health professionals or citizen advocates – become more politically sophisticated than they have been in the past. Only through an awareness of the larger political picture will it be possible to maintain the momentum that now exists for improving the programs and policies that serve children. In particular, it is important for those concerned with children's health to know how to work with community organizations at the local level and with the appropriate leadership at the state level to improve the effectiveness of child health programs and maximize available resources. It will be important to be able to use the media effectively, both to disseminate health education information and to gain wider public understanding about issues affecting children, and thereby to develop a national constituency to support needed child health services. Finally, it is important to realize that in a society as complex as the United States there can be no simple solutions or single way to improve the health and welfare of children. A pluralistic society demands pluralistic solutions to its problems.

Notes

1 The text of the Maternal and Child Health Act can be found in *United States Code,* Title 42, secs. 701 et seq.
2 These percentages were calculated using yearly infant mortality rates from 1965 through 1977 based on materials from the National Center for Health Statistics, Division of Vital Statistics, U.S. Public Health Service, 1979.

References

Bremner, R. H. (Ed.). *Children and youth in America* (Vol. 2: 1866–1932). Cambridge: Harvard University Press, 1971.

Bureau of the Census. *Mortality statistics, 1920.* Washington, D.C.: U.S. Government Printing Office, 1922.

Davis, K., & Schoen, C. *Health and the war on poverty: A ten year appraisal.* Washington, D.C.: Brookings Institution, 1978.

Erikson, E. H. *Childhood and society.* New York: Norton, 1950.

Foltz, A. M. *Uncertainties of federal child health policies: Impact in two states* (DHEW Publication No. [PHS] 78-3190). Washington, D.C.: U.S. Government Printing Office, 1978, p. 24.

Foltz, A. M. Care and carelessness in federal child health policies. *Journal of Public Health Policy,* 1980, *1*(2), 141–149.

Grotberg, E. (Ed.). *Two hundred years of children* (Office of Human Development, Office of Child Development, DHEW Publication No. OHD 77-30103). Washington, D.C.: U.S. Government Printing Office, 1977, pp. 109–110.

Haggerty, R. J., Roughmann, K. J., & Pless, I. B. (Eds.). *Child health and the community.* New York: Wiley, 1975.

Harvard Child Health Project Task Force. *Developing a better health care system for children* (Vols. 1, 2, 3). Cambridge, Mass.: Ballinger, 1977.

Joint Commission on Mental Health of Children. *Mental health: From infancy through adolescence.* New York: Harper & Row, 1973.

Keniston, K., and the Carnegie Council on Children. *All our children: The American family under pressure.* New York: Harcourt Brace Jovanovich, 1977.

Langer, E. Who makes our health policy? *Physicians' Forum,* June 1967, p. 5.

Lesser, A. J. The federal government in child health care. *Pediatric Clinics of North America,* 1969, *16,* 891–900.

Lesser, A. J. *Child health in the 1970s.* Paper presented at the dedication of the Edward A. Park Building, Children's Health Services, Johns Hopkins Hospital, Baltimore, Md., February 23, 1973.

Newberger, E. H., Newberger, C. M., & Richmond, J. B. Child health in America: Toward a national public policy. *Milbank Memorial Fund Quarterly,* Summer 1976, pp. 249–298.

Office of the Assistant Secretary for Health and Surgeon General, U.S. Department of Health, Education, and Welfare. *Healthy people: The surgeon general's report on health promotion and disease prevention* (Surgeon General's Report; DHEW [PHS] Publication No. 79-55071). Washington, D.C.: U.S. Government Printing Office, 1979.

Office of the Assistant Secretary for Health and Surgeon General, Public Health Service, U.S. Department of Health and Human Services. *Better health for our children: A national strategy* (Report of the Select Panel for the Promotion of Child Health). Washington, D.C.: U.S. Government Printing Office, 1981.

Office of Child Health Affairs, Office of the Assistant Secretary for Health, Public Health Service, U.S. Department of Health, Education, and Welfare. *A proposal for new federal leadership in child and maternal health in the United States.* Unpublished manuscript. Washington, D.C., February 23, 1977.

Office of Health Research, Statistics, and Technology, Public Health Service, Department of Health and Human Services. *Health: United States, 1980.* (Publication No. [PHS] 81-1232). Hyattsville, Md.: October 1980.

President's Commission on Mental Health (Vol. 1) (U.S. Supt. of Documents Stock No. 040-000-00390-8). Washington, D.C.: U.S. Government Printing Office, 1978.

Public Health Service, Department of Health and Human Services. *Promoting health/preventing disease: Objectives for the nation* (GPO No. 0-331-669). Washington, D.C.: U.S. Government Printing Office, 1980.

Richmond, J. B. *Currents in American medicine.* Cambridge: Harvard University Press, 1969.

Richmond, J. B. The needs of children. In J. H. Knowles (Ed.), *Doing better and feeling worse: Health in the U.S.* New York: Norton, 1977, pp. 247–259.

Steiner, G. Y. *The children's cause.* Washington, D.C.: Brookings Institution, 1976.

21   Drug policy: the American evolution

David F. Musto

A faith in elixirs and nostrums has characterized much of American social policy toward "the drug problem." Early patent medicines, often laced with opiates or cocaine, promised relief across a wide spectrum of complaints; 80 years later, hallucinogens were marketed with a zealous enthusiasm for their alleged capacity to generate visionary delight. Government efforts to control illicit drugs have frequently been tainted by an equivalent idiom of deliverance, and fire has been fought with fire. The appeals of narcotic-induced stupor or exhilaration are so compellingly seductive that only a counterforce of messianic potency can afford resistance: Such a premise long endured as the conceptual substratum of official programs. Although at various times the crusade has marched under the banner of legal sanctions, supply interdiction, or political and educational reforms, and although the cadence of the drumbeat has modulated according to the prevailing national mood, the search for a fix has proceeded, until very recently, without halt.

At best, shifts in policy have occurred in peripheral response to knowledge acquired about patterns of substance abuse or the pharmacological dynamics of illicit drugs. The pursuit of scapegoats has, by and large, been far more avid than the pursuit of scientific truth. Conspiracy theories abound, elaborated with equal fanaticism by proponents of libertarian or rigidly punitive approaches. Evidence has been educed for arguing that drug control is a façade behind which lurk a host of nefarious schemes: racist demagoguery, hostility to youth and cultural innovations, CIA machinations. Alternately, fundamentalist orthodoxy has accounted for the persistence of narcotics by conjuring up plots devised by the Red Chinese, the Mafia, and other sundry corrupters and profiteers.

In a field teeming with magical thinking, where spokesmen tend to impute to their ideological opponents not just bad judgment but also membership in some cabal, the pull of partisanship has often proved irresistible, even for those investigators who begin with a commitment to detached inquiry. Because the subject of drugs arouses passion commensurate with the value-laden nature of the conflicts that policy disagreements reflect (spontaneity vs. repression, abstinence vs. consumption, individual pleasure vs. civic and familial responsibilities), the refusal to pick up arms on such a battleground may seem like an act of cowardice masquerading as evenhandedness. However, while it is true that melodrama is far more dramatically satisfying than factual analysis, since it holds out the promise for some penultimate resolution, readers addicted to exposé and anxiously waiting for "Mr. Big" to be revealed will find this chapter disappointing stuff. But in sneering at, or burlesquing, past efforts to proscribe or regulate drug abuse, we flatten experience, making it one-dimensional, and thereby cheat ourselves of a wealth of insight about our own policy choices and dilemmas.

There is a certain plausibility in arguing that the government struggle against drugs has resembled a case of institutional countertransference, or even folie à deux; however, the motives behind the various campaigns of control should not be demeaned or trivialized. Despite mischievous or misconstrued techniques of paternal oversight, the government's felt obligation to safeguard the moral and physical integrity of its citizens must nonetheless be taken seriously. How government established the legitimate and feasible scope of its authority over individual conduct and how this scope expands or contracts are continuous themes played out in reaction to a complex of cultural and political pressures in the history we are about to examine.

Drug use in the nineteenth century and the background of the regulatory movement

Narcotics, in the form of opium and its various tinctures, were familiar to Americans as early as the eighteenth century. Prescribed as a broad-spectrum anodyne for everything from delirium tremens to depression, venereal disease, fevers, and stomach disorders, opium occupied a preeminent place in the armamentarium of the early physician; a standard medical text from the middle of the nineteenth century declared opium to be "undoubtedly the most important and valuable remedy in the whole Materia Medica" (quoted in Musto, 1973, p. 20). Even though addiction was a recognized phenomenon, professional opinion by and large held that only the weak-willed succumbed to overindulgence. Morphine, whose discovery in 1805 was followed in turn by the rapid development of other alkaloid derivatives, lent itself to controlled dosages difficult to achieve in opium preparations of irregular strengths. The invention of the hypodermic syringe coincided with the availability of cheap, powerful morphine mass-produced by drug companies; the confluence of these factors accounts for the narcotic's widespread popularity. Even though morphine addiction was called "the army disease," in reference to the numbers of wounded Civil War veterans who were treated with the drug, consumption rates, as inferred from statistics on the import of crude opium for processing, had in fact been climbing steadily from 1840 and did not reach their peak until the mid-1890s (Musto, 1973, p. 2).

Opiates proliferated in the United States during the late 1800s, not only because of promiscuous dispensing by physicians, but also because of the profusion of patent medicines hawked through the mail or sold retail. With labels that promised wholesomeness ("Mrs. Winslow's Soothing Syrup") but failed to list the actual ingredients, psychotropics developed a mass and, to some degree, unwitting clientele, attracting users who could ingest opium or cocaine as a cold remedy while at the same time continuing to serve, in good faith, as loyal soldiers in temperance organizations.

State regulation of drug use had begun as early as 1860, when Pennsylvania restricted the sale of morphine; during the last two decades of the nineteenth century, other states, caught up in the national political tide that was sweeping the country toward alcohol prohibition, passed laws that forbade opium smoking and limited the outlets for cocaine to physicians' and dentists' offices. Legislation amounted primarily to rhetorical statements of principle rather than enforceable mandates. Medical professionals remained on an honor system, since the inspection of prescriptions – the chief policing device as established in local ordinances – was notoriously casual. "Dope doctors" and their counterparts among pharmacists were still free to practice their profitable trade.

It was actually commerce on a different scale that triggered the movement toward federal drug control. The Spanish–American War marked the first great triumph of the United States as a world power; a few hundred casualties yielded the Philippines, Guam, Cuba, and Puerto Rico. On the grounds that these territories were ill prepared for self-rule, American troops suppressed Filipino guerillas with a force far exceeding that required to liberate the islands from Spanish colonialism. Rebutting suspicions that the United States had ousted the European exploiters simply to further its own economic advantage, a regime of impeccable moral consistency was established. Among the array of officials who arrived from the United States to preside over the tutelage of the now-pacified natives, one of the most influential was the first Episcopal bishop of the Philippines, Charles Henry Brent. Quickly, he came to regard as a test of America's altruistic dominion the curtailing of the opium monopoly that the Spanish had operated. Encouraged by a 1901 Supreme Court's decision that states' rights did not apply to U.S. possessions, Brent joined an investigating committee that produced a series of recommendations: Opium dens were to be shut down, their "habitués" registered, and drug education introduced into the schools. In 1905, Congress, enacting the first federal drug control statute, ordered for the islands a prohibition on all nonmedical consumption of opium (Musto, 1973, p. 28).

Soon afterward, humanitarian zeal once again converged with economic self-interest, this time facilitating penetration into the presumably lucrative markets of China, where the United States supported the nationalist struggle against opium. At the behest of Bishop Brent, President Roosevelt ordered the State Department to convene an international meeting at which facts about the worldwide drug problem could be aired and at which America could align itself with China's prohibitionist campaign. As Dr. Hamilton Wright, an American delegate to the 1909 Shanghai Opium Commission, later remarked to the secretary of state, "Our move to help China in her opium reform gave us more prestige in China than any of our recent friendly acts toward her. If we continue and press steadily, China will recognize that we are serious in her behalf, and the whole business may be as oil to smooth the troubled water of our aggressive commercial policy there" (quoted in Musto, 1973, p. 39).

The 14 nations assembled at the Shanghai meeting refused to fall in behind the United States' vanguard and adopt the strict ban on opium that Dr. Wright so passionately espoused. Far from discouraging Dr. Wright, this failure merely convinced him that moral flaccidness was internationally endemic and that the United States must continue the campaign to extirpate a global vice. But if the United States was to exercise this leadership effectively, then its own internal policies had to embody discipline and statutory coherence. As matters stood, such consistency was impossible given the diverse and often lax narcotics laws that existed from state to state. Though foreign nations seemed to shrug at drugs, regarding them as a nuisance rather than a menace, most other countries at least had comprehensive ordinances on the books, no matter how casually they might be enforced. The United States – the self-appointed ethical mentor – was proselytizing abstinence even as drug consumption, according to people like Dr. Wright, was beyond control within its own borders. To reconcile such an embarrassing contradiction and bring domestic behavior into accord with the virtuous sobriety the rest of the world was being urged to adopt, the United States had to reform itself.

Pressures for a federal drug control program thus partly grew out of a perceived necessity that American citizens had to be subjected to the same high-minded treatment that was being exported abroad. A law of impressive scope and robustness would make the integrity of national commitment unequivocal and help persuade other, fainter hearts to follow suit and take the cure. But the movement to consolidate and strengthen regulatory systems was not simply a regimen of moral athletics intended to enhance the United States' prestige or ammunition for a foreign policy of coercive benevolence. Beyond the importance of federal codes as an example for others, a legal apparatus of increased reliability was also felt to be required in order to curb a genuine domestic problem.

Changing view of drug use and the Harrison Act

Until the late nineteenth century, drugs had been present in the United States without inspiring a sense of urgent popular jeopardy or a concerted effort at control. Though in 1900 the addict population was probably a quarter of a million (Musto, 1973, p. 5), the per capita use of opiates was in fact declining; that narcotics came to be defined as a serious problem during a period of reduction in consumption suggests that changes in the social environment primarily accounted for shifts in regulatory policy. The lens of the social looking glass was being adjusted, and behavior that before had been viewed as simply peculiar or pitiful now assumed a far more ominous cast.

The years directly before and after the turn of the century formed a watershed in the growth of the United States as a world power and in so doing brought into sharp focus questions about national values and purposes. Debates between imperialists and antiimperialists exposed a layer of deep uneasiness about the threat to traditional and stable modes of life posed by the choice of empire. The foes of colonialism warned that the maelstrom of foreign involvement would eventually disorient and corrupt America; adventures abroad risked infecting the home with various contagions. It was to guard against such an influx of disease that increasingly severe drug control measures were advocated.

Opium and cocaine were imports, literally and symbolically. They were substances redolent with the violent exoticism of their primitive origins; their use conjured up Lascars, Chinamen, and South American Indians. Narcotics were quintessentially un-American. Even though a powerful antialcohol movement had been a fixture of American politics since the 1830s, there was always a national ambivalence about drinking, and beer and spirits had a historical legitimacy that never was true for drugs.

Drunkenness produced devastating sequelae; at the same time, drinking was a ritual that marked collective activities. It was precisely this capacity to incorporate dual and contradictory elements – social hospitality and personal and familial abandonment – that caused drinking to be so problematic. Narcotics failed to arouse the same kind of ambivalence. The analgesic qualities of drugs were kept discrete and did not overlap into socially acceptable recreational use. The tippling house and grogshop in the eighteenth century, and the saloon in the nineteenth and twentieth, were places protean in their signification, serving both as a snare that enticed men to dissipate and debauch as well as providing a locus for them to conduct serious business or perfect the conversational arts. Whether or not it is true that the taverns of Boston served as headquarters for the planning of the Revolution, the strength of the legend suggests that Americans believed that drinking and purposeful action could coexist. "Dope-dens," on the other hand, were always portrayed as the exclusive haunts of the morally derelict; drugs dulled social sentiment by making the individual's own body an instrument for self-delight. And not only did these magical substances emanate from backward lands, but they also attracted, it was feared, a clientele of "habitués" most at risk to loss of control.

The momentum for a national drug policy gathered strength during a period when isolationist opposition to foreign entanglements coincided with rising hostility toward the horde of urban polyglots and the masses of black field workers stirring on the landscape of the rural South. It was generally perceived that these lower orders and racial minorities, poised on the brink of anarchic violence and never fully accepting the constraining norms of the dominant culture, could topple back into the abyss, and drugs were seen as a triggering mechanism for this regression, with particular substances inducing a specific form of depravity. Cocaine, favored by blacks, aroused them from their natural good-natured stupor, replacing it with an aggressive euphoria. As Jim Crow laws became enforced with a vengeance and lynchings grew epidemic, the dread of "cocomania" spread. Opium was morally lethal for the Chinese, encouraging predatory sexual behavior toward white women. Heroin, first marketed in 1898, became stereotyped as the drug of choice for youth; it was described as having "a very pronounced stimulating effect, and for that reason is largely used by boys and young men as a means of dissipation" (quoted in Musto, 1973, p. 101).

The impetus for a national drug policy went beyond a wish to clamp down on antisocial elements; it must be recalled that the early 1900s was a time both of racist and xenophobic hysteria as well as of growing confidence in the redemptive capacity of government. The mainstream reform position, visible as early as 1900, argued that a benevolent social policy required expanded state intervention. As David Rothman observes:

> To realize the promise of American life, the public sector would have to dominate the private sector. The state, not the individual, would define the common good and see to its fulfillment. In short, the major tenet of Progressive thought was that only the state could make the individual free. Only the enlarged authority of the government could satisfy the particular needs of all the citizens. [Glasser, Marcus, & Rothman, 1976, p. 74]

Pure-food-and-drug laws, legislative concern for the physical environment, restrictions on child labor, penal reform – all manifested this faith in the government as moral arbiter.

In the area of drug policy, this emphasis on government regulation as a humane and rational device at first held sway over punishment-oriented tendencies. Programs of local control initiated during the period 1908–1914 placed stress on fact finding, prevention, and treatment. Abuses were to be registered, a process that would measure the extent of the public health problem; unscrupulous doctors and pharmacists were to be more effectively policed, thereby cutting off the chief source of illegitimate supply; and rehabilitation care, either institutional or ambulatory, was to be provided to the addict. There was no prescription for how these ingredients were to be mixed, and when the Harrison Act was passed in 1914 by Congress as the country's basic narcotic law, it incorporated rather than resolved this sense of legislative experimentalism.

Immediately following the passage of the act, the freedom of doctors to maintain patients on addictive drugs was attacked. Despite protests from physicians, outraged that their practice of medicine was being subjected to government interference, and despite a Court ruling in 1916 (*U.S.* v. *Jin Fuey Moy*) that temporarily restricted the act's policy powers and reaffirmed the doctor's discretionary privilege to prescribe narcotics, the law tightened inexorably. By 1920 the formerly acceptable, or arguable, view that addicts might be allowed to continue as addicts, given appropriate professional supervision, became outlandish, even dangerous.

The shift in judicial outlook resulted from a combination of factors: the enactment of national prohibition, World War I, and the "Red Scare," that aroused a panicked vigilance against subversive conspiracies. With the reinterpreting of the *Jin Fuey Moy* decision in March 1919, the Treasury Department unleashed its agents to arrest doctors and pharmacists who had been supplying addicts. In New York City, a concerted effort was made by local hospitals and the Health Department to absorb the population whose access to drugs had been terminated. Cure rather than maintenance was to be provided, but the availability of institutional beds soon became overwhelmed by demand. Responding to this shortage, the Treasury Department proposed a federal system of short-term, emergency in-patient treatment, operated through a series of model clinics that the Public Health Service would help administer. However, Congress rejected this scheme in a decision influenced both by financial exigencies and the clinical nihilism of the Public Health Service itself. The U.S. surgeon general had become wary of committing Public Health Service resources to treat a condition for which there seemed no cure. This alleged intractability of the narcotics habit had grown to be an article of faith by 1920; a social problem whose handling once fell between the domains of medicine and judicial authority became, more and more, the responsibility of the police.

As a group, physicians did not abruptly abandon their responsibility for the care of addicts. But under the pressure of legal harassment and prosecution, many doctors withdrew from the fray. Though Supreme Court rulings until the mid-1920s still left moot the entire question of the goverment's right to prescribe medical treatment – "What constitutes bona fide medical practice must be determined upon consideration of evidence and attending circumstances," the justices declared in the *Linder* case (Brotman & Freedman, 1968, p. 1) – the Narcotics Division, formed in 1920 as a separate unit within the Internal Revenue Bureau, ignored such ambiguity and mobilized a full-scale campaign against most instances of maintenance (Brotman & Freedman, 1968, p. 5). In the face of enormous professional risks posed by the threat both of actual conviction and the embarrassment and financial costs of legal defense as well by a distaste for addicts themselves, only a handful of practicing doctors continued to see addicts as patients.

Intimidation of the individual doctor was only one element in an overall strategy of enforcement; another key target was the network of dispensaries and clinics set up in 44 cities around the country. Despite the refusal of Congress to provide federal funding for these dispensaries, local municipalities still believed that medical treatment for drug addiction was both humane and practical. Habitual users who before had been supplied by physicians could not, it was felt, be deprived all at once of drugs without endangering their own physical health as well as the safety of the public. The actual results of this local approach were extremely uneven; the program of a city like Shreveport, Louisiana, was considered exemplary, supported by the police as an effective crime-prevention tool and praised by the addicts themselves for delivering a range of ancillary services that went beyond simply maintenance. Political corruption, poor administration, and community resistance marred the performance of other cities. Despite the relative success or failure of these local initiatives, all of the clinics were shut down through government action by 1925. The battle cry of the Narcotics Division in its attacks on the system of local clinics was that these outlets spawned addicts instead of supervising and eventually curing them. The government also argued a philosophic point, insisting that the basic conceptual coherence of the Harrison Act required a rigid maintenance ban. If the character of a substance could shift with the mode of its supply, if the identical drug could be both a medicine officially prescribed to treat a disease syndrome and an illicit moral toxin sought out as a means for depraved delight, then there was a dangerous paradox. If it was not resolved, the ambivalence would continue to debilitate policy application. Referring to the split between the medical and criminal justice models, Charles Terry, who pioneered a public health approach to addiction in Jacksonville, Florida, observed:

> If the Harrison Narcotics Act and its regulations and administrative policies are based on the assumption that addiction is little more than an expression of a vicious criminal habit or desire . . . then the Bureau is right to counter with exclusive handling . . . If, on the other hand, addiction consists of a pathological entity beyond the individual's power to control . . . how can the Government be expected to control it? [Quoted in Wakefield, 1963, p. 25]

The years of strict enforcement

Federal control policy and those enforcement agencies mandated to implement it could not tolerate ambiguous or conflicting statements of mission. But while the move to define the problem, and the Narcotics Bureau's proper role, proceeded with inexorable logic, the government, even as late as 1928, still made gestures to reconcile punishment and cure. As federal penitentiaries became swamped by an influx of drug offenders – a group that came to comprise the largest criminal class in the prison system (out of 7,500 men in three institutions, almost a third were there via the Harrison Act) – wardens demanded relief (Musto, 1973, p. 204); Congress complied in 1929 by creating two "narcotics farms," one at Lexington, Kentucky, and the other at Fort Worth, Texas. These facilities, which in the mid-1930s were relabeled "hospitals," never lived up to their official billing as model treatment environments.

During the late 1920s and up into the next decade, drug policies increasingly abandoned even a rhetorical sympathy for the addict; a punishment-oriented perspective no longer had to pay lip service to a rehabilitative ideal. Richmond P. Hobson, a charismatic organizer in the struggle against alcohol, turned to the menace of drugs after the victory of Prohibition. He spawned a series of citizens groups that could alert the public to the national peril of narcotics; he was an indefatigable political lobbyist, used the radio effectively, and after having Narcotic Education Week declared, addressed the nation on the threat posed by heroin:

To get this heroin supply the addici will not only advocate public policies against the public welfare, but will lie, steal, rob, and if necessary, commit murder. Heroin addiction can be likened to a contagion. Suppose it were announced that there were more than a million lepers among our people. Think what a shock the announcement would produce!

Yet drug addiction is more incurable than leprosy, far more tragic to its victims, and is spreading like a moral and physical scourge.

Most of the daylight robberies, daring holdups, cruel murders and similar crimes of violence are now known to be committed chiefly by drug addicts, who constitute the primary cause of our alarming crime wave. [Quoted in Musto, 1973, p. 191]

For Hobson, the prototypic moral entrepreneur, fear was a perfectly legitimate commodity to monger. From his background in the antiliquor crusade, he understood that stirring the public to commit itself emotionally to a cause required spectacular images and statistics.

Pressure for repeal of Prohibition accompanied the deepening economic collapse; it was hoped that a revived brewing and distilling industry would provide employment for thousands. The reactivation of this industry was accompanied by a huge advertising campaign, not to "stop the leaks" but to encourage leaks and even to create them. With this activity went an abandonment of the nineteenth-century dry ideal; policy makers understood that abstinence was no longer the preeminent virtue; personal sovereignty inhered in freedom of consumption and self-restraint. This ideological shift emerged through gradual and intuitive reassessment. As Samuel Gompers, leader of the American Federation of Labor, observed: "Prohibition is not a matter of right or wrong. It is not a question of whether you approve of drinking or not. It is a habit, and when you invade a man's habit, you unsettle him. You find that the man who has heretofore been contented to labor as he has been laboring, becomes restive and is discontented" (quoted in Grant, 1932, p. 5).

Unlike alcoholic beverages, narcotics had always been on the outskirts of American economic and cultural life; there was no institutional or financial base that could be mobilized to soften controls, and no plausible social benefits could result from a laissez-faire approach. Indeed, the relegitimization of drinking created a particular need to preserve the stigma of drug use. Any social policy aims at achieving some equilibrium; the opening of one safety valve must often be compensated by the tightening of another.

A new federal Bureau of Narcotics was established in 1930 to consolidate international and domestic drug control. Its first commissioner, Harry J. Anslinger, who held his post for more than 30 years and demonstrated a consistent punishment-oriented approach, moved quickly to increase the severity of sentencing for offenders. The politically astute Anslinger felt that opiates and cocaine should be the bureau's targets; America, he felt, should equate drugs with "the hard stuff." However, despite Anslinger's view that the dread of narcotics should be carefully marketed, a campaign developed, without the sponsorship of the bureau, to "crack down" on marijuana.

In 1937, Congress passed the federal Marijuana Tax Act in order to calm a groundswell of regional fear. Concentrated in the Southwest, panic about marijuana was rooted in racial paranoia. Mexican immigrants were seen as the habitual users; under the influence of the drug, it was fervently believed, violence and sexuality, always lurking just below the surface among "primitive" groups, were released. To guard against such eruptions and to control a racial minority whose migrant work became economically superfluous during the Depression, appeals were made to the federal government.

The federal ban on marijuana was a symbolic gesture rather than a purposive law. The enacted legislation did not improve methods of control; enforcement continued to be left in the hands of the state. In essence the act affirmed a cultural standard of conventionality.

Until the mid-1960s, drug control policy worked to feed the demand of such rituals. A symbiotic relationship was maintained between the agencies of control and modes of national dread. The Bureau of Narcotics did not give shape to the configurations of anxiety; it merely ratified what had grown to be a self-generating sense of menace. During the decades of the 1940s and 1950s, drug abuse conjured up the unrepentant deviant and the belligerent outsider. The McCarthyite hysteria, which coincided with the passage of increasingly severe mandatory sentencing for heroin possession, resurrected the image of a vast underground system of pipelines through which enemies of America pumped their moral pollutants. Drug abuse was an adaptable fetish that could be appropriated to ward off a whole range of disturbing and complex social realities.

The reassessment of the 1960s

Yet the power of this fetish to disarm and enchant disappeared. A drug policy that for more than 30 years – from 1930 up into the mid-1960s –

had emphasized punishment and international and domestic quarantine eroded and finally collapsed. Violent, fracturing realignments of the cultural and institutional substratum marked the decade of the 1960s and caused at least a temporary shift in the dominant paradigm of drug control.

The reconceptualizing of "the drug problem" was brought about by the failure of a rigid criminal justice model to assimilate and adjust to rapid changes in the social environment. The pattern of marijuana arrests and dispositions from 1960 to 1967 indicates the nature of the convulsive changes that overwhelmed a torpid ideology of containment. In California during this period, annual adult arrests for marijuana offenses increased 525%, from 4,245 to 26,527; in Chicago, the increase was 3,278%, from 63 arrests to 2,128. Beginning in 1963, dispositions showed a gradual downward spiral in the frequency of convictions; while these trends are of course a function of the entire judicial process, including informal procedures adopted by the police and prosecuting attorneys, what is revealed here is the breaking down of a control apparatus (Grupp & Lucas, 1970, p. 255). Subsequent evidence would confirm what these figures suggest: Marijuana use became so massive, and so overran the traditional perimeters of class and race, that punitive sanctions were no longer credible. To use the disease idiom so favored by antidrug crusaders, the cancer had metastasized, and radical surgery, which before had been recommended to treat the offender, could not feasibly be performed on a large fraction of society.

The inability of punitive codes to contain the torrent of marijuana use was infectious in its destabilizing impact. As young people violated the law and demystified the threat of deterrence, they began to reassess the purported moral toxicity of other drugs. As the civil rights movement, the emergence of a national youth culture, and the war in Vietnam all accelerated a crisis of legitimacy whose fault lines cracked structures of authority, fissures exposed a framework for drug policy that was already disintegrating. It made sense for the architects of the New Frontier and Great Society, men committed to innovation and reform, to reconceptualize the meaning of drug abuse as a social problem and redesign the government's interventionist role.

Consistent with the approach assumed to juvenile crime and poverty during much of the decade of the 1960s, drug abuse was regarded as a symptom of dysfunctional social relations. To interrupt the cycle of deviance and alienation, the ingenuity of the "best and the brightest" would be brought to bear; an ebullient confidence, bordering on hubris, developed in the capacity of behavioral sciences to effect both individual and collective reform. Community mental health centers were to serve as catalysts, coordinating the delivery of treatment services, "interfacing" with schools and local institutions, emphasizing preventive psychiatry and continuity of intervention. In the refulgence of a rehabilitative ideal that had been in vogue half a century before, a similarly belligerent optimism took hold. The high-echelon personnel who shifted back and forth between Pentagon and Department of Health, Education, and Welfare (HEW) shared a faith in the techniques of "human engineering," whether applied to "nation building" in Vietnam or the revitalizing of neighborhood life in American ghettos.

An idiom of scientific benevolence flourished; in the field of drug abuse, social pathologists, devoted to exploring the complex etiology of deviant behavior, rapidly displaced moral overseers. "Dope fiends" became "clients" to be offered a range of treatment modalities. The rejected policies of control through ostracism and criminal sanction were blamed for mystifying a problem that was amenable to dispassionate inquiry. Retrospective critiques of the now discredited, medieval Anslinger era began to appear, with titles like *History of a Nightmare* and *Torture by Law*. Drug abusers, according to such tracts, were physically sick and psychologically alienated, victimized by social prejudice and driven to a life of crime (Wakefield, 1963, chaps. 1 & 2).

It soon became clear that getting at the "root causes" of socially destructive behavior was an elusive goal. Organized altruism, even when administered by a coalition of experts, proved incapable of arresting a dramatic increase in the actual frequency of drug abuse and in the rise of public dread. During the decade of the 1960s, the indices of deviance continued to record changes that can justify, at least metaphorically, the description of an epidemic: The population of heroin users in Boston rose 10-fold; narcotic-related deaths, which stabilized at around 100 a year in New York City during the 1950s, reached 1,200 per year by the end of the 1960s; robbery, which public consciousness came to link to drug abuse, was 51.2 per 100,000 population in 1959 and 131.0 nine years later (Wilson, 1975, p. 7). Such staggering statistics were bad enough; what made them appear even more sinister was the coherence of the malignity that they were seen to reflect. Against a backdrop of domestic tumult, many Middle Americans identified drugs as a talisman for aggressive defiance of authority. The Woodstock Nation, the Black Panthers, campus militants, rebellious soldiers in Vietnam: Drugs seemed the common denominator, the sacrament that played an integral part in diverse rituals of defilement.

The new enforcement and ongoing reorganization of the federal control effort

By the time President Nixon came into office, the reform synthesis, with its faith in government as the agent of social harmony, had already begun to deteriorate. The assumption of a commonweal in which interests were symmetrical and conflicts, always subjective, were open to negotiated settlement was challenged by a grim vision in which one group's advantage could only be purchased at the expense of another's. From this "zero-sum game," rebels and misfits were effectively disbarred; the moral credit that liberalism had extended to certain outcast groups would no longer be honored.

Fighting the "war at home" did not translate into a simple shift from a model of drug control emphasizing rehabilitation to one that was avowedly punitive; policies are not reversed by throwing a switch, and administrators, furthermore, rarely made dichotomous choices. Social policies are composites; the basic ingredients of the solutions may remain fairly constant, even as the way they are combined is altered. Under Nixon, the admixture showed a significantly increased concentration of restrictive and retributive elements.

Supply interdiction became a priority; officials identified foreign sources as the origin of the contagion that was attacking America, and they once again invoked the "outside agitator" theory of deviance. Pressure was exerted on the governments of opium-producing countries to curb cultivation, and "plugging the pipeline," especially in Turkey, did have an impact. The flow of drugs into the processing centers of Marseilles was interrupted and the availability and purity of heroin in the United States consequently reduced; in four years, from 1969 to 1973, heroin's street price doubled, while its strength was cut to 2% or 3% (Wilson, 1975, p. 149).

Along with an international campaign to destroy the base camp for the invasion force of drugs, there was a simultaneous effort to increase pressure domestically. Treatment services, especially methadone, were expanded, and the early 1970s saw enormous leaps in funding levels from $87 million in 1971 to $196 million a year later (Drug Abuse Council, 1980, p. 105). However, the auspices and tone of this care changed. The National Institute of Mental Health (NIMH), which under Kennedy and Johnson had coordinated the deployment of treatment dollars, came to be viewed by the Nixon White House as excessively narrow in its psychiatric frame of reference. Through executive order, Nixon, in 1971, created the Special Action Office for Drug Abuse Prevention (SAO-

DAP); this group terminated NIMH's management responsibility for federal treatment programs, eventually transferring such authority to HEW and its National Institute on Drug Abuse (NIDA).

The White House, during the Nixon years, sought to maintain centralized control over all aspects of drug policy and envisaged treatment as an adjunct to a dominant law-enforcement strategy. According to the conceptual scheme that came to prevail, it was a dangerous mistake to regard drug abusers – including heroin addicts – as victims either of a physical disease or pathogenic social conditions. People who took drugs did so as volunteers; choice was the critical factor distinguishing the counterfeit from the genuinely sick (i.e., cancer patient). And whereas the spread of a disease cannot be deterred by threats, the motives of a drug abuser could be structured through incentives and disincentives. Deviants and criminals proceeded on the basis of enlightened self-interest; the thieves and addicts who displayed calculating wit in the pursuit of their vices were alert to risk factors. It was this inherent, intuitive capacity of offenders to apply cost/benefit analysis that the pure medical model of drug abuse had ignored; even those who were apparently out of control, driven by some implacable craving, were Benthamites at heart, and their behavior could be influenced by a judicious application of the carrot and stick.

This "moral realism" was also the undergirding for the administration's war on drugs. Command of this war did at times break down; bureaucratic rivalries were ferocious during Nixon's constant reorganizing of federal enforcement agencies, which began in 1968 with the abolition of the Bureau of Narcotics and its replacement by the Bureau of Narcotics and Dangerous Drugs (BNDD) and culminated in the establishment of the Drug Enforcement Agency (DEA) in 1973. Between 1969 and 1974, the budget for fighting drugs rose nearly 10 times, from $81.4 million to $784.7, feeding competitiveness among the agencies that were continually proliferating and continually being amalgamated (Havemann, 1973, p. 653). According to a commission that Nixon appointed to investigate drug abuse, "The rapid increase in federal spending made 'drug abuse' a 'hot' area, where money was available with little exercise of control. Persons involved in other big government-spending programs where funds were drying up (for example, the poverty programs) switched into the drug field and became instant 'experts,' " (quoted in Havemann, 1973, p. 653). Their report warned further that the vast and sudden expansion of the federal drug bureaucracy brought with it a risk that "short-term programs would become never-ending projects. . . . To justify on-going programs," the commission observed, the drug bureaucracy must simultaneously demonstrate that the problem is being effectively attacked and that it is not diminishing. Increased seizure and arrest statistics in the area of law enforcement demonstrate a more effective law-enforcement response and also justify requests for more resources, because those same statistics suggest a growing problem. [Quoted in Havemann, 1973, p. 654]

But while Nixon's commitment to "destroy the menace of drug abuse, which is America's public enemy number 1" (quoted in Bonafede, 1971, p. 1417) unquestionably gave rise to bureaucratic profiteering, expedient and misleading use of statistics, and, at times, casual attitudes toward Fourth Amendment restraints, the movement did have an impact. The drop in heroin use that all U.S. cities began to report in 1974 is by no means exclusively the result of addicts being pressured into available treatment programs through effective law enforcement and supply interdiction. Other variables intervened: black nationalist mobilizing against drugs, an enervation of social rebelliousness, shifting fads in the national youth culture. But a substantial degree of credit can be attributed to federal policy. Even with all the profligacy that accompanies zealous endeavors, it can nonetheless be argued that the crusade was crudely efficient. The first Strategy Council, set up under the Drug Abuse Office and Treatment Act of 1972 to develop a comprehensive federal approach, articulated the premises that gave direction to the drug war. The council argued that government is powerless to modify the underlying social conditions that encourage people to use drugs; instead, "availability is the one factor over which society can exert the most direct control. . . . when all other factors are held constant, the abuse of a drug is directly related to its availability" (quoted in Havemann, 1973, p. 654).

The Nixon administration was able to devote vastly increased resources to stop drug abuse because it could rely on the public to support such initiatives. Of course, President Nixon, who felt a visceral animus toward everything that drug abuse symbolized, took the lead with a vengeance. But while the crusade became highly politicized, providing rich opportunities to expand and inveigh against a clique of executive powers – moral quislings ("soft-headed" judges, etc.) – the popular mandate that Nixon invoked was not manufactured. There was spontaneously generated ·widespread and deep-seated societal reaction to illicit drugs; a national survey conducted in 1969 revealed that 42% of all parents would report their children to the police if drug abuse was discovered (Drug Abuse Council, 1980, p. 129); in 1971, a Gallup poll indicated that the drug problem ranked a close third among national concerns, after Vietnam and the economy, and that the percentage of Americans who listed drugs as their leading concern had doubled since the year before. Government policy channeled this panic

(Bonafede, 1971, p. 418). Drug abuse was potent as a national issue because it crystallized an authentic dread of disorder and cultural discontinuity. When President Nixon told his "New Majority" that the struggle against drugs "was a struggle to preserve America's body and soul," he was describing what his audience already felt to be a moral conflict.

In the fall of 1973, the president announced that "we have turned the corner on drug addiction in the United States" (quoted in Drug Abuse Council, 1980, p. 42). As the war in Vietnam was being wound down, so too was the war against drugs; in neither case did disengagement signify victory. Heroin use had indeed been decreased, in some measure because of President Nixon's law-enforcement strategy. There is, however, evidence suggesting that curbing the supply of opiates led to a pattern of substitution of other illicit drugs (Drug Abuse Council, 1980, p. 92); the dispersal of abuse became confused with actual control. But the rapid decline of public hysteria about the drug problem did not occur because of some political sleight of hand; again, it is important to remind ourselves that policy makers – artisans rather than sorcerers – cannot at will conjure up and exorcise demons of collective dread. The rapid waning of obsessive concern about drugs reflected America's emotional exhaustion. There was a wish for respite; after years of killing abroad and turmoil at home, Americans wanted to be brought together.

By 1976, President Ford could joke about marijuana; tight-lipped moralizing had become more relaxed. The new political culture, informal and avowedly "populist," emphasized an easygoing tolerance for alternative life styles. Drug taking was no longer considered a symbolic act of defiance that required punitive controls. Regulation, particularly of "soft" drugs, was more and more pursued through de facto acceptance; marijuana use grew routinized and thereby denatured of its virulence. A "get tough" approach to "hard drugs" also lost much of its political currency. In 1976, the Bar Association of New York City issued an evaluation of Governor Rockefeller's 1973 drug law; this law had contained severe mandatory minimum sentencing and sharply reduced the possibility for plea bargaining. The report found the law ineffective, unenforceable in practical terms, and misconstrued conceptually:

Whether or not drug abuse is for the most part a medical concern as some contend, it is incontrovertibly rooted in broader social maladies. Narcotics use in particular is intimately associated with, and a part of, a wider complex of problems that include family break-up, unemployment, poor income and education, feeble institutional structures, and loss of hope. . . . It is implausible that social problems as basic as these can be effectively solved by the criminal law. [Quoted in Drug Abuse Council, 1980, p. 141]

Once again, attention reverted back to "root causes." Under President Carter, federal strike forces continued to attack the organizational infrastructure of the heroin trade by going after major domestic traffickers, and DEA and State Department efforts kept apace to stem foreign supplies; however, the messianic zealotry of an earlier period had faded.

Changes in the content and style of drug education provide an index of the shift between the alarmist crusade against "public enemy number 1" and the more dispassionate tone of recent policy. During the 1960s, when drug education came into vogue and was encouraged by state and federal authorities, the curricula specialized in such Grand Guignol approaches as grisly pictures of dead junkies, dire warnings of genetic damage caused by LSD, and statements that marijuana smoking leads inexorably to heroin addiction. Police would come to schools and were often accompanied by ex-abusers whose lurid tales fascinated impressionable youngsters. This approach, as Wald and Abrams (1972) reported, only produced "disrespect, skepticism, and resistance to all advice on drugs" (p. 125), and it offered only one choice – abstinence.

During this period, there was an enormous outpouring of drug education kits and curricula; by 1972, at least $100 million a year was spent on such materials (Pizza & Resnik, 1980, p. 21). When the accumulation was at last evaluated by the National Coordinating Council on Drug Education, only 13 of the 800 items studied were deemed free of bias or inaccuracy, and by 1974 the federal government ceased funding such materials, concluding that their distortions and propagandistic approach were self-defeating. A new set of guidelines was later issued stipulating that messages no longer include "the fear element."

In 1976, Dr. Helen Nowlis, director of the Alcohol and Drug Abuse Education Program in the Office of Education, and her colleagues put forth a different conceptual model based on a pyschosocial perspective focusing on a broad range of ecological influences. Instead of imparting information on the deleterious effects of particular drugs through the exaggerated and sensationalistic approach of the drug education programs of the 1960s, the new approach attempted to understand the meaning of drug abuse as experienced by youth themselves (Nowlis, 1976, p. 11). Young people seek to satisfy their developmental needs in either healthy or destructive ways; drug abuse education, according to Nowlis's construct, must emphasize positive options for self-fulfillment. The issue thus became less how to deter youth from deviance than how to engage them in "achieving their full human potential." The promotion of critical inquiry on the part of youth cannot be achieved through applying a single formula; Nowlis stressed that each community must operate in symmetry with its own specific environment, drawing upon local resources to implement a strategy tailored to the dynamics of the indigenous youth population. School-based personnel, trained to function as teams of "change agents," were to advocate and negotiate for youth within diverse contexts: family, neighborhood institutions, legal systems, and so forth. The partnership between this special cadre of teachers and administrators, on the one hand, and youth in search of creative independence, on the other, was designed to generate reciprocal trust: Members of the school team learn to reach out effectively to students; students, in turn, develop new respect for adults and for the structure of authority they represent. As young and old listen to each other, share feelings, and plan democratically, a mutual sense of competence and self-worth is fostered. Dr. Nowlis imagined that the pleasure of human cooperation would displace drug abuse:

People take drugs because they want to, and they will stop using drugs or use less, if they find something better that will serve the same function. . . . The key to the effectiveness of alternatives to drug use is that they provide a more satisfying . . . way of achieving and responding to the particular experiences sought with drugs. [Nowlis, 1976, p. 19]

Dr. Nowlis's strategy has gained a wide following; drug education now proceeds on the premise that enhancing the self-identity of youth is ultimately a far more effective approach to control than judgmental proscription. If youth are left free to choose, it is assumed some drug use – particularly of marijuana – may be inevitable. The psychosocial model abandons abstinence as the goal and instead encourages moderate behavior. Responsible consumption of drugs thus becomes linked to responsible drinking, responsible sexuality, responsible driving, and so forth. By demystifying drug use, the aim is to undermine its negative prestige; once drugs are made matter-of-fact, no longer surrounded with the aura of the forbidden and exotic, then they grow more accessible to cultural regulation.

By 1981 the essential tenets espoused by Dr. Nowlis characterized much of government drug policy. There is no rhetoric about doing battle against "public enemy number 1"; there is no sense of national panic about drugs, and the federal response is basically to let sleeping dogs lie. In part, this attitude reflects a recognition that previous crusades may have intensified domestic turmoil; there is a fear of repeating past mistakes.

Note

This work was supported in part by a Research Scientist Development Award (DA 00037) from The National Institute on Drug Abuse.

References

Bonafede, D. White House report: Nixon's offensive on drugs treads on array of special interests. *National Journal,* 1971, *3*(27), 1417–1423.

Brotman, R., & Freedman, A. *A community mental health approach to drug addiction* (DHEW, Social and Rehabilitation Service, Office of Juvenile Delinquency and Youth Development). Washington, D.C.: U.S. Government Printing Office, 1968.

Drug Abuse Council, *The facts about drug abuse.* New York: Macmillan, 1980.

Glasser, I., Marcus, S., & Rothman, D. *Doing good.* New York: Pantheon, 1976.

Grant, E. A. The liquor traffic before the Eighteenth Amendment. *Annals of the American Academy of Political and Social Sciences,* 1932, *163* 1–9.

Grupp, S. E., & Lucas, W. C. The "marijuana muddle" as reflected in California arrest statistics and dispositions. *Law and Society Review,* 1970, *5*(2), 251–269.

Havemann, J. White House report: Reorganization establishes unusual management group. *National Journal,* 1973, *5*(18), 653–659.

Musto, D. F. *The American disease: Origins of narcotic control.* New Haven: Yale University Press, 1973.

Nowlis, H. Strategies for prevention. *Contemporary Drug Problems,* 1976, *5*(1), 11–20.

Pizza, J., & Resnik, H. S. *The school team approach: Preventing alcohol and drug abuse by creating positive environments for learning and growth.* Washington, D.C.: U.S. Department of Education, Alcohol and Drug Abuse Education Program, 1980.

Wakefield, D. *The addict.* New York: Fawcett, 1963.

Wald, P. M., & Abrams, A. Drug education. In *Dealing with drug abuse: A report to the Ford Foundation.* New York: Praeger, 1972.

Wilson, J. A. *Thinking about crime.* New York: Basic Books, 1975.

Part VI

The future

22   Beyond policies without people: an ecological perspective on child and family policy

Urie Bronfenbrenner and Heather B. Weiss

As this volume testifies, child and family policy, like the family itself, is "here to stay" (Bane, 1976), both as a social institution and as an object of scientific inquiry. Under these circumstances it seems appropriate, indeed obligatory, for social scientists to examine this emergent phenomenon and its consequences for those it is intended to serve – families and children.

This chapter presents such an analysis from a particular scientific perspective, one that, like child and family policy, has come into prominence only over the past decade: an ecological approach to the study of human development. The orientation was chosen for two reasons. First, it constitutes the perspective from which the authors have been working as scholars and researchers. The second, more defensible ground is that the framework is appropriate to the question being addressed. The ecology of human development has been defined as the "scientific study of the progressive, mutual accommodation between the developing person and the changing properties of the immediate and broader contexts in which the person lives" (Bronfenbrenner, 1979b). Public policy now constitutes one of these broader contexts.

What is the effect of policy on children and families? This issue was defined early on as a principal task of research on child and family policy (Bronfenbrenner, 1974a, 1975). Since that time, events have overtaken recommendations. As documented in this volume, policy research is now a thriving enterprise encompassing such diverse and essential topics as legislation at national, state, and local levels; the evolution and nature of programs serving families and children; educational policies and practices; legal and judicial procedures; policies governing mass media; the role of advocacy in the policy process; the development of strategies for dealing with drugs, child abuse, and other social problems; the construction of childhood social indicators; and analyses of the policy process itself. Least salient in this newly evolving field is a concern that emerges as central in an ecological perspective on human development – namely, how do policies affect the experience of those whom they are intended to serve? To put the issue more succinctly: What is the nature of the interface between policies and people?

This interface can be viewed as having three facets. First there is the question of how policy, both in principle and practice, defines the status of the families and children to whom it is addressed. Second, how does policy influence families and other social institutions carrying responsibility for child care? Finally, there is the ultimate criterion of how policy affects the well-being and development of children.

After describing the effects of current policies on children and families, the chapter proceeds to the question of what these effects should be if policies are to fulfill their proper function. Along with scientists, practitioners, and others concerned with the well-being of our nation, we must take a stand on ways to improve the condition of American families, and through them the whole fabric of American society. Five "preposterous" yet hard-headed proposals conclude the chapter. They respond to the need for imaginative and flexible family-oriented arrangements in all aspects of public life.

How policy defines families and children: the deficit model

There have been few, if any, systematic studies of how policies, explicitly or implicitly, define the status of the families and children they are intended to serve. In the absence of hard data, the following archival evidence, spanning a period of 100 years, is offered. Recently, a major social agency in a large American city celebrated its first centennial. For that occasion, the planners of the celebration did something original and rather daring: They reprinted the brochure that the agency had published in its first year of operation 100 years ago. In its debut, the agency had left no mystery either about its own role or that of its clientele. Both were proudly emblazoned in two introductions on the front cover:

The Friend of the Sick
and Poor

———————————

The Worry of the Tramp
and Beggar

Within its covers, the brochure expanded on these two themes. Here are some representative excerpts:

We investigate the cases of all who are sent to us from out of the city, give them food to relieve their immediate wants, ask the railroads for tickets, and send them back to the place from which they came. . . . TRAMPS, BEGGARS, AND LAZY PEOPLE hate the [agency] and condemn it for heartless treatment. It is one with the police force in making things unpleasant for them.

This is how we approached such problems 100 years ago. These were "encounters of the first kind." On the same occasion, the agency also distributed copies of its most recent brochure. Here are some excerpts:

Services are available to all: the married and unmarried, couples, singles, youths living away from home, single-parents, the separated, the divorced, and widowed, all income levels and all races.

The rest of the booklet contains a series of paragraphs under such headings as Individual Counseling, Marriage and Relationship Counseling, Family Counseling, Parent–Child Counseling, Separation and Divorce Counseling, and so forth. These are "encounters of the second kind." They are clearly an improvement over their predecessors – less condescending, more sophisticated, more humane. But the basic operating principle remains the same: Those who have problems are to be helped by those who have the needed resources; Lady Bountiful has merely yielded place to the trained professional.

In more general terms, our policies and practice, past and present, are based on what can be called a "deficit model" (Bronfenbrenner, 1979a). The model pervades all types of social services, but its distinctive properties are revealed in highest relief in our welfare system. To qualify for help, potential recipients must first prove that they and their families are inadequate – they must do so in writing, a dozen times over, with corroborating documentation, so that there can be little doubt that they, and their children, are in fact the inadequate persons they claim to be. Moreover, our mode of service is categorical: To obtain needed help, potential recipients must first be classified into the types of problems they represent. The only way in which they become whole human beings again is to have enough things wrong. Then they can be defined, and dealt with, as "problem children," or better still for bureaucratic purposes, as "multi-problem families."

The influence of policies on families

An exploratory study

What is the effect of the deficit model on its intended beneficiaries? Once again policy research has not ventured so far in pursuing the trail of policy consequences. How people receive, perceive, and interact with the services designed to assist them is an open, empirical question, and one about which there is little contemporary or historical information (Weiss, 1979). The research that does exist has frequently been plagued by problems of inadequate conceptualization and methodology (McKinlay, 1972; Weiss, 1979). McKinlay emphasizes the "need for a number of hypothesis-generating . . . exploratory studies" (p. 139) to prepare the ground for subsequent investigations on a broader scale. Work being done presently by the authors of this chapter is based on interviews conducted in the course of an investigation of the environmental stresses and supports experienced by 276 families, each with a preschool child, living in a medium-sized city in upstate New York. Preliminary qualitative analyses suggest that the deficit model, especially as manifested in the welfare system, takes a substantial toll on the individual's self-esteem and the family's capacity to function. One woman echoed the sentiments of a dozen others when she said, in response to a question about use of welfare, "No, no, no, no. I was on welfare years ago and I'd *never* go on it again. I would fight for some way to get my own living for my kids without being on welfare and [being] classified as a welfare case. I wouldn't want them running me anyways – that's what they did years ago."[1]

The extensive data collected from families in this study highlight the "catch-22" situation of many families living at or near the poverty line. Those who received public assistance feel the full weight of the deficit model, while those who do not receive aid face a desperate struggle for survival. Also reflected in the interviews is the American's commitment to individualism and self-sufficiency. Those who resist turning outside the family for assistance of any kind speak proudly of that fact.

Many families who do receive financial aid, child care, or counseling help from outside sources have mixed feelings. As one married mother put it, "I guess in the beginning [getting help from my sister-in-law] caused a little problem because I felt we should be independent and shouldn't have to count on anybody for help, but that's just totally unrealistic." In sum, this study suggests that the effects of a deficit model strategy in American society need to be understood in the context of the values of the larger culture.

Some paradoxical conclusions for today's society

Since these interpretations are based on subjective opinions expressed by parents, they leave unanswered the critical issues of whether and how policies and programs influence the capacity of the family to care for and foster the development of its children. Despite the absence of hard evidence, the authors propose that existing knowledge justifies two general, somewhat paradoxical conclusions about the adequacy of present policies and practices affecting children and families in American society: (1) If the well-being of American families and children is to be ensured, it is absolutely essential to develop and implement feasible alternatives to services and programs based, explicitly or implicitly, on a deficit model; (2) until such feasible alternatives are actually in place on a broad scale, Americans cannot afford to abandon existing services and programs.

In the early 1980s, there was considerable consensus among political leaders of both parties, and among the general public, that large-scale cuts must be made in government spending and that most of these should occur in the sphere of domestic programs rather than national defense. The readiness to reduce domestic programs was fired by the widely shared belief that resources and services are being wasted on many who are not "truly needy," and that even those who are might be better served by removing the crutch of dependency, stimulating them to fend for themselves. Indeed, it is not difficult to detect in this contemporary rhetoric a continuity, in substance and even in style, with the orientation so prominently displayed on the cover of the agency brochure published 100 years ago. It would appear that "encounters of the first kind" are experiencing something of a rebirth as they enter their second century.

The world in which they are thriving, however, has changed substantially. The changes that are most relevant for public policy are those that have occurred in recent decades. These have been traced, and their implications drawn, in a number of books and articles published in recent years (Bronfenbrenner, 1975; Keniston, 1977; National Academy of Sciences, 1976). Today the facts are all well known to the general public. Whereas a few years ago only experts were aware of, let alone concerned about, the rapid transformations taking place in American society, today just about everyone has read or heard about the "changing American family." We all know about the rapid rise in single-parent homes (today a fifth of the nation's children reside within them), the decline in extended family households (they are almost gone now, save among blacks and other ethnic minorities), and falling birth rate (except among unwed teenage girls). In short, American families have been getting smaller.

As far as the development of the young is concerned, the most consequential change continues to be the rise in maternal employment. The increase has proceeded at an accelerating pace since World War II. By 1978, the majority of American mothers were in the labor force. In recent years, the increase has been greatest among mothers of children under age three, but regardless of the age of their children, the majority of employed mothers are under pressure to work full-time. Given current economic strains and aspirations, few have any other choice.

The effects of policies on children

Environmental principles of development

What are the implications of mass societal changes for the development of children? To address this issue, it is necessary to know what the environmental and social conditions are that are most crucial for the development of human beings from early childhood on. One of the authors (Bronfenbrenner, 1979b) has sought to bring together available knowledge on this topic and found it sobering to discover that the principal conclusions from these data could be summarized in two tentative propositions. Shorn of their technical terminology, the two propositions do not sound very earthshaking. But when applied to our present world, they may shake us up nevertheless.

Proposition 1. In order to develop normally, a child needs the enduring, irrational involvement of one or more adults in care and joint activity with that child.

In short, somebody has to be crazy about that kid. But that is not all the proposition stipulates. Someone also has to *be there,* and to be *doing something* – not alone, but together *with* the child. This brings us to the next proposition, which defines a second environmental condition equally essential if development is to occur:

Proposition 2. The involvement of one or more adults in joint activity with the child requires public policies and practices that provide opportunity, status, resources, encouragement, stability, example, and above all, *time* for parenthood, primarily by parents, but also by other adults in the child's environment, both within and outside the home.

Assuming these propositions to have some validity, they can be used as a frame of reference for evaluating the implications for human development of the changes that have been taking place in the American family and its position in society over recent decades.

The phenomenon of working mothers

Contrary to the rhetoric one hears, especially on college campuses, there is no clear evidence as yet of any marked compensatory trend for husbands to take a greater share in family responsibilities: to come home earlier, cook the meals, scrub the floor, or do 20 things at once, as so many women learn to do as necessary skills for the survival of their families. Husbands do not appear to be taking over in significant degree (Bronfenbrenner & Crouter, 1982; Weiss, 1976). As many more mothers go to work, and fathers do not go back into the home, there are fewer adults left in the household to look after the child. In ever more families, there is only one parent, who is usually the breadwinner, working full-time and living in an independent household. What is the significance of this set of conditions for the requirement stipulated in proposition 2 of "opportunity, status, resources, encouragement, stability, example, and above all *time* for parenthood"? What does this complex of circumstances imply in turn for proposition 1? To be sure, when parents are working full-time, their irrational involvement with the child may not diminish, it may even increase, but what happens to joint activity?

Some light is shed on this question by the results of a survey of 200 working mothers in both single- and two-parent families (Kamerman, 1980). The principal findings are reflected in the title of the volume: *Parenting in an Unresponsive Society*. Two themes emerging from the analysis have special significance for these concerns. The first is the severe stress reported both by single parents and two-worker families around the issue of obtaining satisfactory child care. In contemporary American society, providing for such care often requires a delicately or-chestrated schedule combining the use of day-care centers, babysitters, and shifting parental responsibilities. The strains generated by the task of establishing and maintaining these complex arrangements are docu-mented both in statistical data and case study vignettes. The second theme emerging from the survey relates to the heightened stress experi-enced by the mother in single-parent households, where all the burdens of work, child rearing, and coordinating child-care arrangements fall on her shoulders.

Regrettably, a few investigators have not yet taken the next step of examining the impact of familial stress on the behavior and development of children. In the area of parental work, a recent research review (Bron-fenbrenner & Crouter, 1982) revealed some evidence that conflict be-tween work and family roles reduces both quantity and quality of parent–child interaction and is associated with lower achievement in school, par-ticularly among sons. The studies in this area are weakened, however, by the failure to establish the successive causal links among the objective conditions at work and at home, the degree and nature of stress gener-ated by these conditions, their effect on family functioning, and the resultant impact on the behavior and development of the child. This causal chain is now being delineated in relation to single-parent families, principally through the work of Hetherington and her colleagues (Hetherington, Cox, & Cox, 1978, 1979). These investigators traced the progressive deterioration in mother–child interaction following divorce and its disruptive carryover effects on the social behavior and academic performance of children in school.

Secular trends in children's data

At a more global and speculative level, it is instructive to examine secular trends in data on children, trends paralleling those that have taken place for families. The most salient statistics are the time series data reflecting the impaired well-being and development of children as manifested in declining levels of academic performance and rising rates of child homicide, suicide, teenage pregnancy, drug use, and juvenile delinquency (Bronfenbrenner, 1975; National Academy of Sciences, 1976). Recent figures indicate that these trends are still continuing.

Many of these trends find their strongest expression in the nation's schools. The situation was summarized by the title of a report of the U.S. Senate Committee on the Judiciary (1975), now already behind the times: *The Nation's Schools: A Report Card: "A" in School Violence and Vandalism.* The report revealed that the pattern was not restricted to larger cities, slum areas, or particular ethnic groups. As the title implies, school violence is a national phenomenon. Every school now has its security budget and often a security force. As Wynne (1980) has documented, the American school has become a major breeding ground of alienation, vandalism, and violence.

These trends constitute danger signs for American society. Three additional features are especially disquieting. First, all of the demographic changes are occurring more rapidly among younger families with small children, and are increasing with the degree of economic deprivation and urbanization, reaching their maximum in low-income families living in the central core of our large cities (Bronfenbrenner, 1975; National Academy of Sciences, 1976). Second, the rate of change has not been constant, but has accelerated markedly since the mid-1960s. It was precisely during this same period that the scope and budgets of federally sponsored programs directed at low-income families were expanded on a massive scale. Yet it is clear that this expansion was not adequate to arrest, let alone reverse, the demographic trends reflecting disarray in the lives of families and children. The third and perhaps most telling fact revealed in the secular data is that the general trend is not limited to the urban poor; it applies to all strata of society. Indeed, in terms of the proportion of working mothers, number of adults in the home, single-parent families, teenage pregnancy, falling achievement scores, or exposure to vandalism and violence in the schools, the experiences of middle-class families today increasingly resemble those of low-income families of the 1960s. It is this expanding pattern of secular change that makes the search for new strategies an imperative for those who are concerned with the well-being and development of children in the 1980s. As a society, Americans need to find their way to "encounters of the third kind."

Alternative family-oriented policy models

Flexible work policies and family benefits

The place to start the search is within American society. Alternatives to the deficit model are beginning to emerge in two spheres. The first is in the world of work. As documented in a recent review by Kamerman and Kingston (1982), an increasing number of public and private employers are offering their employees fringe benefits designed to be responsive to family needs. Among them are such provisions as maternity leaves, family health plans, on-site day care, part-time jobs, job sharing, sick leave for parents when children are ill, and flexitime. The last involves a schedule whereby employees work full-time, but have some freedom in determining hours of arrival and departure. Nollen and Martin (1978) estimate that 2.5 to 3.5 million workers (6% of the total labor force) are in some variant of flexitime.

Although family benefits associated with employment offer promise as an alternative to deficit models, they are still at an early stage of development in the United States. In comparison with supports provided in other industrialized countries, they exist only on a limited scale. This contrast is reflected in the following statement of preliminary findings from an ongoing project directed by Dr. Sheila Kamerman and Dr. Alfred J. Kahn:

Mothers of very young children are working outside the home in growing numbers in all industrialized countries. Two-parent two-wage-earner families (and single-parent, sole-wage-earner families) are increasingly the norm. . . . Some countries are expanding child care services as well as cash benefits to protect child and family life. However, the United States lags far behind such European countries as France, Sweden, and the Federal Republic of Germany in the West, and the German Democratic Republic and Hungary in the East in providing either. [Kamerman & Kahn, 1978][2]

A second problem derives from the fact that, in the United States, the provision of family benefits associated with work has been concentrated primarily in large corporations, whose employees are already in a more favored economic position. By contrast, those most in need of such benefits, such as heads of single-parent households or of large families, are likely to have low-paying jobs or no jobs at all. This circumstance therefore serves to widen the already existing gap between the rich and the poor.

Finally, there is some evidence that in the present social context in the United States, work-associated family benefits may not, by themselves, have much impact on the capacity of families to function effectively in their child-rearing role. For example, Bohen and Viveros-Long (1981) obtained measures of family strain and of participation in home activities from employees working in two federal agencies, one of which operated with flexible hours. Ironically, significant differences favoring flexitime were found for only one group of families – those without children. Two explanations are proposed for the absence of effects on families with children: first, that the arrangement did not go far enough to meet the complex scheduling problems experienced by today's parents; second, that child-rearing values were not sufficiently salient to ensure that the flexible time would be used for parental activities. Unfortunately, no data were available to permit further investigation of these possibilities.

Informal supports for families

More promising results have been emerging in another sphere. An increasing number of studies have pointed to the constructive role played by informal support systems, particularly relatives and similarly situated others, in sustaining family life. In her study of working mothers in single- and two-parent families, Kamerman concludes: "Although they frequently mention neighbors or friends as providing important help, it is clear from the interviews that the single most important source of help for working mothers are relatives and family. Whether for child care purposes, emergencies, advice, or just encouragement and sympathy, most of these women view 'family' as an essential support system" (Kamerman, 1980, p. 108). A decade ago, Hill and his colleagues (Hill et al., 1970) studied approximately 300 families distributed across three generations: grandparents, parents, and children. The results provide impressive evidence of the degree to which family members help one another. When Hill added exchanges with extended family members such as siblings and cousins, kin exchanges accounted for 70% of all reported instances of help. When the families were asked where they preferred to turn for assistance in a crisis, each generation's first choice was kin. The initial results of our ongoing study of 170 Syracuse, New York families similarly indicate the importance of the extended family. In response to a question about where they would turn in the event of a family emergency, including financial problems, the majority of the respondents mentioned relatives, pointing out that relatives care, are reliable, and help without being asked.

Carol Stack (1974) documented the ways in which a community of poor black families and friends helped one another. She found that kin, as well as nonkin regarded as kin, built a cooperative and interdependent network engaging in a complex and long-term pattern of reciprocity and exchange that allowed them to survive severe economic deprivation. There were costs, as well as benefits, to this survival strategy, however. Individuals were encouraged to forego upward and geographical mobility and marriage in order to keep the system of reciprocal exchanges in operation.

The power of friends and associates is also reflected in the results of a recent early childhood intervention effort (Weiss, 1979). The data come from a series of intensive interviews with a sample of mothers who participated in the Brookline Early Education Project (BEEP), a research and demonstration project providing a variety of diagnostic and educational services to approximately 300 children and their families in Boston and Brookline, Massachusetts. The mothers were asked whom they turned to for child-care information when the study child was born. "Other mothers with young children" were the source most frequently named. This finding points to the importance of "similarly situated" friends as the most relied on agents of help and advice. Qualitative content analysis of the interview data further indicated the powerful ways in which the mothers supported one another, whether in informal conversation or more organized parent group meetings.

Interviews with BEEP mothers also revealed another benefit of participation: a sense of reciprocity, of giving as well as taking. Mothers reported that it felt good to be able to help others and to have others value their experience and suggestions. The way such informal groups are labeled – as self- or mutual-help groups – perhaps conveys part of their essential power; one is doing for oneself at the same time one is doing for others.

The development of parent support and self-help groups of the type that occurred in the BEEP program is reported, often as an unintended effect, in a number of early intervention projects (Bronfenbrenner, 1974b). These projects also produced in children cognitive gains that were still perceptible after entry into school (Darlington et al., 1980). Such an association of course does not establish informal support systems as a causal factor. Direct evidence on this score is sparse but encouraging. For example, in a study of child abuse and neglect, Giovannoni and Billingsley (1970) identified as specific preventive factors a functional kinship network and church attendance. Corroborative findings come from a large-scale correlational analysis of child abuse reports and socioeconomic and demographic information for the 58 counties in New York State. "A substantial proportion of the variance in rates of child abuse/maltreatment among New York State counties . . . was found to be associated with the degree to which mothers do not possess adequate support systems for parenting and are subjected to economic stress" (Garbarino, 1976, p. 185).

A new paradigm

The foregoing studies deal with the impact of already-existing family support systems. From a public policy perspective, a more cogent issue is whether, and how, effective informal support systems can be introduced where they do not now exist in sufficient strength. One study that deals directly with this phenomenon is Mildred Smith's 1968 experimental intervention, which sought to introduce changes in the relation between family and school in American society. The program was designed to improve school performance of low-income minority pupils in the elementary grades. The project involved approximately 1,000 children from low-income families, most of them black, attending public elementary schools. The principal strategy employed for enhancing children's school performance was including the child's "significant others" – the parent and the teacher – as *partners,* not competitors, in the child's learning process. Parents mobilized other parents to become involved in the school. Parents were urged to provide supports for their children while teachers' in-service sessions focused on the influence of environmental factors in children's classroom behavior and performance. Essentially, support systems were established for all participants in the program.

This strategy contrasts sharply with one based on a deficit model that involves a one-way transmission, from the powerful to the powerless. It is regrettable that the innovativeness of Smith's intervention strategy was not matched by equal originality in the selection of outcome measures. Results in quantitative form were limited to significant gains on tests of reading achievement and to overwhelmingly favorable attitudes expressed toward the program in a questionnaire that brought a gratifying response rate of 90%. Despite its limitations, the Smith program represents the closest approximation we have been able to find to a newly emerging paradigm for child and family policy in American society; it is an instance of "encounters of the third kind." The common and complementary elements of these past examples point to a basic principle underlying the new paradigm. The principle can be stated in a general form that reveals its dialetic nature: *The need is to create formal systems of challenge and support that generate and strengthen informal systems of challenge and support, that in turn reduce the need for the formal systems.*

Five "preposterous proposals": a forward look

In his treatise on social policy and social philosophy, Richard Titmuss makes the point that "social policy, in one of its potential roles, can help to actualize the social and moral potentialities of all citizens" (1970, p. 238). Titmuss's point is particularly relevant now. Thought needs to be given to the way policy contributes to the *voluntary* ways people help one another – to social policies that recognize, maintain, and strengthen such efforts. We need to create social forms that encourage and allow us to help one another, to experience giving *and* receiving. In the absence of hard data, neither scientists nor policy makers have any other course but to rely on their imaginations if progress is to be made. The following hypothetical cases are addressed to three crucial contexts affecting the well-being and development of children in contemporary society: the school, the family's social networks, and the parents' world of work. These three domains are the principal sources both of Americans' gravest problems and of their most promising and powerful counteractive strategies. Nevertheless, the strategies have a serious and perhaps fatal shortcoming: Given the present state of American society, they can only be implemented gradually, if at all. For this reason, we refer to them as "preposterous proposals."

Preposterous proposal 1

It is now possible for a young person to graduate from an American high school without ever having had to do a piece of work on which someone else depended. It is also possible for a young person, female as well as male, to graduate from high school, college, or university without ever having held a baby for longer than a few seconds; without ever having had to care for someone who was old, ill, or lonely; without ever having had to comfort or assist another human being who needed help. Yet all of us, sooner or later, will desperately require such comfort and care, and no society can sustain itself unless its members have learned the motivations, sensitivities, and skills that such caring demands.

One way to counteract these gaps is to introduce a *curriculum of caring* in the schools, from the earliest grades onward. The purpose of this curriculum would be not to learn about caring, but to engage in it; that is, all children would be asked to take responsibility for spending time with and caring for others – the elderly, the young, the sick, and the lonely. The curriculum for caring has special significance for the increasing numbers of older children who are in fact caring for their younger brothers and sisters in the absence of adequate and affordable day-care services in our country. Obviously, such caring activities cannot be restricted to the school; they have to be carried out in the community itself. It would be desirable to locate caring institutions, such as day-care centers, adjacent to or even within the school, but it would be even more important for the young caregivers to come to know the environments and the other people in the lives of their charges. For example, older children taking responsibility for younger ones should become acquainted with the latter's parents and with the places where their charges live by escorting them home from school. In this way, children would come to know firsthand the living conditions of the families in their community. This is surely an essential aspect of public education in a free society; yet it is one that Americans have neglected almost completely.

Preposterous proposal II

This proposal extends the curriculum for caring into the adult world. It builds on the development of parent self-help and mutual support groups of the type found in the Smith project, but provides them with greater momentum and scope by drawing on a distinctively American institution for their implementation. That institution is the Cooperative Extension Service, which is supported by federal and state funds in every section of the nation, urban as well as rural. This program represents an already-existing alternative to the deficit model, since it operates on the principle of mobilizing and relying on local initiatives and resources. The role of Extension personnel is to facilitate process and to supply needed technical information. The experience of the Extension Service in working with families and youth groups at a community level makes it well suited to the task of building and strengthening informal family support systems.

A pilot experiment along this line, under the direction of Moncrieff Cochran, is currently being conducted. Known as Family Matters, it involves a total of 150 families with schoolchildren distributed over 12 neighborhoods. In each neighborhood, a team of 2 field workers employs a mixed strategy of home visits and group meetings to involve families in common activities in behalf of themselves and their children. *The aim of the experiment is to enhance parent empowerment through the creation of supportive social networks that not only link family members to each other but also provide access to needed resources and to centers of power within the community* (Cochran & Woolever, 1980).

Ongoing field observations indicate that informal social networks can be developed and that families who participate in them do experience a sense of enhanced support and self-sufficiency. But the creation and maintenance of these informal systems encounters a serious obstacle in contemporary American society. To function effectively, they require the participation of relatives, friends, and neighbors who are available on an enduring and reliable basis. How can such time and dependability be assured in a highly mobile society in which most able-bodied people are working in full-time jobs?

Preposterous proposal III

The crucial role of work in today's families derives from what seems to be a distinctive feature of American life. From a developmental perspective, there are two kinds of activities that appear particularly salient for our species. The first is work, transforming our environment through the use of our heads and hands. The second distinctive characteristic is the way in which we raise our young. To a greater extent than for any other living creatures, the capacity of human offspring to survive and develop depends on care and close association with older members of the species.

At this point in human history, Americans have developed a pattern in which these two centrally human activities are placed in conflict with one another. A person finds it extremely difficult to do a good job in one sphere without making sacrifices in the other. At the present time, less by decision than by default, Americans are allowing their families, and their children, to pay the price.

One solution to this problem requires a radical change in the American way of life so that the prevailing pattern of employment for both men and women would be to *work three-quarters-time.* The remaining quarter would be free for family activities, visiting friends and relatives, participating in the life of one's neighborhood and community, and looking at the sunset – in short, a quarter of one's life for living. The introduction of such a pattern would have the additional fringe benefit of reducing unemployment, since new cadres would be needed to maintain national levels of production. Under what circumstances could such a revolutionary proposal be adopted in American society? This query brings us to the next and even more outlandish proposal.

Preposterous proposal IV

In order for families to meet the needs created by the rapid and profound social changes that have taken place in recent years, it will be necessary to introduce significant changes in public policy and practice in domains outside the family itself. Such innovations will require broad vision and hard-headed decisions by those persons who occupy positions of power and responsibility both in the public and the private sectors. Despite the impressive achievements of the women's movement, the fact remains that the overwhelming majority of persons in such influential positions today are men.

Given the prevailing pattern in the upbringing of children and youth in American society, males are particularly likely, from earliest childhood, to have been isolated from experiences of caring or from close association with those needing care (Gilligan, 1977). As a result, men are less able to understand the needs of such persons, the circumstances in which they live, their human potential, the necessity and nature of the support systems required to realize this potential, and the very practical social and economic gains that would be achieved as a result. In contrast, those in our society who possess such experience and knowledge are predominantly women, primarily because women confront these situations more often than men in the course of their lives. Women, however, typically do not occupy the positions of power that would permit their experience and knowledge to be translated into public policy and practice. *This state of affairs calls for a substantial increase in the number of women in positions of decision making and power both in the public and private sector.*

Preposterous proposal V

The basis for this final and most pressing recommendation is found in a research trajectory reaching back half a century. Beginning in the mid-1930s, a series of investigators (Angell, 1936; Cavan & Ranck, 1938; Komarovsky, 1940; Morgan, 1939) analyzed the impact on the family of the father's loss of a job during the Great Depression. The principal effects documented in these investigations were loss of status by the father, marked increase in family tensions and disagreements, and withdrawal from social life outside the family. Children appeared in these early studies only as participants in the father's drama rather than as persons themselves affected by the experience. Four decades later, however, Elder (1974, 1979; Elder & Rockwell, 1979) exploited archival data from two longitudinal studies in order to focus on the impact of the Great Depression on the subsequent development of children whose families had been subjected to severe economic stress.

Elder took advantage of this natural experiment to divide each of the two samples into two otherwise comparable groups, differentiated on the basis of whether the loss of income as a result of the Depression exceeded or fell short of 35%. The fact that the children in one sample were eight years older than those in the other permitted a comparison of the effects of the Depression on children who were adolescents when their families became economically deprived versus those who were still young children.

The results for the two groups presented a dramatic contrast. Paradoxically, for youngsters who had been teenagers during the Depression years, the family's economic deprivation appeared to have a salutary effect on their subsequent development. They did better in school, were more likely to go to college, had happier marriages, exhibited more successful work careers, and in general achieved greater satisfaction in life, both by their own and by societal standards, than did nondeprived children of the same socioeconomic status. These favorable outcomes were more pronounced for adolescents from middle-class backgrounds, but were evident among their lower-class counterparts as well. Elder hypothesized that the loss of economic security forced the family to mobilize its own human resources, including those of its teenagers. The youths had to take on new responsibilities in order to help get and keep the family on its feet. This experience provided them with effective training in initiative, responsibility, and cooperation. In the words of Shakespeare's banished duke, "Sweet are the uses of adversity."

Adversity was not so sweet for children who were still preschoolers when their families suffered economic loss. Compared to controls from nondeprived families, these youngsters subsequently did less well in school, showed less stable and successful work histories, and exhibited more emotional and social difficulties, some still apparent in middle adulthood.

Facing the future

The pertinence of Elder's research for the current scene is underscored by recent census figures and research findings. The official U.S. Census report on family income for 1980 documented what it described as "the largest decline in family income in the post World War II period," resulting in the addition of 29.3 million persons below the poverty level, for a total of 13% of the U.S. population (U.S. Bureau of the Census, 1981, p. 1). By 1981, this figure had risen to 31.8 million (U.S. Bureau of the Census, 1982, p. 1) As revealed in the tables accompanying the report, the poverty rates for children were even higher, especially for the very young. Specifically, as of March 1981, more than a fifth (22%) of all children in America up to the age of six were living in families below the "poverty line," compared to 13% for the population as a whole and 16% for those under 65. The poverty line is based on the minimum income sufficient to meet the cost of the Department of Agriculture's economy food plan. The index is adjusted to reflect the different consumption requirements of families based on size, composition, and other relevant demographic factors.

The effects of this most recent economic turndown are already being reflected in research findings. Steinberg, Catalano, and Dooley (1981) studied the effects of inflation on 8,000 families in California in a longitudinal design. Correlational analyses of data over a 30-month period revealed that increases in child abuse were preceded by periods of high job loss, this confirming the authors' hypothesis that "undesirable economic change *leads* to increased child maltreatment" (p. 975). An Associated Press report on this research begins with the lead sentence: "The toll of children battered, maimed, and slain by parents and other relatives is climbing, and experts say the economy – especially unemployment – appears to be a key factor." Alas, for once the media did not exaggerate the facts.

Such findings give added significance to the growing number of children being cast into poverty in our own time. They also raise questions about the severe cuts that have been put in force affecting programs and resources made available to low-income families and their children in the United States. There can be no question that the United States must learn to live within its means; to do otherwise is to court national disaster. It is also clear, as we have previously noted, that some existing programs have been wasteful, ineffective, and severely criticized even by the very families they were supposed to help. But there are other programs that have been working and are now showing important long-range effects. Like the well-known project Head Start, these programs are based on what we have called "encounters of the third kind"; instead of labeling families as inadequate and making them dependent, these strategies treat their recipients as competent human beings who can and do take active responsibility for themselves and for their children. Another key element in these aproaches is that they build family and community. Yet these programs, too, are in jeopardy.

But even more destructive is the United States' failure to recognize the importance of jobs for the survival of families, not only economically, but – what is even more important – psychologically. By tolerating growing unemployment now, the United States risks creating new generations of unemployable Americans in the years ahead. The most effective programs for strengthening our families and children are those that create jobs. Hence our final proposal. It calls for *maintaining and increasing existing federal programs to ensure jobs and viable incomes to all families with young children.* Economize we must, but in doing so we must not betray our distinctive values and strengths as a nation.

There are those who say that that is exactly what we are doing, that Americans have ceased to care about one another. Such critics claim to see the rise of a new separatism across the land, a turning away from a concern with the problems of others to a preoccupation with maintaining and maximizing the status and power of particular groups. To be sure, such phenomena are occurring in some segments of American society, but we do not believe that they constitute the broader and deeper streams and strengths of contemporary America. They are merely filling a vacuum during a period of temporary inertia in the historical movement of the United States in pursuit of its ideals. At this moment, the best of America is conscience-stricken and confused. The country is momentarily immobilized by the conflict between the distinctive values derived from its past and the dissonant realities created by the economic and social changes taking place not only in the United States, but around the world. The vacuum created by this temporary inertia leaves the field open to destructive forces that can divide the nation. Once again the Union is threatened, not the political union of the states, but the spiritual union of the basic parts of our pluralistic society – the diverse families, communities, generations, and religious and cultural groups that make the magic of America. The nation was founded, and has thus far been sustained, on the principle of *e pluribus unum*. What has happened to the *unum*? What is the state of the *union*?

These questions would seem to take us far beyond the domain of child and family policy. This very fact points to the heart of the problem. One telling criterion of the worth of a society – a criterion that stands the test of history – is *the concern of one generation for the next.* A nation's child and family policy is the measure of that concern. Under these circumstances, what is the responsibility of the developmental researcher concerned with policy issues at a time of national crisis? The answer to that question leads in two directions. Social scientists are subject to an ethical code that prohibits them from exposing children to situations that are injurious to their welfare. Unfortunately, there is no such restriction on the nation as a whole or on its duly empowered leaders and policy makers. The latter are free to run their economic and social experiments without such niceties as prior parental consent or review by qualified professionals. It remains the responsibility of researchers, however, to monitor these experiments and give an early warning of any unintended effects. What will be the consequences of cutting back funds for prenatal care, child nutrition and health, day care, and recreational and vocational programs for school-age children? In assessing these effects, researchers must use the best scientific methods at their command. There may be difficulties in finding matched control groups, but there should be no problem with sample size. It is the irony and limitation of our science that the greater the harm done to children, the more we stand to learn about the environmental conditions that are essential for the human condition. It therefore becomes our professional obligation to employ the most advanced research designs at our disposal in order to forestall the tragic opportunity of significantly expanding our knowledge about the limits of the human conditions for developing human beings.

The responsibilities of the researcher extend beyond pure investigation, especially in a time of national crisis. Scientists in our field must be willing to draw on their knowledge and imagination in order to contribute to the design of social inventions: policies and strategies that can help to sustain and enhance our most precious human resources – the nation's children.

Notes

1 This and the quotation in the second paragraph below are taken from an interview with a family as a part of research being conducted under the auspices of the Comparative Ecology of Human Development Project, Cornell University, 1979.
2 For a fuller explication, see Kamerman and Kahn (1978, 1981).

References

Angell, R. C. *The family encounters the Depression.* New York: Scribner, 1936.
Associated Press. Child abuse rises, economy blamed. *Ithaca Journal,* July 21, 1982, p. 18.
Bane, M. J. Here to stay: American families in the twentieth century. *Carnegie Quarterly,* 1976, *24*(4), 1–3.
Bohen, H. H., & Viveros-Long, A. *Balancing jobs and family life: Do flexible work schedules help?* Philadelphia: Temple University Press, 1981.

Bronfenbrenner, U. Developmental research and public policy. In J. M. Romanyshyn (Ed.), *Social science and social welfare*. New York: Council on Social Work Education, Inc., 1974. (a)

Bronfenbrenner, U. Is early intervention effective? *Teachers College Record*, 1974, *76*, 279–303. (b)

Bronfenbrenner, U. Reality and research in the ecology of human development. *Proceedings of the American Philosophical Society*, 1975, *119*, 439–469.

Bronfenbrenner, U. Beyond the deficit model in child and family policy. *Teachers College Record*, 1979, *81*(1), 95–104. (a)

Bronfenbrenner, U. *The ecology of human development: Experiments by nature and design*. Cambridge: Harvard University Press, 1979. (b).

Bronfenbrenner, U., & Crouter, A. C. Work and family through time and space. In S. B. Kamerman & C. D. Hayes (Eds.), *Families that work: Children in a changing world*. Washington, D.C.: National Academy Press, 1982.

Cavan, R. S., & Ranck, K. H. *The family and the Depression: A study of 100 Chicago families*. Chicago: University of Chicago Press, 1938.

Cochran, M., & Woolever, F. *A family support strategy: Fusing family and neighborhood components*. Report to the National Institute of Education. Ithaca, N.Y.: Cornell University, April 1980.

Darlington, R., Royce, J. M., Snipper, A. S., Murray, H. W., & Lazar, I. Preschool programs and later school comparisons of children from low-income families. *Science*, 1980, *208*, 202–204.

Elder, G. H., Jr. *Children of the Great Depression*. Chicago: University of Chicago Press, 1974.

Elder, G. H., Jr. Historical change in life patterns and personality. In P. Baltes & O. Brim (Eds.), *Life-span development and behavior* (Vol. II). New York: Academic Press, 1979.

Elder, G. H., Jr., & Rockwell, R. C. The life-course approach and human development: An ecological perspective. *International Journal of Behavioral Development*, 1979, *2*, 1–21.

Garbarino, J. A preliminary study of some ecological correlates of child abuse: The impact of socioeconomic stress on mothers. *Child Development*, 1976, *47*, 178–185.

Gilligan, C. In a different voice: Women's conception of self and of morality. *Harvard Educational Review*, 1977, *47*(4), 196–204.

Giovannoni, J., & Billingsley, A. Child neglect among the poor: A study of parental adequacy in families of three ethnic groups. *Child Welfare*, 1970, *49*, 196–204.

Hetherington, E. M., Cox, M., & Cox, R. The aftermath of divorce. In J. H. Stevens, Jr. & M. Mathews (Eds.), *Mother–child, father–child relations*. Washington, D.C.: National Association for the Education of Young Children, 1978.

Hetherington, E. M., Cox, M., & Cox, R. Play and social interaction in children following divorce. *Journal of Social Issues*, 1979, *35*(4), 26–49.

Hill, R., Foote, N., Aldous, J., Carlson, R., & Macdonald, R. *Family development in three generations*. Cambridge, Mass.: Schenkman, 1970.

Kamerman, S. B. *Parenting in an unresponsive society*. New York: Free Press, 1980.

Kamerman, S. B., & Kahn, A. J. Personal correspondence, 1978.

Kamerman, S. B., & Kahn, A. J. *Family policy: Government and families in fourteen countries*. New York: Columbia University Press, 1978.

Kamerman, S. B., & Kahn, A. J. *Childcare: Family benefits and working parents*. New York: Columbia University Press, 1981.

Kamerman, S. B., & Kingston, P. Employer responses to the family responsibilities of employees. In S. B. Kamerman & C. D. Hayes (Eds.), *Families that work: Children in a changing world*. Washington, D.C.: National Academy Press, 1982.

Keniston, K., and the Carnegie Council on Children. *All our children: The American family under pressure.* New York: Harcourt Brace Jovanovich, 1977.

Komarovsky, M. *The unemployed man and his family.* New York: Dryden Press, 1940.

McKinlay, J. B. Some approaches and problems in the study of the use of services: An overview. *Journal of Health and Social Behavior,* 1972, *13,* 115–152.

Morgan, W. L. *The family meets the Depression.* Minneapolis: University of Minnesota Press, 1939.

National Academy of Sciences. *Toward a national policy for children and families.* Washington, D.C., 1976.

Nollen, S., & Martin, V. *Alternative work schedules.* Part I: *Flexitime.* Part II: *Compressed work weeks and permanent part time employment.* New York: AMICOM, 1978.

Smith, M. B. School and home: Focus on achievement. In A. H. Pasow (Ed.), *Developing programs for the educationally disadvantaged.* New York: Teachers College Press, 1968.

Stack, C. B. *All our kin: Strategies for survival in the black community.* New York: Harper & Row, 1974.

Steinberg, L. D., Catalano, R., & Dooley, D. Economic antecedents for child abuse and neglect. *Child Development,* 1981, *52,* 975–985.

Titmuss, R. M. *The gift relationship: From human blood to social policy.* London: Allyn and Unwin, 1970.

U.S. Bureau of the Census. *Current population reports* (Series P-60, No. 127). *Money income and poverty status of families and persons in the United States, 1980.* Washington, D.C.: U.S. Government Printing Office, 1981.

U.S. Bureau of the Census. *Current population reports* (Series P-60, No. 134). *Money income and poverty status of families and persons in the United States, 1981.* Washington, D.C.: U.S. Government Printing Office, 1982.

U.S. Senate Committee on the Judiciary. *Our nation's schools – a report card: "A" in school violence and vandalism* (Preliminary report of the Subcommittee to Investigate Juvenile Delinquency). Washington, D.C.: U.S. Government Printing Office, 1975.

Weiss, H. B. *The effect of a wife's employment on the division of household and child care tasks.* Wellesley, Mass.: Center for Research on Women, 1976.

Weiss, H. B. *Parent education and support: An analysis of the Brookline Early Education Project.* Ed.D. dissertation, Harvard Graduate School of Education, 1979.

Wynne, E. *Looking at schools: Good, bad, and indifferent.* Lexington, Mass.: Heath Lexington, 1980.

23   Shaping child and family policies: criteria and strategies for a new decade

Sharon L. Kagan, Edgar Klugman, and Edward F. Zigler

Throughout this volume, the authors have described the complex relationship between knowledge about children and families and the construction of social policy in the United States. Some have treated the subject from a historical perspective, some have focused on alternate perspectives from which policy can be analyzed, and some have traced the development of specific child and family policies through a series of political and legislative maneuvers. To conclude the volume, our discussion will focus on the field of child and family development and social policy as a totality. We will explore its current status and the feasibility of developing family policies by addressing the questions: Does the United States have a cogent child and family policy? Can and should the United States have such a policy? If so, what criteria should guide policy development? Finally, what specific strategies will foster the implementation of constructive policies for children and their families?

Does the United States have a family policy?

The press for the development of a national family policy reached a crescendo during the presidential campaign and subsequent administration of Jimmy Carter, the 39th president of the United States. Carter's pronouncements that he would construct an administration that would reverse trends that have led to the breakdown of the family, and that his administration would "design programs and policies that support families and ensure that future generations . . . will thrive and prosper" (Carter, 1979, p. H302), coupled with his creation of an Office for Families and a White House Conference on Families, ushered in the era when family policy became a public issue.

Carter's concerns about the American family were not new. They had been addressed previously by legislative activity on behalf of children, by

415

scholarly work prepared in the academic community, and by the work of advocates and practitioners throughout the nation. Scholars, long the deliverers of "expert" congressional testimony, explored the relationship between knowledge about children and their families and social policy. Some attested that knowledge about children and families should be used as a cornerstone for legislative and judicial actions. Others called for a more comprehensive approach, seeking a consistent body of legislation that could be considered "family policy." Others looked to foreign countries to see what, if any, lessons could be garnered from cross-national investigations. Advocates and practitioners looked toward the establishment of "networks" and "hotlines" so that the public could be quickly mobilized to support child and family initiatives.

Given a president who was concerned about children and families, an academic community ready to influence policy, and an advocacy–practitioner body on its way to being mobilized, the late 1970s seemed to hold great promise for the enactment of legislation and for the establishment of programs and guidelines that would support the family. However, existing concurrently and perhaps stimulated by the emergence of family policy as a public issue, many unresolved issues surfaced. Coalesced in large part by the Moral Majority, a growing number of Americans began to decry the government's involvement in family matters, including the issues of abortion, divorce, homosexuality, and the use of contraceptives. A well-articulated media and direct-mail strategy catapulted both the Moral Majority and the perspectives it represents into the public and legislative arenas. Mixing religion and politics, the Moral Majority successfully motivated its constituency to pray, register, become informed, help elect godly people, and vote (Ellerin & Kesten, 1981).

During the Carter administration, and most poignantly during the deliberations surrounding the White House Conference on Families, divergent perspectives emerged on the family, including the very definition of family. Although the U.S. Census Bureau defined a family as a group of two or more persons residing together who are related by blood, marriage, or adoption, demographic trends and value preferences necessitated a rethinking of the basic definition of "family." Structural elements were considered: Precisely who constitutes a family? Functional elements were also reconsidered: What does a family provide for its members, and which members perform what functions? Definitions incorporating new structural and functional elements emerged, thereby expanding the de facto conception of family beyond census definitions. Still unresolved, debate over the definition of family and families continues to rage on with regularity, and, as if dulled by repetition, citizens have become immune to its importance. Without a common conception of family or families, the possibility of constructing a cohesive family policy remains questionable.

The lack of clarity regarding the definition of family is not unique: Definitions of *policy* are equally cloudy. Policy may be equated with programs. In 1977 there were 63 federal programs that contained the word *family* in their titles or in their stated objectives (Family Impact Seminar, 1977). In addition to these programs, there were and are many governmental policies, seemingly unrelated to child and family life, that do in fact affect, and in some cases shape, the nature of family life. Not only do family-related programs exist at the federal level, but there are a myriad more at state and local levels.

Gil (1976) warns against equating social policies with social welfare programs. This leads to a fragmented approach to the development and analysis of social policies. It is easier, Gil advises, to address each problem in isolation. Although different policies may be inconsistent, together and through interactions with one another they shape the conditions of living for society as a whole and for each of its members. "The common domain of all social policies can consequently be identified as the overall quality of life in society, the circumstances of living individuals and groups, and the nature of all intra-societal human relations" (Gil, 1976, p. 13). More concretely, social policy is, for some, concerned with the allocation of rights, privileges, labor, and resources within a society.

Another response to the "What is policy?" question focuses on policy as a body of law that consists of statutes dealing with child and family issues: marriage, divorce, custody, adoption, child abuse, and so on. Policy, for others, is that which emanates from what is practical. For this group, policy is not so much a program or body of law, but rather a set of practices made to expedite business at hand. In schools, for example, attendance procedures may be formal and written with known consequences for deviation. In business, flexitime, paternity leaves, and support for families in transition may be corporate practices codified into policy. Collectively these diverse visions include policy as programs, laws, or practices under governmental or private aegis.

Conversely, the nonexistence of a program or practice constitutes policy as well. A nonpolicy has consequences, just as does a policy. For example, that the country does not have a uniform cash assistance or children's allowance program reveals important information regarding the country's commitment to universal family support. That a company doesn't have a flexitime practice may generate as many consequences as would the policy itself. The point is that a nonpolicy can itself be a policy.

Policy may also be considered in the abstract. It has been considered both as an instrument or facilitator of social change and as a reflector of social values. As an instrument of social engineering, policy has a life, a raison d'être, beyond the functions it explicitly states. This perspective, for example, regards the provision of child care not simply as another service to needy families, but as the vehicle that allows mothers to enter the workforce. Child care is an instrument of labor force participation – a means to greater employment, not simply an end in itself. Income redistribution policies that favor large families not only provide more support for larger units, but provide incentives for the very existence of larger families. Income incentives are instruments of social change. Alternatively, those who view policy as a reflector of societal mores and values see its evolution within the historical fabric of American life. For example, the ethic of family privacy has yielded a noninterventionist, nonuniversalist policy stance. In fact, in our country, this ethic has shaped the amount and nature, the quantity, and the quality of family policy.

Another approach to policy, perhaps emerging in response to the concrete and abstract perspectives, is the model-building approach. In an effort to explicate complex policy perspectives and/or to create a common language of policy that will clarify and create further discussion, organized policy models have emerged. Some focus on approaches to the policy-making process (Marmor, chap. 3, this volume; Brewer, chap. 4, this volume). Others have focused on the context of policy itself. A well-known perspective is that of Kamerman and Kahn (1978) who define policy as "everything that government does to and for the family" (p. 3). Within family policy, Kamerman and Kahn suggest two categories: (1) explicit policy; and (2) implicit policy. Explicit family policies are further divided into two subgroups: (a) specific programs and policies designed to achieve specified, explicit goals regarding the family; and (b) programs and policies that deliberately do things to and for the family, but for which there are no agreed-upon overall goals regarding the family. Implicit family policy includes "governmental actions and policies not specifically or primarily addressed to the family, but which have indirect consequence" (Kamerman & Kahn, 1978, p. 3). Another approach distinguishes between social and public policies. From this perspective, social policies are those policies that affect humans, be they directly focused on children (day-care or public school policy), families (adoption, foster care, and Aid to Families with Dependent Children), or improving the general quality of life (energy or transportation policy). Public policy from this perspective includes those policies that have been developed by the government and have its imprimatur.

Given various perspectives on "families" and on "policies," it is no wonder that scholars debate the very existence of child and family policy. Bane (1978) stated it succinctly: "Perhaps the easiest answer one could give to the question 'What is the family policy of this country?' is there is none" (p. 1). Bane acknowledges the existence of programs and family law, but she indicates that, short of the Constitution, there is no coherent guiding philosophy that could yield a single set of child and family policies (Bane, 1978). Steiner (1981) goes a step further and states, "Family policy is simply a description of a bundle of government programs, and hence inevitable" (p. 214). It is, he says, "not a coherent program awaiting formal approval. . . . Family policy is unifying only so long as the details are avoided. When the details are confronted, family policy splits into innumerable components. It is many causes with many votaries" (Steiner, 1981, p. 215). Bane and Steiner would agree, as would the authors, that currently, and in spite of much attention, there is no coherent American family policy. That it does not exist should surprise no one, given the complexities of policy making coupled with the American ethic of privacy and the disparate definitions of family that currently abound.

Can the United States have a family policy?

Beyond the question of whether or not comprehensive family policy exists in the United States today is the question of the political and intellectual viability of an American family policy for the future.

The basic building block of American society is the family. It is the first socializing unit for the infant, and has the potential to remain the single ongoing institution that provides support and nurturance throughout life. Throughout the debate on family policy, the viability of the family remains uncontested.

For all its strengths, the American family is in an era of rapid change. It is no longer an isolated institution, remote from other societal forces. Rather, it is an institution at once in transition and in a position of tremendous power. Given the complex interactions between the family and other social forms, and given the constant changes in family patterns, the development of a single unified family policy is not realistic. No matter how comprehensive, a single family policy in America remains unattainable and undesirable. What is needed is incremental reform of existing policies and new policies that are based on a set of principles or criteria grounded on the best information available. In addition to criteria for reframing and constructing policy, implementation strategies must be considered.

The need for considering family policy criteria and strategies will not be diminished by the current devolution of fiscal and programmatic authority to states. To the contrary, the new federalism will demand careful scrutiny of policies, thereby eliminating some and reshaping or creating others. Precisely because of rapid changes in governmental roles and because of rapid changes in family structure, the need for criteria coupled with specific strategies becomes more urgent.

Criteria for formulating policies

The shaping of American child and family policy, as previous chapters have indicated, has been a patchwork. Often developed to meet pressing needs of "underprivileged," economically disadvantaged, or handicapped populations, specific child and family policies have been explicitly targeted. As problems that are of concern (e.g., drug and alcohol abuse, teenage sex and pregnancy, juvenile crime, and adolescent suicide) increase and also cross subgroups, the very nature and audience for policy initiatives may change drastically.

A more universal need for policy exists in spite of, and perhaps because of, a weakened political infrastructure. Although political advocates for children and families exist, their impact historically has been weak, especially when compared with other organized lobbies, including those representing labor, the aged, and farmers. That there is no cabinet-level position representing child and family interests indicates a lack of governmental commitment in this area. Increased problems affecting a broader spectrum of the nation's children, a comparatively weak advocacy system, and a limited governmental infrastructure to create, fund, and monitor child and family policy are factors that amplify the need for reconsidering the relationship between government policy and child and family life.

Several assumptions have guided the positions espoused herein. First, we assume that there is an important role government can take in fostering child and family well-being. Surely the government is not solely responsible for the family, but eliminating the government from any role in child and family policy is both unwise and unrealistic. Second, we assume that there are bodies of knowledge that can be brought to bear on the construction of policy, thereby improving it conceptually and practically. Third, we assume that changes in American society will necessitate new visions of both the structure and function of policy. Specifically, new perspectives on policy will need to be embraced so that emerging problems, faced by individuals regardless of income, can be ameliorated. Constructive social policies can no longer be directed solely at the poor.

Given these assumptions, upon what should child and family policy be based, and what criteria should be considered when developing policy? For years those who have recommended and created policy have turned recurrently to several sources. Policy makers look to concrete data and to projections emanating from data to determine the extent of current and projected societal problems and societal needs. Concrete data include census figures, research studies, scholarly reports, and social indicator information. In addition to data that give quantitative information, policy makers have been guided by bodies of literature that have developed over time. Occasionally, a single study will influence policy decisions, but more frequently policy will be guided by a large body of work emanating from divergent sources. Rarely codified for the policy maker, this knowledge exists as "general information." As such, it provides the context for policy discussion, and only sometimes the basis for policy decisions. Our recommendation is that these sources – demographic data and scientific knowledge – continue to be used as guides for framing child and family policy. To enhance their utility, however, demographic data must be presented and analyzed so that major trends can be extrapolated from the data, and scientific knowledge must be codified into a reasonable set of generally agreed-upon principles of child and family life. The use of demographic data as criteria for policy will be discussed by focusing on fertility, mobility, divorce, and working women. It will be followed by a discussion of principles of child and family life.

Demographic data

The construction of policy is a complicated undertaking that calls for the synthesis of data from many sources. Demographic data, because of their breadth and scope, are particularly useful in stemming parochialism and dissuading inherent and natural value biases. Although it would be impractical and unwieldy to discuss all forms of demographic data and to sort out all the trends that affect children and families, a discussion of four major trends that affect family life will demonstrate how demographic data can be used to illuminate the background against which policy is shaped.

Fertility rates. The raw fertility rate (the average number of children per woman) according to the 1980 census was 1.9. This is less than the 2.1 children needed for the natural replacement of the population (Bureau of the Census, 1981). Not only is the number of children per woman decreasing, but so is the average family size. In 1947 the average family size was nearly 4 persons, but by 1978 the mean size had decreased to closer to 3 (Treas, 1981). Some demographers predict that the average family size will fall to about 1.5 children by the turn of the century, and zero population growth will be achieved during the first third of the twenty-first century (McFalls, 1981).

Although the reasons are complex and intertwined, there are three major causes for the decline in family size. First are financial factors. It has been estimated that it now costs between $50,000 and $100,000 to raise one child. Although children represent a major economic investment, they do not provide a financial return on investment and no longer guarantee security for their parents in old age. Second, delays in marriage coupled with increased divorce rates cause more women to spend less time raising children. Women, spending more time in work roles, are finding viable alternatives to marriage and motherhood. Third, the variety, availability, and reliability of contraceptives decreases the number of unplanned pregnancies. Legalized abortion mitigates contraceptive error.

Women are electing to remain unmarried in increasing numbers. In 1980, some 50% of all women 20 to 24 were unmarried compared to 33% in 1970 and 25% in 1960. By the year 2000, this figure could approach 70% (McFalls, 1981). The proportion of women who remain single and childless between the ages of 25 and 29 doubled from 10.5% in 1970 to 21% in 1980. Not only is there a trend to delay marriage, but many women who do marry elect not to have children. "It seems likely then that the process of delaying childbearing may provide women with the opportunity to develop life styles and other interests that may be competing with their role as a mother" (Bureau of the Census, 1980b).

Although the rate of fertility among 20- to 24-year-old women is decreasing, two dichotomous trends are emerging. One trend is the "30-year-old panic" where couples, realizing the woman is approaching the limit of her child-bearing years, attempt pregnancy (Parker, Peltier, & Wolleat, 1981). Many become midlife parents, but others, discovering that they are unable to conceive, turn to adoption (Rapoport, Rapoport, & Strelitz, 1980). The other trend, at the opposite end of the spectrum, is teenage pregnancy. About 10% of all females between the ages of 15 and 19 become pregnant annually, accounting for 1.1 million pregnancies and about 600,000 births. Of these, about 250,000 children are born out of wedlock (Levitan & Belous, 1981). Overwhelming as these figures are, the concomitant problems associated with teenage pregnancy must not be overlooked. Teenage motherhood is associated with reduced educational and occupational attainment, higher marital instability, and higher subsequent fertility.

In addition to these changes, it is predicted that the number of children in each family will be reduced. For example, among women born between 1931 and 1935, 37% had four or more children. If present trends continue, perhaps fewer than 10% of child-bearing women of this generation will have that number of children. Among couples who will have children, it is also expected that 20% will have only one child. By 1990, only half of all husband–wife couples will have children under 15 living at home (Masnick & Bane, 1980). Given the demographic trends, attention must be directed toward the strengths and vulnerabilities of children growing up in smaller families and as only children. Attention must also be paid to the increased number of aging adults living without children. "Children in an 'old' society are in danger on the one hand of being toys for adults and on the other of being pressed into premature adulthood" (Bane, 1976, p. 113).

Thus, despite low fertility rates, the population, because of the sheer numbers of women entering their child-bearing years, will increase into the twenty-first century. Families will be smaller and the population older, signaling new needs in terms of socialization patterns for both children and adults. Decreasing family size will increase the importance of friendships, neighborhoods, and organizations as sources of support and personal ties. The idealization of the nuclear family with two children can no longer be the model for the policy maker. Diverse life styles coupled with adults more freely choosing to become parents will become the norm.

Mobility. Because America is a mobile society, policy makers need to comprehend not only the numbers of families who move, but the rationale and consequences of their decisions to do so. At least 40 million Americans change their residence once a year, and the average person will move 14 times in his or her lifetime (Gordon, 1976). Although moves are traditionally associated with career or financial change, society often neglects the emotional consequences of mobility. Although moving may be beneficial, it can occasion multiple losses to the individual (e.g., important social ties, familiar living patterns, security, and even income), potentially contributing to the development of depression from loneliness (Weiss, 1973). During the 1970s, 41% of all families moved from one location to another (Bureau of the Census, 1980c), creating a paradox in the nuclear family system. Because the family is shrinking in size and moving away from traditional familial and communal supports, it is becoming increasingly isolated. Conversely, as it calls on schools, hospitals, and other social services, the family is becoming more dependent on formal institutions to provide needed support and services.

Over the years there have been consistent trends in family life. In the

1920s households were fairly heterogeneous, with several generations living together. In the post–World War II period, a time of affluence and independence, the nuclear family flourished (Masnick & Bane, 1980). Growth of the nuclear family has been associated with suburban growth and urban decline. In 1950 the suburbs grew by 45.9% (Bureau of the Census, 1980c). More recently, however, accompanying the trend toward smaller families, a rural renaissance, embracing a growth revival in small cities and towns, has emerged. Families are moving away from cities and suburbia to "exurbia" (Kirst, 1981).

Underlying reasons for migration to exurbia are varied. Nonmetropolitan employment options, particularly in energy and recreation industries, have become more plentiful. This decentralization of manufacturing to nonmetropolitan areas is particularly attractive to industry because of reduced transportation, labor, and land costs. In addition to issues of life sustenance, issues of life style have been an equally important precipitant of nonmetropolitan growth. Trends toward early retirement, a more leisurely lifestyle (Morrison, 1981), and an environment where traditional values of home and family can be easily affirmed have supported the rise in nonmetropolitan living.

Migration studies reveal not only where people move, but a great deal about the characteristics of individuals who do move. Analyses show very high levels of residential mobility in the first few years after divorce or separation, but not after widowhood. Only 16% of those over 65 made changes of residence. Conversely, 46% of all single parents moved in the 1970s (Masnick & Bane, 1980).

In *Aspects of the Present,* Margaret Mead stated, "What we have failed to realize is that even as we have separated the single family from the larger society, we have expected each couple to take on a range of obligations that traditionally have been shared within a larger community" (Mead, 1980a, p. 102). The loss of support from families and community ties necessitates a greater role for peers and for institutions. New alliances and supports, as well as mechanisms for accessing services, are needed to replace the "kin" of former times. Mobility data shape not merely the location of public programs, but the very nature of policy alternatives.

Divorce rates. Often divorce has been charged with causing the collapse of family life in the United States. Kamerman and Kahn (1978) point out that the "number of divorces exceeded one million in 1975, the highest number ever in U.S. history in a one-year period, while the number of marriages, two million, was the lowest since 1969" (p. 43). A 65% increase in the number of divorces over the course of the 1970s has resulted in the reality that one out of every five children has separated parents. This trend is expected to continue into the 1990s when one out of every three youngsters will have parents who divorce (Bane, 1976).

This high rate of divorce is forcing structural changes in family patterns. Today only 6% of all American families fit Talcott Parsons's 1940s' definition: working husband, wife at home full time with two children (Rapoport et al., 1980). Consequently, roles for adults and children are becoming increasingly varied: single parents, with or without custody or with joint custody; solitary parent; stepparent; or married parent. The child may have one home with two parents, one home with one parent, two homes between two parents, or two homes with four parents as well as a combination of siblings and stepsiblings. "One outcome of this is that more and more children are expected to adapt themselves not once and for all to one set of parents, brothers and sisters but twice or even several times to new family constellations" (Mead, 1980b, p. 133).

One important consequence of divorce is the rise of the single-parent family. Over the 1970s single-parent households increased by 73% while married households declined by 4%. In 1979, of all families 19% were single-parent households; of these, 17% were female-headed. Female-headed households were the largest subgroup below the poverty level, with more than half dependent on welfare (Bureau of the Census, 1980a).

The rate of remarriage is keeping up with the rate of divorce. Some 67% of all people who divorce remarry, indicating that there remains a strong desire for a compatible marriage and family life (Norton & Glick, 1979). Of these remarriages, 60% involve children, making transitions potentially more complicated and stressful (Garfield, 1980). Problems arising from children's feelings of rivalry, envy, and conflicts regarding the replaced or displaced natural parent are common. Given these trends, it is reasonable to assume that divorce, and its stressful concomitants, will continue.

The rationale for divorce has received increased attention as incidence has increased. The feminist movement receives its share of blame when the question "Why divorce?" is posed. Antifeminists contend that women are too concerned with themselves at the expense of the family. Economists argue that it is the expense of raising a family that propels women into the labor market, increasing stress in marriage. Social scientists point out correlations between education and marriage. The lower the educational level, the greater the incidence of divorce, except for women with more than four years of college (Spanier & Glick, 1981). Others believe that because we live longer now, relationships cannot be expected to last such an extended period of time (Bettelheim, 1980). Finally, conservatives argue that since divorce has been easier to obtain, the rate has climbed. The stigma of divorce has vanished. In fact, many corporations now pay a higher premium for the divorced man. Because he is mobile, the company doesn't have to concern itself with relocation problems of the family (Glieberman, 1981).

Research results regarding the effects of divorce are varied and reveal complications regarding the application of social science research to policy. On the one hand, research indicates that divorce has initial negative effects on children. Hetherington (1979) indicates that "even children who later are able to recognize that the divorce had constructive outcomes initially undergo considerable emotional distress with family dissolution" (p. 851). Other work indicates that children are no longer considered victims of broken homes, and that in the course of adjusting to divorce children have been shown to acquire strengths and responsibilities, highlighting the fact that divorce need not be a traumatic experience for all children (Kurdek & Siesky, 1980, p. 99). These perspectives indicate that the final word on divorce effects is not in as yet, and support a call for additional research. Policy makers faced with discordant results are hard-pressed to convert scholarly research to constructive policy.

Working women. In 1980, for the first time in history, more than 50% of American women participated in the paid labor force: A full 52% of women were gainfully employed (Bureau of the Census, 1981). Female workforce participation has its root in history and its reasons in contemporary times. Historically, women have always been a part of the labor force. At the turn of the century, 20% of all women over the age of 16 worked, and the percentage has been rising ever since ("Superwoman squeeze," 1980). Currently, economists point to expanding work opportunities, higher styles of living, and inflationary times as strong incentives to labor force participation. Sociologists cite changing sex-role attitudes, rising divorce rates, and falling birth rates. Historians point to the parallel between the trend toward more women working outside the home and the growth of industrialization and technology.

Whatever the rationale, the rise of women in the workforce has created challenges for individuals and institutions. Juggling work and married life is a reality for 25% of all married women, creating the "superwoman squeeze" ("Superwoman squeeze," 1980). Whereas women work outside the home, their work is not equal to men in terms of pay or occupational status. By the end of the 1970s, some 80% of all clerical workers and 62% of all service workers were women. Only one out of every five women held professional/managerial positions. Typically, women earn only 60%

of what men do (Levitan & Belous, 1981), and the average wife's earnings represent only 26% of the total family income.

The most striking change in demographics related to working women is the increased employment of working mothers. Currently 44.9% of mothers with children under age 6 are in the labor force, compared to 18.6% in 1960. Of mothers with children between the ages of 6 and 17, fully 62% are currently in the labor force in contrast to 39% in 1960 (Bureau of the Census, 1981). Although working mothers confront many issues (e.g., guilt, perceptions of self-worth, fatigue), the single largest problem is child care.

Currently only 10% to 15% of all preschool children of working mothers are cared for in day-care centers. The rest are cared for individually or in small groups in their own homes or in the home of a caretaker who may or may not be related to the child (Hofferth & Moore, 1979). For many others who cannot afford or find after-school care, the alternative becomes the key: "Latchkey children," those unsupervised by an adult after school, are estimated to number 4 million. This unfortunate trend is exacerbated by fertility rates: Smaller family size decreases the likelihood of having adolescents and young children at home during the same years. Increased popularity of retirement villages removes the elderly, traditional sources of child care, from the community.

Demographers and sociologists predict that by 1990 the labor force will consist of 56 million women and 66 million men. This means that 70–80% of all women 20–25 years old will be working (Masnick & Bane, 1980). In addition to creating policies that promulgate increased child care through public or private sector initiatives, business and industry will need to create environments and policies that support working adults.

Principles of child and family life

In addition to using demographic data as criteria for policy formulation, principles of child and family life are of equal importance. Emanating from scholarly research done over time, basic conceptions of child and family interactions have evolved. Although not free from debate, these ideas are shared and generally accepted by researchers and scholars in the field, and as such can guide policy development. It should be pointed out that although discussed individually, the principles and associated practices are often interrelated.

The principle of family integrity and continuity. Children and families benefit if the integrity and continuity of the family can be maintained.

The principle of continuity is not new, particularly in its application to young children. It is axiomatic that very young children benefit from the presence of a loving provider who remains in the child's environment over time. Continuity for children as they make the transition from home to school and even from grade to grade has long been espoused and has even been the focus of a federal demonstration program (Project Developmental Continuity, 1975).

Given knowledge and research about the benefits of child and family continuity, it is troublesome indeed that until very recently, policies affecting the most troubled children in the United States fostered the breakup of the family. Children have been consigned to institutions for a variety of reasons: delinquency, misconduct, disability, and parental failure. An alternative to institutionalization has been the foster-care system. Foster care, by definition, is temporary or transitional. Foster parents are therefore not encouraged to develop long-term attachments for the children in their care. Children in foster care are often placed in one home or another, with only 15% to 25% ever returning to their own homes (Keniston & Carnegie Council, 1977). Not only can this approach be detrimental to children and their families, but it is costly as well. Although federal dollars have been available to support the room and board (maintenance) of children in out-of-home placements, until the passage of Public Law 97–262, the Adoption Assistance and Child Welfare Act of 1980, limited federal money was used to provide supports (respite care, homemaker services, etc.) aimed at keeping the family together. With enactment of this legislation, incentives exist for states to provide services to sustain the integrity and continuity of the family. Incentives for adoption of foster-care children for whom there is no possibility of a return to the natural home are also included in the legislation.

Although a single piece of legislation cannot modify policy and practice in total, it can, through a system of financial incentives, alter the way federal, state, and local governmental agencies serve many of the most troubled children and families.

The principle of heterogeneity. Children and families are heterogeneous, and they vary on every measurable characteristic. Due to this variability, children and families have diverse needs.

Growing diversity in American families has been an underlying theme of this chapter. New definitions, both structural and functional, have accompanied changes in demographic trends and value preferences. Structurally, new family forms have emerged: Single-parent, two-worker, serial, homosexual, unmarried, and communal families abound. Functionally, family roles are being shared by spouses and by children. Increasingly, youngsters are assuming adult roles by providing after-school care to younger children or by providing emotional support to parents at stressful periods during divorce and separation. Family functions are being assumed by nonfamily members. "It is less often recognized that even in our own society with its emphasis on the autonomy of the nuclear family, there are a range of caring other figures who are involved in parental or quasi-parental roles" (Rapoport et al., 1980, p. 24). In transient and nontransient communities, nonfamily members often play important roles. A neighbor, a fellow day-care parent, or a business associate can provide support often unavailable from distant kin. The growth of self-help, self-education, and peer-exchange groups all point toward changing patterns in family functioning.

Whether or not new family patterns are or should be socially sanctioned is a matter of value preference. Traditionalists, growing in visibility and effectiveness, call for a return to basic values of fidelity, loyalty, and chastity – a system where moral norms, once defined, remain operative without exception (Marshner, 1981). A more liberal position, in contrast, encourages change that perpetuates individual freedom and choice. Irrespective of strong value preferences, decisions that precipitate changed family patterns may be other than value-motivated. Pushed by economic necessity, women return to the workforce. Women look to their jobs and professions for the security previously afforded by marriage (Friedan, 1979). Families "take in" relatives who are often too old or too poor to provide their own care. Taken together, changes in family organization, whether motivated by value or necessity, characterize the growing pluralism evident in American family life.

The implications of family pluralism are abundant. Kamerman and Kahn (1978) indicate that "American political and cultural diversity . . . has precluded explicit family policy and is behind current hesitancy" (p. 503). The prevalence of divergent views regarding family structure, coupled with the intensity with which they are held, indicates that reconstructed or new family policies must be broadly conceived so that the varied values and needs of American children and adults can be accommodated. No single family pattern can constitute the norm. Rather, policies must acknowledge that family pluralism is a reality. Operationally, this means that child and family policies must be structured so that, wherever possible, options are afforded. Although this is not feasible in all legislative actions or judicial decisions, creators of policy must nevertheless create options so that policy users can modify practice to best fit their unique and diverse needs.

The family and the influence of other institutions. The most important influence on the development of the individual is the family, but the family is only one of many institutions shaping the individual.

In the effort to support family functioning, policy makers and advocates must consider that the family, although the primary influence on the child, is itself shaped by a complicated economic, political, and social structure. Existing at the nexus of formal and informal institutions, a body of law, and a body of theory, the family becomes a mediator, a mediating structure, negotiating and modifying society's impact. Within a rapidly changing world, the family is called on to perform its historic functions: nurturing the development and providing the basic needs of its members while inculcating moral and ethical values. These functions take place in the foreground, often surrounded by a background that may contradict, modify, or usurp family influence.

Because of the confluence of forces that affect children and families, policies created in their behalf must be made in the context of the broader society by the broader society. The government is not and should not be the sole harbinger of family policy. Rather, the private sector, along with the nonprofit and religious sectors, must become aware of the magnitude of their roles in affecting family life. With more businesses and industries committed to changes in the work structure and to flexible benefit packages, a broad-based effort to support the family is under way.

Beyond providing direct benefits to families, corporate and public policies must facilitate networking among institutions and families. Consideration must be given to bridging the gap that exists between families and the institutions that serve them. Schools must become more receptive to involving and helping parents. Strategies for this, which have been elaborated elsewhere (Zigler & Kagan, 1982), include provisions for accessing family support services like information and referral services and after-school and infant care. This is not to say that public schools should directly provide all programs, but school personnel can act as effective advocates for parents in negotiating services already available in the community or in advocating for their establishment.

Minimum environmental level. Children and families who experience an environment that falls below some minimal level of quality will be damaged by that environment.

Environment is generally regarded as physical space connoting a facility – a home, a school, a place of work. In addition, our definition of environment incorporates the totality of one's milieu, one's social and nonsocial environments. With regard to social environments, there is a concern that basic standards of safety must be guarded. That the United States, after a decade of debate, still has no national day-care requirements is inexcusable. Daily, throughout the nation, parents leave children in settings that are environmentally unsafe. Schools, while generally maintaining safe physical plants, undermine children's healthy development by sanctioning corporal punishment. The mere existence of corporal punishment is a tacit acceptance of violence and physical aggression as an appropriate model for human behavior. That corporal punishment is sanctioned may paradoxically liberate students to engage in violence targeted at the school facility itself. Reports of increased property violence and violence to school personnel should be sufficient impetus for educational policy makers to reevaluate their internal practices regarding corporal punishment.

Child abuse continues to perplex scholars and policy makers. Although it is difficult to provide precise statistics on child abuse – perhaps because definitional issues abound (Zigler, chap. 19, this volume) – its incidence is large and its effects costly. Roughly 2,000 children each year die of child abuse (Martinez, 1977). The scholarly community is learning more about child abuse incidence and etiology, but it remains a persistent personal threat to the social and emotional well-being of children and their families.

Other environmental hazards less elusive than child abuse can be and have been rectified. As the number-one killer of children, accidents are receiving increased attention. The use of lead-free paint, safety bottle caps, window guards, and seat belts have been instituted with positive effects. Childhood immunizations and "no shots – no school" policies have reduced the incidence of childhood diseases drastically. Still, more work is needed in the area of accident prevention if a healthy environment for children is to be achieved. The United States has the highest rate in the world of accidental death due to firearms for children between the ages of 5 and 14. Motor vehicle accidents account for the greatest number of childhood deaths. Policies and practices available to all that help create a safer environment remain sorely needed.

Disparity of child and family needs. The needs of children and their families may not always be consonant.

Historically, it has been assumed that parents or guardians acted as agents for their children. Inherent in this assumption is the belief that parents know and select what is best for the child. It was assumed that parental decisions are "correct," rarely biased by adult self-interest, insufficient knowledge, or discrepancies between child and family interests.

More recently, the myth of the all-knowing rational parent has given way. Perhaps exacerbated by the fast pace of adolescent development or by the many advocacy movements of the 1960s, the need for child advocates, particularly in cases where family functioning has broken down, is now acknowledged. Typically, when families are in extreme situations, in cases of child abuse, or when parents can no longer control their children, child advocates represent the best interests of the youngster. Not only are advocates needed when child and family needs are not synonymous, but when parents and schools are in conflict or when state services to children are contested as inappropriate.

Just where the rights of parents and children part company has been a matter of debate, differing widely from state to state. In some cases, children are removed from their homes against the will of the parents. To combat this and other perceived infringements, some states have instituted rules that protect the rights of parents (Bane, 1976, p. 106). Simultaneously, courts must deal with sets of parents whose wishes are not compatible. Consider cases where parents cannot agree on the upbringing of children or in which custody is contested by parents following divorce. These differences, touching only the surface, present hard dilemmas for policy makers. What must be considered, finally, is that a system that provides for individuals must recognize that the will of one parent, both parents, or the entire rest of the family may not be in consort with a child's best interests. Protections for children, as distinct from their parents or guardians, must be incorporated into policy. While a deterrent to swift policy construction and legislative enactment, individual safeguards are an essential legacy of a thoughtful, caring society.

Strategies for implementing policy

Given the utilization of solid demographic data and adherence to basic principles of child and family life, policy for children and their families should be well formulated. The problem remains that well-conceived policies can effect little change without formal incorporation into the system. This means that not only must legislation be passed, but funds must be appropriated so that the intent of the legislation will be enacted and sustained over time.

As the decade of the 1980s moves on, much of the enthusiasm that characterized Jimmy Carter's hopes for improving family life has waned. Domestic issues, largely economic, coupled with increasing interest in defense have characterized the Reagan administration. The devolution of human services to the states, via the block grant, seems to have been part of a broader plan, leaving the national agenda, not to mention the national media, free to focus on the economy and foreign affairs. Some view decentralization of authority and funds to the states as a way of "passing the buck," of admitting that issues related to children and families are too hot to handle at the national level. Moving them to states takes them out of the national public eye, forestalling organized confrontation while permitting local input. Periodically convened and receiving national attention since 1909, the White House Conference on Children was decentralized in 1981, presumably to provide an additional planning vehicle that would assist states as they assume greater responsibility for human services. In effect, the departure from tradition, carried out with impunity because of the lack of a mobilized child and family constituency, belies the very intent and ultimate value of a White House Conference.

Amid this ever-changing social and increasingly conservative economic climate, child and family advocates, already splintered, are likely to subdivide their efforts not only by issue, but by geographic area: by state or locality. The national consensus that was sought in the formation of important issue-based coalitions of the late 1970s is now even more difficult to achieve, although more necessary. Given these events, discussion of implementation strategies is made extremely complex and important.

Various chapters in this volume have pointed to the idiosyncratic nature of the policy process. Usually rooted in a social problem, policy is formulated using a variety of methods. Yet in cases where policy recommendations have been converted into legislation, several common variables exist. It is our contention that these common elements, once codified, can yield important guidance to those interested in policy implementation.

Stated generally, the common elements that are needed to hasten legislative action include an informed citizenry, generally composed of those affected directly and indirectly by the problem; broad-based constituencies aware of and ready to support legislation; and contact points within the legislative and executive structure.

An informed citizenry

When social legislation is enacted, typically an awareness of the social problems that necessitated the legislation exists not only in the minds of policy makers and those affected by the legislation, but by the public at large as well. How a sense of problem develops among a populace warrants consideration. Currently, in the United States, the public has access to more media than at any time in history. Education is not limited to schooling alone, according to Cremin (1965), and a vast array of institutions serve to inform and educate the public. Cremin cites newspapers, cinema, radio, television, books, and periodicals, not to mention countless youth organizations of local, national, and international character. Says Cremin, "My point is that all these agencies educate the public and no serious discussion of contemporary educational policy can afford to ignore them" (p. 14).

Not only are the information sources readily available, but the American ethos freely endorses the open transmission of information. A fundamental tenet of American democracy was articulated by Jefferson when he explicated the link between education and a free society: "If a nation expects to be ignorant and free in a state of civilization, it expects what never was and never will be" (Jefferson, 1899). Because a democratic system is founded on the premise of universal access to information, its continued success depends on the existence of an informed electorate.

Given the United States' diverse population, developing a consistent perception of need is not a simple matter. An additional impediment to information flow is that, in many cases, many qualified to inform the public do not elect to do so. Caught up in a system aptly characterized as "publish or perish," scholars aspiring for tenure traditionally elect to publish their findings in scholarly journals in spite of the journals' limited audience. If scholarly talent, as one source, would address societal problems in popular periodicals or the press, the American public would be better informed.

Communicating to large audiences requires special skills and a supportive institutional arena. It is not sufficient to advocate that journalists and news broadcasters cover social service issues regularly. The power structure of the American press and broadcast media must regard the reporting of societal problems as fundamental to the public interest and as a corporate responsibility. When these problems are given greater media attention, the public will be more informed and in a better position to become advocates in behalf of legislation important to them.

A mobilized advocacy lobby

Public knowledge of an issue is not sufficient in and of itself to influence policy. Disparate groups and individuals need to coalesce if their collective power is to be felt. Advocacy groups and networks have been established for precisely this purpose, and while useful, they represent only one strategy. Another approach that has been tried with success is that of ad hoc coalitions that mobilize around single issues. A recent and fairly successful example of a coalition strategy is that established to review and modify the 1980 Federal Interagency Day Care Requirements (FIDCR).

Over 30 organizations agreed upon a unified set of regulations that were subsequently signed by Secretary of Health and Human Services Patricia Harris. However, the subsequent failure to implement FIDCR in Congress teaches us that successful coalitions need to couple efforts in the executive branch with lobbying strategies aimed at the legislature.

The advisability of establishing a standing child and family lobby has been debated over the years, with some supporting a national thrust and others advocating a state and local orientation. Complex issues are involved irrespective of governmental level: For which issues will the coalition lobby? Who will gain the right to speak and/or serve children and families? How will membership organizations and special interest groups function within a larger advocacy group? Complex issues of turf, finances, and authority have been impediments to sustaining a national coalition, as evidenced by the demise of the Coalition for Children and Youth. Although there are over 200 organizations in the United States committed to child and family issues, each has its own agenda. Divergent missions make compromise the difficult but necessary ingredient for firmly establishing and maintaining a broad-based national lobby. In spite of the attendant problems at the national level, child and family lobbies are certainly requisite at the state level. In several states, including California and Texas, well-organized lobbies have been effective in shaping legislation and provide good models for potential advocates elsewhere.

Contact points within the system

In order to maximize both general public awareness of child and family issues and the formation of a mobilized advocacy lobby, emphasis has been and must continue to be placed on developing and sustaining contact points within existing systems. Legislatively, both individuals and committees must be cultivated so that child and family issues are fully addressed. Leaders who are knowledgeable about critical problems must be maintained in their positions. New leaders joining the House and Senate must be made aware of current issues needing attention. Constituents, advocacy groups, lobbyists, and concerned individuals share this responsibility. The establishment of a Select Committee on Children, Youth, and Families in the House is a hopeful achievement. This committee can provide a forum for the discussion of pressing social issues. The importance of working closely with legislative aides should not be minimized, nor should the roles of the powerful Senate Finance Committee and the House Ways and Means Committee.

Within the executive branch, two specific strategies should be considered. First, a presidential advisor on child and family life should be appointed. Working with the president, this official would be a liaison with the Congress and the bureaucracy, overseeing efforts on behalf of children and families. Working closely with other advisors, this advisor could heighten the awareness of key decision makers regarding the potential impact of governmental initiatives on children and families. Although the concept is not new – it was suggested publicly by Eleanor McGovern during her husband's 1972 presidential campaign – it remains unimplemented.

The second strategy that must be implemented if the United States is to serve children and families efficiently is a review of the function of the Administration for Children, Youth, and Families (ACYF). Established initially as the Office of Child Development, this agency has decreased in status continually since its inception. Now ACYF must be legislatively legitimized, thereby eliminating the vulnerability of its very existence (Zigler, 1977). Its commissioner should be appointed by the president, and should report directly to the secretary of health and human services. Inasmuch as programs for children are scattered throughout the executive branch and under the jurisdiction of numerous legislative committees, it is essential that this single agency have the authority to take leadership in planning, implementing, and assessing programs for children and families. Support for ACYF must be mobilized so that both the authority and resources are obtained to enable the agency to function effectively.

Conclusion

Although in a period of transition, the American family and the American government are inextricably intertwined. Policies created by the Congress and decisions rendered by the courts have profound influences on family well-being. Policies implemented at the federal, state, and local levels and in the executive, legislative, and judicial branches have always affected and continue to affect children and families. Policy can and should be used to support families – but not to mold families or the services they receive according to one model. Rather, the government's role should be to ensure that child and family life is sustained according to a basic standard, regardless of family structure. Policies, when developed or revitalized, must be predicated on the best knowledge available. Finally, it is our guiding premise that the development and enactment of constructive social policies for children and families remains feasible and necessary.

References

Adoption Assistance and Child Welfare Act of 1980 (Public Law 96-272). *Weekly Compilation of Presidential Documents* (Vol. *16*[25]). Washington, D.C.: U.S. Government Printing Office, June 17, 1980.

America's small town boom. *Newsweek,* July 6, 1981, pp. 26–37.

Bane, M. J. *Here to stay: American families in the twentieth century.* New York: Basic Books, 1976.

Bane, M. J. *Family policy in the United States: Toward a description and evaluation* (Working Paper #52). Cambridge: Joint Center for Urban Studies of the Massachusetts Institute of Technology and Harvard University, July 1978.

Bettelheim, B. Untying the family. In E. Douvan, H. Weingarten, & J. Schieber (Eds.), *American Families.* Dubuque, Iowa: Kendall/Hunt, 1980, pp. 166–172.

Bureau of the Census. Families maintained by female householders, 1970–1979. *Current Population Reports* (Series P-20, No. 107). Washington, D.C.: U.S. Government Printing Office, 1980. (a)

Bureau of the Census. Fertility of American Women, June 1979. *Current Population Reports* (Series P-20, No. 358). Washington, D.C.: U.S. Government Printing Office, 1980. (b)

Bureau of the Census. Geographical mobility, March 1975–March 1979. *Current Population Reports* (Series P-29, No. 353). Washington, D.C.: U.S. Government Printing Office, 1980. (c)

Bureau of the Census. Population profile of the United States, 1980. *Current Population Reports* (Series P-20, No. 363). Washington, D.C.: U.S. Government Printing Office, 1981.

Carter, J. The supplemental State of the Union message from the President of the United States. *Congressional Record* (daily edition), January 25, 1979, p. 1068.

Cremin, L. A. *The genius of American education.* New York: Vintage, 1965.

Ellerin, M., & Kesten, A. H. The new right: An emerging force on the political scene. *USA Today,* 1981, *109,* 10–15.

Family Impact Seminar. *Toward an inventory of federal programs with direct effects on families.* Mimeographed. Washington, D.C.: George Washington University Institute for Educational Leadership, 1977.

Friedan, B. Feminism takes a new turn. *New York Times Magazine,* November 18, 1979, pp. 40, 90–106.

Garfield, R. The decision to remarry. *Journal of Divorce,* 1980, *4*(1), 1–10.

Gil, D. G. *Unravelling social policy.* Cambridge, Mass.: Schenkman, 1976.

Glieberman, H. Why so many marriages fail. *U.S. News and World Report,* July 20, 1981, pp. 53–55.

Gordon, S. *Lonely in America.* New York: Simon & Schuster, 1976.

Hetherington, E. M. Divorce: A child's perspective. *American Psychologist,* 1979, *34*(10) 851–858.

Hofferth, S. L., & Moore, K. A. Women and their children. In R. E. Smith (Ed.), *The subtle revolution: Women at work.* Washington, D.C.: Urban Institute, 1979, pp. 125–158.

Jefferson, T. Thomas Jefferson to Colonel Charles Yancey, January 1816. In Paul Leicester Ford (Ed.), *The writings of Thomas Jefferson* (Vol 10). New York: Putnam's, 1899, p. 4.

Kamerman, S. B., & Kahn, A. J. *Family policy: Government and families in fourteen countries.* New York: Columbia University Press, 1978.

Keniston, K., & the Carnegie Council on Children. *All our children: The American family under pressure.* New York: Harcourt Brace Jovanovich, 1977.

Kirst, M. Loss of support for public secondary schools. *Daedalus,* 1981, *110*(3), 45–68.

Kurdek, L., & Siesky, A. Effects of divorce on children: The relationship between parent and child perspectives. *Journal of Divorce,* 1980, *4*(2), 85–99.

Levitan, S. A., & Belous, R. S. *What's happening to the American family?* Baltimore: Johns Hopkins University Press, 1981.

Marshner, C. The pro-family movement and traditional values. In S. K. Muenchow & M. L. McFarland (Eds.), *What is pro-family policy? Proceedings of the Bush interest group symposium, May 1981.* New Haven: Bush Center for Child Development and Social Policy, 1981.

Martinez, A. Testimony before the House Committee on Education and Labor, Subcommittee on Select Education concerning proposed extension of the Child Abuse Prevention and Treatment Act. Ninety-fifth Congress, March 11, 1977.

Masnick, G., & Bane, M. J. *The nation's families, 1960–1990.* Boston: Auburn House, 1980.

McFalls, J. A. Where have all the children gone? The future of reproduction in the United States. *USA Today,* 1981, *109,* 30–33.

Mead, M. Can the American family survive? In R. Metraux (Ed.), *Aspects of the present.* New York: Morrow, 1980. (a)

Mead, M. Every home needs two adults. In R. Metraux (Ed.), *Aspects of the present.* New York: Morrow, 1980. (b)

Morrison, P. America's changing population: Demographic trends. *USA Today,* 1981, *110,* 20–24.

Norton, A. J., & Glick, P. C. Marital instability in America: Past, present, future. In G. Levinger & O. Moles (Eds.), *Divorce and separation: Context, causes, and consequences.* New York: Basic Books, 1979, pp. 6–19.

Parker, M., Peltier, S., & Wolleat, P. Understanding dual career couples. *Personnel and Guidance Journal,* 1981, *60,* 14–18.

Project Developmental Continuity. *Guidelines for an implementation year.* Washington, D.C.: Office of Child Development, U.S. Department of Health, Education, and Welfare, 1975.

Rapoport, R., Rapoport, R. N., & Strelitz, Z. *Fathers, mothers, and society: Perspectives on parenting.* New York: Vintage, 1980.

Spanier, G., & Glick, P. C. Marital instability in the United States: Some correlates and recent changes. *Family Relations,* 1981, *31,* 329–338.

Steiner, G. Y. *The futility of family policy.* Washington, D.C.: Brookings Institution, 1981.

Superwoman squeeze. *Newsweek,* May 19, 1980, pp. 72–79.

Treas, J. Postwar trends in family size. *Demography,* 1981, *18,* 321–334.

Weiss, R. *Loneliness: The experience of emotional and social isolation.* Cambridge: MIT Press, 1973.

Zigler, E. Who will speak for children and families? A case for strengthening OCD. *American Journal of Orthopsychiatry,* 1977, *47*(4), 564–567.

Zigler, E., & Kagan, S. L. Child development knowledge and educational policy: Using what we know. In A. Lieberman & M. McLaughlin (Eds.), *Policy making in education.* Chicago: National Society for the Study of Education, 1982.

Editors

Edward F. Zigler is Sterling Professor of Psychology and Director of the Bush Center in Child Development and Social Policy at Yale University. He served as the first Director of the U.S. Office of Child Development and was Chief of the Children's Bureau in the U.S. Department of Health, Education, and Welfare. Serving on many presidential commissions and panels, Dr. Zigler was a member of the original Head Start Planning Committee and recently led the presidentially appointed committee on the future of Head Start. Dr. Zigler has lectured widely and has served as a government consultant in the United States and abroad. He is the author of several books and numerous articles that have appeared in scientific journals and popular periodicals. Among his many honors, Dr. Zigler received the 1979 G. Stanley Hall Award and the 1982 Distinguished Contributions to Psychology in the Public Interest Award from the American Psychological Association.

Sharon L. Kagan is Associate Director of the Yale Bush Center in Child Development and Social Policy and is the Coordinator of the Bush Network of Programs in Child Development and Social Policy. She is an Assistant Professor of Education at the Child Study Center at Yale University. Formerly a Director of Head Start and Project Developmental Continuity programs, Dr. Kagan has lectured and written in the areas of child care, educational policy, parent involvement, parenting education, and institutional change and is currently active on a variety of national and state policy boards.

Edgar Klugman is Professor of Early Childhood Education at Wheelock College in Boston. In 1979–1980 he was awarded a Mid-Career Fellowship at the Yale Bush Center in Child Development and Social Policy. Dr. Klugman recently served as a member of the Governing Board of the

National Association for the Education of Young Children and was Co-Chairperson of that organization's Public Policy Task Group. Dr. Klugman has also been a member of the Steering Committee of the National Campaign for Child Daycare and has written and lectured in the areas of early childhood professionalization, educational policy, and the politics of advocacy.

Contributors

J. Lawrence Aber is Assistant Professor of Clinical and Developmental Psychology at Barnard College, Columbia University. From 1976 to 1979 he served in the Massachusetts state government as a Special Assistant to the Director of the Office for Children. In 1979 he cofounded the Harvard Child Maltreatment Project, a longitudinal study of the nature and causes of child maltreatment and its effect on social–emotional development. He presently conducts policy-relevant research on populations of children at developmental risk in New York City and serves as Director of Research for a National Study Panel for the Future of Services to Children funded by the Edna McConnell Clark Foundation.

Garry D. Brewer is a Professor in the School of Organization and Management, the Department of Political Science, and the Institution for Social and Policy Studies at Yale University. Dr. Brewer has had extensive experience in policy analysis and is the author of numerous articles and reviews. He is the author, coauthor, or editor of seven books.

Orville G. Brim, Jr. is the President of the Foundation for Child Development. His deep interest in the development of social indicators has been instrumental in launching a national movement dedicated to their utilization. He is author or editor of many books, including *Constancy and Change in Human Development* (1980); *Learning to be Parents* (1980); and *Life-Span Development and Behavior,* Volumes II, III, and IV (1979–1982). Dr. Brim is a former President of the Russell Sage Foundation and a past President of the American Orthopsychiatric Association. He is Vice Chairman of the Board of Trustees of the American Institutes for Research and a member of the Social Science Research Council's Committee on Life-Course Perspectives on Human Development.

441

Urie Bronfenbrenner's involvement in social policy began in the early 1960s with his cross-cultural research on child rearing in the Soviet Union and his concern, as a social psychologist, with the cold war. These two aspects of public policy, examining the role of national policy as it affects the lives of children and families and evaluating the psychological factors in international tensions, have been dominant themes in his work ever since. Dr. Bronfenbrenner, formerly a member of the Head Start Planning Committee, is currently Jacob Gould Schurman Professor of Human Development and Family Studies and of Psychology at Cornell University.

Carol Mershon Connor is a Ph.D. candidate in Political Science at Yale University. She has worked as an Assistant in Research at the Center for Health Studies at Yale's Institution for Social and Policy Studies. The recipient of Fulbright and Social Science Research Council fellowships, Ms. Connor has completed field research on Italian industrial conflict.

Pamela Ebert-Flattau earned her doctorate in Experimental Psychology at the University of Georgia in 1974, specializing in visual perceptual development. Following her training, Dr. Ebert-Flattau served as a Congressional Science Fellow working with the U.S. Senate Subcommittee on Children and Youth. In 1975 she joined the National Research Council, where she worked for six years, most recently as Staff Director for the Committee for a Study of the Federal Role in Undergraduate Science Education for Non-Specialists. In September 1981, Dr. Ebert-Flattau joined the National Science Foundation, where she works currently as a science policy analyst in the Science Indicators Unit of the Directorate for Scientific, Technological, and International Affairs.

Susan Shays Gilfillan is a Postgraduate Fellow in Psychiatry (Social Work) at Yale University, Division of Mental Hygiene. She was formerly a Research Assistant at the Yale Bush Center in Child Development and Social Policy.

John I. Goodlad, Dean of the Graduate School of Education at the University of California, Los Angeles, has been an active participant in education conferences and on advisory boards for 25 years and has had a seminal influence on the direction of education in the United States and abroad. A frequent contributor to professional journals, yearbooks, and encyclopedias, Dr. Goodlad is the author or coauthor of 32 books on educational issues and a contributor to approximately 60 books on educational topics.

Edmund W. Gordon is Professor of Psychology and Afro-American Studies and Professor of Psychology (Child Study Center) at Yale University. He is a specialist in the learning and adjustment problems of low-status groups in American society. Professor Gordon was the Director of the Division of Research and Evaluation for Project Head Start in the Office of Economic Opportunity (1965–1967). He has written widely in the fields of education and psychology and taught for many years at Teachers College, Columbia University. Professor Gordon is also Editor of the *American Journal of Orthopsychiatry* and of the *Review of Research in Education.*

John E. Hansan is the Executive Director of the National Conference on Social Welfare in Washington, D.C. Dr. Hansan is an authority on public policy and other developments affecting public welfare. He has served as Director of the Ohio Department of Public Welfare, as Chief of Staff for the Governor of Ohio, and as the Director of Government Affairs and Social Policy for the American Public Welfare Association.

Stephen B. Heintz is Commissioner of the Connecticut Department of Income Maintenance with responsibility for managing the state's public assistance and Medicaid programs. Previously, Mr. Heintz served as Under Secretary for Comprehensive Planning in the Connecticut Office of Policy and Management with responsibilities for state planning and policy analysis. Mr. Heintz was appointed Chairman of the Governor's Interagency Task Force on Block Grants by Governor William A. O'Neill and is active in the work of the National Governors' Association. He also serves as a member of the Connecticut Humanities Council.

Ellen Hoffman has been Director of Governmental Affairs for the Children's Defense Fund since 1977. In that capacity she is responsible for monitoring congressional actions affecting children and for coordinating CDF's legislative agenda and activities on Capitol Hill. From 1971 to 1976 she served as professional staff member and Staff Director of the Senate Subcommittee on Children and Youth chaired by Walter F. Mondale. While there she had responsibility for a wide variety of domestic policy issues in the areas of children and youth, women's rights, education, and the arts. Ms. Hoffman was formerly an education reporter for the *Washington Post* and has taught courses in public policy and legislative affairs.

Juel Janis is Assistant Dean and Adjunct Associate Professor in the School of Public Health at the University of California, Los Angeles. Before that she was Executive Assistant to the Assistant Secretary for Health and Surgeon General in the U.S. Department of Health and Human Services. She was previously Director of the Behavioral Science Program and Associate Professor of Pediatrics at the University of Massachusetts Medical School and Associate Professor of Health Sciences at Florida International University. In the early 1970s, Dr. Janis ran the Head Start program in Dade County, Florida. Her research interests lie in the areas of child studies, the behavioral sciences, and health policy.

Theodore R. Marmor is Professor of Public Health and Professor of Political Science at Yale University and Chairman of the Center for Health Studies at Yale's Institution for Social and Policy Studies. Professor Marmor is an authority on domestic and comparative policy studies, especially in the areas of social security, health insurance, and professional regulation.

Gwen Morgan is a Lecturer at Wheelock College in Boston, where she teaches courses in child daycare and in policy at both the undergraduate and graduate level as well as coordinates advanced seminars on day care administration. She has also been a consultant to many organizations, including Abt Associates, UNCO, American Institutes for Research, the U.S. Office for Human Development, and various state agencies. She is Vice President of the Day Care Council of America, a board member of the National Association for the Education of Young Children, and a board member of the National Campaign for Child Daycare for Working Mothers. She has written extensively on child daycare.

Susan Muenchow is a journalist specializing in child and family concerns and policy. She is a Research Associate in the Department of Psychology at Yale University and is the Head of the Section in Public Education and Media of the Yale Bush Center in Child Development and Social Policy. She has previously worked for the *Christian Science Monitor* and *Time* and currently writes for *Parents Magazine.*

David F. Musto, M.D., is Professor of Psychiatry (Child Study Center) and of the History of Medicine at Yale University. He is Head of the Section in History and Social Policy of the Yale Bush Center in Child Development and Social Policy and the Yale Child Study Center. During the Carter administration he served on the White House Strategy Council on Drug Abuse Policy and more recently as a member of the National Research Council's Panel on Alcohol Policy. In 1973 Yale University Press published his history of drug abuse policy, *The American Disease: Origins of Narcotic Control.*

Peggy Pizzo is an affiliate faculty member at the Bush Center in Child Development and Social Policy at Yale University. She has been an Assistant Director of the White House Domestic Policy Staff, where she concentrated on policy issues related to Head Start, foster care and adoption, child abuse, child care, and other human services. Ms. Pizzo was formerly Special Assistant to the Head of the Administration for Children, Youth, and Families in the U.S. Department of Health and Human Services. *Parent to Parent,* her book on parent self-help and advocacy organizations in the United States, was published in 1983.

Catherine J. Ross is Assistant Professor of History at the Child Study Center of the Yale University School of Medicine. She is Assistant Head of the Section in History and Social Policy of the Yale Bush Center in Child Development and Social Policy and the Yale Child Study Center. She was an editor of *Child Abuse: An Agenda for Action* (1980).

Seymour B. Sarason is Professor in the Department of Psychology and in the Institution for Social and Policy Studies at Yale University. A recipient in 1975 of the Award for Distinguished Contributions to Community Psychology and Mental Health, Division of Community Psychology, from the American Psychological Association, he served as President of the APA's Division of Clinical Psychology in 1978–1979.

Heidi Sigal is a Program Officer of the Foundation for Child Development. Since joining the Foundation in 1972, her primary involvement has been in the areas of childhood social indicators and the social and affective development of children. As Associate Director of the Foundation's intramural research program on indicators of the status of children in New York City, she coauthored (with Trude W. Lash) three volumes: *State of the Child: New York City* (1976), *Children and Families in New York City: An Analysis of the 1976 Survey of Income and Education* (1979), and *State of the Child: New York City II* (1980). She recently developed and directed the Foundation's international program of grants to young scholars investigating social and affective development.

Jeanette Valentine is Assistant Professor of Pediatrics at Boston University School of Medicine. Dr. Valentine has taught and conducted research in the area of social policy for children and families. She was formerly a Research Associate and Lecturer at Yale's Institution for Social and Policy Studies and Department of Psychology and continues to participate in Yale's Bush Center in Child Development and Social Policy. Dr. Valentine is coeditor (with Edward Zigler) of *Project Head Start: A Legacy of the War on Poverty* and is currently involved in research on maternal and child health policies.

Heather B. Weiss is currently a Research Associate in Psychology at the Yale Bush Center in Child Development and Social Policy, where she directs a study of contemporary family support and education. She has been the Director of Research, Development, and Analysis for the Comparative Ecology of Human Development Project at Cornell University and a Research Associate at the Brookline Early Education Project and was a Postdoctoral Fellow at the Bush Center. Dr. Weiss has written on the history and dynamics of parent education and support programs, work and family issues, family policy, and the use of qualitative methodology in family research.

Carol Camp Yeakey is an Associate Professor of Administration and Higher Education at Purdue University. She was a Rockefeller Fellow at the Bush Center in Child Development and Social Policy at Yale from 1981 to 1982 and a National Institute of Education Fellow from 1980 to 1981. She has also taught at Rutgers University Graduate School of Education and at Teachers College, Columbia University. Her speciality is school organizational policy and decision making. Dr. Yeakey has published on that topic in such journals as the *Oxford Review of Education,* the *Journal of Educational Administration,* the *Journal of Collective Negotiations in the Public Sector,* and the *American Journal of Orthopsychiatry.*

Nicholas Zill II is the President of Child Trends, Inc. and a former Senior Staff Scientist with the Foundation for Child Development. He directed the Foundation's National Survey of Children in the United States in 1976–1977 and is one of the principal investigators on a follow-up study to the national survey focusing on the effects of marital disruption on children. Before joining the Foundation, Dr. Zill was one of the original staff members of the Social Science Research Council's Center for Social Indicators Research in Washington, D.C. He has advised the National Center for Health Statistics and other federal agencies on ways to improve the usefulness of national statistics on children.

Name index

Subject index